GREYHOUND
ANNUAL 2008

Edited by Jonathan Hobbs

Interiors designed by Fiona Pike
Cover designed by Adrian Morrish

Published in 2007 by Raceform
Compton, Newbury, Berkshire RG20 6NL

A catalogue record for this book is available from the British Library.

ISBN 978-1-905153-53-4

Printed by Creative Print and Design, Wales.

Contents

HOW TO READ THE FORM

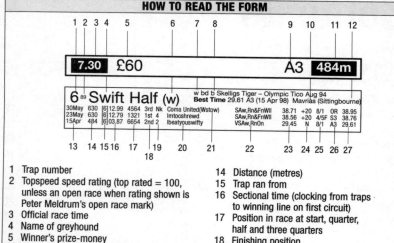

1   Trap number
2   Topspeed speed rating (top rated = 100, unless an open race when rating shown is Peter Meldrum's open race mark)
3   Official race time
4   Name of greyhound
5   Winner's prize-money
6   wide runner. (m) is used for middle, (r) occasionally for rails
7   Breeding line, showing colour, sire, dam and whelp date. Also shows season information for bitches.
8   Shows best recent time over the trip in the last 90 days.
9   Grade of race
10 Trainer
11 Distance of race in metres
12 Trainer location if not the race venue
13 Date of race

14 Distance (metres)
15 Trap ran from
16 Sectional time (clocking from traps to winning line on first circuit)
17 Position in race at start, quarter, half and three quarters
18 Finishing position
19 Distance won/beaten by
20 Greyhound beat/beaten by
21 Venue of race (if other than present venue)
22 Comments-in-running
23 Time of race
24 Going allowance (N-normal)
25 Starting Price
26 Grade of race, the lower the number, the better the grade
27 Calculated time, taking the going allowance into account

GREYHOUND ABBREVIATIONS

A-always, **Aw**-away, **Awk**-awkward, **b**-bitch, **B**-badly, **bd**-brindled, **be**-blue, **bk**-black, **Blk**-baulked, **Bmp**-bumped, **Bnc**-bunched, **Bnd**-bend, **Brk**-break, **Btn**-beaten/beaten for, **CF**-Co-Fav, **Chl**-challenged, **Ck**-checked, **Ckg**-checking, **Clr**-clear, **CmAg**-came again, **Crd**-crowded, **Crmp**-cramped, **d-dog**, **DH**-dead-heat, **Dis**-distance, **Disp**-disputed, **dk**-dark, **DNF**-did not finish, **Drpd**-dropped, **E**-early, **EP**-early pace, **EvCh**-every chance, **f**-fawn, **F**-favourite or fast, **Fcd**-forced, **Fd**-faded, **Fin**-finished, **FlsHt**-false heat, **Fr**-from, **Gng**-going, **GR**-graded race, **H**-hurdle or heavy, **Hcp**-handicap, **Hd**-head, **Hgh**-high, **HldOn**-held on, **Hndy**-handy, **Imp**-impeded, **Inc**-inclined, **IT**-inter-track, **J**-joint-favourite, **Jkt**-jacket, **Jmp**-jump(ed), **KS**-kennel sweep, **Lkd**-lacked, **Ld**-lead/led, **Lm**-lame, **Ln**-line, **Lse**-loose, **m**-metre(s), **Mid/(m)**-middle, **Mod**-moderately, **Msd**-missed, **Mzl**-muzzle, **N**-normal, **Nk**-neck, **Nr**-near, **Nv**-never, **OR**-open race, **Outp**-outpaced, **P**-pace(d), **PR**-puppy race, **Pkd**-pecked, **Pt**-peat, **Q**-quick, **r**-red, **R**-received, **Rec**-record, **ReRn**-re-run, **Rls/(r)**-rails/railed, **Rn**-ran/run, **Rnin**-run in, **RnUp**-run-in, run-up, **S**-slow or stayers (class), **Scr**-scratch, **SH**-short head, **Shw**-showed, **Slp**-slipped, **Sn**-soon, **SP**-starting price, **Ssn**-season, **Ssn?**-season unknown, **Stmb**-stumbled, **Stk**-struck, **Stt**-start, **Styd**-stayed, **Swv**-swerved, **TR**-track record, **T**-to or trial, **Trbl**-trouble, **Th'out**-throughout, **Tk**-track, **Tm**-time, **TN**-trialists & newcomers, **Tp**-trap, **Unatt**-unattached, **V**-very, **w**-white, **W/(W)**-wide, **Whlp**-whelped a litter, **Wll**-well, **Wn**-won, **WtVr**-weight variation.

Foreword

by Lord Lipsey,
BGRB chairman

Few who were there will forget the wonderful scenes in July as Nick Savva, Bob Morton and his family toured Wimbledon Stadium after their third consecutive victory in the Greyhound Derby, this time provided by the brilliant Westmead Lord.

For me people like Nick and Bob encapsulate the true spirit of greyhound racing – competitive and determined yes, but in a truly sporting spirit. You know that if Westmead Lord had lost Nick and Bob would have been the first to shake winning connections by the hand.

Horse racing is often referred to as the King of Sports. If that is right, greyhound racing is its democratic equivalent. It is a sport without hierarchy or class; a sport anyone can afford to enjoy, provided they keep control of their punting; indeed a sport in which nearly anyone can afford to participate, with a share or two in a dog or two and much pleasure to be gleaned from it.

Greyhound racing people, I have found, wear their hearts on their sleeves. Chairing the BGRB has not been a recipe for a quiet life. Everyone wants to give you their take. With most people in greyhound racing, however, this passion is combined with a natural courtesy, and a desire for dialogue.

I have enjoyed my talks with my critics as much as with those (including my board) who have backed me through thick and thin.

I recognise that BGRB does not have a monopoly of wisdom, though contrary to what some people think it doesn't have a monopoly of stupidity either! Opening out the future of our sport to everyone in it is vital to progress.

Lord Lipsey: 'Opening out the future of our sport to everyone in it is vital to progress'

It is not greyhound racing lovers who are the problem. It is the extreme welfarists who fill one's mailbag with their ignorant abuse. Unfortunately for us, wild and sometimes violent extremists have moved into the campaign against greyhound racing, thanks to the government's laws stopping them concentrating on animal laboratories. These people observe none of the principles of fruitful dialogue. They lie about the facts. They twist the arguments.

How a public service broadcaster like the BBC can justify granting Annette Crosbie five, yes five programme opportunities within weeks to spread her myths, without offering us a proper right of reply, I do not know. We have of course lodged an official complaint, whose outcome at the time of writing is not known.

Nor do I know how self-styled animal lovers can be so vindictive to the species homo sapiens as some of the extremists are towards people in greyhound racing. Animal lovers, they may be; people haters, they are, to the core.

Greyhound racing will in future be more and more active in combating their arguments. We shall demonstrate to the general public that greyhounds enjoy a wonderful life while racing and then after racing. We shall expose the extremists for the ignorant dangerous folk they are, and when they break the law we shall see they are brought to justice.

We are coming I hope to the end of a period of organisational turmoil in greyhound racing, which Lord Donoughue has done his best to resolve. We are also having to adapt to the end of a period when the bookmakers' contributions – for which we are grateful – were rising sharply.

In setting budgets the conflicting claims of welfare, prize money and grants to make stadia more attractive to the public are hard to reconcile. For myself I should make it clear that we will never stint on welfare. Our dogs come first.

David Lipsey
Chairman

Government's View

by Gerry Sutcliffe
Minister for Sport

I AM once again grateful to have the opportunity to contribute to the Greyhound Annual. The last twelve months have proved to be an eventful year for the industry. On the one hand we have seen impressive improvements in areas such as kennel staff training and on the other the appalling events in Seaham, which are a stark reminder that the whole greyhound racing community must do more to protect the welfare of both racing and retired greyhounds.

I have made my feelings clear on this matter on a number or occasions in the past. Indeed, the provision of proper welfare and retirement arrangements is one of the principle reasons I worked so hard to convince bookmakers of the need to pay more through the British Greyhound Racing Fund (BGRF). There can be no excuses for not meeting these important welfare issues, now that a significant funding stream is available.

On that note, I welcome the continuing constructive relationship between the Association of British Bookmakers (ABB) and the British Greyhound Racing Board (BGRB), and I was pleased to learn that a contribution rate of 0.6% has been agreed for the next three years. This certainly is good news for the sport and will allow the sport to plan ahead in funding track integrity measures, training and education for industry staff, investing in stadium facilities and of course the improved welfare of racing and retired greyhounds, including the support for the Retired Greyhound Trust.

Gerry Sutcliffe: '2008 will undoubtedly be one of the industry's most challenging years'

I recently spoke at the launch of Vision 2010 and I outlined two priorities for the greyhound industry – welfare and training.

I am glad to note that, following the appointment of a training consultant, much progress has been made in this vital area of work.

The arrival of a track safety and track maintenance training programme should ensure that track preparation is undertaken properly, thereby minimising injuries to dogs. The industry has also seen the introduction of a basic National Vocational Qualification in Animal Care for all kennel staff. This is a major step forward recognising the vital role kennel staff play in the industry, and I am confident that the new scheme will raise training standards across the country and further promote the welfare of the greyhounds who partake in the sport.

The Government also welcomes initiatives such as the 'Welfare Summit' which looked at the way forward for the industry regarding welfare and regulation. It is tragic that it took the events of Seaham to bring forward this initiative, but I am optimistic that the 'Options for Change Committee' that was set up as a result of the summit now has the commitment and courage to successfully implement suitable structural changes to the industry to provide an effective solution for issues such as the plight of retired greyhounds.

The Government believes in self-regulation where appropriate and I know that this has been the favoured approach of DEFRA in its Animal Welfare legislation. DEFRA officials are currently working with the industry and welfare groups to prepare draft regulations which will make a real difference to the welfare of all racing greyhounds. The industry will only have itself to blame if self-regulation is no longer viewed as a viable alternative to statutorily imposed arrangements.

The next twelve months will no doubt be a challenging period for the greyhound industry, even with a secure level of funding there can be little time for complacency. Greyhound stadia themselves must continue to adapt and modernise to meet the increasingly high expectation of the customer and the challenges of other leisure activities. The BGRB has stated that the new funding agreement should ensure that there are enough available resources to go into stadium development and I hope this proves to be the case.

I have made no secret of the fact that I am disappointed to see some bookmakers still not contributing to the Fund and I hope to see more non-payers contributing in the near future. I would also like to express my sincere thanks to those bookmakers who continue to support the voluntary agreement and help ensure that greyhound racing remains a thriving sport and a great evening out.

The arrival of the Gambling Act in September 2007 presents opportunities for the industry, notably expanding the pool betting product into betting shops, but there will also be new competition. I am sure that with the continuing modernisation of all aspects of the greyhound racing product, including the recent television advertising campaign, the industry will have the strength to take advantage of the opportunities to meet any challenges.

Finally, I wish you all the very best for a successful 2007.

Gerry Sutcliffe

Faithful, good-natured male WLTM like-minded family to share his zest for life. Loves animals, children and enjoys most sports.

If only we could give each of our retired greyhounds their own personal ad. But as the RGT re-homes around three thousand dogs a year, it's just not possible.

We always need more people to adopt our dogs, so perhaps you could help? Retired greyhounds are gentle, intelligent animals who have devoted their early years to racing and now need some TLC in a loving family home.

They ask very little in return: regular walks and meals, the odd cuddle and maybe a warm basket by a cosy fire. So if you're looking for a devoted companion to share happy times, look no further. Simply send the coupon, log onto our website or phone us on: **0870 444 0673**

Key organisations

BRITISH GREYHOUND RACING BOARD

The BGRB is the sport's governing body that has responsibility for all aspects of the industry and representation of stakeholders. The BGRB is comprised of the BGRB Board, a Chairman, an Executive Office and the stakeholder associations representing racecourse promoters, greyhound owners, professional trainers and greyhound breeders.

Address: BGRB, 1 Warwick Row, London SW1E 5ER

Website: www.thedogs.co.uk

Phone: 020 7808 7722 (general enquiries)
020 7808 7031 (media enquiries)

Implementation of policy and governance of the sport is managed through four standing committees reporting to the BGRB Board. Each committee comprises a range of individuals with wide industry knowledge and outside expertise.

BGRB Board

The BGRB Board of Directors is representative of all stakeholders in licensed greyhound racing. It is responsible for taking the major decisions on all policy issues, including matters of central funding. All NGRC rule changes require the endorsement of the BGRB Board. The membership represents the whole industry as follows:

Lord Lipsey (Chairman)
Richard Hayler (Secretary)
Independent Non-Executive Directors x 2
NGRC Senior Steward
Racecourse Promoters Representation x 5
Greyhound Owners Representation x 2
Greyhound Breeders Representation x 1
Greyhound Trainers Representation x 1

Executive Committee

This committee is able to take necessary decisions between full board meetings on the whole range of topics covered by the other committees. It was introduced as part of the reforms under Vision 2010 to speed up decision making.

Lord Lipsey (Chairman)
Richard Hayler (Secretary)
Michael Bailey (Independent BGRB Director)
John Curran (Racing Committee)
John Haynes (Welfare Committee)
Clarke Osborne (Commercial Committee)

Welfare Committee

This committee works closely with the NGRC over rules and best practices in the sport. It is particularly focussed on track safety and track improvement work, welfare research, retired greyhounds, the trainers' assistance fund and the training and education programme.

John Haynes (Chairman)
Peter Laurie (Secretary)
Barry Johnson (Veterinary surgeon and Independent BGRB Director)
David Baldwin (Promoters representative – Sheffield)
John Curran (Promoters representative – Kinsley)
Bill Glass (Promoters representative – Reading, Poole & Swindon)
Brian Clemenson (Trainers representative)
Bob Gilling (Breeders representative)
Stuart Locke-Hart (Owners representative)
Frances Allen (President, Society of Greyhound Vets)
Hazel Bentall (NGRC Veterinary Steward)
Alistair McLean (NGRC Chief Executive)

Ivor Stocker (RGT Director)
David Parker (BGRB Training Co-ordinator)

Commercial Committee

The Commercial Committee covers all commercial aspects of greyhound racing from marketing through to IT, intellectual property rights and the Gambling Act.

Clarke Osborne (Chairman)
Simon Levingston (Secretary)
Rachel Corden (Nottingham)
Clive Feltham (GRA)
David Hood (Sunderland
& Newcastle)
Richard Lang (Romford & Hove)
Richard Perkins (Peterborough)

Racing Committee

This committee encompasses all matters of racing not specifically linked to welfare, with a remit that includes close consultation with the NGRC. It also oversees the distribution of the annual BGRF prize-money grant.

John Curran (Chairman)
Richard Hayler (Secretary)
Charles Chandler (Promoters representative – Walthamstow)
Terry Corden (Promoters representative – Nottingham)
Bob Rowe (Promoters representative – GRA)
Bob Gilling (Breeders representative)
Stuart Locke Hart (Owners representative)
Brian Clemenson (Trainers representative)
John Johnson (Representative from BAGS)
Alistair McLean (NGRC Chief Executive)
Tanya Stevenson (Media))
John Haynes (BGRB Welfare Consultant)

NATIONAL GREYHOUND RACING CLUB

The NGRC is the body responsible for regulating the industry in accordance with the Rules of Racing. The NGRC acts as the judicial body for the discipline and conduct of the licensed greyhound racing industry. It licenses racecourses, trainers, owners, kennels and officials and keeps a register of owners and all greyhounds racing at racecourses that it licenses. The Senior Steward of the NGRC is an ex-officio member of the BGRB Board.

Senior Steward: Edward Bentall
Chief Executive: Alistair McLean
Address: Twyman House, 16 Bonny Street, London NW1 9QD
Website: www.ngrc.org.uk
Phone: 020 7267 9256

BRITISH GREYHOUND RACING FUND

The British Greyhound Racing Fund is the official funding body for greyhound racing in Britain licensed by the NGRC. The BGRF collects voluntary contributions paid by bookmakers. Its Board, comprised of bookmaker and BGRB-nominated representatives, accepts or rejects the BGRB's funding proposals and oversees their execution.

BGRF funding covers all aspects of welfare, integrity and development and promotion of the sport and the Fund works closely with the BGRB and NGRC on these matters

Chairman: Charles Lennox-Conyngham
Secretary: Margaret Woodruff
Address: Central Point, 45 Beech Street, London EC2Y 8AD
Website: www.bgrf.org.uk
Phone: 020 7953 9701

Editor's View

By Jonathan Hobbs

FIRST an apology. You are reading this later in the year because of various delays, not least the publication of Lord Donoughue report. It was expected to be in the public domain earlier, but clearly greyhound racing was a far more complicated industry to unravel and understand for the committee, and some 55,000 words later we have a most wide-ranging list of recommendations to take greyhound racing forward.

It has certainly attracted publicity, all of it positive. Some welfare groups have tried to score points, but that has to be expected. Donoughue's appointment of Clarissa Baldwin of the Dogs Trust as an 'assessor' was an early shrewd tactical move by the man I am cheekily calling 'the Dapper Don'.

Government pressure will ensure that the review recommendations will be followed through, although as with similar reports amendments can be expected. The major problem will lie, as it always has, with trying to bring together the various factions of the sport. But the setting up of the Greyhound Board of Great Britain will do a large part of that.

Take time to digest the key recommendations of the Donoughue report www.greyhounds-donoughue-report.co.uk. There is something of interest for everyone connected to the sport, be it as owner, trainer, kennelhand, general enthusiast or, of course, if you work within the industry.

And while the headlines and soundbites talked of a 'last chance saloon' for the sport, do not be alarmed. One man will always want to race his dog against another, and will find a way to do it. It is, though, a last chance for the 'stakeholders', those cogs of the greyhound industry, to come together and drive the business forward.

The leisure industry turns over billions of pounds every year, and we are a major part of the 'night out' scene. Plus there is the added financial interest of being part of the betting industry, another multi-billion pounds industry. We can be key to both.

If promoters respect owners and trainers as much as they do themselves – it is a complaint I hear time and time again – we can prosper together.

Now, talking of stakeholders, the major bodies once again contribute to this annual. But please remember that their submissions were asked for before Donoughue – to seek reaction post-report might have just taken us into 2008! But many second-guessed where we are likely to be, stopping short of saying they would be part of the GBGB. That would have been too presumptuous!

I welcome a first contribution from Gerry Sutcliffe, who succeeded Richard Caborn as Minister for Sport. Gerry has a hard act to follow in terms of how Richard was a friend of greyhound racing, loyally supporting us on many occasions. But encouragingly Gerry's department was first in on deadline day (always a good sign), and his words speak volumes. I bid you welcome, sir!

Lord Lipsey (BGRB), Alistair McLean (NGRC) and Charles Lenox-Conyghan (BGRF) again contribute and remain key figures as the repercussions of Donoughue are digested and plans for the future hatched, as is Jim Reynolds, the Trainers' Association chairman, who submits a first 'report' in his new role.

I also welcome BGRB general secretary Richard Hayler and welfare and PR spokesman Peter Lawrie, two young men with a passion for greyhound racing. Given that only one of their predecessors had, or has, such a love for the game their involvement is also welcomed.

Hayler pens a personal piece, rather than overtly political, and his experiences are required reading for those who want to take us forward.

Bob Gilling of the Breeders Forum took time from guiding Brickfield Class to umpteen successes to update us on British breeding, while David Parker, the sport's Training Co-Ordinator updates us on his very successful seminars.

Having myself spoken in Ireland at a Skillnet event this year, backed by the Irish Greyhound Board, I understand how education in all aspects of the sport is so important to encourage and prepare those who work within, or might seek employment, in the sport.

Emma Johns reports from the Great Greyhound Gathering, a retired greyhounds 'fun day' which she was instrumental in, while we record the background to probably greyhound racing's most positive PR news of 2007, the induction of the great Westmead Hawk into Madama Tussauds. Take a visit to the London tourist attraction, it is hugely worth it.

As for memories of 2007, they are covered with an extensive round-up of all the major races, with particular emphasis on the Blue Square Derby and another triumph for the Savva and Morton team. Both have plenty to look forward to in 2008, and it is great that Nick has sat down (with Floyd Amphlett) to pen his memoirs. Can't wait.

Now to the thank-yous, and regular contributors Richard Birch, Michael Church, Phil Donaldson, John Forbes, Ian Fortune and Patrick Saward have all come up trumps again, while from the industry Robert Henigan and Terry Housden from the NGRC and Margaret Woodruff of the Fund again played important roles.

Julian Brown at Raceform and designer Fiona Pike have kept me on my toes, while the team at the Racing Post have been incredible in what has been a topsy-turvy year.

Last, but by no means least (as they always look!), thanks to Mrs H, Samantha, and the younger members of the Hobbs clan, Jude and Saskia.

Late nights and early mornings all round, now!

CALENDAR OF CATEGORY ONE EVENTS TO MAY 31

JANUARY

Saturday 12 January	PERRY BARR	BIRMINGHAM CUP	1ST ROUND 480
Thursday 17 January	PERRY BARR	BIRMINGHAM CUP	SEMI FINALS 480
Thursday 24 January	PERRY BARR	BIRMINGHAM CUP	FINAL 480

FEBRUARY

Monday 11 February	CRAYFORD	LADBROKES GOLDEN JACKET	1ST ROUND 714
Tuesday 12 February	WALTHAMSTOW	LADBROKES.COM ARC	1ST ROUND 475
Saturday 16 February	CRAYFORD	LADBROKES GOLDEN JACKET	SEMI FINALS 714
Saturday 16 February	WALTHAMSTOW	LADBROKES.COM ARC	2ND ROUND 475
Thursday 21 February	WALTHAMSTOW	LADBROKES.COM ARC	SEMI FINALS 475
Saturday 23 February	CRAYFORD	LADBROKES GOLDEN JACKET	FINAL 714
Tuesday 26 February	WALTHAMSTOW	LADBROKES.COM ARC	FINAL 475

MARCH

Thursday 06 March	MONMORE GREEN	LADBROKES PUPPY DERBY	1ST ROUND 480
Thursday 13 March	MONMORE GREEN	LADBROKES PUPPY DERBY	SEMI FINALS 480
Thursday 13 March	OXFORD	PALL MALL	1ST ROUND 450
Tuesday 18 March	OXFORD	PALL MALL	SEMI FINALS 450
Thursday 20 March	MONMORE GREEN	LADBROKES PUPPY DERBY	FINAL 480
Tuesday 25 March	OXFORD	PALL MALL	FINAL 450

APRIL

Tuesday 01 April	SHAWFIELD	SCOTTISH DERBY	1ST ROUND 480
Saturday 05 April	SHAWFIELD	SCOTTISH DERBY	2ND ROUND 480
Saturday 05 April	WIMBLEDON	GRAND NATIONAL	1ST ROUND 460H
Tuesday 08 April	SHAWFIELD	SCOTTISH DERBY	SEMI FINALS 480
Friday 11 April	HALL GREEN	BLUE RIBAND	1ST ROUND 480
Friday 11 April	ROMFORD	GOLDEN SPRINT	1ST ROUND 400
Friday 11 April	WIMBLEDON	GRAND NATIONAL	SEMI FINALS 460H
Saturday 12 April	SHAWFIELD	SCOTTISH DERBY	FINAL 480
Tuesday 15 April	HALL GREEN	BLUE RIBAND	SEMI FINALS 480
Tuesday 15 April	WIMBLEDON	GRAND NATIONAL	FINAL 460H
Thursday 17 April	HOVE	THE CORAL REGENCY	1ST ROUND 695 E
Friday 18 April	ROMFORD	GOLDEN SPRINT	SEMI FINALS 400
Tuesday 22 April	HALL GREEN	BLUE RIBAND	FINAL 480
Thursday 24 April	HOVE	THE CORAL REGENCY	SEM FINALS 695E
Friday 25 April	ROMFORD	GOLDEN SPRINT	FINAL 400
Tuesday 29 April	HOVE	THE CORAL REGENCY	FINAL 695

Sponsored by the BGRB

MAY			
Thursday 01 May	WIMBLEDON	BLUE SQUARE DERBY	1ST ROUND 480
Friday 02 May	WIMBLEDON	BLUE SQUARE DERBY	1ST ROUND 480
Saturday 03 May	WIMBLEDON	BLUE SQUARE DERBY	1ST ROUND 480
Friday 09 May	WIMBLEDON	BLUE SQUARE DERBY	2ND ROUND 480
Saturday 10 May	WIMBLEDON	BLUE SQUARE DERBY	2ND ROUND 480
Saturday 17 May	WIMBLEDON	BLUE SQUARE DERBY	3RD ROUND 480
Tuesday 20 May	WIMBLEDON	BLUE SQUARE DERBY	1/4 FINALS 480
Saturday 24 May	WIMBLEDON	BLUE SQUARE DERBY	SEMI FINALS 480
Saturday 31 May	WALTHAMSTOW	GRAPHITE (UK) PUPPY DERBY	1ST ROUND 475
Saturday 31 May	WIMBLEDON	BLUE SQUARE	DERBY FINAL 480

Breeding View

by Patrick Saward

When the British Greyhound Stud Book made it appearance, somewhat earlier than usual, as summer was drawing to a close, the retiring Keeper Charles Blanning outlined a far-from-cheerful scenario for domestic breeding in his valedictory preface.

With good reason, as it was delivered against a background of sharply reduced litter and registration figures, to which Blanning added the 'Seaham Affair', media hostility, political sniping, reduced prize-money and increased bureaucracy as factors militating against the sport's prospects.

Paradoxically, his works were penned during a year in which, for the first time ever, the English Derby was won by a home-bred greyhound for the third time in a row. Westmead Lord's victory in the premier Classic clinched a unique treble for his owner Bob Morton and trainer-breeder Nick Savva, the connections of the dual 2005-2006 victor Westmead Hawk.

Westmead Lord (by Doopys Kewell) and Westmead Hawk (by Sonic Flight) are both out the same dam, Mega Delight (Smooth Rumble-Knockeevan Joy), British-bred by Alex McKenzie of Edinburgh. They are rather more than half-brothers, as Droopys Kewell's sire Larkhill Jo and Sonic Flight share the same Savva-bred dam, Westmead Flight.

Mega Delight does not come from one of the traditional Savva dam lines, but as her maternal grandsire Mustang Jack was out of Westmead Fairy (Fearless Champ-Westmead Move), she claims a family tie to the breed developed at the famed Edlesborough range in Bedfordshire.

Third in the 2006 breeders' table, Savva passed the 100-winner mark in late September 2007, two weeks earlier than he had reached his 2006 century and thus on course to better the 138 open-race victories that he clocked up that year.

Also heading for the best-ever tally of open-race wins was the Northumberland breeder Jimmy Fenwick, who entered the final quarter of the campaign with a bag of over 60, boosted by the winning ways of Iceman Brutus.

The son of Toms The Best-Any Chewing Gum included Coventry's Category One Zig Zag Puppy Championship among a string of victories.

Other British breeders to taste Category One success were Mark Currell, with Blonde Buster (Peterborough Derby); Dave Wood, courtesy of Foulden Special (Grand Prix); Keith Howard and David Pearl, whose Hedsor Chipa landed the Swindon Produce stakes; Harry Crapper, breeder of Carling Puppy Classic victor Sibsey Showtime; David Eaton, with Summer Stayers' Classic ace Datona Dandy; and Charles Pickering, who bred Birmingham Cup hero Zigzag Dutchman and registered 30 litters in the 2007 Stud Book , by far the largest number of any domestic breeder.

Pickering's enthusiasm has in no way been dampened by the disastrous fire at his Lincolnshire kennels in December 2006, when some 30 greyhounds perished, including the stud dogs Jamaican Hero and Droopys Honcho.

In the autumn, domestic breeding interests are focused on the Breeders' Forum Produce Stakes at Hall Green, which Nick Savva won in 2005 and 2006 with Westmead Hawk and Dilemmas Flight respectively. His hopes for a three-timer were pinned entirely on Westmead Prince, winner of the Peterborough

Puppy Derby, but this litter-brother to Westmead Lord was eliminated in the semi-finals.

Victory went to Feel Free, bred, owned and trained in Bletchingdon, Oxfordshire, by Richard Baker, who thus recorded his biggest success in a training career of nearly 20 years. A £2,000 breeder's premium accompanied the £15,000 first winner in the race's 25-year history.

Like all the finalists in this and the Swindon Produce Stakes decider, he was sired by an Irish-based stud dog, in his case Droopys Kewell. As the latter's son Droopys Scolari threw the Swindon victory Hedsor Chipa, it was a notable achievement for the two sires, who stand at the Dunphy brothers' range in Co. Waterford.

There are plenty of well-bred, proven stud dogs in Britain, yet they comprised only a quarter of the 31 sires who had runners in the Hall Green feature. The Co. Laois-based Daves Mentor was the most strongly represented of all, with nine starters.

Baker won races with Feel Free's dam Road Princess, a minor open winner at Coventry where she reached A1 grade, and runner-up for the Brighton Belle at Hove. She is by Honcho Classic out of Halls Gold, a half-coursing bred bitch who won on the track at Tralee and raised a few flags whilst engaged in the winter sport, without winning a stake outright.

The 2007 breeders' championship again resolved itself into a contest between Ian Greaves and Sean Dunphy, with the former set fair for principal honours once more, though with a tally short of the record 328 open-race wins gained by his graduates in 2006.

His cardinal big-race success in 2007 came courtesy of Vatican Jinky, who won Belle Vue's Gold Collar in record 590m time, and Walthamstow's Graphite Puppy Derby hero Calzaghe Joe.

Vatican Jinky is by the American dog Hondo Black, while Calzaghe Joe is son of Top Honcho, both sires being located at the Frightful Flash Kennels in Co. Laois; indeed, Greaves patronises no other stud dog establishment.

Sean Dunphy has also achieved excellent results from the FFK sires – he bred the 2004 Derby hero Droopys Scholes from a Top Honcho mating – but around three-quarters of Dunphy-bred open winners are by stud dogs located at the Dunphy range in Co. Waterford.

Such was the case with Opening Artist (by Droopys Scolari), who won the Wimbledon Puppy Derby and reached Graphite Puppy Derby and Carling Puppy Classic finals; Droopys Curbs (by Droopys Shearer) landed Waltamstow's VCbet Puppy Stakes, and Droopys Sheehy (by Droopys Cahill) annexed the Manchester Puppy Cup.

Droopys Cahill has since joined the Lynton Kennels in Essex, swelling the band of Dunphy-bred stud dogs now located in Britain, which includes Droopys Rhys (at Pam Heasman's range), Droopys Ernest (with Pete and Ann Lagan), Droopys Woods and Droopys Corleone (both at Zig Zag Kennels).

While Nick Savva is assured of the third slot in the breeders' championship, the placings below him are closely disputed at the time of press, with John Marks and Liam Dowling heading the contestants.

Marks was represented in the Derby final by Caulry Fast Trap, who finished last, but Dowling was more fortunate in the Scottish version with Fear Haribo, son of Larkhill Jo and the Australian bitch Yamila Diaz, who took the £20,000 purse in record time.

Further down the roster, but sharply in relief in terms of quality, Liam Dwan stands out as the breeder of the Sussex Cup hero Barnfield On Air (by Pacific Mile), probably the fastest dog in the country, who set four track records.

Boherna On Air (by Kiowa Sweet Trey), another Dwan-bred, was twice victorious in Category One finals, at Monmore (Ladbrokes

Barnfield On Air(T3): four track records

Gold Cup) and Sheffield (Steel City Cup). The two hounds are closely related on the bottom line.

After a reign of six years as champion sire, the FFK-based Top Honcho was deposed in 2007 by his son Droopys Vieri – not exactly a palace coup, as the new number one stands at the 'Droopys' stud.

It was no pushover for Droopys Vieri, and the new order underlines the strength of Top Honcho's male line, which boasts another 'top ten' sire in Droopys Woods, and two in the following ten, Droopys Scholes and Fortune Mike.

Walk the Line (Golden Jacket) and Spiridon Louis (Regency, St Leger) embellished Droopys Vieri's scoresheet, while Top Honcho enjoyed one of his best-ever campaigns in Category One finals, notching up seven victories by mid-October. He accumulated ten such titles in 2001.

The deceased Larkhill Jo posted his sixth Category One success of the year when Blitz won the Reading Masters. With the Scottish Derby among his half-dozen, his dynasty claimed supreme honours at both Shawfield and Wimbledon when the Droopys Kewell whelp Westmead Lord took the premier Classic at Plough Lane.

After Top Honcho, the highest-placed Australian import in the stud dog rankings is fifth-placed Daves Mentor, whose principle winners during 2007 were Ballymac Charley (Pall Mall), Blonde Dino (Midland Puppy Derby) and Too Risky (Arc).

He has fallen out of favour with Irish breeders, who were outnumbered in terms of support by their British counterparts in the new British Stud Book, which listed 16 litters by him. One was registered by Mark Currell, owner of Blonde Dino, the 27.81sec record holder at Monmore.

Supposed by some to throw too many offspring of suspect temperament, Daves Mentor has a stamina index of 450m, one of the lowest of any of the Australians.

BGRF

The British Greyhound Racing Fund

THE last couple of years have seen a good deal of activity in greyhound racing. At the time of writing we await the launch of Lord Donoughue's wide-ranging Independent Review into the governance of the sport. This is a reflection of the care we take to ensure the highest standards for ourselves and the sport in which we invest as the major funding body.

Income

Income in 2006 was a record £11.5m following the increase in the rate of bookmaker contribution to 0.6% of greyhound betting turnover. In 2007, the level has dropped slightly largely because people have less disposable income for betting: greyhound racing remains as popular as ever in the betting shops compared to other media.

Charles Lenox-Conyngham: Fund chairman

Welfare

Developments in welfare remain of the highest importance to the BGRF. On our website, www.bgrf.org.uk, we show the historic spend on welfare to the end of 2006 compared to other areas of expenditure and this makes interesting reading.

In 2007, £3.6m out of a budget of £11.5m will go on direct welfare expenditure, including £1.7m to the RGT, £1m towards welfare attendance at racecourses (in support of the racecourse vet, required as a condition of NGRC licensing); also £0.5m towards the BGRB's track safety scheme and £0.2m towards welfare-related training and education initiatives. A further £0.2m was committed to welfare projects and track safety research and development.

The BGRB coordinates welfare on behalf of the sport. Its Welfare Committee is chaired by Fund director John Haynes, and the BGRB employs the sport's first full-time Welfare Officer, Peter Laurie.

I am particularly pleased to report that after homing a record 4,000 ex-racers in 2006, the Retired Greyhound Trust is on target to improve this figure still further in 2007 as we write. This achievement is possible through its national network of homing schemes – which range from hard-working and often self-effacing individuals to racecourse facilities such as Sheffield's magnificent new homing centre. Endless effort goes into raising funds to keep such schemes running, offering temporary kennelling and excellent standards of care whilst good homes are sought.

The RGT exists to help those who are unable to make their own arrangements for re-homing ex-racers in accordance with NGRC Rule 18. Greyhounds make the most brilliant pets and companions in their retirement and the RGT can be contacted on 0870 444 0673.

As well as direct expenditure, many of the grants given by the Fund are closely linked to welfare. However, it is easy to overlook the role of prize-money in supporting the owner and the trainer and ensuring that they, the primary carers of the racing greyhound, can afford to offer the best facilities for their charges.

Integrity

£1.5m is budgeted in 2007 towards areas classed as integrity. These include Newmarket drugs testing and research and racecourse integrity measures. Thanks to the vigilance of the stewards of the NGRC and the high standards of Newmarket testing, the sport remains virtually drugs free.

Racecourses

In 2007, £2m was granted towards racecourse improvements and we expect this to be fully expended by the year end. Major schemes this year include Kinsley's impressive new restaurant facility. The Fund works closely with the industry to improve business planning and make best use of the resources available.

Marketing & IT

The marketing budget is slightly higher this year in an effort to help the sport recover from the effects of the football world cup. This includes a national marketing campaign, as well as regional support to stadia and smaller initiatives. A lot of effort goes into this and we thank our colleagues at the BGRB for undertaking this work.

Administration

The cost of the Fund's administration has not risen in monetary terms over the past ten years, despite the fact that income has increased nearly fivefold. Administration costs are under 2%, meaning that over 98% of all contributions go through to the front line.

A full list of Fund directors and their appointing bodies can be found at www.bgrf.org.uk/who.asp. Margaret Woodruff continues in her role as secretary and can always be contacted for advice.

**Charles Lenox-Conyngham
Chairman,
British Greyhound Racing Fund**

BGRB   The British Greyhound Racing Board
– a personal view from the General Secretary

One Monday night about ten years ago I went with a friend to Crayford. Having been racing at Wembley and Hackney already I wasn't quite a 'six-packer' but nor was I a seasoned greyhound man.

Towards the end of the evening I was talking to my friend, discussing when we should next go racing. Another man at the bar decided to join in the conversation.

"How did you get on tonight lads?"

"Good thanks, we were just talking about visiting some other tracks. I don't suppose you'd have any pointers?"

He sighed. "Well I don't know. I mean take this place, it's not a patch on the old Crayford."

Ten minutes later we'd heard about how Canterbury was "on its knees", Hackney was "never going to get built" and how there would be "no greyhound racing in London in ten years".

As far as I could make out 20 years earlier every track had been full every night, all the punters knew at least three generations of breeding of every participating dog, and the dozens of competing bookmakers bet to about 101 per cent. Honestly, after this gent's speech you'd have forgiven me if I had never gone greyhound racing again.

Don't get me wrong, his predictions were not far off the mark and it was a hammer blow to this London-dweller to also lose Catford so few years later. But I was just a rookie race-goer being friendly and chatting to another punter at the end of good night out. If that was end of a football match I would have been feeding off the enthusiasm of my fellow fans. Instead I was chosen to receive greyhound racing's last rites and I can tell you without

Richard Hayler: BGRB General Secretary

any exaggeration that I have heard variations of that speech well over a hundred times since.

Perhaps the sport needs a holiday. Every sport has a closed season apart from greyhound racing. Maybe because there is always racing none of us are ever given the chance to miss it. The start and end of a sporting season is always the focal point of fans' excitement and we have neither. I wonder what the crowds would be like at Old Trafford if Manchester United had played three football matches a week every week for the last ten years.

Of course nothing is that straight forward. We have, quite rightly, gone beyond being just a sport. We are part of the entertainment industry, and no owner/trainer wants to lose a month of prize money anymore than a promoter wishes to lose out on a month's tote revenue. Other leisure venues such as cinemas don't have a closed season and they seem to be doing okay. Or are they? I grew up in Watford, which apparently had nine cinemas in 1958. In 2008 it has only one. All live entertainment venues are under pressure.

Greyhound racing faces challenges today that could never have been imagined in 1958. You can watch, bet on and talk to others about live greyhound racing every evening in any high street betting shop; and as a greater threat yet, you can do all those things via a computer from the comfort of your living room armchair.

That presumes of course that you even want to bet on greyhounds. In 1958 if you wanted to have a bet in the evening you went to a greyhound stadium and you bet on greyhounds. Of course that is still the sensible choice, but today the range of other options includes floodlit horse racing, roulette machines in betting shops, internet poker, online casinos or betting on any number of other sports featuring on one of 400 satellite TV channels.

In the circumstances the 3.3 million live attendances we achieved in 2006 is a superb result for the sport. Imagine greyhound racing had launched from scratch last year into the modern competitive betting and entertainment market place. Experts would have been astounded at our success. They would have marvelled at the creation of a fast-paced, accessible night out which doubled up as a trustworthy and reliable betting medium, and immediately became Britain's third most popular spectator sport. These are aspects that we have become immune to or taken for granted.

Although I cannot prove it I would bet good money that the number of different people going greyhound racing has increased every year for the last ten years. Total attendances have fallen slightly because ëregulars' are being lured away by the comfort of betting from home; but social interest in going to the dogs and betting on our races is definitely on the up.

There are many dedicated greyhound racing websites; www.thedogs.co.uk is just one, but the number of different individuals visiting the site has grown year on year, month on month. There are twice as many people using the site today as when it re-launched in its present design six years ago.

The commercial challenges to greyhound racing are not shrinking however, and if I was allowed to make one New Year's resolution for the whole sport it would be to get everyone working together. Owners and trainers are racecourse promoters' best customers, and they are potentially the best-placed people to help improve tracks' business performance.

Although not everyone would agree,

> *Greyhound racing faces challenges today that could never have been imagined in 1958. You can watch, bet on and talk to others about live greyhound racing every evening in any high street betting shop; and as a greater threat yet, you can do all those things via a computer from the comfort of your living room armchair.*

Sponsored by the BGRB

owners and promoters are very much on the same team. Each depends on the other. A full track should be heart warming for both parties and an empty one mutually depressing. It would be fantastic if even just one track management and one local owners association began working together to share ideas on how to get the tills ringing on the basis that prize money would rise and fall in agreed ways based on the track's financial performance. An owner would know that every tote bet, every restaurant meal eaten and every guest introduced to the sport was directly contributing to his or her prize money return.

If such a scheme had been in place ten years ago perhaps I would have encountered a more encouraging voice that night at Crayford. Positivity might just become infectious.

Richard Hayler
General Secretary
British Greyhound Racing Board

NGRC

The National Greyhound Racing Club – Chief Executive's report

By the time the Greyhound Annual goes to press Lord Donoughue will have published his Review into greyhound racing and no doubt this will have led to many reactions from greyhound lovers and stakeholders alike.

It is hoped that his review and recommendations will form the basis of a route map for the sport to move forward and help reinvigorate interest and enthusiasm.

As agreed at the outset when nominating Lord Donoughue to be the Chairman of the Independent Review, the NGRC have co-operated fully with the Review Group. I must compliment the thoroughness of their work in first understanding the sport and its stakeholders before considering the best possible future solution. Due to the proximity of the Review it is interesting to reflect on the past year at the NGRC and the enormous amount of work that has continued for the sport and while Lord Donoughue's review group's work has been ongoing we have continued business as usual.

Alistair McLean: NGRC Chief Executive

The NGRC has continued to carry out its function serving the sport, maintaining integrity, welfare and security standards both on and off the track as would have been expected, although in 2007, there have been a few key events which have impacted enormously on greyhound racing. These include the Animal Welfare Act passing through Parliament and the introduction of the Gambling Act.

Animal Welfare Act

Welfare standards and regulation are key issues for the NGRC and we have worked closely with the Department for the Environment, Food and Rural Affairs in the shaping of the Act and on behalf of the industry looking to develop with other stakeholders secondary legislation that will underpin the Act.

This involves detailed consideration of what is required to ensure a minimum standard for safeguarding greyhound welfare across the sport and a proportionate approach as to how it can be achieved without placing undue burden on those affected by the Act.

One of the ways that we do this is through our committee work and as far as welfare is concerned this is through the NGRC's Veterinary, Welfare & Scientific Committee.

This NGRC committee with representatives from the sport and veterinary expertise meet regularly to review current policies as well as carrying out research projects into subjects such spaying and oestrus suppression and the effects on racing bitches.

Many or our initiatives, likes those of the BGRB Welfare Committee, are designed to improve welfare standards for the greyhound and ensure that such initiatives are where necessary aligned to the Animal Welfare Act.

We are continually reviewing how we regulate greyhound welfare and the Stewards continue their resolve to remove those from NGRC racing who demonstrate a disregard for their responsibilities under both the Rules of Racing and the Animal Welfare Act, so that the responsible vast majority should not be continually tarnished by actions of the few.

Gambling Act 2005

The Gambling Act 2005 was fully enacted in September 2007 and brought with it a new 'cheating law' with regulation carried out by the Gambling Commission; not only is it a breach of rules to cheat for financial gain but it is also illegal.

Everybody wants a clean and fair sport so the integrity of racing is another key subject requiring an assured level of regulation and with ever changing betting opportunities we continue to explore the possible negative effects that they can have.

This work has been carried out through improved and regular liaison with betting organisations and changes have been made to the Rules of Racing in respect of betting and laying. One of our committees that deal with this area is the NGRC's Integrity Joint Committee.

Its role is to examine many areas affecting integrity and makes recommendations to the Stewards for any changes or initiatives that it considers would improve regulation in this area. We have also been working closely with other sports through the Integrity in Sports Betting Panel which was launched in 2006 by the former Minister for Sport, The Rt. Hon. Richard Caborn with the aim of encouraging sports regulatory authorities to unite in achieving the objective of safeguarding integrity in all sports and thereby their participants and the betting public.

Changing the Rules of Racing requires great care to ensure that we are improving the Rules of Racing for the good of the sport and not just changing them for the sake of it.

With that objective in mind the Rules Review Committee was set up to see what rules needed altering and what new rules were needed, such as rules on betting and laying. The committee has almost completed its review of the Rule Book and has made a large number of amendments to accommodate the changing times in which we live and work, and to help clarify the interpretation of rules. Its work is ongoing and will continue into 2008 with the

Sponsored by the BGRB

intention of publishing a new complete Rule Book once this first review is complete.

Finally we have the work of the newly created NGRC Appeal Board. For those that will remember, the NGRC was involved in a high court case with Mr Flaherty regarding the decision the Stewards made at an inquiry. What followed was an Appeal Court hearing which ruled in favour of the NGRC and led in part to the NGRC Appeal Board being introduced. This board consists of independently appointed members who sit to determine whether or not the Stewards have made a fair decision. It is an additional safeguard to anyone who if following an inquiry feel that the stewards have made an error, then they can appeal to the Appeal Board. Two cases have been heard by the Appeal Board and while the Stewards' decisions have been upheld on both occasions the Appeal Board have heard each case in full and made a number of important observations. This a good process for the sport to have and give further protection to the regulation and integrity of the sport.

Into 2008

As in all businesses and organisations, our work continues to grow but with it grows our commitment to ensure that along with delivering the everyday functions of registration, licensing and security of welfare and integrity regulation, with the support and expertise from both within the NGRC and the many stakeholders we will maintain our efforts to improve the sport and to overcome the problems of recent years.

Best of luck to all in 2008.

Alistair McLean
Chief Executive
National Greyhound Racing Club

Trainers' Association

by Jim Reynolds, Chairman

2008 should be viewed as a year of opportunity for everyone working in greyhound racing. There has been a sea of change in the last year; we had the passing of the animal welfare bill and Lord Donoughue's report. It is imperative that we use these as a catalyst for positive change as we continue to improve the way we run our sport and show everyone that it has a bright future.

Our world is very different now. Compare it to when I started on the long road in the 1970's working seven days a week for £30 with no internal structures in place to allow for natural development.

There are new initiatives on welfare and education for staff, these must be encouraged and enhanced to demonstrate how professional our industry has become.

Now that we have meaningful qualifications when working in our industry it should go hand in hand that these qualifications are incorporated into a career path to becoming a professional greyhound trainer. This will encourage new skills which will take our sport to new levels.

Track safety and track maintenance is an area that we must continue to improve on. Welfare issues that arise from a poorly prepared track should be a thing of the past, we have the technology and the know-how to prepare good running surfaces; we must all endeavour to ensure that our greyhounds get the best conditions possible to realise their potential and have a long and healthy racing career.

Greyhound racing is a great sport; it is a fantastic evening's entertainment for many thousands of people all year round. Where

Jim Reynolds: Trainers' Association chairman

else can you take your family out together for the evening in a friendly and safe environment? How many owners get great pleasure of going to the kennels every Sunday with their friends and families to walk their greyhound out in the countryside?

The real buzz is getting the greyhound out and watching the way they greet the owners week after week; these are the images that the 'antis' don't want to see, the quality of life with care and attention to their every need. We must endeavour to show that we do care for our greyhounds, and care for them better than any other.

2007 was another great year for 'champion greyhounds' with both Spiridon Louis and Barnfield On Air excelling in all they have done. Any trainer will tell you that is the dream; one day they will have a greyhound of that class and pace. For me there is nothing better than to get a raw novice puppy that is about to embark on its racing career, doing its grading trials, watching it having its first ever race beside five other dogs, seeing it learn race after race growing in confidence and realising its potential in getting its first victory.

The joy of taking it racing each week with heightened anticipation wondering how it will run; will the trap draw be better for it? Will it manage to take the rise in grade and compete beside faster greyhounds or will it improve once it is stepped up to the six-bend trip?

This is what makes our job the best in the world; this is what makes every greyhound in our care our very own 'champion greyhound'.

Looking forward to 2008, every sector of our industry must work together for a stronger and more efficient sport; don't think 'what are they doing', the thought should be 'what can we do'?

Our sport is a great sport with a great history and, with high standards of strength and resolve, it will continue for many years to come.

Jim Reynolds
Chairman
Trainers' Association

Breeders Forum

by Bob Gilling

I am pleased to report British breeding is now at its highest level. Although less litters have been registered recently the quality has improved dramatically.

Three years ago I was fortunate to be on the first 'The Dogs' programme on Sky. As the breeders' representative on the BGRB, I stated then that I was confident the British breeders could produce and rear greyhounds, as good as anywhere in the world.

Since then the last three Derbys have been won by British-breds, namely Nick Savva's Westmeads – Hawk and Lord. Then he has followed this up by breeding the fantastic St Leger winner Spiridon Louis, most ably trained by Lorraine Sams.

Many of our other breeders have also bred

Bob Gilling: Breeders' secretary

BREEDERS FESTIVAL 2006
CATEGORY WINNERS HARLOW, 23 SEPTEMBER

Class 1 (broods destined for stud) Alfa Amour (Top Honcho–Myross Mistress), owner L Steed

Class 2 (broods that have whelped a litter) Half Cool (Cool Performance-New Experience) Best in Show brood owner P Heasman

Class 3 (broods that have whelped a winner) Mollicious (Small Fortune-Java Rose) owner J Zsibrita

Class 4 (broods that whelped an open winner) Sparks Running (Larkhill Jo-Crossleigh Spark) owner S Walton

Class 5 (for retired greyhounds over eight) Best dog Frontier Bob (Sept 96) owner L Parry Best bitch Well Maid (Dec 95) owner J Zsibrita

Class 6 (pups whelped Jan-Mar 07) unnamed (March 07) be d Westmead Hawk-Songbird Gill, owner L Parry

Class 7 (pups Apr-June 06) Black Fly (Mustang Zapper-Chuckle Anita) owner T Pett

Class 8 (saplings July-Sep 06) Old Money (Courts Legal-Queens Shilling) owner W Scoles

Class 9 (saplings Oct-Dec 06) unnamed (Oct 06) Brett Lee-Open Verdict (Best in Show sapling) owner S Poots

Class 10 (progeny as a group) Rapid Ranger-Shelbourne Irene (one dog, two bitches May 06) owner J Hurst

Category One greyhounds.

Mark Currell has been very successful with his Blonde Buster and Dino; Dave Wood with Foulden Special – what a run in the Grand Prix at Walthamstow! – Harry Crapper with Sibsey Showtime in the Puppy Classic at Nottingham; D. Eaton's Datona Dandy in the Summer Classic also at Nottingham.

Keith Howard and David Pearl kept up the good work with Hedsor Chipa winning the Swindon Produce once again this year, while Richard Baker burst on the breeding scene with his home bred feel free in the Produce Stakes at Hall Green.

We all appreciate the financial support from the BGRF to our breeders.

I have had the task of awarding incentives to our successful breeders. This has now appeard to be Fund money well spent. They have all delivered the goods. The whole of the greyhound sport appreciates their efforts, without them there would not be the excitement we experience when we see all these champions perform.

We all look forward to next year. There are a lot of top-class pups ready and waiting.

The hare is on the move!

May all your pups be injury free, and be lucky.

Bob Gilling
Honourary Secretary
British Greyhound Breeders Forum

FBGOA

by John Waldron

THE FBGOA is the voice of greyhound owners at the highest level in the sport. It represents owners' associations and is not open to individuals.

2007 has been a year of writing submissions to various bodies, apart from a report in connection with the Animal Welfare Act, there was a submission to the Donoughue inquiry and sandwiched between these came The Associate Parliamentary Group for Animal Welfare report on greyhound racing.

This august body comprising a group of seven MPs, a Noble Lord and a Baroness asked for information from every Tom, Dick and Harriet within and outside the sport and produced a report, making recommendations as to the future.

We thought that an abbreviated summary to that enquiry would illustrate the contribution that the FBGOA make to the sport.

Re-homing of Greyhounds

The FBGOA. fully supports schemes which involve the homing of greyhounds at track level with member tracks having schemes either within their organisation, or associated with it, which set out to find suitable homes for retired greyhounds. Some organisations are purely homing based and have individual charitable status.

As illustration, to highlight just two tracks, both of which are members of the Federation. Wimbledon Greyhound Welfare occupies kennels at Hersham in Surrey. This started as an adjunct to the Owners' Association and quickly grew, in size and popularity, making it necessary to separate it from the parent body. It was renamed Wimbledon Greyhound Welfare (WGW) with its own independent management committee.

This organisation is staffed by dedicated volunteers and has homed hundreds of greyhounds since its inception. The Owners' Association supports all its fund raising ventures together with the track proprietors, GRA, and to highlight the financial contribution, in the year 2005/6 the Owners' Association contributed £5,359 to WGW.

At Brighton & Hove track, a £30,000 investment in kennels at Albourne in West Sussex has produced accommodation for 35 greyhounds in the homing chain. The rental of the site is in the region of £10,000 p.a. and is financed by the track owners, other sums are raised by a wide range of fund raising activities, generosity of prominent owners and a covenant of £4,000 p.a. donated by the track owners, Coral Bookmakers.

A similar arrangement is in operation at its sister track, Romford. A new scheme of compulsory membership of the Owners' Association for the first year, by new owners at the tracks, recently introduced with half the membership fee being passed on to the retired kennels has substantially increased revenues at both places.

Again, the Brighton Retired greyhound Trust is staffed by dedicated volunteers without whom the whole concept would become financially unworkable.

These are but two examples of what happens at stadia licensed by the N.G.R.C. for greyhound racing and this is replicated across the country to a greater or lesser extent. The standard of accommodation and feeding for the retireds conform to the criteria laid down by the governing body for the racing greyhound so that many owners of ex-racers are content to pay a monthly kennel bill to keep their greyhounds in familiar and secure accommodation for the rest of their lives of until found a home.

Regulation

The Federation believe that layers of additional statutory regulation will drive away large numbers of volunteers in homing schemes who simply love the dogs and generally do not have the background to cope with the inevitable stratas of bureaucracy that statutory regulation would impose.

The governing bodies of the sport have been working hard over recent years to implement, with a large degree of success, the safeguards which are already in existence. There is no compelling reason to create additional statutory rules and regulations from Parliament or from Town Halls.

Greyhound owners and followers of the sport have seen improvements on a wide front in terms of track improvement, kennelling standards, transportation, veterinary facilities and the reduction of injuries. All these improvements which have come about since the voluntary grant to the sport from Bookmaker's greyhound betting turnover, need time to become established as minimum requirements within a self-regulating regime.

For a sport introduced to the U.K. some 80 years ago, old customs are often hard to break down but given time and finance the Greyhound Charter will be seen as a major break-through in greyhound welfare.

The report of the APGAW has now been published and it contains 48 pages of comments, recommendations, statistics and opinions.

One has to search its contents carefully to find any reference to Owners and on page 35 they are mentioned within a section headed 'benefits of independents', wherein it is stated that owners of greyhounds racing on the independent circuit have a greater emotional attachment to their dogs (presumably owners of NGRC-registered dogs have a lesser emotional attachment!).

From the report, one would have thought that owners played no part in the functioning of this sport which is the third largest spectator sport in the UK.

There is no mention that owners support the sport in terms of purchase of greyhounds, kennel expenses and contributions to welfare to the tune of £ 27m p.a. after prize-money or that the betting turnover on greyhounds tops £2 billion p.a. Most greyhound owners find themselves in a 'negative equity' situation even after prize-money so every pound they receive is recirculated within the sport.

Finally, if your track has no owners' association, or if it has but does not belong to the Federation, think about it.

The Federation works closely with promoter, breeder, and trainer bodies, and forms no threat to managements. Indeed, thriving owners' associations bring benefits to tracks with promotional meetings, retired greyhound benefit and social occasions which enhance gate receipts.

Contact can be made directly with the secretary John Waldron, or through our website www.fbgoa.org.uk.

John Waldron
Secretary
Federation of British Greyhound
Owners' Associations

Calculating the age of a greyhound – NGRC Rule 23

Whelping Date	Eligible to trial on: (15 months old)	Eligible for puppy: races until
January 2007	1.04.08	31.12.08
February 2007	1.05.08	31.01.09
March 2007	1.06.08	29.02.09
April 2007	1.07.08	31.03.09
May 2007	1.08.08	30.04.09
June 2007	1.09.08	31.05.09
July 2007	1.10.08	30.06.09
August 2007	1.11.08	31.07.09
September 2007	1.12.08	31.08.09
October 2007	1.01.09	30.09.09
November 2007	1.02.09	31.10.09
December 2007	1.03.09	30.11.09

Welfare and PR

by Peter Laurie

For the BGRB, 2007 has primarily been about greyhound welfare and responding to the pressures and expectation from government, the public, the media and welfare pressure groups for the sport to put its house in order following the abhorrent revelations from Seaham in summer 2006.

But it has also been about getting new people to come greyhound racing and reminding the public that even in an increasingly crowded and competitive leisure market, our sport still offers an accessible, fun and great value source of entertainment.

Whilst some areas of the BGRB's work have understandably been put on hold whilst Lord Donoughue and his team carried out their independent review of the sport's regulation, it has still been a busy year.

Under the Chairmanship of John Haynes, the Welfare Committee has overseen a programme of investment unprecedented in the history of the sport. By the end of 2007, almost £4 million – approximately one third of the sport's annual income – will have been spent on a wide range of welfare improvement initiatives.

Within that budget, almost half a million pounds has been allocated to track safety improvement projects, including alterations to cambers, installation of improved drainage systems and safety curtains and the purchase of new track preparation equipment; all with the aim of reducing injuries and extending racing careers. Almost every NGRC track has benefited and the feedback from owners, trainers and racing managers has been extremely positive.

A programme of welfare research has

Peter Laurie: BGRB Welfare Officer

complemented the track improvement work, to help ensure that more and more decisions are taken on the back of scientific evidence and not anecdotal opinion. It is likely that research will have an increasingly important role to play in the development of future welfare policy.

Headlining the research programme has been the ongoing testing of Viscoride, a potential alternative running surface to sand.

Reports from the Sports Turf Research Institute tell us that the material performs well in all weather conditions and following initial galloping of greyhounds on the test-bed there, it is very likely that the material will now be laid on a full size test track throughout 2008.

Other BGRB-funded research continues at Liverpool University (and is helping to stimulate interest in greyhound racing amongst its student vet population), by track vet Richard Payne, the Society of Greyhound Vets and the NGRC. Mineralogist Dr Terry

Sponsored by the BGRB

Veasey has also completed a valuable survey of the sands used at different tracks and their characteristics.

The BGRB's training and education programme has really gathered pace throughout 2007 and all credit to Training Co-ordinator David Parker whose efforts over the past 18 months are now bearing plenty of fruit. Individuals across the sport now for the first time have the chance to develop and demonstrate their skills and commitment.

In June we congratulated the first two kennelhands to have completed their NVQ qualifications in greyhound care and many more will follow. A series of one-day seminars have been launched covering everything from instruction for newcomers to the sport, human first aid and manual handling to hands-on presentations from distinguished vet Plunkett Devlin.

Training for track groundstaff continues to develop with another popular set of workshops and a series of new initiatives planned for 2008.

The Trainers' Assistance Fund has had a busy 12 months, awarding grants to over 200 trainers right across the country.

Every trainer has been entitled to funding towards air management or air-conditioning systems in their transport vehicles, and towards the cost of new travel cages. It is very pleasing that in just a few years trainers have acted to ensure that welfare of greyhounds-in-transit is safeguarded, and the Government's new transport requirements have been smoothly introduced.

Grants have also been awarded to professional trainers to enhance their facilities or to assist during periods of hardship.

And last but not least on the welfare front, the sport's provision for retired greyhounds continues to improve and it is so pleasing to hear that the number of retired greyhounds that are rehomed each year continues to rise.

The RGT have reported record levels of rehoming in 2007 and a further set of grants have been awarded from the BGRB's Retired Greyhound Fund to support many of the non-RGT rehoming organisations.

Aside from the need for the BGRB to increase resources directed at welfare, it has also had to adjust its strategies to counter post-Seaham negative publicity that is seemingly rarely far away.

The BGRB is now both reacting more strongly than in the past to all inaccurate claims and myths that the sport's critics may make and propagate as well as doing more to promote the many positive sides to greyhound racing.

The BGRB's PR agency, Freerange Communications brought new ideas to the table, from the whacky (such as Ann Summers parties at Wimbledon and Belle Vue) to the serious (for example, press nights for national newspaper journalists).

The BGRB is now both reacting more strongly than in the past to all inaccurate claims and myths that the sport's critics may make and propagate as well as doing more to promote the many positive sides to greyhound racing.

The firm also helped co-ordinate the induction of a waxwork model of Westmead Hawk into Madame Tussauds, an event that saw images of the canine superstar appearing in the national media for the first time since his two Derby victories.

The BGRB commissioned a communications audit in late summer that involved interviews with stakeholders across the sport. The outcomes from the report are helping to direct the introduction of a series of new proactive PR initiatives, the first of which will be unveiled in early 2008.

Elsewhere. the BGRB has continued its sponsorship of Sky's magazine show 'The Dogs' and generally sought to communicate more effectively with stakeholders via the trade media – notably Racing Post and Greyhound Star – and the BGRB website www.thedogs.co.uk, which is likely to be overhauled in 2008.

On the racing front, the issue of prize-money has dominated many of the headlines,

but it should be remembered that the BGRB contribution to graded prize-money was reduced by approximately £2 per runner in its 2007 budget for one reason and one reason only – to allow extra and urgently required spending on welfare, without which the sport would likely be staring down the barrel at costly and restrictive Government regulation.

Whilst the reductions were sorely felt by many greyhound owners and trainers and were exacerbated by some tracks making cuts of their own, the BGRB has worked hard to reduce the impact, for example by diverting money saved by the cancellation of the Top Dog competition to graded racing and an allocation of money to each track for Christmas bonus races.

The open-race calendar has welcomed a number of new sponsors and competitions – Blue Square were popular new backers of the Greyhound Derby and also invested heavily in a series of competitions at Coventry, while William Hill launched a successful Festival of

Westmead Hawk meets his waxwork model at Madame Tussauds, which the BGRB's PR agency Freerange Communications helped to co-ordinate. Nick Savva, trainer of the double Derby champion, is also pictured

Racing in the North East of England complete with a tremendous prize-fund. Trainers and owners of open race greyhounds are spoilt for choice like never before when it comes to races and competitions suitable for their runners.

However, it is vital to the future prosperity of the sport in Britain for it to become more attractive to new audiences. Many tracks are safeguarding their and their trainers' futures, investing heavily in customer facilities and ensuring that a greater percentage still of those who go greyhound racing for the first time will return.

Millions of households across Britain will have seen an exciting and ultimately successful national television advertising campaign on ITV1 that has bolstered attendances across the country. The well-documented Greyhound Sporting Leagues have also proved successful and have helped significantly improve midweek crowds and income at all tracks, and simultaneously raised money for grass-roots sports clubs.

Within the BGRB office itself, Emma Johns, John Petrie and Lauren Duffield all left for pastures new in 2007. Richard Hayler has assumed the role of BGRB General Secretary, while Zekai Kosumcu has joined the team as Finance Manager – and unofficially, as photographer! – and Amanda Duplock is the new Executive Assistant.

I hope this review has given readers a better idea of the focuses of the BGRB throughout 2007.

As the sport enters 2008, the challenge is for the organisation to continue to derive maximum benefit for the sport from the resources available to it, whilst incorporating the findings of the Donoughue review.

Constructive ideas and suggestions to help us achieve this are, as always, welcome.

Peter Laurie
Welfare Officer and PR Spokesman
BGRB

Education

by David Parker

As a child I was much taken with the Apollo moon landings. An avid viewer and collector of newspaper cuttings I dreamt that one day I would walk on the moon. Unfortunately by 1972 it was all over. A total of 12 men had walked on the moon and I was not one of them, my career as an astronaut was over before it had begun.

Why you ask does this have any relevance to the readers of the BGRB Greyhound Annual? Well, because even at that tender age I realised that times change and that in order to keep up and move on you need to be flexible and learn new skills. My most recent change has been to join the BGRB and work with a whole range of new people.

The past two years have seen some fairly major changes within the greyhound racing world.

A new focus on animal welfare and proposed changes to the regulation of the sport has left many feeling that their career will be as long as an Apollo astronaut. But of course that will not be the case.

Change presents a wide range of challenges and in order to meet these challenges we need to change the way we go about things, develop some new skills and ensure that the way that we do our job meets the need of the new world.

Training plays a major role in the promotion of the change. The development of new skills and qualifications can offer a new perspective and a new confidence to succeed.

During 2007 the BGRB has been very much in the business of offering new skills and qualifications. The year has seen us register over 50 kennel hands onto the NVQ

David Parker: Training Co-ordinator

scheme. These people are leading the way in a sport in which staff will increasingly expect to be able to further develop their knowledge and skills in the workplace.

The Government is proposing to ensure that all young people are either in education of some sort until the age of 18. Some of these people will be attracted to our kennels if they see that there are educational opportunities. The provision of these opportunities will see the continuation of Government funding coming into the sport for education.

Linked to the NVQ scheme we have tried to offer basic skills training in First Aid and Manual Handling as well as offering an Introductory Course for new entrants. These courses are available at tracks all around the country and whilst predominantly aimed at younger workers, are suitable for all. Frankly these courses have not been as well received as I had hoped.

They cover skills that should be a basic requirement of every worker in any industry; namely a basic understanding of the business and what it does, the confidence to address an accident whilst at work and the knowledge to keep injury free. All of these skills produce a more reliable, knowledgeable and engaged worker – exactly what I would have thought that the sport requires.

As to those that have told me that ìit's not worth training because no one stays for longî. Perhaps you should ask yourself why? The more we encourage and offer opportunities to people the better the return will be.

And if that is not sufficient encouragement to ensure that you take up the training that is currently on offer, look at the world around us. Pick up any newspaper on any day and you will find stories from the law courts about those that have had accidents at work or feel they have been unfairly treated.

As employers and indeed as employees it is vital that our employment practices are up to scratch. For those unsure of what these might be, we will be introducing a new resource for trainers and employers in the new year that will clearly outline the responsibilities under law.

Another area where it is vital to ensure that those new to the sport have a clear understanding of their role is in customer service. Each and every track relies on its ability to offer the paying public an experience they will wish to repeat which ensures that the sport thrives.

During 2007 we have been working with our friends at Belle Vue to develop a computer based training programme that will be available to all tracks in 2008.

Add to this the work that has been done in recognition of the new gambling regulations,

the development of track maintenance staff skills and knowledge and the impending introduction of a track ground staff accreditation scheme in 2008. Change and the influence of training has been at work in all of the fundamental areas of the sport.

You will note that to date this article has focused entirely on the people working in the sport rather than the greyhounds that are it's lifeblood. But fear not, for in 2007 we were delighted to welcome Plunkett Devlin to deliver seminars at Romford and Sheffield where the dogs were the stars of the show.

Over 175 people attended these two events and it was pleasing to see how many of them were young people. Some were clearly the sons and daughters of old hands others were working in professional kennels and wanted to improve their knowledge and skills. Whilst there continues to be an enthusiastic and knowledgeable group of young people working in the sport we will be able to take the changes, that are inevitable, in our stride and introduce the improvements that will be required as racing moves into the new century.

As I write this there is a news storey that Wayne Rooney has taken on a tutor and is studying for his GCSE in Maths and English. Some people think that this is amusing but Wayne is showing us all the way. Whoever you are, whatever you do, ensuring that you have the skills required to meet the demands of life or indeed to catch up with those that you might have left behind is a vital part of thriving in the modern world.

So the next time you see a BGRB course being organised at your track and you think "should I go?", make sure that the answer is YES.

It might not make you an astronaut, but how about a time traveller?

David Parker
BGRB Training Consultant

Racing Manager
Peter Miller
By Phil Donaldson

Peter Miller, Hove's racing manager, looks across as the 515m traps pop open and two trial dogs are put through their paces. It's a typically cold but bright Monday afternoon in November as we sit and chat at the Coral-owned track.

Miller laughs as he answers my opening gambit about his age. "Yes, believe it or not I'm 43. It's the job, you see, it puts years on you!"

As I, personally, left the same position at Catford some seven years back, I nod wisely. While my racing office career took me from Wembley to the former Adenmore Road venue, Miller has a few more miles on his clock.

His racing office journey started at Ramsgate as a teenage office assistant and moved via Oxford, Wembley, Powderhall and Romford, until he landed at Hove on the retirement of Jim Layton back in spring 1994.

So what was it that kick-started his life in greyhound racing?"Well," he replies, "like many in the game, I was brought up with dogs. My dad, George, was a trainer at Southend and Ramsgate, and it was a way of life to go racing."

It was while studying for his A-levels that Miller was offered a job at Ramsgate, working under RM Geoff Jeffcoate, but after six months at his local track, promoters Northern Sports requested he transfer to what was then Dumpton Park's sister-track, Oxford.

"I saw it as a progressive move, and took up the challenge," recalls Miller. "I was there for two-and-a-half years, and for some of that time I was able to get involved with the grading, too, when briefly filling in as racing

manager, although technically I was too young for the job – I don't think the NGRC were impressed!"

The Miller bandwagon rolled on, and in April of 1984, our man landed up at Wembley stadium – one of the big guns in greyhound racing at the time. A strong tradition of competitive graded racing, a regular menu of top-class open racing, and a betting ring featuring Tony Morris, Dougie Tyler and the infamous John Power, made Wembley an exciting place to be, and Miller remembers his time there largely with affection.

"I initially worked under joint-racing managers in Ron Fraiser and Jim Cremin," he recalls, "while Terry Norman was the other member of the team. It was a busy place to be, and I can still vividly recall the rush of Monday mornings, which was when the opens for Friday would close."

Younger readers out there may find this hard to believe, but in those days there was no fax machines, let alone emails and formpacks, so all formlines were collated long-hand over the telephone.

"The worst call to make was Harringay. Woe betide anyone who got Ginger Lee on the line. He used to rattle them off at about five lines per second. It was a nightmare!"

Miller remembers a strong training strength too, with the likes of Tom Johnston, Ted Dickson and Terry Dartnall enjoying some lively battles around the famous track.

However, when the GRA moved in to buy the operation, Miller felt his feet start to itch. "To be honest, I never really took to the GRA, and in my opinion, Wembley was never the same once they got involved."

Fortunately for Miller, another phone call resulted in another job offer, as Coral came calling with news of a racing manager's vacancy at their Edinburgh track Powderhall, and as a single, 25-year-old he did not take much persuading.

"They were a happy couple of years, and I really enjoyed the craic," Miller admits. "The outside Bramich hare took a bit of getting used to – as did the Scottish hunger for handicap racing – but the banter with the locals was great. It was a fair gallop too, with loads of potential."

It was also in Scotland that Miller met his wife Mayann, so you could say the move paid off big style! All was set fair in Edinburgh, until Coral were approached by Eddie Ramsay, who made an offer for the place.

Miller agreed to remain in position whilst the take-over went through, but crunch-time came as Coral prepared to hand over the keys. With no specific vacancy as such they offered a floating role back down south between Hove and Romford.

Miller decided instead to stay put – but just a month later the Barking firm were back with a proper job offer – that of Romford RM, as the infamous Jim Simpson race-fixing scandal was exposed.

"It was a hard decision, as Mayann had to be happy about it too," he says. "Happily, she moved down south with me, and I entered the hectic world of Romford."

The five-meetings-a-week schedule at that time was a bit of a shock to Miller's system, although he laughs as he adds "they have a minimum of six now so good luck to Peter O'Dowd!

"To be honest, it was hard work, as when you're new you tend to want to be there all the time. I've learnt now that you can't be, which is why it's important to have a team you can trust."

And there's plenty of experience in the Hove racing office, with Jeff Piper filling the slot of very able deputy, assisted by Andy Leaney "a Coral man for 28 years who has worked his way from the ground staff, via the print shop, to the racing team."

Ricky Kirtin provides office back-up, Louise Smith is an evening steward, while Miller counts himself fortunate to have former racing office stalwart Philip Grimstone to call on whenever staffing levels are low.

So getting personal for a bit, I wonder if the generally mild-mannered grader ever loses his rag. "Very rarely," he admits, "but I can't stand people who are constantly moaning. Honestly, I used to think it was compulsory for trainers to have a degree in moaning before they could get a licence!"

Backtracking slightly – possibly at the thought of offending his contracted handlers – Miller swiftly adds: "To be fair, there is much more pressure on trainers these days, particularly financially, as the number of owners dwindles. I suppose they have to filter their frustration through to us!"

So where does Miller go to get away from what can be a consuming vocation? "Horseracing is my idea of a relaxing day out. I'm fortunate that Plumpton, Goodwood, Brighton, Fontwell and Lingfield all in easy reach."

And what keeps a man of 25-years-plus experience still in love with the game? "I love

> *The worst call to make was Harringay.*
> *Woe betide anyone who got Ginger Lee on the line.*
> *He used to rattle them off at about five lines*
> *per second. It was a nightmare!*

our big nights. The two Sky meetings in 2007 were tremendous nights, and in Spiridon Louis [Regency] and Barnfield On Air [Sussex Cup] we had a couple of half-decent champions!

"I also enjoy Ballyregan Bob Memorial night. He was, and still is, my all-time favourite greyhound. He was unbelievable to watch, and I'm delighted as Hove racing manager to help maintain our pride in his achievements. The card also features the final of the Jimmy Jupp National Hurdle – named after an owner that no track regular will forget."

2007 wasn't a bad year at all for Hove. Miller admits that while like most tracks, the midweek crowds have suffered, Saturdays are still booming. "We're fortunate in that we've secured 31 Tuesday BAGS fixtures, as that was our weakest night.

"But overall, things are going well. I don't believe in putting pressure on people to get results. We are one of the few UK tracks to maintain 12-race evening cards, and our 12 trainers are not told how many dogs they must provide.

"People want to work at different volumes, and as long as I can maintain around 350 dogs on the strength then I'm comfortable. And if I'm comfortable, I'm happy – which is what it's all about really!"

Trainer Profiles
Barry Draper
By John Forbes

WHEN Clan Draper reviews 2007 they can indulge themselves in a smile of satisfaction at a job well done. Trainer Barrie, his assistant and brother, Trevor, and father, Albert, devised a plan a few years ago to start their own breeding operation and the Rotherham-based family are reaping their reward.

A combination of their own breeding system, and a few shrewd purchases from tried and trusted sources saw them dining at the top table and heading for their highest finish in the Trainers' Championship.

Barrie Draper says: "With greyhound prices rising, we sat down a few years ago and decide what action we had to take.

"It was obvious that we had to look to the future and we decided that we should invest in setting up our own breeding plan. With that in mind we bought went out and bought good bitches that we could race and then breed from afterwards and we went to the Dessie Loughrey and the Dunphy brothers.

"We had bought from them before and they had supplied us with some good greyhounds."

It was the same story at the end of 2006 when the Drapers started looking to the forthcoming year.

Barrie says that it was not a conscious decision, but suddenly the kennel was starting to fill up with some very nice looking young talent as the former occupants came towards the end of their racing days.

For the first time in many years, the kennel was not chasing the 'Holy Grail' of the Derby, in fact, the Classic went past without so much as a blink from the kennels at Poultry Farm, but other plans were beginning to hatch.

"We didn't plan it like that. It just happened," commented Barrie. "When the Derby came round the greyhounds that we had in the kennel were either too young to be considered for the Derby or they were not

Skybet Gymcrack winner Farloe Hurricane with his owners, from left: Albert Draper, Kath and Charles Buddery, and Stuart Shaw. Trainer Barry Draper completes the line up.

really the Wimbledon type.

"I am a great believer in horses for courses and if I don't think that dogs will be suited by a particular track then I won't run them there. It doesn't make sense in running greyhounds if you don't believe that they have a chance of winning.

"We could have gone to Wimbledon and spent a few thousand pounds or so in entry fees and expenses going back and forward for trials and maybe a couple of rounds, but that wouldn't have made sense.

"So, while everyone went to Wimbledon we went elsewhere."

The Draper team really got into the action with the likes of Farloe Hurricane and Boherna On Air the main standard bearers as they planned their sorties with care.

Just three days after the Derby final, they landed their first Category One of the year as Farloe Hurricane led home kennelmate

Boherna On Air in the final of the Skybet Gymcrack at Hall Green.

Boherna On Air then picked up the standard and added two more prizes from the top shelf, the Ladbrokes Gold Cup at Monmore and the William Hill Steel City Cup at Sheffield.

But there was plenty of help from other quarters with another 29 racers contributing in some way to the total that took Barrie Draper comfortably into a the top ten in the Trainer's Championship table.

And, while the focus was on the young guns, there was an important contribution from one of the longer serving inmates, Farloe Hobbs.

The 2003 son of Top Honcho and She Knew faced the starter on 23 occasions in 2007, winning 11 times, including competitions at Nottingham in Sheffield.

"He was a great servant to us," says Barrie,

"and he has now been retired."

Barrie has no hesitation when it comes to naming the best greyhound that has gone through his kennels in the past 20 years – He Knows.

Runner-up to Some Picture in the 1997 Derby, he won the Blue Riband the following year and was also a winner of the Dransfield Invitation in a career that set Draper up as an open trainer.

"Without a shadow of doubt, He Knows is the best greyhound that I have ever trained," he states with absolute certainty. "He was an exceptional in every way and he opened up new areas of training for me," says Draper.

Now he dreams that, just maybe, there might be another star lurking in the team that has been assembled for the 2008 campaign.

Draper comments: "I have around 40 young greyhounds in the kennel, ranging from saplings to those around 17 months that I am just getting ready for the track. I don't like to race my young dogs before they are 18 months old."

"It is early days yet, but one or two are starting to look promising, but they are like young footballers, they can look like worldbeaters at 15 but a couple of years later they are going nowhere.

"I have been there before and I know that it is a long way down when there are disappointments, but I am very hopeful that I won't have to go out splashing out with the chequebook."

Graham Hutt

By Richard Birch

GRAHAM HUTT enjoyed a wonderful 2007 campaign, his best since taking out a licence six years ago, and highlighted by four winners from four runners in the first round of the Blue Square Derby.

"That was absolutely incredible," the genial Scot recalls. "We entered four dogs for the Derby – Droopys Tobey, Nervous Woody, Manic Mile and Drimeen Dasher – and came away with four winners.

"Three of them won on the first night at odds of 7-1, 5-1 and 7-2, and then Manic Mile [2-1] completed the four-timer 24 hours later. We won a few quid, too, having done them all in multiples.

"We'd taken them down to Wimbledon the previous week to give them experience, and they ran well then. We knew they'd all come on for the run, particularly Nervous Woody, but to have all four win was a dream come true."

Hutt still gets excited when remembering the Derby experience. "To just have greyhounds good enough to take part in the Derby was a phenomenal experience," he says.

"Wimbledon is a tremendous track, and the atmosphere was electrifying; it gave me a major buzz. The hairs on the back of my neck were standing up."

Hutt, 46, who is assisted by Jimmy and James Wright ("both of whom love the game and have worked tremendously hard"), trains at Baltree Farm Kennels in Kincross, Scotland, and, sensibly, stayed with Rab McNair in the south at various times during the first and second rounds rather than travel back and forth all the time.

High hopes that Nervous Woody, 28.59sec winner of his second-round heat, could reach the latter stages of the premier Classic, were dashed in a quarter-final featuring eventual Derby champion Westmead Lord and runner-up Loyal Honcho.

"He was just a two-year-old at that time," says Hutt. "He had the pace, but wasn't

Graham Hutt's Go Edie Honda (T1) holds Romford Car Two (T4) to win the William Hill Grand Prix at Sunderland and land his handler his biggest win yet as a trainer

experienced enough. We were disappointed when he went out, but it will just make us try that little bit harder next year."

Hutt runs a small, but select open-race team of about a dozen greyhounds. There's room for several more, but the trainer believes 12 is "a nice number".

"What we're always striving for is to get the better-class of greyhound," Hutt says. "We've had a phenomenal year, and the likes of Go Edie Honda, Nervous Woody and Manic Mile have really helped to put us on the map.

"Good dogs are hard to come by. Fortunately we've got some nice owners, such as Robert Keir, the breeder of Mama Chico, who have helped out enormously. We're always looking for good dogs. We want to progress things – to keep taking our operation forward."

Go Edie Honda contributed Category One success for Hutt when landing the inaugural William Hill Grand Prix at Sunderland from Romford Car Two, a matter of weeks before the Derby began in earnest.

"That was a fantastic night," Hutt recalls.

"Sunderland put on a superb festival – catering for all types of dog. William Hill deserve the highest praise possible for what they did there.

"Go Edie Honda's race was worth £20,000 and the William Hill Classic double that. The Grand Prix was the richest six-bend race in the country in 2007; absolutely fantastic. We'll definitely be targeting those competitions again next year."

Go Edie Honda also reached the final of the Totesport Gold Collar at Belle Vue. "He was a bit unlucky there," says Hutt. "The three [Vatican Jinky] cut across him that night, otherwise we feel he'd have gone mighty close from trap one."

Manic Mile also made a big contribution to Hutt's memorable year. In addition to beating Blonde Sheriff in the the Gorton Cup final at Belle Vue, he represented the Kincross team in the Scottish Derby final, won by brilliant Fear Haribo.

"He's one of the fastest dogs in the country on his day," says Hutt. "An absolute aeroplane, blessed with fantastic pace. The only trouble is he rarely came out of the box running."

Droopys Tobey, narrowly denied the 2006 William Hill All England Cup final at Newcastle by the Charlie Lister-trained prolific scorer, Geordie Parker, subsequently finished runner-up in the Birmingham Cup at Perry Barr to another Lister flier, Zigzag Dutchman.

"He has phenomenal early pace, but hasn't been easy to train," reveals Hutt. "We've had to hold him back a bit. At the start of the year we felt he'd be our major player, but little niggles interrupted his progress."

Mama Chico, a winner at Belle Vue, Nottingham, Shawfield, Sunderland and Coventry, and Boherash Patriot have both made important contributions.

"Mama Chico has been a bit unlucky in finals, finishing second several times," Hutt says. "Boherash Patriot has reached three finals, and will always nick the odd open here and there."

Hutt has recently taken charge of Barnfield Weeman, ex-Sam Poots. "He's no superstar, but will win plenty of races," Hutt says. "Darran [Keefe] recommended him to us. We certainly like what we've seen so far."

There's no doubt who the apple of Hutt's eye is, though. Asked to nominate a greyhound to follow for 2008, the reply is instant. "Nervous Woody," he says. "For pure pace. He's still lightly raced, and 2008 could be his year."

Graham Hutt (right) and assistant Jimmy Wright after Droopys Tobey's Derby heat win

Few have as much enthusiasm for greyhound racing as Hutt. He's grateful to his wife, Margaret, for "putting up with me and letting me travel around the country watching dogs".

There's plenty to look forward to, and, if the new campaign brings as much success as 2007, Hutt seems sure to have lots of fun, and make every mile travelled worthwhile.

Peter Sallis

By Jonathan Hobbs

WITH victories in the Guineas at Nottingham, Golden Sprint at Romford and Midland Champion Hurdle at Hall Green, Paul Sallis could be forgiven for remembering 2006 more fondly than 2007 – and that despite having in the kennel 'the fastest dog I've put a lead on'.

That greyhound was Westmead Syd, who shot to prominence in the Gymcrack two years ago at Sallis's 'home' track Hall Green, but whose efforts on the track were restricted through injury. A Derby trial stakes victory was followed by a second in the first round, but injury forced his withdrawal from the premier Classic. He returned for the Produce Stakes later in the year but broke a wrist in winning his qualifying trial.

"He was 10 lengths clear at one point, broke his wrist, and still won the trial in 28.80sec. He looked to be on for a 28.10sec or something, but that was the measure of the dog," said Sallis.

"I remember once when he trialled at Hall Green. He did 14.26sec on slow going, absolutely took off. They thought the dog behind had gone wrong it was that fast. He tore his shoulder though in that trial, and you just think sometimes there are dogs that are too fast for their own good.

"I have to say his owners have been great about it. They lived through the frustaration, too. Dave Gregory is a great supporter of mine and the kennel, and Syd Forster is a terrific character, a real buzz. Down the line I'm sure we'll have a litter from him, remember he's bred by the guvnor [Nick Savva], and the Westmeads haven't done too badly in recent years!

"It's just a shame for us it hasn't been Westmead Syd, but it's been a topsy-turvy year. There were the flying trials, then the

Paul Sallis: helped prepare Ballyregan Bob

disappointment of the Derby. Then we thought we had him okay for the Produce, and then there was this nightmare week. We lost Driving Up Hasty on one of the Sky races at Belle Vue and, while I was on the phone to the vet there, someone called me over to say at Hall Green to say they'd seen Farloe Peach break a hock. For Hasty, a good young dog, it was fatal, but we'll breed from Peach here."

But Sallis, still some way short of 40, has learned to be philosophical after spending most of his life in and around greyhound racing. There are are few in the game who could boast of helping to prepare the legendary Ballyregan Bob, but Sallis is one of them.

He spent his formative years with the legendary George Curtis and spent time as assistant trainer to Brian Clemenson and the late Gordon Hodson. It was clearly a successful apprenticeship as he once again sits atop Hall Green's trainer standings.

Graded racing is the 'bread and butter', of course. But Sallis soon carved himself a reputation as an open-race trainer of some repute, with a knack of placing his dogs extremely well. Look at the Sallis runners who have won first time out at tracks, and it's a record any handler would be proud.

Drive Up Boss and Driving Up Henry both won first-time up at Walthamstow – "we had a 270-1 double that night, Henry won by four lengths and Boss by nine!" – Farloe Peach did the same at both Romford and Wimbledon; while Star Of Twilight [Peterborough], Driving Up [Walthamstow] and Jills Fault [Romford, Reading] were other 'first-timers' for Sallis.

"I'd like to think it shows we know the dogs, and the tracks they are likely to run first time. The owners like it – some of the prices they've got have been pretty tasty. That night at Walthamstow Henry was 20-1 and Boss 12-1!"

Sallis's partner is Esther Driver, a former kennelhand of the year. They met while Driver was working for Derek Knight, and have a three-year-old son Henry. With Sallis an erstwhile member of Ballyregan Bob's backroom staff, and Driver an BGRB award-winner, are they not one of the sport's 'golden couples'?!

"I don't know about the golden couple bit, but we work well. We've both done our time at some of the best kennels in the sport and, call it an apprecticeship, an education, and that experience must count for something. We've tried to take bits from the kennels we've worked for, and I think the overall package has worked."

The family moved into Shortwood Farm, in Overseal, Derbyshire after Henry was born in

Jills Fault, a flag-bearer of the Paul Sallis kennel, won the Northern Hurdle in 2007

August 2004. There is 15 acres of land – "Henry's covered most of it already!" – with numerous paddocks, runs, a gallop, kennel blocks – and newly-built whelping-down blocks. The pair have plans to establish a breeding operation from the site and, with Westmead Syd and Driving Up Rob, have two well-bred potential sires at their disposal.

"We have great facilities here and, importantly, plenty of space. It's the perfect place to train in terms of what we have to work with, and situation – we're only 40 minutes from Hall Green. But it's also great for pups. Esther is taking great pride with her work with the broods and the pups, and it's something else we can establish and build on."

But back to those earlier years, with George Curtis and the former world record holder. Ballyregan Bob was the biggest name in greyhound racing when the sport, with his help, featured everywhere from the local Evening Argus to the Nine O'Clock News on the BBC.

Curtis's ability to place his greyhounds for success in open races was never better illustrated than with Ballyregan Bob. His then record of 32 straight wins was acheived at a number of tracks, and his tutelage is rightly looked back on fondly by Sallis.

"It was my first job out of school," he said, "and they were great days. But they taught me almost everything I know today. The way I do things with the dogs is very much based around what I learned with George. He was, and still is, a true 'dog man'. He would get under a dog's skin, knew the things to bring out their best, and knew when to leave them alone. His relationship with [Ballyregan] Bob really was father-and-son like.

"I joined George when I was 17, and at that time Bob's record was at 21 and he just broken the British record for conseculive wins. I remeber arriving and hoping I wasn't a bok to them! Anyway, he kept on winning and the rest is history. He had amazing back legs,

that's where his power came from."

Sallis first took out a licence on his own while based at Milton Keynes in 2004. And the fastest dog he has trained since has been the unlucky Westmead Syd and Driving Up Rob.

"Driving Up Rob, who retired this year, put the kennel on the map. He won the Guineas at Nottingham, but it took bookmakers, and maybe punters, too, a while to get the hang of him. He wasn't until his 24th race that they made him favourite, and that after he had beaten the likes of Droopys Shearer and Velvet Rebel. He'd also gone one spot off the clock at Swindon in beating One Yard.

"I remember being at Nottingham the second night Rob ran, and Charlie Lister turned to me and said 'you've got a right good dog there'. That was a great boost for us all here, and says a lot about the man's ability to spot a dog, of course."

With a graded contract at Hall Green and an ever-expanding open-race kennel, Sallis now oversees a sizeable business.

It requires an approachable manner and a knack of dealing with owners, especially. "Brian [Clemenson] is particularly good with that side of the business, he's a good PR man for the sport, and I've tried to use that experience I had with him.

"It's so important these days to have a relationship with the people that provide your living. Every owner wants to know how his dog is, where it's running and any future plans. I try and set aside time to deal with that, and it makes for a more tight-knit kennel, and generally my owners support one another."

Sallis's time with Clemenson culminated so successfully with victory in the Trainers' Championship meeting at Sittingbourne. "Brian had chickenpox and had to miss the meeting, but was watching as myself and Lyn [Clemenson's partner] sent out the last three winners to pip Linda Jones."

So he knows the good times, be it being involved in a Trainers' Championship meeting success, or from the successes of greyhounds like Westmead Syg, Driving Up Rob and, recently that stalwart of the Sallis kennel, Jills Fault, in the Northern Hurdle at Sheffield.

"What a dog he's been for us," added Sallis, "and we'll be looking for more of the same from the rest of the dogs in 2008 – the likes of Star Of Twilight, Keljo Keane, Caulry By Two and Keljo Cheveyo, a very promising puppy, should do us proud we hope.

"We've got some great owners who have bought some new exciting dogs. We've got the breeding side of the business doing good, and we'll be kicking on Hall Green as usual. But we still need the luck, more we had in 2007!"

> *I joined George when I was 17, and at that time Bob's record was at 21 and he just broken the British record for conseucutive wins. I remember arriving and hoping I wasn't a bok to them*

Owner Profile
Centaur Greyhounds

WITH the rising costs of ownership, syndicates and partnerships are very much seen as a way forward in terms of attracting more people into the sport. They help spread the cost and, by their very nature, can lead to more social occasions at tracks – the only downside seems to be the arguments post-victory about just who takes home the trophy!

The Champagne Club has been one of the most successful such larger syndicates in recent years, their 'Bubbly'-prefixed winning plenty of open races and the non-profit operation – any proceeds are reinvested in stock – continues to build on a large membership.

Interviewed in the Racing Post by Phil Donaldson last year, the Champagne Club's Steve Fluin famously said: "I want Fred the plumber, or whoever, to be able to stand on the line with guys like Roy Felmingham and know what it feels like to pick up a big trophy."

And a number of successes for the 'Bubbly' dogs has helped that to happen, from the likes of Bubbly Pebbles, Bubbly Chester, Bubbly Tojo and Bubbly Classic, through to marathon star Bubbly Kate. The Champagne Club remains one of greyhound racing's longest-running and successful syndicates.

The 'Centaur' prefix has also begun to feature more and more on the greyhound scene.

From the early successes of Centaur Corker and Centaur Para through to the more recent triumphs of Centaur Striker, Centaur Decree and Centaur Trooper, they have largely been owned by the Centaur Greyhounds Partnership, of which Scott Fraser, part-owner of 2006 Yarmouth Derby and All England Cup winner Geordie Parker, is a director.

Like Geordie Parker, most of the Centaur dogs are bred by the company's stud manager, Jimmy Fenwick.

Fenwick is based at Morpeth in Northumberland and was already a successful breeder with that most prolific of brood bitches, Ladys Guest, putting him on the map as a British breeder of note. His friendship and then business partnership with the founder of the Centaur syndicates, Keith Sobey, aims to continue the early impetus achieved by the greyhound who put the prefix into the minds of open-race fans, Centaur Corker.

Winner of the Ladbroke Golden Jacket and Coral Marathon in 2003, Centaur Corker was a first foray into greyhound ownership of Sobey's company FF Racing Services and the Brian Clemenson-trained dog was one of the best stayers of his generation with track records at Crayford and Hove underlining his talent.

Sadly, it was to prove an all-too-brief track career because of injury, but it was a nevertheless a brilliant one and gave Sobey and his team, already successful in horse racing with the likkes of Hasty Prince and Overstrand, a taste of what could be achieved and enjoyed in greyhound racing.

Centaur Corker had been bought from Ireland, but he would now kick-start their bid to nurture home-grown talent. Fenwick, in the meantime, had bred a cracking litter by Brett Lee out of his own Lydpal Louise, which included Geordie Parker. He is owned by Fenwick and Fraser, a former professional footballer now property developer.

Fraser is one of four directors of Centaur Greyhounds, along with Sobey, financial expert Ian Craig and estate agent, Michael Gill.

The presentation after Centaur Trooper's Monmore success, with 'Centaur' members Scott Fraser, Andrew Cork, Ian Craig, Michael Gill and Keith Sobey, plus Matt Dartnall

"We are all businessmen, with plenty of experience in the finance and property world. But for all four of us it's the love and passion we've got for the sport of greyhound racing that is driving us on," said Fraser. "Yes, we've got a business plan in terms to building the operation through attracting other owners and partners, but with that will hopefully come success and you can already see from the likes of Centaur Striker [National Sprint] and Centaur Trooper [Spring Festival Stayers], which we bred, that we are going the right way.

"Jimmy, as well as our stud manager, is also our breeding consultant, and he has our own stud dogs to use, which are Centaur Corker and Centaur Para. Our brood bitches include Up In Lights, Morphes Pearl, Murlens Chance, Centaur Trooper and Centaur Spirit, while our now retired brood Ballybeg Pumpkin produced a total of 30 pups for us in 2004 from which we produced two competition winners in Trooper and Striker. Indeed, from those litters there were a total of 13 open-class animals which is a 43.34 per cent strike rate, a fantastic ratio and a testament to Jimmy's judgement and the skill of the people rearing/schooling the pups for us namely Tommy Cooke, Michael Shanaghan and Mike Gallagher."

Murlens Chance gave Centaur Greyhounds the top-class sprinter Centaur Striker from her only racing litter to date, although the partnership is currently excited by a Droopys Scholes batch, whelped in Aug 06, who are starting their careers at Walthamstow, Belle Vue, Monmore and Newcastle. Murlens Chance recently whelped a litter to Droopys Scolari.

Fenwick handles many of the puppies at racing age, with the likes of Mark Wallis, Charlie Lister and Terry Dartnall among Centaur's current trainers.

Up In Lights threw Centaur Trooper, who won competitions at Crayford and Monmore before breaking a wrist in a solo trial at

Reading. Centaur Trooper has since had a litter by Geordie Parker, while Up In Light's other open-race progeny include Centaur Rover, Centaur Stag and Genesis Sister.

"She also has an August 06 litter on the ground to Elite State, who have recently arrived in the UK and in September she whelped a litter of 12 to Droopys Vieri," added Fraser, who is excited by those on the track and those being reared.

"Myself and the other directors are pretty hopefull given the quality of the litters we've had that the 'Centaur' prefix will be well represented at tracks across the country for the next few years." And it is that which Fraser and his colleagues hopes will attract more people into the business.

"We look for 'owner partnerships' rather than actual syndicates under the Centaur umbrella. These partnerships consist of no more than four partners, of which Centaur Greyhounds will always be one, and we offer pups for sale either as outright purchase or 50 per cent ownership at any stage of their rearing from 12 weeks onwards, and it was particularly pleasing to find that all 23 of our 2006 pups were snapped up by our existing owners/partners.

"That tells me we must be doing something right and that these owners, of whom a number were new to greyhounds, many succesfully converted from racehorse ownership, must be thoroughly enjoying the experience.

"To build the profile even more, though, you got to have the quality, and we made a decision that we needed to (a) have the appropriate quality of greyhound and (b) have associations with some of the best trainers in the business. And we believe we have.

"Geographically, we are pretty strong to suit a spread of owners and, while delighted with the success of our breeding operation, we still occasionally purchase young greyhounds on the recommendation of our trainers – the best example being Centaur Decree, who we have high hopes for in 2008.

"Decree gave us some great moments in 2007, getting to the Eclipse final at Nottingham late on in the year was superb. He was purchased in a 50/50 partnership, and all co-owners were, and are, kept fully up to date on their greyhound's racing plans via phone, text and e-mail.

"We enjoy mixing the business with the hobby, and I'm sure that there are exciting times ahead for Centaur Greyhounds.

The Great Greyhound Gathering

September 2007 saw the first ever national dog show and family fun day for the Retired Greyhound Trust. More than 500 dogs and some 2,000 people attended the Great Greyhound Gathering at Nottingham Horse Racecourse, Colwick Park and for the first time the RGT Retired Greyhound of the Year was chosen. The GGG was organised for the RGT by former BGRB press officer Emma Johns, accompanied by her ex- racer Go Running Whip. Here is her account of the day itself, and those leading up to it.

The sun shone and the rain clouds whizzed overhead faster than a greyhound. The MP, Sheriff and Deputy Lord Mayor of Nottingham were all on hand but the GGG was officially opened by a pair of canine thoroughbreds ceremonially chomping through a 'ribbon' of cooked sausages.

The GGG was about promoting the breed as pets and awareness and it was great to have such a good turn out – and especially to have so many supporters from the sport itself on the day.

Living in Kent and organising a major show in Nottingham meant 'Whippy' enjoyed the odd night away staying in dog-friendly hotels

The crowds gather for the various dog shows at the Great Greyhound Gathering

and we were interviewed by BBC Radio Nottingham countless times and also live on the Sky Sports greyhound show twice. Down at Brighton & Hove Stadium he was more interested in the food at the restaurant tables nearby than the action on the track!

One of his TV appearances led to sponsorship of £5,000 from the betting exchange Betfair for the RGT Greyhound of the Year. Each RGT branch was asked to nominate a representative – a dog they had rehomed able to attend the show with their family – with the cash prize going back to that original branch of the charity. Every dog is special and every dog attending the GGG, non-greyhounds were welcome too, received a commemorative rosette just for being there. There was extra interest in the class to decide the RGT Greyhound of the Year and a wonderful entry but there could be only one winner; Sunny – racing name Come on Flo.

Together with owner Karen Woods, Sunny wowed Crufts judge, Afghan breeder and Belle Vue owner Keith Thornton in the ring and represented Greyhoundhomer, an RGT branch in Essex. Karen and husband Greg from Letchworth in Hertfordshire had lost a previous pet greyhound when they went to see Pat Philpott at Greyhoundhomer about taking on a new dog.

Karen said: "He is a big boy at weighing 40 kilos but has got on with our 18-year-old cat right from the start. He also soon discovered the joys of home life – from sofas to beds and learned to play with toys. For me the best part of adopting an ex-racer is watching their personality develop as they settle into their new life as a family pet.

"Sunny has become a lot calmer and relaxed, as well as more playful and affectionate."

Since being declared RGT Retired Greyhound of the Year, Sunny has been quite the celebrity with interviews on Sky Sports and coverage in newspapers nationally and at home in Hertfordshire.

Karen added: "It was fantastic and unbelievable to win and to be able to provide the funding for Pat and the branch and most of all help spread the word about greyhounds as pets. Sunny is the perfect ambassador!"

**For more information about
the Retired Greyhound Trust
to find your local branch details
see www.retiredgreyhounds.co.uk
or telephone 0870 4440673.**

Best of British

Westmead Hawk at Madame Tussauds

ON October 18, 2007, dual Derby champion Westmead Hawk, the acclaimed 'wonderdog' of modern greyhound racing, became the first animal athlete to make it into Madame Tussauds.

The real Westmead Hawk gave a big 'paws up' to his waxwork figure when he came nose to nose with it ahead of the world famous attraction's 'Best Of British' week, at which he starred. Cheering his champion dog on from the sidelines was owner, entrepreneur and racing enthusiast Bob Morton.

"He is truly a special dog but I never dreamed he'd end up in Madame Tussauds," commented Morton. "When the call came saying they wanted to include him I was speechless for a second or two. Then it sank in and I was of course, absolutely delighted. 'The Hawk' will go down in history as one of the great champions and this is a wonderful accolade for a world-class athlete," he said proudly.

"We are delighted to welcome The Hawk to Madame Tussauds, London," said head of marketing, Drew Potton. "Greyhound racing is a wonderfully British and hugely popular sport, thrilling millions of fans every year. He is the perfect star to open our 'Best Of British' season where we will be celebrating all of the Great Britons in the attraction"

The creation process, involving a team of some 20 artists, took four months to complete, and presented unique challenges – not least the Hawk's glossy coat, which required four intensive weeks of specialist attention.

Westmead Hawk, the waxwork version

"Undoubtedly, some of our celebrities have more hair than others but Westmead Hawk is certainly the hairiest star we've ever created!," said Jim Kempton of Madame Tussauds Studios. "It meant we had to adopt different production techniques, adding eurythane skin to the Hawk's fibre glass core, which was then painstakingly flocked with hair just a few millimetres long. This has ensured the figure is fantastically realistic, and very real to the touch."

 Sponsored by the BGRB

The RGT

The Retired Greyhound Trust

What is the Retired Greyhound Trust?

Founded over 30 years ago, The Retired Greyhound Trust (RGT) is the only UK charity dedicated to finding homes for ex-racing greyhounds.

Our devoted volunteers work tirelessly across the UK from 70 branches which have found homes for almost 40,000 ex-racing greyhounds to date.

We undertake a thorough rehoming process and conduct checks to ensure that new homes are suitable for dogs.

After the initial meeting we will recommend a greyhound that best suits the owner and their lifestyle and conduct full health checks to make sure they are ready for life as a pet.

What we do and why?

We believe that all greyhounds deserve a happy retirement and that our work is crucial to the sustainability of the industry.

By protecting the welfare of retired greyhounds we are providing a better future for the sport.

The RGT works hard to encourage owners to take their responsibility seriously by ensuring their dogs are properly cared for when they retire. We advertise in national and trade publications to promote greyhounds as pets.

Our volunteers are always out and about at dog shows and in their communities spreading the good word. Their effort and encouragement has seen more and more people adopting retired greyhounds.

How you can help?

You can support us and make arrangements for your greyhounds to stay in kennels until the RGT can find them a home.

Make sure your dog is in good health and neutered before handing them over to the RGT, as this helps us to find them a home sooner.

You can also assist by making others aware of the need to find homes for retired greyhounds and encourage them to adopt one.

Why not consider becoming an RGT volunteer and conduct home checks or even transport dogs?

A better future for ex-racing greyhounds means a better future for the industry.

Please play your part and get involved. We are always seeking sponsorship or donations to help those greyhounds that haven't found a home and take care of future retirees.

To find our more about how you can help contact the RGT's national office on 0844 826 8424.

Call the Retired Greyhound Trust on 0844 826 8424or visit www.retiredgreyhounds.co.uk to find your nearest branch.

LIST OF RGT BRANCHES NATIONWIDE

Scotland

Borders/Berwick	Sonia Graham	07967 057759
West Lothian	Beth Haley	01501 753224
Edinburgh	Ian Carmichael	0131 4760069
Glasgow	Caroline Finnett	01292 263493
Isle of Skye	Mandy Reid	01470 511705

North East/North West

Alnwick	Diane Gibbinson	07859 888384
Bridlington	Lynette Philips	01262 609343
Cumbria – Millom	Marcia Stroud	01229 771135
Cumbria – Workington	Tom Edgar	01900 872776
East Riding	JayJensen	01482 503944
Hollinhall (Durham)	Alison Waggott	01388 768385
Hull	Sue Markham	01482 223228
Manchester (Kersal)	Dave Heaton	01617 366923
Manchester	Liz Murphy	0870 8407502
North East/Durham	Lesley Eagleton	01207 299311
North Yorkshire	Karen Fraser	01609 761014
Pelaw Grange (Co Durham)	Janet Brass	01325 360197
Sheffield	Lynda Cattlin	0114 2334000
Shropshire	Sue Tipton	01743 872395
West Yorkshire	Kath Armitage	01924 848121

Midlands/East Anglia

Birmingham (Hall Green)	Pat Chan	0121 426 4810
Birmingham (Perry Barr)	Ruth Boswell	0121 782 7702
Birmingham (Thistle Grove)	Ann Williams	0121 603 5350
East Anglia	Ann Brandon	01406 331267
Eastern Counties	Ingrid Wright	01508 550910
Henlow (Stadium)/Bedford	Keith Mellor	01462 851850
Lincolnshire	Kevin Stow	01522 569825
Melton Mowbray/Leicester	Clair Wallace-Sims	01664 812361
Midlands (Newark)	John Morton	01636 822032
Mildenhall/Suffolk	Ann Raymond	01638 176578
Milton Keynes	Jenny Wakeling	01908 379470
Monmore (Wolverhampton)	Alison Bandurak	01922 412212
Northampton	Mandy Hooker	01327 830250
Nottingham	Michelle Eastment	01159 655434
Oxford	Jenny Hebborn	01865 374792
Peterborough (Brambleberry)	Sharon Saberton	07843 655003
Peterborough RGT	Jan Ruffle	01832 205363
Peterborough Welfare	Carol Whaley	07737 683969
Rugby & Coventry	Sari Pearce	01788 833855
Shropshire & Borders	Sue Tipton	01743 872395

Sponsored by the BGRB

Worcester	Kim Holmes	01299 861514
Worksop	Doug Wright	01909 721234
Yarmouth	David Jones	0845 4583797

Wales/South West

Cornwall – Bude	Mike Bowman	01288 352656
Cornwall – Launceston	Stephen Gurr	01566 782842
Devon/Somerset	Tracey Seymour	01237 451677
Homesafe – Nationally	Ann Shannon	01624 861408
Poole	Rita Price	01747 854042
South Wales	Paula Ambrose	01633 892846
South West Sight Hounds – Bristol	Sue Selleck	01454 632333
Swindon	Caroline Gomersall	01793 729043

Jersey

| Jersey | Malcolm Hickmott | 01534 742619 |
| Jersey | Debbie Paisnel | 01534 638121 |

London/South East

Brighton & Hove	Jenny Bunting	01444 881788
Catford	Bill Maynard	01634 220131
Crayford	Peter Bussey	01322 408977
Essex – Basildon	Sue Kirkman	01268 415716
Essex – Brentwood	Joy Hardy	01277 373799
Essex – Maldon	Steve Cobb	01621 788315
Greyhoundhomer (Essex)	Pat Philpot	01708 551689
Greyhoundhomer (Herts/Beds)	Elaine Richards	01279 501899
Greyhoundhomer (Suffolk)	Kevin Baalham	01473 420232
Greyhound Lifeline	Marie Harris	07828 138378
Harlow	Doreen Macarthur	01279 426804
Kent	Cheryl Miller	01474 815273
Portsmouth	Liz Redpath	01730 893255
Romford	Steve Simmons	07956 686480
Sittingbourne	Julie Wilson	01795 438438
Southampton	Sue Thurlby	02380 619225
Walthamstow	Johanna Beumer	0208 444 9649
Walthamstow	Joy Battley	01992 890540
Wimbledon	Denise Dubarbier	01932 224918

Isle of Wight

| Isle of Wight | Sue Shearer | 07933 785696 |

The Writer's View

Michael Church, a previous Special Projects Manager at Racing Post *is an author of ten books on racing related subjects. In addition, his latest offering,* The Derby Chart 1780-2007, *traces the male lineage of every Epsom Derby winner back to their Founding Fathers.*

A greyhound fan from a small boy, he now fronts the syndicate 'Sir Ivor's Survivors' with dogs trained by Mark Wallis.

Here follows a story from his Ripping Gambling Yarns – Tales of a Misspent Youth. *Church, an 18-year-old in the RAF, visits Liverpool's three dog tracks in 1954, only to find all the races are four-dog handicaps.*

"Scrape those meat tins out before you go, Church. I want to see them gleaming before you put one foot outside this camp." Sergeant Thompson's voice boomed across the 'tin room' at the back of the canteen.

Thompson, the catering sergeant at RAF West Kirby, had promised the Commanding Officer that he would win the all-England award for the best and cleanest RAF canteen. And here was I, five weeks into my National Service, released from square bashing and band practice (3rd cornet) to assist in bulling up the canteen. To make matters worse, this evening was my first off-camp pass, for which I had planned to visit Seaforth Stadium, one of Liverpool's three greyhound tracks.

Two hours later, with the help of half a dozen Brillo pads, I presented eight large meat tins for inspection.

"Call those clean, Church? They look bloody mankey and smell bloody mankey. Get them into boiling water and this time use wire wool."

It took a further hour's drudgery before I was released but, with great determination, I caught the bus and train to get to Seaforth for the last three races.

To my surprise, all the races were four-dog handicaps, the traps placed at intervals; trap four at the front on the outside and trap one at the back on the rails, with an inside hare.

Punters had to have a degree in maths to work out the comparative times, but the finishes were usually close and the forecast was the most popular bet. After two failed attempts at the forecast, I decided to back trap four to win the last race.

Joining the back of a queue, I eventually got to the tote window just as the dogs were being put into the traps and, having a slight stammer, my attempts to spit out "One win four," became "Wer-wer-one." Before I could finish, a ticket whirred out, my pound was taken, the lights went out and the sellers hatch slammed down. Surprised and annoyed, I banged on the hatch, shouting:

"What about my change?"

Now, with the dogs already racing, I checked my ticket under one of the down lights on the terrace. It read £1 WIN TRAP ONE. One pound! I only wanted two shillings and that was on the four dog.

Looking across at the greyhounds, four led the other three into the last bend. But then, running wide, he let in the one-dog who powered up the straight to win by a length. Still in shock, I waited for the official result and tote dividends.

"Win number one, seven pounds ten shillings."

The rest I never heard – seven pounds ten, three weeks wages!

I dashed over to the payout and could now clearly see the £1 sign over the window. Handing over my ticket with a trembling hand, the young lady said: "Feeling better now – you were getting in a right state." Just behind me, I heard a grumpy old man mutter, "Where do these young Airman get their money?" I would have liked to have told him but it might have taken me all night to spit it out.

The following week I went to Liverpool's White City, a narrow track with the spectators undercover all the way round and standing on floor boarding. It looked then as if it had seen better days and only had six bookmakers. Once again, the races were four-dog handicaps, but tonight, there were two inter-track races with another Liverpool track – Stanley.

I suppose there was acute rivalry between these tracks, but I wasn't aware of this, at least, not until the second of the heats. In the first race, the White City favourite won, but their other dog finished last, so, because points were alloted on a four-three-two-one basis, the tracks were tied at five all. In the second heat, a Stanley dog was favourite – a fast-starting brindled bitch in trap four.

Standing near the fourth bend, the race already in progress, and with the four dog about six lengths clear, I noticed a tall, swarthy man nearby, remove his large cape-like raincoat. Just as the dogs turned into the home straight, he threw it, like a matador's cape over the leading bitch. A pile-up followed, with the last two dogs convinced the hare was also under the coat. The man then ran off, pursued by two officials, one of which caught and held him fast until a policemen arrived.

It seemed the villain had claimed mistaken identity, but one of his pursuers called on the policeman "to get the young airman over to identify him." This I was duly pressurised into, and signed a short statement, before the culprit was handcuffed to another police officer and taken away. The race was declared void and soon after the punters settled down to studying the next.

Leaving the track half-an-hour later, I spotted two shady-looking men in a doorway opposite.

"That's him, the airman," I heard one of them say. I took off.

After running 40 yards or so, I joined a bus queue and removed my peak-cap. My heart was still pounding when they caught up with me before the bus arrived.

"We're from the Liverpool Echo; would you give us the story?"

I never returned to White City, but instead visited the Stanley track twice during my last week at West Kirby. Meanwhile, Sergeant Thompson's dream came true as the camp's canteen won the all-England award. Photographs of its modern furniture with latticed dividers, highly polished floors and flowers on every table, appeared in the Echo alongside 'Airman Identifies Culprit in Greyhound Scandal!'

Part of the excitement of going greyhound racing whilst in the RAF was the freedom of mixing with civilians – ordinary people, who would gladly chat to you about the dogs. This, compared with the strict ordered routine of the camp, seemed to me like paradise. On both my trips to Stanley, I transferred over to the 'posh side.' On one occasion, standing alone by the winning post, I was asked by a lady in a fur coat who I was going to back in the next.

"Roller Coaster," I replied.

"Oh that's ours," she said. "Trevor and I own it."

Just then, Trevor appeared in a bright camel coat, nodded on our introduction and then buried his head in the Greyhound Express. I drifted away and so did Roller Coaster, finishing third of four.

Later that week I saw Trevor and Sadie again. This time, they had been drinking and he raised his hat.

"Trevor's on a roll," Sadie said, "He's backed the last three winners."

"Quiet dear; let's hear what the Royal Air Force fancy for the next." "Well, I think the scratch dog's got too much to do and both three and four will fade, so it's got to be two."

"Trap two – Young Hazard," he laughed, "Young Hazard it is then. I'll cut you in for a quid."

We watched the race together, the blue jacket the focus of our attention under the bright lights. Three led four into the straight, but two finished like a train, with the three of us jumping up and down and shouting him home.

After the last race, I was invited to meet their friends in the owners' bar, a rare treat for me, especially as all of them wanted to buy me a drink. "This was more like it," I thought, putting the meat-tin episode behind me and downing my fifth gin and tonic.

All too soon, Trevor and Sadie were driving me back to camp in their new Jaguar, and the inevitable sight of the barbed wire fences and rows of wooden huts brought me back to earth. Pulling in at the main gate, we were approached by a Military Police Sergeant. Trevor wound down his window.

"Oh it's you sir! Sorry, didn't recognise the new car – oh and thank you for the case of whisky for the canteen celebrations."

"I hope you were able to enjoy a drop," Trevor said graciously.

"Is that one of our Airmen with you sir?" the Sergeant enquired.

"Yes."

"Has he been in any trouble sir?"

"No, on the contrary!."

The Sergeant peered into the car.

"It's you Church, I see. Been on another one of your crusades against crime have you?"

Moments later, he eyed me with suspicion, as, with assumed dignity, I attempted to walk in a straight line through the main gate.

Later, safely in my narrow bed, I dreamt of myself gracing the owners' bar once more, this time, as the proud owner of a string of successful greyhounds.

Travelling the Tracks

by John Forbes

"Get a life," groaned Mrs F as I searched cyberspace for a Derby that hadn't got Nick Savva or Charlie Lister's names on it. Mission impossible some might say, but there it was – or rather, there they were – two of them. In Hamburg.

The Internationales and Deutsches Derbys were due to be settled at the Norddeutscher Windhundrennvere at Sieker Landstrasse, some ten miles out of the city centre.

Armed with the bits of information that my schoolboy German – and I went to school when Tom Brown was head boy – I set out to find out what it was all about.

On the Saturday morning, the day of the Internationales Derby, I was picked up near my hotel by one of the racecourse officials, Hans Rogmans, and taken to the track, hidden away in an industrial estate.

At first glance I thought that there must be some mistake, for it looked more like a caravan park than a greyhound track, with vans and campers all around the circuit and an overflow on an adjoining factory car park, plus a small tented village.

However, it soon became evident that they were very necessary for they also served as racing kennels, there being none on the track.

The racecourse was a sand surface with

two trips – 350 and 480 metres – with a strange hare powered by petrol and driven by one man in the centre of the circuit, with a type of control system usually used for model aircraft.

The track was well served by a very pleasant clubroom, with kitchen serving light meals, and a barbecue and bar area outside for those who did not want to retire to their caravans.

Racing started at 9am (not much chance of bumping into any Racing Post colleagues then) and it quickly became obvious there were plenty more shocks in store.

As the fields started to assemble there were a few greyhounds, but far more whippets, Afghans, Salukis and a breed called the Magyar Agar from Hungary, which looked for all the world like a greyhound but was, I was reliably informed, two seconds slower (I think I own one of those!).

No Dachshunds, however. Maybe sand burns on the belly are a problem with this breed? And the only German Shepherd in the vicinity treated the whole thing with an air of complete disdain.

Greyhounds are a much more popular breed in the far south of the country and there were, in fact, only six entries for the Internationales Derby, so with rather untypical logic for Germans, they split them into two heats of three, all three in each heat going to the final.

Worse was to follow, for Nick Savva and the Irish had actually beaten me to the punch! Into the final sailed Coolakenny Maggi, and she duly won very comfortably in 28.27sec, a record for the 480 metres.

A closer examination revealed this was a daughter of Toms The Best, who was trained Nick Savva to win the English and Irish Derbys, out of Aunt Maggie, bred in County Tipperary by Olive Ryan. In fact, the winner is a litter-sister to the Gary Baggs-trained Silver Collar winner, Westminster Taj.

However, persuading the Savva camp to make a more personal raid on the event might be a bit more difficult as it costs 20 Euros to enter and there's no prize-money, just a presentation jacket.

The Deutsches Derby poses an even greater problem as the greyhound has to be German-bred and, furthermore, it is in the rules that a greyhound can only win it once. So no Savva or Bob Morton, then!

Clearly, racing in Germany is very much an amateur affair and that is the way they want to keep it. There is no betting whatsoever, and that's the way that the locals like it.

Hans Rogmans says: "If we were to have betting on the races then it would become professional and we are not sure that would be good for the dogs."

People came for all over Germany, the Netherlands, eastern Europe and France with their greyhounds, hence the large camp-site

A closer examination revealed this was a daughter of Toms The Best, who was trained Nick Savva to win the English and Irish Derbys, out of Aunt Maggie, bred in County Tipperary by Olive Ryan. In fact, the winner is a litter-sister to the Gary Baggs-trained Silver Collar winner, Westminster Taj.

and there was no doubting their enthusiasm – nor that of their animals – as they meetings developed.

The morning session consisted of races for all the different grades within the breeds and then there was a break of a couple of hours, while everyone had their lunch, and then the finals were run off in the afternoon.

When I say that everyone had their lunch during the break, I think that the runner-up in the Internationales Derby might have done better had he not had two pieces of cake! No drugs flying squad here.

The track stages just three two-day meetings a year and the remainder of the time it is used as a training track for the local racers.

The land is owned by the city of Hamburg and the club make their money from fees charged for trials and races, the catering and bars and it does just enough to keep it ticking over.

Enjoyable though the time was spent at the track, it just didn't seem the same without being able to have a bet.

The irony was that on the way back I was able to stop off at the betting shop near my hotel and have a bet in the 5.44pm at Oxford. A loser of course.

Some things never change, no matter where you are.

Big Races of 2006

WILLIAM HILL LAURELS

CLASH HARMONICA never really looked comfortable at Belle Vue, but his genuine class saw him strike gold in the final of the £10,000 Betfred Laurels at the Manchester venue.

Trained by Charlie Lister for The Boys From Leicester syndicate, Clash Harmonica was stopped in his tracks as he made his run on two of three occasions, but came through late on to triumph in a close finish – favourite Fear Haribo flashed home to finish fourth after stumbling badly at the traps.

Ironically, after racing news filtered through that the last-named. the Gymcrack winner, was to join Lister ahead of his 2007 campaign, after Carly Philpott relinquished her trainer's licence.

Winning breeder: Mairead McGrath, Cappagh, Waterford

Finish	Trap	Names	Price	Time/Dis
1	1	CLASH HARMONICA	3/1	27.88
2	2	Fantasy Tiger	12/1	1/2
3	3	Dalcash Sweettea	12/1	1/2
4	4	Fear Haribo	5/4F	1/2
5	5	Manic Mile	9/2	1
6	6	Noirs Duke	7/1	1 1/4

BEDFORDSHIRE DERBY

CANARY SKY landed a hugely emotional victory when taking a competitive and classy Bedfordshire Derby at Henlow in late October.

A few weeks after the January 2004 had prevailed in a close finish, having provided his trainer with her biggest win, Jackie Taylor lost her battle against serious illness, aged just 47.

Her partner Steve Cooper was on hand to parade the dog and collect the trophy with the son of Top Honcho's owners Steve Albiston and Diane Weise.

Taylor had for years been associated with the old Milton Keynes track and trained the likes of Koko Bandit, Super Trooper, Who Knows, Tarmon Tia, Vatpack Brandon and Three Way Ebony.

Winning breeder: Oliver Walsh, Ballylinan, Co. Kildare

Finish	Trap	Names	Price	Time/Dis
1	1	CANARY SKY	5/2	28.20
2	2	Whitegate Jet	2/1F	HD
3	5	Davdor Dashing	7/2	1 1/4
4	3	Weeton Weapon	20/1	3/4
5	4	Castlekerry Blue	3/1	1 1/4
6	6	Sparta Fire	10/1	HD

GOLDEN MUZZLE

BLAKES WORLD carved his own special niche within the open-race calendar when winning the Golden Muzzle, the famous old competition commendably revived by Portsmouth towards the end of 2006.

A switch from the inside to the outside hare had seen a few changes to the track, including the introduction of the revised one-lap trip over 430m. During the competition the track record was broken twice, including Blakes World's 26.27sec in the £4,000 decider.

Trained by Jo Burridge, it was the fourth win for the Dorset-based trainer in the event, having previously scored with Chocolate Drink (1987), Tingling Star (1991) and Springville Hoff (1997), and was the product of a mating between two of Felmingham's stars, Blue Gooner (Circuit, Golden Crest) and Killeacle Phoebe (TV Trophy).

Winning breeder: Roy Felmingham, Meopham, Kent

Finish	Trap	Names	Price	Time/Dis
1	4	BLAKES WORLD	9/4JF	26.15TR
2	5	Darbystown Liz	3/1	2 3/4
3	1	Old Macdonald	9/4JF	3/4

4	2	Coolside Lucky	5/2	SH
5	3	Barra Silk	33/1	1 1/4
6	6	Moses Bridge	14/1	1 1/2

WILLIAM HILL ST LEGER

NINJA BLUE edged out Westmead Olivia to win the William Hill St Leger, in one of the closest and most exciting finishes the stayers' Classic has ever seen.

The Terry and Elaine Coveney-owned, Charlie Lister-trained runner had looked a decent stayer when making the final of the Summer Classic at Monmore earlier in the year, but was withdrawn through injury come the decider.

Led by Blissful Classic, the eventual winner struck a blow with his middle pace when the leader moved wide off the second and went on, holding Westmead Olivia's late flourish by the minimum margin after a nervous wait before the judge's announcement.

Winning breeder: Pat Larkin, Derry

Finish	Trap	Names	Price	Time/Dis
1	5	NINJA BLUE	11/4	41.52
2	4	Westmead Olivia	5/1	SH
3	6	Blissful Classic	7/1	1/2
4	1	Fabulous Sophie	7/2	2 1/4
5	3	Blackmagic Guy	10/1	SH
6	2	Daisyfield Seani	9/4F	3 3/4

COVENTRY ST LEGER

WESTMEAD SWIFT led home Westmead Olivia for yet another big-race one-two for Nick Savva in 2007 in the Tom Fruit St Leger, worth a superb £15,000-to-the-winner.

Owned by Bob Morton, and a litter sister of dual Derby champ Westmead Hawk, Westmead Swift had made the final of the Grand Prix only to find trouble after a wide draw.

Ironically, a wide tag worked the oracle at Coventry and she trapped well in both semifinal and final, and led what what a high-class field — featuring St Leger and Grand Prix finalists aplenty — in the decider.

The final also saw yet another final appearance for Daisyfield Seani in 2006, the Matthew Etherington-owned bitch having also made the deciders of the St Leger, Cesarewitch, Grand Prix and Golden Jacket.

Winning breeder: Nick Savva, Dunstable, Beds

Finish	Trap	Names	Price	Time/Dis
1	5	WESTMEAD SWIFT	11/2	42.77
2	6	Westmead Olivia	7/4	1 3/4
3	4	Blackmagic Guy	8/1	2 1/2
4	3	Daisyfield Seani	5/4F	1/2
5	1	Swift Jade	9/1	3/4
6	2	Larkhill Bird	13/2	1 3/4

BETFRED ECLIPSE

CLASH HARMONICA, one of two runners in the final for the in-form Charlie Lister camp, added to successes already landed in the Laurels and Napoleons Invitation when completing an unbeaten run through the Betfred Eclipse at Nottingham.

Favourite for the final was the also unbeaten Zigzag Dutchy, but his chance was lost at the start as Broadacres Rob led up and it was left to 'The Boys From Leicester'-owned runner to wear down the leader down the far side and kick on off the third bend for an easy win.

Not comfortable around Belle Vue, despite winning, the Nottingham victory once more underlined the August 2004's dog claims to the BGRB Newcomer of the Year award.

Winning breeder: Mairead McGrath, Cappagh, Waterford

Finish	Trap	Names	Price	Time/Dis
1	4	CLASH HARMONICA	5/2	29.50
2	3	Broadacres Rob	5/1	4 1/4
3	1	Zigzag Dutchy	11/10F	1 3/4
4	2	Mackrel Sky	33/1	2 3/4
5	5	Corleones Rammi	12/1	1/2
6	6	Eye Onthe Veto	9/2	HD

CORAL ESSEX VASE

EYE ONTHE VETO made it a double in the event for owner John Keefe when winning the Coral Essex Vase at Romford in December.

The son of Kiowa Sweet Trey and Pennys Cloud had been installed a red-hot favourite after brilliant performances in heat and semi-final, and was made a 4-5 chance on the night to follow up Keefe's win with 16-1 poke Eye Onthe Ball a year previously.

But he was made to work hard after Bubbly Casino had taken a flyer from traps. Eye Onthe Veto's middle pace saw him collar the leader bby the third bend and he then stretch clear, but need to with powerful Westmead Aoifa now in full stride after being held up at the Pavilion turn. She finished fast but could not get to the winner.

In finishing second, however, Westmead Aoifa took the Top Dog honours for the year, earning £25K for top bitch and £25K for overall.

Winning breeder: Eugene Price, Newtown, Co. Kildare

Finish	Trap	Names	Price	Time/Dis
1	5	EYE ONTHE VETO	4/5F	35.99
2	3	Westmead Aoifa	9/4	3/4
3	4	Bubbly Casino	20/1	3 3/4
4	1	Willington Spot	20/1	1 3/4
5	6	Blissful Classic	6/1	HD
6	2	Ninja Blue	12/1	3 1/4

CORAL PUPPY DERBY

ROSWELL STARSHIP ran out a comfortable winner of the Coral Romford Puppy Cup final, landing back-to-back wins in the event for his trainer Mark Wallis and continuing a fantastic run of success for his owner, Evan Herbert.

Herbert, a long-time owner of Wallis and his mother-in-law Linda Jones, the former licence holder at Imperial Kennels, had seen his January Tiger win the Grand Prix at Walthamstow a fortnight earlier, while Wallis was following up his win with Fear Assasin 12 months previously.

Trapping well, the favourite made all to post the fastest final time in the Puppy Cup for the last 10 years and was continuing a rich vein of form which saw him reach two

Walthamstow puppy finals and the semis of Wimbledon's Puppy Derby.

Winning breeder: Vicki Moloney, Upper Garryvoe, Co. Cork

Finish	Trap	Names	Price	Time/Dis
1	4	ROSWELL STARSHIP	7/4	24.36
2	1	Astute Gift	8/1	2 3/4
3	6	Wills Burno	12/1	3 3/4
4	2	Jangos Hero	6/1	5
5	3	Chakalak Paris	6/4F	1
6	5	Ninas Capone	5/1	2 1/4

WILLIAM HILL NORTHERN PUPPY

DROOPYS McANDREW gained a narrow and thrilling victory over Vatican Jinky in the £8,000 William Hill Northern Puppy Derby over 450m at Sunderland, the shortest of short-heads separating the pair.

Droopys Mcandrew, one of two Ted Soppitt-trained finalists, was always prominent but had to withstand the rally of Vatican Jinky, after he was chopped off when challenging at the third bend, the runner-up just failing to peg back the 27.24sec winner.

The victory of the November 2004 son of Velvet Commander and Droopys Kristin gave Durham-based Soppitt not just a four-timer on the night, but back-to-back successes in the puppy event having scored in 2005 with Calzaghe Boyo.

The highlight of the supporting card was the record-breaking run from Ballymac Rooster in the 261m sprint open.

Winning breeder: Michael Dunphy, Portlaw, Co. Waterford

Finish	Trap	Names	Price	Time/Dis
1	1	DROOPYS MCANDREW	9/4	27.24
2	2	Vatican Jinky	5/4F	SH
3	3	She Said No	12/1	1 1/2
4	4	Calzaghe Geordie	6/1	1
5	6	Nearly Broke	4/1	2 1/2
6	5	Apache Dawn	14/1	SH

WILLIAM HILL OAKS

DILEMMAS FLIGHT won a high-class William Hill Oaks to credit Nick Savva with his fourth win the bitches Classic

and, in doing so, land the Dunstable trainer/breeder with the Oaks/Derby double after Westmead Hawk's triumph earlier in the year.

In a fantastic race, Dilemmas Flight, still in puppy status as she went to traps in late November, finished best to edge out Cleenas Lady and Jazz Hurricane and do what her dam Early Flight, a beaten Oaks finalist herself, could not pull off.

The semi-finals had been won the Cleenas Lady and top Irish bitch Deanridge Vixen and, while the latter missed her break and struggled to strike a blow thereafter, Cleenas lady, the Select Stakes champion, produced a terrific back-straight run after crowding to hit the front off the fourth bend.

However, both Jazz Hurricane and Dilemmas Flight used their stamina to range upsides off the last and, in a ding-dong finish, it was the Savva bitch who forged ahead.

The Jack and Andy Elias-owned runner had earlier struck gold in the Produce Stakes at Hall Green (Early Flight also made the final there!) before claiming the bitches' Classic, to add to previous Elias victories in the Derby (Moaning Lad) and St Leger (Kens Dilemma/Dilemmas Lad).

In doing so, the December 2004 whelp (by Droopys Vieri) added to the successes of the litter, which included Westmead Alec (Sussex Puppy Trophy/Racing Post Festival) and Spiridon Louis (Walthamstow track record).

Ironically, on the night Savva chose not to go to Wimbledon, instead heading for Henlow to see some puppies trial, as he eyed further glory in 2007 and beyond!

Winning breeder: Nick Savva, Dunstable, Beds

Finish	Trap	Names	Price	Time/Dis
1	2	DILEMMAS FLIGHT	7/1	28.96
2	1	Cleenas Lady	11/8F	1
3	6	Jazz Hurricane	5/1	NK
4	5	Chakalak Paris	20/1	2 1/2
5	4	Deanridge Vixen	2/1	6 1/4
6	3	Africa	25/1	NK

ALL ENGLAND CUP

GEORDIE PARKER ended the year on a high for connections when edging Droopys Tobey in a thriller for the William Hill All England Cup final at Brough Park.

Trained by Charlie Lister for part-owners Scott Fraser and breeder Jimmy Fenwick, the Yarmouth Derby winner had to battle back when led by the Graham Hutt-trained runner-up down the far side after just shading his rival for early pace.

Proving the stronger on the run-in, the British-bred Geordie Parker also landed his trainer the Sky/Hills trainers' championship for live-on-Sky meeting, and earned 20-1 quotes from the major bookmaking firm for the 2007 Derby.

Lister, who had sent out a 1-2-3 in the 2005 All England Cup, also fielded prolific-scoring Clash Harmonica in the final, but the Laurels champion found crowding and hit the rails at the bend.

On the undercard, Ted Soppitt's Calzaghe Frisby maintained his unbeaten record over six bends to gain outright honours in the Sky Sports/William Hill race to be winning-most greyhound on Sky in 2006.

Winning breeder: Jimmy Fenwick, Morpeth, Northumberland

Finish	Trap	Names	Price	Time/Dis
1	4	Geordie Parker	1/1F	28.83
2	6	Droopys Tobey	14/1	HD
3	6	Gee Vee	20/1	1/2
4	2	Count Gelignite	33/1	1/2
5	1	West Tipp	9/2	4 1/4
6	3	Clash Harmonica	6/4	SH

XMAS FESTIVAL STAYERS

JETHART JOE completed a great day for the Pat Rosney camp when landing a surprise but deserved win in the £5,000 Ladbrokes Christmas Festival Stayers final at Monmore.

In what was a high-class line-up, Jethart Joe followed up his 12-1 heat success to lead home the likes of Westmead Olivia, Westmead

Swift and Spiridon Louis after a fast start and a first-bend lead.

Since arriving from Ireland, the May 2004 son of Larkhill Jo and Lydpal Frankie had been running on over four bends in A1 contests, but relished the step up in trip to make it a treble for local handler Rosney on the day. He also sent out Fourcuil Moth to win the Bitches 480 event and supporting card winner Jethart Silver.

Winning breeder: Jimmy Fenwick, Morpeth, Northumberland

Finish	Trap	Names	Price	Time/Dis
1	4	JETHART JOE	8/1	37.86
2	6	Lady Three Star	12/1	4 1/2
3	5	Westmead Olivia	7/2	NK
4	3	Westmead Swift	4/5F	1/2
5	1	Fabulous Sophie	10/1	3/4
6	2	Spiridon Louis	7/2	1/2

HARRY HOLMES MEMORIAL

KYLEGROVE TOP capped a great year for Julie Bateson when taking the £5,000 Harry Holmes Memorial to land the Lancaster-based handler with her biggest win as a trainer.

Bateson had scored near-misses with the likes of Teds Anchor and Halcrow Prince, both big-race finalists in 2006, but it was the son of Top Honcho and Bangor Shirley who earned 'black type' for the kennel in the Sheffield feature.

Owned by Anthony Rhodes and Howard Jenkinson, Kylegrove Top made all to strike from favourite Droopys Sami.

Winning breeder: Peter Burgon, Templemore, Co. Tipperary

Finish	Trap	Names	Price	Time/Dis
1	1	KYLEGROVE TOP	3/1	29.12
2	6	Droopys Sami	5/4F	3 1/2
3	5	Ballymackey Lark	12/1	1/2
4	4	Mountview Ranger	9/2	1 1/4
5	2	Portant Lady	12/1	1 1/4
6	3	Navigation Jack	11/2	2

NATIONAL SPRINT

CENTAUR STRIKER upset the odds on his kennelmate and red-hot favourite Ningbo Jack when landing the Stadium Bookmakers National Sprint, the traditional pre-Xmas treat at Nottingham.

The 14-1 chance, owned by the Centaur Corker Stud, broke smartly from trap five and was never headed and, despite running wide off the second bend, went clear from the remainder, most of whom were involved in crowding.

Ningbo Jack, as planned for the start of the competition, was retired to stud afterwards following a fantastic career including 40 wins from 76 starts, six sprint track record, a Laurels triumph and a place in the the 2005 Derby final.

Winning breeder: Jimmy Fenwick, Morpeth, Northumberland

Finish	Trap	Names	Price	Time/Dis
1	5	CENTAUR STRIKER	14/1	17.82
2	3	Cherryhill Power	66/1	2 1/2
3	4	Ningbo Jack	4/5F	1/2
4	1	Banjo Kazooie	14/1	NK
5	2	Blonde Cindy	4/1	1/2
6	6	Star Display	7/1	DIS

Racing Post Festival

Grand Finals night, Walthamstow, 14 November 2006

THE 2006 Racing Post Festival at Walthamstow broke all records and went down as one of the best yet in its now well-established history.

A fantastic crowd on the concluding Tuesday, following ten days-plus of high-quality action, not to mention a TV audience courtesy of Sky's coverage, saw some cracking racing from start to finish – although punters definitely found it hard this time!

The defeat of 1-7 chance and new track-record holder Spiridon Louis in the final of the Racing Post Festival Puppy Stayers kicked off a miserable first three-quarters of the card for favourites backers, as Seamus Cahill's Swift Maggie took advantage of the 'jolly' finding trouble after a slow start.

Gary Baggs was another Stow-based trainer to strike on the night, and his Annes Honcho defied her years.

The fact that she is the mother of a July 2005 batch of pups, by coming through in the RP Veterans final for part-owners Bill McLuskey and Peter Rider.

McLuskey would also enjoy success with Killeen Tom in a six-bend hurdles contest, but it was Maxine Locke who struck in the Maidens Derby final with Forest Express reversing semi-final form with Farloe Rooney.

And her fellow Romford-based handler Martyn Wiley then weighed in with Westdale Blue in the Totesport London Scurry as a fast start saw him deny hotpot Myella Honcho the lead.

The Racing Post's Chris Smith (right) presents the Festival Veterans trophy to owners Bill McCluskey and Peter Rider after Annes Honcho's success. Trainer Gary Baggs, Anne and Sam Rider are also pictured

And on what completed a fantastic evening for Romford trainers, the VCbet Marathon final went the way of another big-priced runner as En It outstayed Blackmagic Maisy for the spoils.

Spiridon Louis' litter-brother Westmead Alec struck back for the family in the Totesport Puppy Stakes final after breaking well from three, before the fast-finishing Raging Jack denied Countrywide Steels & Tubes Goodwood Cup winner Lambstown Blue another Festival victory in the VCbet Invitation.

TV viewers had to wait to the final live race, the showpiece Festival Stayers, for a first successful favourite as new six-bend star Calzaghe Frisby kept up his unbeaten record over the longer trip in holding off Romford Car Two, with Grand Prix winner January Tiger in third.

Thats The Bullet then had punters back on good terms with themselves when landing the odds in the Festival Hurdles final, before Slaneyside Demon proved himself the king of the maxi-marathon dogs in the 10-bend event.

Wheres Yer Man, the Scurry winner 12 months previously, again unleashed ferocious early speed to make all in the Carlisle Brass British-Bred final, before the gambled-on Confident Foe outstayed her rivals in the Dual Distance finale.

THE 2006 FESTIVAL FINALS

FESTIVAL MAIDEN DERBY FINAL

Finish	Trap	Names	Price	Time/Dis
1	1	FOREST EXPRESS	3/1	28.84
2	2	Farloe Rooney	11/8F	HD
3	6	War Of Attrition	6/1	1 1/4
4	4	Go Princess	20/1	3 3/4
5	3	Monksland Mike	6/1	HD
6	5	Milldean Storm	8/1	1

TOTESPORT LONDON SCURRY

Finish	Trap	Names	Price	Time/Dis
1	6	KILLEEN TOM	14/1	40.74
2	4	Top Personality	14/1	HD
3	5	Baran Nelson	8/1	NK
4	1	Droopys Campo	5/4F	3/4
5	3	Flying Frank	7/2	3/4
6	2	Skippers Crew	3/1	2 1/2

VICTOR CHANDLER MARATHON FINAL

Finish	Trap	Names	Price	Time/Dis
1	4	EN IT	8/1	53.10
2	2	Blackmagic Maisy	7/4JF	1 1/4
3	5	Seathwaite Robby	7/2	1/2
4	3	Patch Of Blue	10/1	3 3/4
5	6	Lady Minstral	7/4JF	1 1/4
6	1	Knockaun Megan	8/1	1 3/4

FESTIVAL PUPPY STAYERS FINAL

Finish	Trap	Names	Price	Time/Dis
1	6	Swift Maggie	8/1	39.91
2	1	Spiridon Louis	1/7F	HD
3	3	Westmead Suzie	33/1	1 3/4
4	4	Miselar Custard	14/1	DH
5	5	Vatican Skye	10/1	3 1/2
6	2	Westmead Sam	25/1	1 1/4

FESTIVAL HURDLE FINAL

Finish	Trap	Names	Price	Time/Dis
1	6	KILLEEN TOM	14/1	40.74
2	4	Top Personality	14/1	HD
3	5	Baran Nelson	8/1	NK
4	1	Droopys Campo	5/4F	3/4
5	3	Flying Frank	7/2	3/4
6	2	Skippers Crew	3/1	2 1/2

FESTIVAL VETERANS FINAL

Finish	Trap	Names	Price	Time/Dis
1	2	ANNES HONCHO	4/1	29.34
2	1	Loughteen Bandit	7/2	1 3/4
3	5	Purple Monkey	6/4F	2
4	4	Ronnies Flight	11/4	2 1/2
5	3	Strong Flow	8/1	3/4

Racing Post Festival

Grand Finals night, Walthamstow, 20 November 2007

VCbet's Neil Wilkins presents the trophy to Barnfield On Air's part-owners Mark Hodgson and Steve Murphy after his Racing Post Festival grand finals' night triumph

THE 2007 Racing Post Festival came to an outstanding conclusion at Walthamstow when even dreadful weather conditions failed to dampen the spirits after a series of brilliant performances, topped off by Spiridon Louis in the marathon final and Barnfield On Air in the invitation.

The two VCbet-backed contests ended proceedings for those watching on television and arguments about the pair's Greyhound of the Year aspirations raged long into the night!

First up was Spiridon Louis as Lorraine Sams's Regency and St Leger champion made all over 835m to win as he liked from Shine Fantasy and Centaur Fuji.

Barnfield On Air was soon in command in the invitation and Sam Poots's Sussex Cup and Blue Square 480 champion, a multiple track record holder including over the 475-metre Stow trip, ran his rivals ragged.

The wet conditions precluded any exceptional times, but Barnfield On Air still clocked the fastest time of the night, his 28.75sec for the one lap three spots quicker than Toosey Blue, who helped make it a one-two for John Mullins in the British Bred final as he led home Blonde Buzz. Later, Blonde Jeannie made it a good night fo Mullins, winning the bitches' stake.

Tony Collett landed the Racing Post Festival Stayers final with St Leger second Lenson

Joker; Gary Baggs struck for the locals and owner Steve Baran in the Maiden final, while Ted Soppitt was thrilled with his Droopys Totti in the Racing Post Festival Puppy Stayers final.

Droopys Totti had kicked off the 14-race gala with a facile success, while Kildare Lark then made up for his trainer Jason Foster missing out on the Irish Grand National when winning the Racing Post Festival Hurdle. The winner had made the final at Harold's Cross.

Danas Black landed something of a touch for Andrew Peacock when turning a fine, running-on second in his 475m heat into a brilliant win in the final over 640m, upsetting the odds on Lenson Earl.

The Morton family's Westmead Tina shaped well for her Oaks campaign by pouncing late on to beat Mustang Garcia in the Totesport Puppy Stakes final, while the Wright family's evergreen Legal Major struck for Ernie Gaskin in the London Scurry

Ninja Blue, winner of the 2006 St Leger, won an exciting Racing Post Seniors for trainer Charlie Lister and owners Terry and Elaine Coveney, while Roy Towner's grand servant Slaneyside Demon late on repeated his maxi-marathon success, him and Rosshill View serving up a terrific race over 1,045m, the winner just getting up.

It was the perfect race to end a perfect evening for open-race fans.

THE 2007 FESTIVAL FINALS

FESTIVAL MAIDEN DERBY FINAL

Finish	Trap	Names	Price	Time/Dis
1	5	Baran Pedro	3/1	29.02
2	3	Barnfield Woody	1/1F	3/4
3	2	Ronnies Hotstuff	7/2	1
4	4	Millwards Summit	20/1	2 1/4
5	6	Chakalak Fortax	14/1	1/2
6	1	Tilly	12/1	1

TOTESPORT LONDON SCURRY

Finish	Trap	Names	Price	Time/Dis
1	4	Legal Major	9/4	26.00
2	2	Westmead Prince	2/1F	1 1/4
3	1	Black Taxi	9/4	4 1/4
4	5	Fivestar Oak	12/1	1
5	6	Perceptive Pacey	4/1	1 3/4

VICTOR CHANDLER MARATHON FINAL

Finish	Trap	Names	Price	Time/Dis
1	2	Spiridon Louis	4/9F	53.48
2	5	Shine Fantasy	16/1	3
3	6	Centaur Fuji	16/1	3/4
4	3	Genesis Alix	20/1	3 1/2
5	1	Bubbly Kate	2/1	2
6	4	Malbay Thumper	33/1	1 1/2

FESTIVAL PUPPY STAYERS FINAL

Finish	Trap	Names	Price	Time/Dis
1	4	Droopys Totti	10/11F	39.66
2	2	Droopys Attracta	20/1	5 1/2
3	1	Rebourne Again	7/2	4 1/2
4	3	Rough Rose	5/1	1 1/2
5	5	Dangerous Lady	7/2	3/4
6	6	Unique Picture	50/1	DIS

FESTIVAL HURDLE FINAL

Finish	Trap	Names	Price	Time/Dis
1	3	Kildare Lark	7/2	29.22
2	6	Custom Paul	7/1	3 1/2
3	4	Snazzy Time	7/2	1/2
4	1	Nevada Blue	5/4F	7 1/2
5	2	Dixies Woods	12/1	SH
6	5	Tommy Bahama	9/2	DIS

FESTIVAL STAYERS FINAL

Finish	Trap	Names	Price	Time/Dis
1	6	Lenson Joker	4/6F	39.63
2	5	Directors Chair	4/1	2
3	1	Big Brett Coal	7/2	2
4	2	Heavy Weather	20/1	3 1/2
5	4	Fear Robben	12/1	HD
6	3	Tiger Scot	33/1	3 1/4

PREVIOUS RACING POST FESTIVAL WINNERS

RACING POST FESTIVAL HURDLE

1998	Kingswell Sport	7-2	29.65	J Page
1999	Catunda Leonardo	9-1	29.85	T Dartnall
2000	Tuttles Minister	11-8F	29.71	T Foster
2001	Born To Go	4-1	29.32	T Foster
2002	Patriot Man	7-4F	29.52	B Clemenson
2003	Later	8-1	29.73	P Rosney
2004	Oklahoma Jo	5-2	29.66	T Foster
2005	Lethal Rumble	1-5F	29.58	M Wallis
2006	Thats The Bullet	2-5F	29.57	E Gaskin
2007	Kildare Lark	7-2	29.22	J Foster

RACING POST FESTIVAL VETERANS

1998	Clear Prospect	9-2	29.11	L Mullins
1999	Rebel Leader	15-8	29.20	B Clemenson
2000	Level Mover	5-2JF	29.35	R Jones
2001	Glowing Wave	6-1	29.01	B Wileman
2002	Simply Fabolous	11-4	29.39	B Capaldi
2003	El Ronan	11-8F	29.46	C. Lister
2004	Droopys Corleone	11-10F	29.03	D Riordan
2005	Ballymac Kewell	11-8F	29.02	CPhilpott
2006	Annes Honcho	4-1	29.34	G Baggs
2007	Ninja Blue	7-4F	29.05	C Lister

VICTOR CHANDLER MARATHON

1998	Thornfield Bob	10-1	53.14	B Murfin
1999	Spenwood Wizard	5-4F	53.58	R Hough
2000	Spenwood Wizard	2-7F	53.66	J Burridge
2001	Jennie Come Home	6-1	52.95	B Draper
2002	Smoking Baby	EvsF	53.31	D Knight
2003	Roswell Juliette	25-1	53-92	L Jones
2004	Blues Highway	11-2	53.99	B Clemenson
2005	Star Of Dromin	4-9F	52.84	M Wallis
2006	En It	8-1	53.14	D Mullins
2007	Spiridon Louis	4-9F	53.48	L Sams

RACING POST FESTIVAL STAYERS

1998	Dans Sport	7-4JF	39.77	C Lister
1999	Palace Issue	1-2F	39.51	L Mullins
2000	Palace Issue	2-5F	40.01	L Mullins
2001	Frisby Fassan	6-4F	39.85	H Crapper
2002	Frisby Folly	11-4	40.25	H Crapper
2003	Erinaceous Flyer	7-2	40.29	E Gaskin
2004	Solid Money	8-11F	39.68	D Knight
2005	Slick Kid	16/1	40.65	M McCool
2006	Calzaghe Frisby	4-7F	39.50	T Soppitt
2007	Lenson Joker	4-6F	39.63	T Collett

RACING POST PUPPY STAYERS

1998	Palace Issue	4-7F	40.05	L Mullins
1999	Lamerie	5-2	40.21	L Mullins
2000	Kegans Flyer	13-8	40.62	L Jones
2001	Kinda Sleepy	7-4JF	39.86	L Jones
2002	Keltie Sparkler	11-8F	39.98	J Mullins
2003	Mora Star	6-1	40.56	J. Mullins
2004	Never Can Tell	8-1	40.22	P Garland
2005	Hondo Blue	1-4F	39.81	J Ball
2006	Swift Maggie	8-1	39.91	S Cahill
2007	Droopys Totti	10-11F	39.66	T Soppitt

The Derby

by Jonathan Hobbs

Three-in-a-row for Savva and Morton

WE had been here before, gloriously been here before. An historic third straight Derby victory for breeder/ trainer Nick Savva and owner Bob Morton, Westmead Lord followed the feat of his half-brother, the mighty Westmead Hawk, in winning the Blue Square Derby on a night of high emotion at Wimbledon in July.

For a new sponsor, the 77th running of the Classic could not have gone better. Decent crowds, high levels of betting, on and off-course, plus the added interest of a quality Irish entry meant that the premier Classic kept greyhound fans on the edge of their seats from the first round, to the final.

From Graham Hutt's early successes, to those of John Mullins and the quite storming performances of the Irish-trained runners helped make a Derby without Westmead Hawk still a brilliant one, and quite an international one with runners from England, Scotland and Ireland ultimately lining up in the quest for greyhound racing's greatest prize.

But as already alluded to, once again the build-up the Classic centred around the aforementioned 'special one', Westmead Hawk.

Winner of the previous two Derbys, Nick Savva's superstar had recovered from the broken hock he suffered the previous July in a trial at Hall Green, ironically as he prepared for

They've done it again! Westmead Lord and connections celebrate a Classic treble

a 'roadshow' series of appearances at tracks. He had rehabilitated in Ireland, serving bitches at the Dunphys' Portlaw establishment in the interim.

To all intents and purposes, though, his career was over.

Savva travelled over to Ireland intermittently and was quietly encouraged with what he saw. He galloped him, first in Ireland, and then 'behind closed doors' back at home at the Westmead Kennels where he was born. Connections played it down, but there was obviously still hope and the news coming out of the Edlesborough kennels was positive.

He trialled and then raced in the heats of the Greyhound Stud Book Trophy at Monmore. Second in the heats, he was also second in the final behind Fear Robben, but Savva was still not entirely happy. He felt he needed more runs before any decision to seek an unprecedented third straight Derby success – he wanted to see the 'spark' of a champion. Westmead Hawk had two Derby trial stakes at Wimbledon. He won the first in a workmanlike fashion, coming through off the last bend. Those at Wimbledon roared him home, of course, the champion was back. But to Savva's trained eye something was still missing.

He returned the following week and finished second, albeit a staying-on one. Savva spoke afterwards with Morton and the decision was taken to retire him. For the record, Talkspot, the greyhound owned by

radio station Talksport, was the last greyhound to beat him.

Savva told the *Racing Post*'s Richard Birch: "Westmead Hawk was a dream, and we just woke up. He's not the dog we know. He's way behind his best. That was his fourth run back this year, and he went into the race very fit and very well.

"He runs more and more like a stayer now. Of course, that's what he was equipped for, and that's why he was so special, so unique – he could beat the best on a regular basis over a trip that was too short for him.

"It's understandable. Age and injury have taken a toll. 99 out of 100 lose that vital bit extra after such an injury. Hawk wants to do it, but he can't any more. You can see that.

"He showed nothing up to the third bend. He would win races over six bends, but personally I think it's right to retire him. I've made my decision. The dog has run his last race. He won't be entered for the Derby."

The sport had clamoured for the return of the master of the off-the-pace, last-gasp performance. Westmead Hawk had become only the fourth greyhound to do the Derby double, and the fact his was a British-bred success counted for a whole lot more. In fact, Hawk's domination might just have been the catalyst for the most serious assault on the English Derby in years – from Ireland!

Indeed, when Wimbledon closed entries on the 2007 Blue Square Derby, the total number

of entries stood at 191 with 18 entries from Ireland. These were 18 very strong entries, headed by Ian Reilly's Phoenix Paddy, Fraser Black's Droopys Robinho, Paul Hennessy's Tyrur Lee and Seamus Graham's Loyal Honcho. All were heavily punted in the run-up to the first round.

But if Ireland's challenge looked strong, Scotland's was all-conquering in the first batch of heats with Graham Hutt weighing in with a treble courtesy of Drimeen Dasher, Nervous Woody and Droopys Tobey.

Having celebrated at the Ashford, Kent, kennels overnight of compatriots Liz and Rab McNair, he then returned the very next night to make it four from four from his entry with Manic Mile obliging.

But time-wise, and for sheer individual brilliance, the first-round clockings of Phoenix Paddy and Tyrur Lee set the standard. Both stopped the clock at a fastest-of-the-31-qualifiers 28.46sec and, having finished first and second in the e50,000 Cox Cup at Newbridge, the form of that particular event got a massive boost.

Other high points across the three-night schedule of the first round included wins for Killer Keane, the unexposed and highly-rated Directors Chair, local star Side Leg and Paul Hennessy's Ullid Conor. The latter, a much-travelled, experienced sort, beat Westmead Lord, Hawk's half-brother, in a heat which would ultimately have most bearing on the Classic.

Into the second round, and Ireland's strong team of greyhounds turned the screw. Droopys Robinho, always likely to improve for his first round defeat, now began to show the sort of form which made him a heavily-backed leading contender for outright honours as he won well, with more improvement likely.

Westmead Joe, a finalist 12 months before, showed trackcraft reminiscent of his half-brother Westmead Hawk after powering home in his heat; Eye Onthe Veto built on his first round effort by leading home Express Ego, while Ullid Conor prove he was the real deal with another solid effort.

Blonde Dino also raised eyebrows with his terrific run in a tough eliminator, but it was Savanna Highlands who posted a brilliant 28.43sec.

However, two major players left the Derby. Fear Haribo had won the Scottish Derby, having annexed the Gymcrack as a pup in 2006. He found himself in a 'heat of death' featuring

Phoenix Paddy and Westmead Lord among others, but came up short and was afterwards found to be wrong. He did, however, come back very strongly later in the year.

Barnfield On Air, another who later in the year became a real player, also bowed out after a troubled run in the second round after a very impressive heat run.

Into the third round, and the last 48 session with eight Derby heats packing them into Wimbledon.

From Dilemmas Flight's success in heat one to Blonde Jeannie's in the eighth, the night oozed quality but also had its fare share of shocks, with Eye Onthe Veto, Savanna Highlands, Tyrur Lee, Westmead Joe and Greenwell Flash bowing out.

Dilemmas Flight clearly had her sights set on the elusive Oaks/Derby double; Farloe Premier continued to make great progress from the same owner/trainer team (Lister/Bates) who had succeeded with Farloe Verdict; Fear Me rolled back the years, again for the Lister camp; Bens Court built on his second round win with defeat of Blonde Dino for Claudia Wray and her father Steve; Full Bloom had Portsmouth trainer Robin Thorn in raptures with another gutsy win; Blonde Jeannie continued to make it a great Derby for 'Team Mullins', while Droopys Robinho was at his sparkling front-running best.

However, again it was Phoenix Paddy who had the clock-watchers drooling with a sensational 28.33sec win, the run of the competition thus far, and a time which would not be bettered in the 2007 Blue Square Derby. It was pace and power all rolled into one, and trainer Reilly had another Droopys Scholes on his hands, if luck would hold. Sadly, it didn't.

The quarter-finals, as always, form the middle leg of the three runs in eight days schedule for the Derby. It is what makes the English version unique, with the demands helping to make it for many the greatest greyhound race in the world, and certainly the toughest. The formbook was strong, but the script was well and truly torn up now.

First out of the competition was Droopys Robinho. He missed the break, roared to the bend but found a wall of greyhounds in front of him, in particular Blonde Dino. They collided and there was no way back for either as Dilemmas Flight strode majestically away to win in 28.68sec. Directors Chair and Ballymac Charley also made it through to the last 12.

Now it was time for the 'Derby king' Charlie Lister to strike. Farloe Premier had been a greyhound who had flirted with six bends and, just as it had not stopped Westmead Hawk's progress over four, the strapping black powered to victory from Forest Scholes and Greenwell Storm. But again, there would be a sting in the tail ahead of the semis for the winner.

The third quarter-final and, in scenes reminiscent of Premier Fantasy, there was heartbreak for an Irish-trained favourite when Phoenix Paddy broke down on the run to the bend. Ian Reilly, who enjoyed great joy with Droopys Scholes, now suffered the lowest point of his career, but was commendably philosophical. "He won't race again. What can you say? It's an absolute sickener, but these things happen in greyhound racing."

Kanes Blue had made the quarter-finals 12 months previously for Keeley McGee, but sold into Chris Allsopp's kennel was now back for more Wimbledon joy and he took chief advantage of the situation to lead home Ullid Conor and Blakes World.

The fourth quarter-final saw Loyal Honcho post the quickest time as he led up from Westmead Lord and was always holding that rival to win in a speedy 28.46sec. The runner-up, though, performed with credit after not leading. Caulry Fast Trap grabbed third.

The bandwagon rolled on to the semi-finals, and the unfortunate withdrawal of Farloe Premier, who suffered a bad injury following the quarter-finals. It left just 11 dogs in the hunt for glory.

Loyal Honcho wins his quarter-final in brilliant style

The Irish pair of Ullid Connor and Forest Scholes ensured that third-placed Westmead Lord made the final without a win in the event in a scrappy opening semi-final. The winner recorded 28.90sec.

The second semi saw the bitch shine again, as Dilemmas Flight powered her way home to deny Loyal Honcho another success. Outsider Caulry Fast Trap booked his place in the final with a spirited display, leaving connections of all six dreaming of Saturday, July 7.

Once again, the Westmead Kennels were dominant in the final. Not just providing two runners of their own (Dilemmas Flight, Westmead Lord), both also bred there, they were again playing host to Irish-based trainers Fraser Black (Forest Scholes) and Seamus Graham (Loyal Honcho).

The *Racing Post*'s special Derby pullout had played humorously on the fact – labling Savva and his lodgers Graham and Black the 'Three Amigos'! But they had the last laugh by filling the first four places in the decider.

Despite speculation all week as to who would go off favourite, it was Graham's Loyal Honcho who headed the market at 6-4. Westmead Lord had showed great early pace

in the early rounds but seemed short on stamina. He made the final without winning a heat, although that had been no obstruction to the likes of winners Tartan Khan and Allen Gift. Nevertheless, on the night, he was almost friendless in the betting market as the runners came on parade.

He appeared to spook slightly at the larger crowd and commotion of Derby final night. The youngest runner in the field took a sideways step away from the hordes on the terraces, but Savva 'gave him his lead', he relazed and trotted towards trap five runner

The Derby roar, or more likely Savva's genius, sparked Westmead Lord into life out of the traps after those missed breaks in quarter-final and semi-final. He was away to a flyer and ther youngest runner in the field, by some five months no less, was away

He stretched clear, being pursued by the gallant favourite throughout. As they rounded the last, his back-straight advantage had been eroded, but for those on the leader the line came in time, as he flashed home half-a-length ahead of Loyal Honcho.

The win brought the house down, such is the popularity of the Savva/Morton combination, and the Union Jack was once

Westmead Lord (T6) in front on the dash to the bend and on his way to Derby glory

again hoisted to celebrate the British-bred winner.

Morton said: "Nick is simply the best. He doesn't just train Derby winners – he breeds them too. He's a great credit to British breeding." And of the winner: "I never lost confidence in him. In fact, I've been praying to the Lord, for 'the Lord', for the past two weeks. It worked!"

Indeed, for Bob and Sue Morton, it continued a terrific run of success after persuading Savva to come out of retirement, take out his trainer's licence again, and address the fact that the family had come so close in the Classic with Special Account 1982 and Sonic Flight, Westmead Hawk's sire, in 2001. But even they could never have envisaged three in a row.

Savva paid tribute afterwards to the team at Westmead Kennels, notably assistant trainer Gary Slater, long-time friend and Savva team member, Billy O'Connor, and Alan Calder.

As Patrick Saward said in his incomperable Breeding Lines column in the *Racing Post*, it was "not long since we were moping at the prospect of a Derby without Westmead Hawk,

but we need not have been downcast. Nick Savva, the undisputed king of British breeding, produced the retired champion's half-brother Westmead Lord to take the sport's most coveted title back to Edlesborough in Bedfordshire for the third successive year, seeing off in brilliant style a gallant and worthy Irish challenge which has been a major factor in making this one of the most memorable of Derbys."

Westmead Lord was from a litter of three by Droopys Kewell, an Irish Derby finalist and Irish Leger and Champion Stakes winner, with Peterborough Puppy Derby winner Westmead Prince already putting the batch on their map.

Lightly-raced coming into the event, he had won the Paddy Dunne Memorial Puppy Cup at Henlow before the plan was hatched to contest the Derby. The plan came off, despite his inexperience and tender years, and once again the 'Westmead' name had been carried to Classic glory.

With natural improvement, talk afterwards soon turned to 'the Lord', just like 'the Hawk', defending his title in 2008 when the general consensus was that he would be even better!

Trap 1: FOREST SCHOLES
Trainer: Fraser Black
Owner: John Poynton
Breeder: Patrick Kehoe, Co. Wexford

QUICKLY repaid the faith – and the investment! – of new owner John Poynton by lining up in the final. Poynton, an owner of both horses and greyhounds for many years, bought the son of 2004 Derby winner Droopys Scholes just two weeks before, so impressed was he with the performances of the heavyweight. Over the Cheltenham fences, Poynton, the former Coventry City chairman, cheered on the likes of Browne's Gazette and Landing Light, but the Jersey-based businessman now cheered on his runner in the quest to land a Greyhound Derby. Scotsman Black, twice a winner of the Irish Greyhound Personality of the Year award and based 'across the water' at Rathangan, Co. Kildare, had already won a Scottish Derby with Droopys Marco in 2005, and now looked to Farloe Scholes to makeup for the disappointment of seeing hotpot Droopys Robinho go out in the quarter-finals.

Trap one: Forest Scholes

Trap 2: ULLID CONOR
Trainer: PJ Fahy, Co. Galway
Owner: Paul Hynes
Breeder: P J Fahy, Co. Galway

Had been away from home with his handler, 17-year-old son of leading Irish trainer Paul, young Kevin Hennessy, for the duration of the Classic. They lodged with the Kent-based husband-and-wife training team of Seamus and Teresa Cahill, and Kevin, while not young enough to 'train' an English Derby finalist, was 'under age' when it came to attending the Derby Lunch, which was held in a London casino! By the Co. Kilkenny-based Hennessy family's brilliant former tracker Late Late Show, Ullid Conor was a winner of over 575 yards in Ireland, and also 640m at Sunderland. For the trip to the north-east, Kevin lodged again, this time with Willie Frew, in Scotland. "Thankfully, he's the type of dog who settles well," adds Kevin. "He's only a little dog, around 28 kilos, but covers the ground quickly, off the front and staying on to qualify when needed."

Trap two: Ullid Conor

Trap 3: DILEMMAS FLIGHT
Trainer: Nick Savva, Henlow
Owner: Jack Elias
Breeder: Nick Savva, Edlesborough, Beds.

WAS aiming to rewrite the record books in the final, as she bid to not only join a select band of bitches to win the premier Classic but also complete a famous, historic double by adding the Derby to the Oaks crown she won at Wimbledon in 2006. Bred at the famous Westmead Kennels in Dunstable, the two-year-old's owner Elias, a retired north London hotelier, had enjoyed Derby success as a member of the syndicate which owned 1995 winner Moaning Lad. Elias's son, Andy, who now helps run the family business, followed his father's greyhounds the length and breadth of the country, with victories in two St Legers, first with Kens Dilemma in 1995 and then with her son Dilemmas Lad in 1999, helping to swell the mantelpiece! Aimed to become only the sixth of her sex to be added to the roll of honour. Also won the Produce Stakes as a puppy.

Trap three: Dilemmas Flight

Trap 4: CAULRY FAST TRAP
Trainer: Elizabeth McNair
Owner: KSS Syndicate
Breeder: John Marks, Co. Tipperary

CAULRY FAST TRAP thrilled the husband-and-wife training team of Liz and Rab McNair by reaching the final - and the Scottish couple were more than happy for their three-year-old to play the underdog."He's got so much guts, keeps doing it, and we're in the final. It's a great feeling," said Rab befofrhand, adding: "I know the Derby roar won't bother him, he's

such an easy-going dog. In fact, I hope it's as loud as the London Underground. It might help us!" The McNairs left their Scottish base a few years previously to take up residency at kennels in Ashford, Kent. "It's meant the travelling to Wimbledon has been that much easier," said Liz. Caulry Fast Trap was already a Derby winner, having won the Rye House version last year. He is owned by the KSS Syndicate of Brendan Keogh, Simon Senyk and Mark Boble, and is out of a former Seamus Graham-trained bitch, Queen Survivor.

Trap four: Cauldry Fast Trap

Trap 5: LOYAL HONCHO
Trainer: Seamus Graham, Ireland
Owner: Noel Ryan
Breeder: Terence Gollogly, Co. Armagh

LOYAL HONCHO continued a trend for Irish trainer Seamus Graham, who was having his fourth English Derby finalist in three years after Mineola Farloe (twice) and Blue Majestic. Twelve months previously, his Mineola Farloe led from traps to near the line until a certain Westmead Hawk pounced. Graham, with three Irish Derby wins, five Consolations, plus a host of other big-race wins, was bidding to win the Derby for his friend Noel Ryan, 82 "When I took out my license in 1984, it was Noel who owned the first dog I trained," said

Graham. "Noel was a member of the syndicate which owned Dipmac, our first Irish Derby winner, so all these years later to be in a Derby final with him is just great." Loyal Honcho had been third to Ardkill Jamie and Razldazl Billy in the Easter Cup at Shelbourne Park.

Trap five: Loyal Honcho

Trap 6: WESTMEAD LORD
Trainer: Nick Savva
Owner: Bob Morton
Breeder: Nick Savva, Edlesborough, Beds.
WESTMEAD LORD's family credentials always warranted a place in the Derby final, given that his older half-brother Westmead Hawk had won the last two Classics! Also bred and trained by Nick Savva and owned by the Jersey-based Morton family, Bob and Sue, plus sons Andrew, Edward, Charles and Robert, Westmead Lord was from the June 2005 batch by Mega Delight. "And of the three in the litter, he was always the one who looked extra special, even though [Westmead] Prince won the Peterborough Puppy Derby," said Robert Morton. Bob Morton added: "Lord is only just two, and it's just great to be involved once again and helps makes up for the disappointment of Hawk's retirement. Savva, himself, was still modestly surprised at events. "I can't believe I bred a dog with so much natural speed!" he joked. "He's a big dog, 37 kilos-plus, and hasn't had a lot of racing really. He won a puppy event at Henlow in memory of my great friend Paddy Dunne, and then we targeted Wimbledon."

Trap six: Westmead Lord

PRIZE-MONEY

Winner: £100,000 & Trophy
2nd: £12,000
3rd: £6,000
4th: £4,000
5th: £3,000
6th: £3,000

HOW THEY FINISHED

Fin	Trap	Name	SP	sect.	Time/Dis
1	6	**Westmead Lord**	6/1	4.79	28.47
		bk d Droopys Kewell-Mega Delight Jun-2005			
		(Trainer: N Savva, Henlow)			
		Comment: QAw, ALd			
2	5	**Loyal Honcho**	6/4F	4.91	1/2
		bkw d Top Honcho-Midway Crystal Oct-2004			
		(Trainer: S Graham, Ireland)			
		Comment: Mid, ChlRnln			
3	1	**Forest Scholes**	8/1	5.00	NK
		bdw d Droopys Scholes-Colorado Tine Jan-2005			
		(Trainer: F Black, Ireland)			
		Comment: Rls, RnOn			
4	3	**Dilemmas Flight**	2/1	5.03	1
		bkw b Droopys Vieri-Early Flight Dec-2004			
		(Trainer: N Savva, Henlow)			
		Comment: CrdStt, RnOn			
5	2	**Ullid Conor**	5/1	4.90	SH
		bk d Late Late Show-Tyrur Gillian Jul-2004			
		(Trainer: P Hennessy, Ireland)			
		Comment: Rls, ClrRun			
6	4	**Caulry Fast Trap**	33/1	5.05	1 3/4
		bk d Spiral Nikita-Queen Survivor Oct-2003			
		(Trainer: E Mcnair, Unattached)			
		Comment: CrdStt			

Going Allowance: +20

FIRST ROUND

Finish	Greyhound	Trap	SP	Sec.	Time/Dis
1	Drimeen Dasher	3	5/1	5.03	28.90
2	Two Nicks	1	4/1	5.07	3 1/2
3	Iceman Vader	2	5/2	5.12	3/4
4	Snoozys Palace	4	6/1	5.09	NK
5	Debbies Choice	6	6/4F	5.08	SH
6	Days Of Speed	5	20/1	5.18	2 3/4

Finish	Greyhound	Trap	SP	Sec.	Time/Dis
1	Forest Scholes	1	7/2	5.10	28.90
2	Discreet Cat	4	8/1	5.16	3 1/4
3	Pacey Macy	3	16/1	5.04	SH
4	Anycrackjack	2	7/4F	4.99	1/2
5	Mango Tango	5	2/1	5.17	1/2
6	Kindred Sparky	6	6/1	5.09	1 3/4

Finish	Greyhound	Trap	SP	Sec.	Time/Dis
1	Ballymac Charley	6	3/1	4.89	28.96
2	Astute Gift	4	9/4	5.05	3 1/4
3	Blakes World	5	12/1	5.02	3/4
4	Pin Head	1	5/1	5.06	1 1/4
5	Southview Dan	3	14/1	5.00	8 1/2
6	Catunda Deano	2	7/4F	5.10	1 1/4

Finish	Greyhound	Trap	SP	Sec.	Time/Dis
1	Nervous Woody	3	7/2	4.93	29.14
2	Corleones Rammi	6	5/1	4.99	1/2
3	Smoking Again	5	14/1	4.97	4 1/4
4	Bigbadassassian	4	14/1	5.04	4 3/4
5	West Tipp	2	1/1F	5.18	1 1/2
6	Jo Shuffle	1	7/2	5.14	8 1/4

Finish	Greyhound	Trap	SP	Sec.	Time/Dis
1	Savana Highlands	1	5/4	4.99	29.03
2	Express Ego	2	4/6F	4.97	SH
3	Moving Charlie	6	33/1	4.91	6 1/4
4	Did She	4	50/1	5.19	1/2
5	Bonville Buster	3	20/1	5.16	1 1/4
6	Tanner Butler	5	33/1	5.03	1 1/4

Finish	Greyhound	Trap	SP	Sec.	Time/Dis
1	Droopys Tobey	6	7/1	4.89	28.83
2	Fear Haribo	4	1/2F	4.97	SH
3	Highbury Lao	5	9/2	5.02	1
4	Upper Hand	1	25/1	5.04	1/2
5	Fear Armani	2	7/1	5.03	1/2
6	Lilywhite Paddy	3	33/1	4.98	2 1/2

Finish	Greyhound	Trap	SP	Sec.	Time/Dis
1	Kanes Blue	6	7/4F	4.88	28.92
2	Pilot Pretender	5	10/1	4.99	HD
3	Lenson Express	1	9/4	5.09	SH
4	Beatties Best	2	7/1	5.01	3/4
5	Brooklyn Bridge	4	5/1	5.00	1 3/4
6	Hedrivesmemad	3	7/1	4.98	4 1/2

FIRST ROUND

Finish	Greyhound	Trap	SP	Sec.	Time/Dis
1	Farloe Jester	1	1/1F	5.11	28.80
2	Gotabetem	2	12/1	4.93	3
3	Astronomic	6	5/2	5.04	3/4
4	Butterbridge Ali	5	4/1	5.09	1
5	Mattos	3	20/1	5.15	1
6	Airtech Spur	4	33/1	5.10	1 1/4

Finish	Greyhound	Trap	SP	Sec.	Time/Dis
1	Droopys Fabregas	6	6/4	5.05	28.93
2	Westmead Liz	5	1/1F	5.08	3
3	Stonewall Cert	3	16/1	5.03	1 1/2
4	Tristar Blue	4	6/1	5.09	HD
5	Rusheen Boss	1	20/1	5.17	2
6	Roman Emperor	2	10/1	5.15	1

Finish	Greyhound	Trap	SP	Sec.	Time/Dis
1	Eye Onthe Veto	4	5/4F	4.87	28.55
2	Caulry Fast Trap	3	2/1	5.05	SH
3	Hooter Macooter	6	14/1	5.01	4
4	Raging Jack	2	9/4	5.19	6 3/4
5	Astral Jazz	5	25/1	5.12	1 1/4
6	Rocket Launcher	1	16/1	5.09	1/2

Finish	Greyhound	Trap	SP	Sec.	Time/Dis
1	Phoenix Paddy	3	7/4	4.82	28.46
2	Geordie Parker	5	4/5F	4.86	5
3	Orange Disorder	6	12/1	4.90	1 3/4
4	Funtime Chunky	4	10/1	4.86	2 3/4
5	Postle Supreme	2	20/1	5.00	2 1/4

Finish	Greyhound	Trap	SP	Sec.	Time/Dis
1	Tyrur Lee	1	4/7F	4.86	28.46
2	Fabregas	2	33/1	4.95	3 1/2
3	Fine Plan	3	25/1	4.92	2 1/2
4	Who Needs Wings	5	2/1	5.08	3/4
5	Rio Tuxedo	6	5/1	5.01	HD

Finish	Greyhound	Trap	SP	Sec.	Time/Dis
1	Dilemmas Flight	6	6/4F	5.09	28.94
2	Full Bloom	1	7/2	5.10	SH
3	Minnies Premier	4	5/1	5.06	NK
4	Cobra Striking	3	5/2	4.96	HD
5	Exclusive Lee	2	14/1	5.07	4 1/4
6	Droopys Top Lad	5	20/1	5.09	1 3/4

Finish	Greyhound	Trap	SP	Sec.	Time/Dis
1	Iceman Ross	6	1/2F	4.88	28.63
2	Westmead Syd	3	5/1	4.84	3
3	Mullaghmore Man	2	5/1	5.04	1 1/4
4	Coolsville	4	16/1	4.04	3 3/4
5	Cuil Tiger	1	14/1	5.16	1 1/4
6	Eye Onthe Flame	5	16/1	4.98	1 3/4

Finish	Greyhound	Trap	SP	Sec.	Time/Dis
1	Manic Mile	1	2/1F	5.10	28.91
2	Rough Gerrard	2	5/1	4.96	3/4
3	Wayward Ted	4	4/1	5.09	2 3/4
4	Droopys Lippi	3	12/1	5.04	1/2
5	Temple Lad	5	6/1	5.11	HD
6	Get Up Ditto	6	3/1	5.00	1/2

Finish	Greyhound	Trap	SP	Sec.	Time/Dis
1	Barnfield On Air	2	5/4	HT	28.58
2	Blonde Dino	4	4/5F	0.00	4 1/4
3	Lenson Earl	3	7/1	0.00	1 3/4
4	Westmead Nicole	5	10/1	0.00	3 1/4
5	Stepaside Budgie	1	16/1	0.00	1 3/4

Finish	Greyhound	Trap	SP	Sec.	Time/Dis
1	Droopys Wells	6	5/1	4.90	28.99
2	Fear Me	3	4/1	4.90	Shd
3=	Classy Star	5	20/1	1 1/4	
4	Express Comet	2	10/11F	5.01	1 1/4
5	Betwithoutpete	1	25/1	5.11	3 1/4
6	Vipar Totti	4	4/1	1 1/4	

Finish	Greyhound	Trap	SP	Sec.	Time/Dis
1	Jaxerback	1	10/11F	4.92	28.62
2	Westmead Alec	4	6/1	4.99	2 3/4
3	Swift Pirate	6	5/1	5.01	HD
4	Masterpiece	3	9/2	5.16	1
5	Fear Daniel	5	10/1	4.99	1 3/4
6	Danas Black	2	33/1	5.17	5 1/4

Finish	Greyhound	Trap	SP	Sec.	Time/Dis
1	Larkhill Jim	3	9/4	4.96	28.89
2	Cahercrin Lad	5	7/1	4.98	4
3	Rio Jericho	1	5/1	5.02	1
4	Casino Valentine	6	20/1	5.09	HD
5	Corleones Flash	2	4/1	5.03	HD
6	Blonde Sheriff	4	2/1F	5.09	1

Finish	Greyhound	Trap	SP	Sec.	Time/Dis
1	Farloe Premier	3	11/8F	4.99	28.58
2	Directors Wish	4	9/4	5.01	6 3/4
3	Pagoda Tarbert	5	9/2	4.97	1 1/2
4	Allenbuild Flyer	1	8/1	5.09	1 1/2
5	Geldrops Stride	6	50/1	5.17	HD
6	Droopys Silva	2	5/1	5.08	2

Finish	Greyhound	Trap	SP	Sec.	Time/Dis
1	Loyal Honcho	6	4/5F	4.88	28.57
2	Heroic Assassin	2	20/1	5.03	7 1/4
3	Coyote Justine	5	6/1	4.98	1/2
4	Big Brett Coal	3	5/1	5.11	1 1/2
5	Rev Counter	1	6/1	5.13	SH
6	Westcountry Lady	4	9/2	5.06	4 3/4

Finish	Greyhound	Trap	SP	Sec.	Time/Dis
1	Meenala Cruiser	5	1/3F	4.93	28.65
2	Courts Ad Queen	1	3/1	5.04	4
3	Miselar Custard	3	10/1	5.26	Nk

4	Knockskagh Snap	2	20/1	5.05	SH
5	Schofield Star	6	10/1	5.02	3 3/4

Finish	Greyhound	Trap	SP	Sec.	Time/Dis
1	Ullid Conor	1	4/1	5.12	28.65
2	Westmead Lord	5	4/5F	4.95	1
3	Alibulk Rocket	6	9/4	5.03	1 3/4
4	Caressed	3	50/1	5.02	4
5	Newtown Koala	4	9/2	5.03	1 3/4
6	Westdale Blue	2	50/1	5.17	2 1/2

Finish	Greyhound	Trap	SP	Sec.	Time/Dis
1	Congo Romeo	6	20/1	5.05	28.98
2	Deanridge Vixen	2	11/4	5.05	3 1/4
3	Gandisranger	1	20/1	5.03	2 1/4
4	Droopys Electric	3	1/1F	5.13	HD
5	Pond Astronaut	5	9/2	5.15	1/2
6	Kilsheelan	4	12/1	5.21	4 1/2

Finish	Greyhound	Trap	SP	Sec.	Time/Dis
1	Blonde Jeannie	1	6/4F	4.90	28.81
2	Love Forever	3	8/1	5.10	1 1/4
3	Calzaghe Boyo	2	8/1	5.10	1 3/4
4	Talkspot	5	9/4	4.96	1 1/4
5	Trade Plate	6	7/2	5.22	HD

Finish	Greyhound	Trap	SP	Sec.	Time/Dis
1	Bonville Podge	1	5/1	4.97	29.00
2	Champ Woodward	4	8/1	4.92	1
3	Farloe Black	3	1/1F	5.06	3/4
4	Airtech Avit	5	25/1	4.99	3 1/2
5	Heavenly One	6	20/1	5.02	1 1/2
6	Journey North	2	9/4	5.08	1 1/2

Finish	Greyhound	Trap	SP	Sec.	Time/Dis
1	Toosey Blue	6	8/1	4.86	28.84
2	Westmead Joe	3	11/10F	5.02	HD
3	Macniler	1	4/1	5.00	2
4	Cleenas Lady	2	7/2	4.89	1/2
5	Gee Vee	5	20/1	4.94	3/4
6	Moss Row Mick	4	8/1	5.06	2

Finish	Greyhound	Trap	SP	Sec.	Time/Dis
1	Blonde Joey	1	12/1	4.98	28.89
2	Greenwell Flash	4	6/4JF	5.04	NK
3	Ballygarron Hope	2	33/1	5.07	SH
4	Rooster Nosey	6	12/1	4.91	HD
5	Winetavern Henry	3	6/1	5.16	1 3/4
6	Centaur Decree	5	6/4JF	5.03	HD

Finish	Greyhound	Trap	SP	Sec.	Time/Dis
1	Killer Keane	1	6/1	4.90	28.73
2	Greenwell Storm	4	7/4F	5.11	1
3	Fear Robben	2	3/1	5.08	1 1/4
4	Roxholme Ryan	6	2/1	4.91	1
5	Alternative Plan	5	16/1	5.16	4
6	Directors Tale	3	33/1	5.11	1 1/4

Finish	Greyhound	Trap	SP	Sec.	Time/Dis
1	Directors Chair	3	3/1	4.91	28.70
2	Droopys Robinho	2	4/5F	4.92	1 3/4
3	Zigzag Dutchy	5	4/1	4.98	HD
4	Bens Court	6	6/1	4.98	HD
5	Risk Related	4	25/1	4.98	2 1/2
6	Knockna Kirka	1	25/1	5.08	3

Finish	Greyhound	Trap	SP	Sec.	Time/Dis
1	Side Leg	6	1/2F	4.96	28.71
2	Droopys Kolo	2	6/1	4.91	1 1/4
3	Cloheena Ami	3	8/1	5.07	2 1/4
4	Forest Express	1	6/1	4.98	HD
5	Trained Assassin	4	8/1	4.96	1/2

SECOND ROUND

Finish	Greyhound	Trap	SP	Sec.	Time/Dis
6	Greenfield Hero	5	12/1	5.06	1 3/4

Finish	Greyhound	Trap	SP	Sec.	Time/Dis
1	Larkhill Jim	2	3/1	4.96	28.94
2	Congo Romeo	6	10/1	5.00	2
3	Calzaghe Boyo	5	20/1	5.03	2
4	Two Nicks	1	7/1	4.96	3 1/4
5	Killer Keane	3	5/2	5.09	HD
6	Jaxerback	4	6/4F	5.75	4 1/2

Finish	Greyhound	Trap	SP	Sec.	Time/Dis
1	Pilot Pretender	4	7/1	4.96	28.87
2	Minnies Premier	5	7/1	4.98	2 1/4
3	Farloe Premier	1	11/10F	5.11	1 1/2
4	Toosey Blue	6	3/1	5.00	HD
5	Love Forever	3	10/1	5.08	3/4
6	Westmead Alec	2	6/1	4.99	DIS

Finish	Greyhound	Trap	SP	Sec.	Time/Dis
1	Nervous Woody	4	9/2	4.84	28.59
2	Astronomic	5	5/2F	4.99	4 1/4
3	Lenson Earl	2	3/1	4.97	NK
4	Coyote Justine	6	10/1	4.99	2 1/4
5	Fabregas	1	6/1	5.01	2 1/2
6	Droopys Kolo	3	4/1	4.97	3/4

Finish	Greyhound	Trap	SP	Sec.	Time/Dis
1	Droopys Robinho	2	6/4F	4.91	28.82
2	Droopys Tobey	4	7/1	4.98	2 3/4
3	Greenwell Flash	6	7/4	5.08	NK
4	Westmead Liz	5	6/1	4.93	1 1/4
5	Courts Ad Queen	1	14/1	4.98	1
6	Directors Wish	3	8/1	5.05	1

Finish	Greyhound	Trap	SP	Sec.	Time/Dis
1	Corleones Rammi	6	6/1	4.91	29.02
2	Farloe Jester	1	1/2F	5.10	SH
3	Moving Charlie	5	20/1	4.92	4 1/2
4	Blonde Joey	3	8/1	5.11	2 1/2
5	Gotabetem	4	8/1	5.27	NK
6	Rough Gerrard	2	8/1	5.21	SH

SECOND ROUND

Finish	Greyhound	Trap	SP	Sec.	Time/Dis
1	Westmead Joe	2	5/4JF	5.19	29.30
2	Pagoda Tarbert	5	33/1	5.00	3 3/4
3	Lenson Express	3	7/1	5.06	NK
4	Cahercrin Lad	6	14/1	5.01	1/2
5	Deanridge Vixen	4	8/1	4.93	1
6	Farloe Black	1	5/4JF	5.06	3/4

Finish	Greyhound	Trap	SP	Sec.	Time/Dis
1	Phoenix Paddy	2	1/1F	5.02	28.72
2	Westmead Lord	3	3/1	4.95	1 1/2
3	Droopys Wells	6	10/1	4.97	NK
4	Fear Haribo	4	7/2	5.08	1 3/4
5	Astute Gift	1	12/1	5.07	SH
6	Smoking Again	5	100/1	5.03	2 1/2

Finish	Greyhound	Trap	SP	Sec.	Time/Dis
1	Bens Court	6	6/1	4.93	28.85
2	Swift Pirate	4	6/1	5.08	2 1/4
3	Directors Chair	2	4/9F	5.04	3 1/2
4	Mullaghmore Man	1	6/1	5.08	3/4
5	Orange Disorder	5	14/1	5.04	1

Finish	Greyhound	Trap	SP	Sec.	Time/Dis
1	Blonde Dino	5	2/1	4.88	28.63
2	Loyal Honcho	6	4/7F	4.99	2 3/4
3	Ballymac Charley	3	5/1	4.98	1 1/4
4	Discreet Cat	4	20/1	4.99	1 1/4
5	Rio Jericho	2	25/1	5.06	3/4

Finish	Greyhound	Trap	SP	Sec.	Time/Dis
1	Ullid Conor	2	4/1	4.91	28.74
2	Fear Me	4	4/1	4.94	1/2
3	Forest Scholes	3	10/1	5.00	2 1/4
4	Droopys Fabregas5	8/1	5.06	1/2	
5	Barnfield On Air	1	4/7F	5.04	1 1/4
6	Classy Star	6	50/1	5.04	1 1/2

Finish	Greyhound	Trap	SP	Sec.	Time/Dis
1	Alibulk Rocket	6	2/1	5.09	28.91
2	Hooter Macooter	5	8/1	5.02	1 1/2
3	Allenbuild Flyer	3	25/1	4.89	1 1/2
4	Gandisranger	2	33/1	4.93	3 3/4
5	Meenala Cruiser	4	4/7F	5.00	HD
6	Heroic Assassin	1	16/1	4.99	3 1/2

Finish	Greyhound	Trap	SP	Sec.	Time/Dis
1	Highbury Lao	4	9/4F	4.96	29.10
2	Caulry Fast Trap	5	7/1	5.08	2
3	Kanes Blue	6	3/1	4.94	NK
4	Fear Robben	3	4/1	5.00	2 3/4
5	Macniler	2	6/1	5.00	2 3/4
6	Champ Woodward	1	6/1	4.99	1 1/2

Finish	Greyhound	Trap	SP	Sec.	Time/Dis
1	Savana Highlands	1	2/1	4.90	28.43
2	Dilemmas Flight	6	9/2	4.93	1 1/2
3	Tyrur Lee	3	4/5F	4.99	1/2
4	Wayward Ted	5	33/1	5.09	5 1/2
5	Miselar Custard	2	25/1	5.18	1 1/4
6	Drimeen Dasher	4	10/1	4.99	3 1/2

SECOND ROUND

Finish	Greyhound	Trap	SP	Sec.	Time/Dis
1	Eye Onthe Veto	6	7/2	4.86	28.65
2	Express Ego	1	11/10F	5.00	1 1/2
3	Zigzag Dutchy	3	8/1	4.94	3/4
4	Ballygarron Hope 2	100/1		5.06	NK)
5	Geordie Parker	4	4/1	4.88	1 3/4
6	Iceman Ross	5	8/1	5.04	1/2

Finish	Greyhound	Trap	SP	Sec.	Time/Dis
1	Greenwell Storm	5	5/2	5.04	28.71
2	Full Bloom	2	5/1	5.13	4 1/4
3	Fine Plan	1	25/1	5.01	1 1/4
4	Iceman Vader	3	8/1	5.01	1
5	Side Leg	4	11/10F	5.01	3/4
6	Butterbridge Ali	6	4/1	5.07	SH

Finish	Greyhound	Trap	SP	Sec.	Time/Dis
1	Blonde Jeannie	2	1/1F	5.04	29.18
2	Blakes World	6	8/1	4.95	3/4
3	Manic Mile	4	3/1	5.19	NK
4	Bonville Podge	3	5/1	5.02	3/4
5	Stonewall Cert	1	16/1	5.04	1
6	Pacey Macy	5	14/1	5.00	3/4

THIRD ROUND

Finish	Greyhound	Trap	SP	Sec.	Time/Dis
1	Dilemmas Flight	6	3/1	4.89	28.58
2	Zigzag Dutchy	3	4/1	5.01	3 1/2
3	Blakes World	2	25/1	4.91	NK
4	Highbury Lao	1	9/2	5.05	SH
5	Moving Charlie	4	25/1	4.99	6 3/4
6	Eye Onthe Veto	5	5/4F	4.99	8 1/4

Finish	Greyhound	Trap	SP	Sec.	Time/Dis
1	Fear Me	3	9/2	4.95	28.68
2	Westmead Lord	5	6/4F	4.86	NK
3	Ullid Conor	1	5/2	5.00	4 1/4
4	Alibulk Rocket	6	9/2	5.04	1 1/2
5	Lenson Earl	2	16/1	5.05	SH
6	Astronomic	4	10/1	5.05	1 1/2

Finish	Greyhound	Trap	SP	Sec.	Time/Dis
1	Phoenix Paddy	4	6/4F	4.87	28.33
2	Loyal Honcho	6	3/1	4.94	4 1/4
3	Express Ego	2	3/1	4.95	1
4	Droopys Wells	5	14/1	4.98	2 3/4
5	Larkhill Jim	1	12/1	5.04	4 1/4
6	Farloe Jester	3	8/1	5.07	1/2

Finish	Greyhound	Trap	SP	Sec.	Time/Dis
1	Farloe Premier	1	7/4F	5.05	28.80
2	Forest Scholes	3	5/2	5.03	NK
3	Caulry Fast Trap	5	7/2	5.14	2 1/2
4	Allenbuild Flyer	4	33/1	5.19	4
5	Manic Mile	2	3/1	5.27	1 3/4

THIRD ROUND

Finish	Greyhound	Trap	SP	Sec.	Time/Dis
1	Bens Court	5	12/1	4.88	28.83
2	Blonde Dino	3	1/1F	4.90	SH
3	Directors Chair	2	6/1	4.99	5 3/4
4	Corleones Rammi	6	10/1	4.97	2 1/2
5	Savana Highlands	1	6/4	4.99	5 3/4
6	Congo Romeo	4	33/1	5.03	4 3/4

Finish	Greyhound	Trap	SP	Sec.	Time/Dis
1	Full Bloom	2	7/2	HT	29.10
2	Ballymac Charley	3	7/4F	0.00	1
3	Kanes Blue	5	9/2	0.00	HD
4	Fine Plan	1	20/1	0.00	1 1/2
5	Pilot Pretender	6	3/1	0.00	2 1/4
6	Hooter Macooter	4	7/1	0.00	3 1/4

Finish	Greyhound	Trap	SP	Sec.	Time/Dis
1	Droopys Robinho	2	9/4F	4.94	28.61
2	Greenwell Storm	5	3/1	5.06	3 3/4
3	Nervous Woody	3	4/1	5.01	NK
4	Droopys Tobey	4	8/1	5.01	3/4
5	Swift Pirate	6	20/1	5.17	1 1/4
6	Tyrur Lee	1	5/2	5.01	SH

Finish	Greyhound	Trap	SP	Sec.	Time/Dis
1	Blonde Jeannie	1	11/4	5.02	29.10
2	Lenson Express	3	14/1	5.02	1/2
3	Calzaghe Boyo	2	25/1	5.12	3/4
4	Pagoda Tarbert	5	33/1	5.13	3 1/4
5	Greenwell Flash	6	2/1	5.24	6 1/2
6	Westmead Joe	4	5/4F	5.15	SH

QUARTER-FINAL

Finish	Greyhound	Trap	SP	Sec.	Time/Dis
1	Dilemmas Flight	6	5/2	5.05	28.68
2	Directors Chair	1	12/1	5.13	4
3	Ballymac Charley	5	16/1	5.03	2 1/4
4	Blonde Dino	4	5/1	5.03	SH
5	Full Bloom	2	25/1	5.10	1 1/4
6	Droopys Robinho	3	4/6F	5.09	1 1/2

Finish	Greyhound	Trap	SP	Sec.	Time/Dis
1	Farloe Premier	2	5/1	5.01	28.52
2	Forest Scholes	3	5/1	5.01	3 3/4
3	Greenwell Storm	6	5/2F	5.15	1/2
4	Zigzag Dutchy	4	7/2	5.03	NK
5	Bens Court	5	3/1	5.00	SH
6	Lenson Express	1	7/1	5.09	1

Finish	Greyhound	Trap	SP	Sec.	Time/Dis
1	Kanes Blue	6	10/1	4.83	28.83
2	Ullid Conor	2	8/1	4.97	2
3	Blakes World	4	50/1	4.89	NK
4	Fear Me	3	9/2	5.01	1 3/4
5	Blonde Jeannie	1	8/1	5.02	1
6	Phoenix Paddy	5	1/2F	5.03	DIS

QUARTER-FINAL

Finish	Greyhound	Trap	SP	Sec.	Time/Dis
1	Loyal Honcho	6	9/4	4.91	28.46
2	Westmead Lord	5	9/4	4.99	3 3/4
3	Caulry Fast Trap	4	25/1	5.02	1 1/2
4	Calzaghe Boyo	2	50/1	5.06	2 1/2
5	Express Ego	1	2/1F	5.10	1 1/4
6	Nervous Woody	3	5/1	5.02	5 1/2

SEMI-FINALS

Finish	Greyhound	Trap	SP	Sec.	Time/Dis
1	Ullid Conor	2	2/1	4.93	28.90
2	Forest Scholes	3	5/1	4.97	NK
3	Westmead Lord	6	4/5F	4.93	2 3/4
4	Ballymac Charley	5	10/1	4.93	3 1/2
5	Blakes World	4	16/1	4.95	3

Finish	Greyhound	Trap	SP	Sec.	Time/Dis
1	Dilemmas Flight	3	7/2	4.92	28.74
2	Loyal Honcho	5	10/11F	5.05	2 1/2
3	Caulry Fast Trap	4	25/1	5.07	1
4	Greenwell Storm	6	6/1	5.13	2 1/4
5	Kanes Blue	2	14/1	4.96	3/4
6	Directors Chair	1	4/1	5.05	3/4

DERBY ENTRIES OVER THE YEARS

Year	Total	Irish
2007	191	18
2006	178	11
		(2 others)
2005	195	16
2004	194	13
2003	207	14
2002	173	8
2001	149	0
2000	172	8
1999	153	11
1998	167	2
1997	156	11
1996	201	17
1995	198	15
1994	208	10
1993	197	20
1992	197	19
1991	187	16
1990	213	11
1989	200	10
1988	195	19

Sponsored by the BGRB

The Greyhound Derby History

500 yards (White City)

1927

1ST	ENTRY BADGE	(5)	1-4F
2nd	Ever Bright	(1)	100-6
3rd	Elder Brother	(4)	100-8
4th	Toftwood Micksack	(3)	10-1
5th	Dereham Boy	(2)	20-1
6th	Banderloo	(6)	100-8
29.01	6, 1/2		J Harmon
			(White City)

525 yards (White City)

1928

1ST	BOHER ASH	(1)	5-1
2nd	Fabulous Figure	(2)	11-10F
3rd	Musical Box	(4)	5-1
4th	Bendeemer	(3)	100-8
5th	Moorland Rover	(5)	4-1
6th	Baby Elephant	(6)	20-1
30.48	1/2, nk		T Johnson
			(Edinburgh)

1929

1ST	MICK THE MILLER	(4)	4-7F
2nd	Palatinus	(2)	3-1
3rd	En Tomb	(3)	9-2
4th	Beadsman	(1)	25-1
29.96	3, 2, 3		P Horan
			(Dublin)

1930

1ST	MICK THE MILLER	(1)	4-9F
2nd	Bradshaw Fold	(3)	100-8
3rd	Mick McGee	(2)	100-6
4th	Dresden	(5)	100-6
5th	So Green	(6)	100-6
6th	Jack Bob	(4)	8-1
30.24	3, hd, 2, 2 1/2		S Orton
			(Wimbledon)

1931.(Re-Run)

1ST	SELDOM LED	(4)	7-2
2nd	Golden Hammer	(1)	3-1
3rd	Micks Fancy	(3)	6-1
4th	Mick The Miller	(6)	1-1F
5th	Brunswick Bill	(5)	100-8
6th	Vacant		
30.04	4, 1, 1, 1		W Green
			(West Ham)

1932

1ST	WILD WOOLLEY	(6)	5-2
2nd	Future Cutlet	(5)	8-13F
3rd	Fret Not	(1)	10-1
4th	Barrack Bridge	(3)	33-1
5th	Dee Tarn	(4)	66-1
6th	Disorder	(2)	20-1
29.72	nk, 10, 7, 1, 1		J Rimmer
			(White City)

1933

1ST	FUTURE CUTLET	(3)	6-1
2nd	Beef Cutlet	(5)	2-1
3rd	Wild Woolley	(6)	6-4F
4th	Roving Loafer	(2)	100-6
5th	Lutwyce	(1)	7-1
6th	Deemsters Mike	(4)	33-1
29.80	sh, 5, 2, 5, 10		S Probert
			(Wembley)

1934

1ST	DAVESLAND	(4)	3-1
2nd	Grey Raca	(3)	6-4F
3rd	Wild Woolley	(6)	5-1
4th	Brilliant Bob	(1)	3-1
5th	Kumm On Steve	(5)	100-7
6th	Denham Peter	(2)	3-1
29.81	2, 1, 4, 1, 4		H Harvey
			(Harringay)

1935

1ST	GRETA RANEE	(3)	4-1
2nd	Curleys Fancy II	(1)	2-1F
3rd	Stout Heart	(6)	5-2
4th	Bosham	(5)	100-8
5th	Maidens Delight	(4)	7-1
6th	Fresh Judgement	(2)	8-1
30.18	3/4, 3/4, 11/2, 1, 2		A Jonas
			(White City)

1936

1ST	FINE JUBILEE	(3)	10-11F
2nd	Itchok	(5)	8-1
3rd	Curley's Fancy II	(4)	6-1
4th	Raven Arms	(2)	33-1
5th	Grand Flight II	(1)	5-2
6th	Diamond Glory	(6)	33-1
29.48	6, 1/2, 2, 1/2, 4		M. Yate
			(Private)

1937

1ST	WATTLE BARK	(6)	5-2
2nd	Shove Halfpenny	(1)	7-4F
3rd	Grosvenor Bob	(4)	11-2
4th	Maidens Delight	(5)	20-1
5th	Avion Ballerino	(2)	10-1
6th	Top Of The Carlow Road	(3)	11-2
29.26(TR)	11/2, 4, hd,		J Syder
	hd, hd		(Wembley)

1938

1ST	LONE KEEL	(3)	9-4
2nd	Melksham Numeral	(1)	8-1
3rd	Wattle Bark	(4)	20-1
4th	Bealtaine	(6)	100-6
5th	Demotic Mack	(2)	7-2
6th	Manhattan Midnight	(5)	7-4F
29.62	1/2, sh, 5, 2, dnf		S. Wright
			(Private)

1939

1ST	HIGHLAND RUM	(6)	2-1JF
2nd	Carmel Ash	(2)	2-1JF
3rd	Demotic Mack	(3)	10-1
4th	Mister Mutt	(5)	100-8
5th	Junior Classic	(1)	5-2
6th	Vacant		
29.35	21/2, 12, hd, 1		P. Fortune
			(Wimbledon)

525 yards (Harringay)

1940

1ST	GR ARCHDUKE	(1)	100-7
2nd	Duna Taxmaid	(4)	8-1
3rd	Rock Callan	(2)	7-4F
4th	Keel Creamery	(6)	5-2
5th	Irish Rambler	(5)	13-2
6th	Roving Youth	(3)	3-1
29.66	nk, 1/2, 1, 1, 2		C. Ashley
			(Harringay)

(1941-1944 not run)

525 yards (White City)

1945

1ST	BALLYHENNESSY SEAL	(1)	1-1F
2nd	Rhynn Castle (Res)	(4)	20-1
3rd	Magic Bohemian	(3)	3-1
4th	Tamarisk	(2)	8-1
5th	Duffys Arrival	(5)	8-1
6th	Celtic Chief	(6)	10-1
29.56	5, 1, 2, 2, 3		S. Martin
			(Wimbledon)

1946

1ST	MONDAYS NEWS	(3)	5-1
2nd	Lilacs Luck	(2)	2-1F
3rd	Plucky Hero	(6)	6-1
4th	Celtic Chief	(1)	9-2
5th	Dante II	(4)	10-1
6th	Shannon Shore	(5)	9-2
29.24	7, 11/2, 3/4, 5, 3		F. Farey
			(Private)

1947

1ST	TREVS PERFECTION	(2)	4-1
2nd	Mondays News	(5)	9-4F
3rd	Slaney Record	(6)	100-7
4th	Trevs Jackie	(4)	10-1
5th	Lacken Invader	(3)	4-1
6th	Patsys Record	(1)	7-2
28.95	2, 11/2, 1, 2, 221/2		F.Trevillion
			(Private)

1948

1ST	PRICELESS BORDER	(1)	1-2F
2nd	Local Interprize	(5)	6-1
3rd	Sheevaun	(3)	9-2
4th	Doughery Boy	(6)	100-8
5th	Rathattan Ben	(4)	100-1
6th	Baytown Stork	(2)	100-1
28.78	2, 2, 2, nk, 11/2		L. Reynolds
			(Wembley)

1949

1ST	NARROGAR ANN	(2)	5-1
2nd	Dangerous Prince	(5)	100-7
3rd	Sailing At Dawn	(1)	9-2
4th	Local Interprize	(4)	3-1
5th	Glencloy Regent	(3)	9-4F
6th	Saft Alex	(6)	11-2

28.95   11/4, 21/2, 11/2,   Reynolds
nk, 10L   (Wembley)

1950

1ST	BALLYMAC BALL	(4)	7-2
2nd	Quare Customer	(5)	9-2
3rd	Captain The Killer	(6)	100-8
4th	Drugoon Boy	(1)	10-3
5th	Magna Hasty	(3)	50-1
6th	Ballycurreen Garrett	(2)	7-4F

28.72   31/4, 51/2, 3, 2, 4   S. Martin
(Wimbledon)

1951

1ST	BALLYLANIGAN TANIST		(1)

11-4

2nd	Black Mire	(3)	9-4F
3rd	Rushton Smutty	(2)	4-1
4th	Atomic Line	(6)	4-1
5th	Rapid Choice	(4)	100-8
6th	Mad Miller	(5)	10-1

28.62   21/2, 23/4, 2, 1/2,   L. Reynolds
23/4   (Wembley)

1952

1ST	ENDLESS GOSSIP	(6)	1-1F
2nd	Drumman Rambler	(2)	7-2
3rd	Shaggy Newshound	(1)	25-1
4th	Dashboard Dan	(5)	7-1
5th	Caseys Seal	(4)	100-8
6th	Paddys Dinner	(3)	9-2

28.50   31/2, 3, 21/2, 3, dnf   L. Reynolds
(Wembley)

1953

1ST	DAW'S DANCER	(5)	10-1
2nd	Galtee Cleo	(1)	4-5F
3rd	Small Town	(3)	11-2
4th	Tonic	(6)	100-8
5th	Glittering Look	(4)	4-1
6th	Baytown Caddie	(2)	8-1

29.20   1/2, 21/4, 11/4,   P. McEvoy
1/2, 1/2   (Private)

1954

1ST	PAULS FUN	(3)	8-15F
2nd	Leafy Ash	(5)	33-1
3rd	Title Role	(6)	3-1
4th	Clever Count	(1)	33-1
5th	Ardskeagh Ville	(2)	100-8
6th	Ashcott Boy	(4)	100-7

28.84   31/4, 13/4, 5,   L. Reynolds
3/4, dis   (Wembley)

1955

1ST	RUSHTON MAC	(2)	5-2
2nd	Barrowside	(3)	1-2F
3rd	Coolkill Chieftain	(4)	100-7
4th	Gulf Of Honduras	(6)	8-1
5th	Home Straight	(1)	100-6
6th	Duet Leader	(5)	10-1

28.97   3/4, 41/2, 1, 13/4, 3   F. Johnson
(Private)

1956

1ST	DUNMORE KING	(3)	7-2
2nd	Duet Leader	(2)	8-1
3rd	Gulf Of Darien	(6)	10-1
4th	Northern King	(4)	6-4F
5th	Granbally Shaun	(5)	100-6
6th	Quare Fool	(4)	3-1

29.22   1/2, dh, 1, 3, 13/4   P. McEvoy
(Clapton)

1957

1ST	FORD SPARTAN	(1)	1-1F
2nd	Highway Tim	(2)	11-2
3rd	Land Of Song	(3)	100-8
4th	Highwood Sovereign	(6)	9-2
5th	Gallant And Gay	(5)	33-1
6th	Quare Fool	(4)	3-1

28.84   nk, 1, 3, 11/4, 3   J. Hannafin
(Wimbledon)

1958

1ST	PIGALLE WONDER	(1)	4-5F
2nd	Northern Lad	(5)	25-1
3rd	Mile Bush Pride	(3)	5-2
4th	Gentle Touch	(4)	100-6
5th	Slimmer Down Pal	(2)	50-1
6th	Outside Left	(6)	6-1

28.65   2 3/4, nk, 4, 43/4, 1   J. Syder
(Wembley)

1959

1ST	MILE BUSH PRIDE	(4)	1-1F
2nd	Snub Nose	(6)	5-1
3rd	Crazy Parachute	(1)	10-3
4th	Coolkill Racket	(3)	100-7
5th	Bryans Hope	(2)	10-1
6th	Dancing Sheik	(5)	33-1

28.76   nk, hd, 7, 21/2, dis   H. Harvey
(Wembley)

1960

1ST	DULEEK DANDY	(4)	25-1
2nd	Clonalvy Romance	(5)	11-2
3rd	Mile Bush Pride	(1)	4-5F
4th	Caramik	(6)	100-6
5th	Wheatfield Swan	(2)	50-1
6th	Clonalvy Pride	(3)	2-1

29.15   21/4, 1, 51/4,   W. Dash
11/4, 3/4   (Private)

1961

1ST	PALMS PRINTER	(1)	2-1
2nd	Oregon Prince	(2)	6-4F
3rd	Winter Bell	(5)	50-1
4th	Spider Hill	(6)	3-1
5th	Luxury Liner	(4)	10-1
6th	Clopook	(3)	100-8

28.84   11/4, 11/4, sh,   P. McEvoy
11/2, dis   (Clapton)

1962

1ST	THE GRAND CANAL	(5)	2-1F
2nd	Powerstown		
	Prospect	(4)	7-1
3rd	Dromin Glory	(6)	9-2
4th	Master McMurragh	(2)	3-1
5th	Nash Recorder	(3)	10-1
6th	Trip To Dublin	(1)	6-1

29.09   1, 1, hd, 11/4, 3   P. Dunphy
(Ireland)

1963

1ST	LUCKY BOY BOY	(1)	1-1F
2nd	Greenane Wonder	(2)	4-1
3rd	Barronstown King	(6)	25-1
4th	Hack It About	(3)	4-1
5th	Misty King	(5)	8-1
6th	Bulgaden Glory	(4)	20-1

29.00   63/4, 1, 12,   J. Bassett
21/2, 11/4   (Clapton)

1964

1ST	HACK UP CHIEFTAIN	(1)	20-1
2nd	Die Cast	(2)	2-1F
3rd	Runpuninni	(5)	3-1
4th	We'll See	(4)	9-4
5th	Crazy Platinum	(6)	8-1
6th	Scamp Boy	(3)	5-1

28.92   13/4, 3, 13/4,   P. Stagg
11/4, 2   (Belle Vue)

1965

1ST	CHITTERING CLAPTON		(6)

5-2

2nd	Sunbow	(1)	2-1F
3rd	Shy Prairie	(3)	9-1
4th	Creggan Bush	(4)	3-1
5th	Flash Solar	(5)	100-8
6th	Greenane Flame	(2)	11-2

28.82   53/4, 3, 4, 6, dis   A. Jackson
(Clapton)

1966

1ST	FAITHFUL HOPE	(3)	8-1
2nd	Greenane Flash	(6)	4-1
3rd	Dusty Trail	(5)	6-1
4th	I'm Quickest	(1)	5-2
5th	Maryville Hi	(4)	13-8F
6th	Kilbeg Kuda	(2)	4-1

28.52   41/4, 13/4, 43/4   P. Keane
(Clapton)

1967

1ST	TRIC TRAC	(1)	9-2
2nd	Spectre II	(6)	2-1F
3rd	Mel's Talent	(2)	6-1
4th	Shady Parachute	(3)	9-2
5th	Silver Hope	(5)	5-2
6th	Ambiguous	(4)	100-8

29.99   1, 43/4, 11/4,   J. Hookway
43/4, 5   (Sheffield)

1968

1ST	CAMIRA FLASH	(4)	100-8
2nd	Witch's Smoke	(2)	100-7
3rd	El Campo	(6)	13-2
4th	Shady Parachute	(5)	4-6F
5th	Shady Begonia	(1)	6-1
6th	Winning Hope	(3)	7-2

28.89   1, nk, 3, 3, sh   R. Singleton
(White City)

1969

1ST	SAND STAR	(4)	5-4F
2nd	Kilbelin Style	(1)	6-4
3rd	Ploverfield Dan	(2)	100-8
4th	Petrovitch	(5)	20-1
5th	Hard Held	(6)	13-2
6th	Barrack Street	(3)	11-2

28.78   2, 11/2, 1, 5, 4   H. Orr
(Ireland)

1970

1ST	JOHN SILVER	(2)	11-4
2nd	Little County	(4)	7-4F
3rd	Corral Romeo	(3)	50-1
4th	Hymus Silver	(6)	14-1
5th	Sirius	(5)	11-2
6th	Moordyke Spot	(1)	9-4
29.01	1, 5, 11/4,	B. Tompkins	
	13/4, 21/2	(Private)	

1971

1ST	DOLORES ROCKET	(2)	11-4
2nd	Supreme Fun	(6)	6-1
3rd	Leap And Run	(3)	3-1
4th	Moordyke Champion	(1)	6-1
5th	Cobbler	(5)	20-1
6th	Ivy Hall Flash	(4)	7-4F
28.74	1/2, 3/4, 1, 21/2,	H. White	
	13/4	(Private)	

1972

1ST	PATRICIAS HOPE	(5)	7-1
2nd	Ballylander	(4)	16-1
3rd	Micks Pride	(6)	25-1
4th	Scintillas Gem	(1)	7-1
5th	Super Rory	(3)	4-9F
6th	Proud Life	(2)	8-1
28.55	31/4, sh, 11/4,	A. Jackson	
	1, 31/2	(Clapton)	

1973

1ST	PATRICIAS HOPE	(5)	7-2
2nd	Softly	(4)	12-1
3rd	Say Little	(6)	6-4F
4th	Forest Noble	(1)	3-1
5th	Black Banjo	(3)	5-1
6th	Breakaway Town	(2)	10-1
28.68	1/2, nk, nk,	J. O'Connor	
	41/4, dis	(Wimbledon)	

1974

1ST	JIMSUN	(2)	5-2
2nd	Myrtown	(3)	2-1
3rd	Ballymaclune	(6)	5-1
4th	Soft Light	(4)	6-1
5th	Backwater Champ	(5)	13-8F
6th	Handy Hi	(1)	20-1
28.76	11/4, 1/2, hd,	G. DeMulder	
	1, 21/2	(Hall Green)	

500 metres (White City)

1975

1ST	TARTAN KHAN	(2)	25-1
2nd	Sallys Cobbler	(1)	3-1
3rd	Pineapple Grand	(6)	4-1
4th	Myrtown	(3)	10-11F
5th	Foreign Exchange	(5)	10-1
6th	Vacant		
29.57	11/4, 1, 13/4, 11/4	G. Lynds	
		(Bletchley)	

1976

1ST	MUTTS SILVER	(4)	6-1
2nd	Ballybeg Prim	(5)	4-5F
3rd	Westmead Myra	(6)	20-1
4th	Xmas Holiday	(1)	5-1
5th	Jackies Jet	(2)	7-1
6th	Westmead Champ	(3)	3-1
29.38	21/4, 31/2, hd,	P. Rees	
	2, 3/4	(Wimbledon)	

1977

1ST	BALLINISKA BAND	(5)	1-1F
2nd	El Cavalier	(1)	5-1
3rd	Pat Seamur	(4)	5-1
4th	Ballybeg Grand	(3)	16-1
5th	Westmean Manor	(6)	8-1
6th	Saucy Buck	(2)	7-1
29.16	21/2, 41/2,	E.Moore	
	1/2, 13/4, 11/4	(B Vue)	

1978

1ST	LACCA CHAMPION	(3)	6-4F
2nd	Backdeed Man	(6)	6-1
3rd	Ali Wit	(5)	7-1
4th	Superior Model	(1)	5-1
5th	Glenroe Hiker	(4)	9-4
6th	Great Ali	(2)	16-1
29.42	13/4, 21/2, sh,	P. Mullins	
	11/2, 3/4	(Private)	

1979

1ST	SARAHS BUNNY	(6)	3-1
2nd	Lacca Champion	(5)	10-1
3rd	Desert Pilot	(3)	9-4
4th	First General	(4)	14-1
5th	Tyrean	(1)	15-8F
6th	Tough Decision	(2)	9-2
29.53	13/4, 41/2,	G.DeMulder	
	21/2, sh, hd	(Hall Green)	

1980

1ST	INDIAN JOE	(6)	13-8JF
2nd	Hurry On Bran	(5)	13-8JF
3rd	Young Breeze	(1)	7-2
4th	Fred Flinstone	(2)	7-1
5th	Corduroy	(3)	14-1
6th	Iskagh Ruler	(4)	20-1
29.68	1, 11/4, 1, 13/4, 1/2	J. Hayes	
		(Ireland)	

1981

1ST	PARKDOWN JET	(6)	4-5F
2nd	Prince Spy	(2)	33-1
3rd	Rahan Ship	(1)	2-1
4th	Clohast Flame	(4)	7-2
5th	In Flight	(5)	33-1
6th	Barleyfield	(3)	14-1
29.57	3/4, 11/4, 13/4, 2, dis	G. McKenna	
		(Ireland)	

1982

1ST	LAURIES PANTHER	(1)	6-4F
2nd	Special Account	(4)	7-2
3rd	Duke Of Hazard	(5)	9-2
4th	Supreme Tiger	(3)	3-1
5th	Pineapple Barrow	(6)	16-1
6th	Killimy Ivy	(2)	14-1
29.60	3/4, hd, 11/4,	T. Duggan	
	3/4, dis	(Romford)	

1983

1ST	IM SLIPPY	(4)	6-1
2nd	On Spec	(3)	33-1
3rd	Debbycot Lad	(5)	3-1
4th	Game Ball	(2)	1-1F
5th	Real Miller	(1)	25-1
6th	Amazing Man	(6)	9-2
29.40	nk, nk, 3/4, 13/4, 3	B. Tompkins	
		(Coventry)	

1984

1ST	WHISPER WISHES	(4)	7-4F
2nd	Morans Beef	(5)	9-4
3rd	Proud Dodger	(6)	7-1
4th	The Jolly Norman	(3)	20-1
5th	House Of Hope	(1)	12-1
6th	Spartacus	(2)	9-2
19.43	3/4, 1/2, 11/2,	C. Coyle	
	3/4, 61/2	(Maidstone)	

480 metres (Wimbledon)

1985

1ST	PAGAN SWALLOW	(5)	9-1
2nd	Jack The Hiker	(3)	10-1
3rd	Carrigeen Chimes	(6)	11-2
4th	Walstone	(1)	3-1
5th	Smokey Pete	(2)	8-11F
6th	House Hunter	(4)	20-1
29.04	11/2, hd, 2, 1/2, 3/4	P. Rees	
		(Wimbledon)	

1986

1ST	TICO	(5)	6-4JF
2nd	Master Hardy	(6)	18-1
3rd	Sunley Express	(1)	12-1
4th	Fearless Action	(4)	6-4JF
5th	Easy Prince	(2)	9-1
6th	Murlens Slippy	(3)	5-1
28.69	51/2, 1/2, 1/2,	A. Hitch	
	sh, 11/2	(Slough)	

1987

1ST	SIGNAL SPARK	(4)	14-1
2nd	Tapwatcher	(5)	11-10F
3rd	Rikasso Tiller	(3)	3-1
4th	Slaneyside Speed	(6)	7-1
5th	Eneceee	(1)	5-1
6th	Stouke Whisper	(2)	12-1
28.83	sh, 3, nk, 3/4, 31/2	G. Baggs	
		(Walthamstow)	

1988

1ST	HIT THE LID	(6)	3-1
2nd	Stouke Whisper	(3)	7-1
3rd	Curryhills Gara	(1)	6-4F
4th	Make History	(4)	3-1
5th	Gino	(2)	12-1
6th	Comeragh Boy	(5)	6-1
28.53	11/4, 11/2, 1,	J. McGee	
	nk, 51/4	(Canterbury)	

1989

1ST	LARTIGUE NOTE	(2)	1-1F
2nd	Kilcannon Bullet	(6)	2-1
3rd	Castleivy Mick	(1)	10-1
4th	Early Vocation	(5)	10-1
5th	Cooladine Style	(3)	25-1
6th	Catsrock Rocket	(4)	7-1
28.79	51/4, nk, 21/4,	G. McKenna	
	1, 21/4	(Ireland)	

1990

1ST	SLIPPY BLUE	(4)	8-1
2nd	Druids Johno	(6)	4-7F
3rd	Fair Hill Boy	(1)	4-1
4th	Fires Of War	(5)	10-1
5th	Galtymore Lad	(3)	20-1
6th	Burnt Oak Champ	(2)	14-1
28.70	31/4, hd, 3/4,	K. Linzell	
	133/4, nk	(Walthamstow)	

1991

1ST	BALLINDERRY ASH	(5)	5-1
2nd	Itsallovernow	(6)	5-1
3rd	Dempsey Duke	(1)	6-1
4th	Fearless Mustang	(3)	1-1F
5th	Summerhill Super	(2)	14-1
6th	Dunmurry Brandy	(2)	14-1
28.78	13/4, 3/4, 31/4, sh, 11/4	P. Byrne (Wimbledon)	

1992

1ST	FARLOE MELODY	(6)	6-4F
2nd	Winsor Abbey	(4)	7-1
3rd	Siostaloir	(5)	6-1
4th	Pennys Best	(3)	33-1
5th	Glengar Ranger	(1)	7-4
6th	Gentle Warning	(2)	6-1
28.88	33/4, hd, nk, 1/2, 43/4	M O'Donnell (Ireland)	

1993

1ST	RINGA HUSTLE	(3)	5-2
2nd	Sullane Castle	(1)	7-1
3rd	Hypnotic Stag	(6)	7-2
4th	Greenane Squire	(2)	15-8F
5th	Lassa Java	(4)	7-2
6th	Ceadar Mountain	(5)	50-1
28.62	21/4, 21/4, sh, 1, 3/4	A. Meek (Hall Green)	

1994

1ST	MORAL STANDARDS	(2)	9-4F
2nd	Ayr Flyer	(6)	3-1
3rd	Moaning Lad	(5)	7-2
4th	Up The Junction	(1)	3-1
5th	Flag The Fawn	(3)	16-1
6th	Callahow Daly	(4)	12-1
28.59	11/4, 1/2, sh, 11/2, 11/2	A. Meek (Hall Green)	

1995

1ST	MOANING LAD	(3)	5-2
2nd	Summerhill Joy	(6)	3-1
3rd	Curryhills Fancy	(5)	50-1
4th	Pearls Girl	(1)	2-1F
5th	Mustang Joe	(2)	5-1
6th	Heres Seanie	(4)	5-1
28.66	3/4, 11/2, 31/4, 2, sh	T. Mentzis (Milton Keynes)	

1996

1ST	SHANLESS SLIPPY	(3)	4-9F
2nd	Night Trooper	(2)	16-1
3rd	Batties Rocket	(5)	5-2
4th	Everloving Eddie	(6)	16-1
5th	Checkpointcharly	(4)	50-1
6th	Be Bopa Lola	(1)	20-1
28.66	23/4, 13/4, sh, 31/4, hd	D. Ruth (Ireland)	

1997

1ST	SOME PICTURE	(6)	8-13F
2nd	He Knows	(4)	3-1
3rd	Stows Val	(3)	10-1
4th	Annies Bullet	(5)	7-1
5th	Charpaidon	(1)	33-1
6th	Heres Andy	(2)	7-1
28.23	61/2, 3/4, 4, 1/2, 31/4	C. Lister (Unattached)	

1998

1ST	TOMS THE BEST	(4)	4-5F
2nd	Tuesdays Davy	(6)	6-1
3rd	Tullerboy Cash	(1)	8-1
4th	Jaspers Boy	(5)	9-4
5th	Honour And Glory	(2)	7-1
6th	Vacant		
28.75	41/4, 5, sh, 1/4	N. Savva (Unattached)	

1999

1ST	CHART KING	(6)	8-11F
2nd	Frisby Full	(5)	66-1
3rd	Deerfield Sunset	(1)	11-10
4th	Secret Crystal	(4)	25-1
5th	Pottos Storm	(2)	66-1
6th	Pure Patches	(3)	16-1
28.76	11/2, hd, 21/2, sh, dis	K. Hewitt (Ireland)	

2000

1ST	RAPID RANGER	(2)	7-4F
2nd	Rackethall Jet	(3)	7-1
3rd	Greenfield Deal	(4)	14-1
4th	Deerfield Sunset	(1)	2-1
5th	Smoking Bullet	(5)	8-1
6th	Farloe Club	(6)	3-1
28.71	31/2, 2, nk, 63/4, 21/4	C. Lister (Unattached)	

2001

1ST	RAPID RANGER	(4)	7-4
2nd	Sonic Flight	(3)	10-11F
3rd	Castlelyons Dani	(2)	14-1
4th	Countrywide Tams	(1)	14-1
5th	Smoking Bullet	(5)	10-1
6th	Droopys Honcho	(6)	7-1
28.71	31/4, 11/2, hd, 31/2, hd	C. Lister (Unattached)	

2002

1ST	ALLEN GIFT	(5)	16-1
2nd	Call Me Baby	(6)	8-1
3rd	Crack Him Out	(1)	9-4
4th	Blue Gooner	(4)	5-1
5th	Pilot Alert	(3)	2-1F
6th	Windgap Java	(2)	5-1
29.04	3/4, 11/4, 3/4, 13/4, 3/4	C. Gardiner (Hove)	

2003

1ST	FARLOE VERDICT	(2)	12-1
2nd	Top Savings	(6)	4-7F
3rd	Farloe Pocket	(4)	33-1
4th	Man Of Cash	(1)	3-1
5th	Larkhill Bullet	(5)	6-1
Disq	Droopys Hewitt	(3)	16-1
29.04	3/4, NK, 31/4, Sh, disq	C. Lister (Unattached)	

2004

1ST	DROOPYS SCHOLES	(3)	7-2
2nd	Big Freeze	(5)	10-1
3rd	Tims Crow	(6)	4-1
4th	Rhincrew Seagal	(4)	2-1F
5th	Ballymac Kewell	(2)	7-2
6th	Fire Height Dan	(1)	6-1
28.62	3/4, 1/2, nk, 23/4, 3/4	I. Reilly (Ireland)	

2005

1ST	WESTMEAD HAWK	(4)	5-4F
2nd	Blonde Mac	(1)	33-1
3rd	Blue Majestic	(3)	6-1
4th	Mineola Farloe	(5)	7-1
5th	Ningbo Jack	(2)	3-1
6th	Geldrops Touch	(6)	7-2
28.56	1 3/4, 3, 1/2, 3/4, shd	N Savva (Henlow)	

2006

1ST	WESTMEAD HAWK	(4)	4-7F
2nd	Mineola Farloe	(2)	7-2
3rd	Amarillo Slim	(5)	6-1
4th	Westmead Joe	(3)	7-1
5th	Cleenas Lady	(1)	25-1
6th	Clash Darby	(6)	33-1
28.44	3/4, 3/4, 3/4, 1, 2	N Savva (Henlow)	

Big Races in 2007

EXPRESS EGO was a most impressive winner of the first major event of 2007, the Racing Post Juvenile Championship at Wimbledon.

The 'wildcard' entry, trained by Owen McKenna, had won the National Puppy Stake consolation at Shelbourne and Champion Unraced at Enniscorthy, and arrived with his kennel companion In The Bag, and both sparkled in prep trials.

Hitting the boxes, the 36-kilo February 2005 son of Top Honcho and Airport Express powered to the first bend and was never headed, winning by four lengths from the gallant Cobra Striking, after which former Wimbledon handler McKenna outlined the English Derby as a target.

And those who raced in to support the Irish dog, the youngest runner in the line-up, gained confidence in hearing that the winning time of 27.42sec was the fastest ever winning time in the event's history.

On the supporting card, Jazz Hurricane reversed form with her Oaks conqueror Dilemmas Flight, prevailing after a great back-straight tussle but then having to withstand In The Bag's huge finish.

Winning breeder: Michael Dalton, Golden, Co. Tipperary

Finish	Trap	Names	Price	Time/Dis
1	2	EXPRESS EGO	6/4F	27.42
2	5	Cobra Striking	4/1	4
3	6	Iceman Ross	5/2	1 1/4
4	4	Roswell Starship	6/1	1 1/2
5	1	Courts Ad Queen	10/1	4 1/2
6	3	Fear Robben	12/1	SH

EYE ONTHE VETO began the year as he ended the last with victory in the valuable Emerald Cup at Coventry.

Bad weather in early February proved tough on tracks and the early rounds of the £7,000 event saw wide runners with a huge advantage, although come the final it was largely a level playing field.

Breaking well, the Mark Wallis-trained, John Keefe-owned runner was soon in front and powered clear to win a shade comfortably from staying-on, tough-as-teak Iceman Ross.

Winning breeder: Eugene Price, Newtown, Co. Kildare

Finish	Trap	Names	Price	Time/Dis
1	5	EYE ONTHE VETO	9/2	29.15
2	4	Iceman Ross	9/4	3 1/2
3	6	Droopys Wells	7/2	SH
4	3	Well Tutored	7/2	SH
5	1	Cleenas Lady	4/5F	3/4
NR		Tomll Fix It		

WESTCOUNTRY LADY scored a popular win for her trainer Jo Burridge in the final of the Stadium Bookmakers Trafalgar Cup over 450 metres.

The prestigious puppy competition had been won 12 months earlier by subsequent Scurry Gold Cup winner Horseshoe Ping, and it was a similar burst of early pace that saw the June 2005 daughter of Top Honcho and Pats Flight lie handy before pouncing off the second bend as leaders Kilsheelan and Pea Ball came together.

In winning, Westcountry Lady was scoring for owner Mark Croker, who also owned by the Burridge-trained winner's dam.

Finish	Trap	Names	Price	Time/Dis
1	5	WESTCOUNTRY LADY	7/1	27.14
2	4	Kilsheelan	6/4F	NK
3	3	Pea Ball	5/2	1 3/4
4	6	Romeo Jamie	10/1	1 3/4
5	2	Saigon Hero	8/1	1
6	1	Fabulous Tears	7/2	3/4

BETFAIR SPRINGBOK

BLACKMAGIC JAMIE made it 13th time lucky in a major final for his owner Jamie Langley (Blackmagic Guy, Maisy etc) when scoring a rare win in a big-race hurdles competition for trainer Ernie Gaskin in the Betfair Springbok at Wimbleon.

Thats The Bullet had performed well for 'Team Gaskin' in 2006, but it was the novice who now starred for the Nazeing kennel – now exclusively an open-race one following 'young' Ernie's decision to leave Walthamstow – as he prevailed in an early-paced battle with Tommy Bahama.

Just shading his rival into the turn, the pair had a rare battle down the far side, pulling clear from the remainder, and Blackmagic Jaime was never headed.

Executive Memo, impressive in the semis, was never a factor in the final after missing the break.

Winning breeder: Stephen Casey, Kildangan, Co. Kildare

Finish	Trap	Names	Price	Time/Dis
1	3	BLACKMAGIC JAMIE	8/1	28.82
2	4	Tommy Bahama	11/8F	NK
3	2	Sorrento Woods	5/1	4 3/4
4	1	Building Boom	40/1	2
5	5	Executive Memo	6/4	2
6	6	Amazing Aces	16/1	1/2

LADBROKE GOLDEN JACKET

WALK THE LINE became the second Crayford-trained winner of the Kent track's biggest event when the Patsy Cusack-handled runner made all in the Ladbroke Golden Jacket final.

The December 2004 daughter of Droopys Vieri and Ballycahane Zoie had been a 50-1 chance at the start of the 714m event and, while finishing second in both heat and semi-final, was punted at big prices on the day of the final, from 20-1 overnight to 8-1 on the morning of the race.

A fast start saw Walk The Line seize of a first bend lead and kept up the gallop all the way to the line.

Winning breeder: ?
ccc

Finish	Trap	Names	Price	Time/Dis
1	2	WALK THE LINE	8/1	46.00
2	3	Daisyfield Seani	7/4F	2
3	4	Blackmagic Guy	6/1	3/4
4	1	Local Knowledge	6/1	1 1/2
5	6	Zattah Pips	5/2	3/4
6	5	Swift Maggie	6/1	6 3/4

WILLIAM HILL PRESTIGE

LARKHILL BIRD came again to deny Westmead Olivia in a pulsating £5,000 Betdirect Prestige final at Hall Green – and continue her rise up the stayers' rankings.

In 2006, Michael Walsh's bitch won the Yorkshire St Leger at Doncaster and the Midland Oaks at Hall Green, the first event over six bends and the second over four.

Back to the longer distance at the Birmingham track, Larkhill Bird led home a bitches 1-2-3-4 in the 645m annual, given the boost of a new sponsor in 2007.

Purchased from Australia at 12 weeks old by Pat Whelan, the 'Larkhill' man won a race with her in Ireland before the August 2003 daughter of Stately Bird and Elle's Army was purchased by Walsh and part-owner Derek Clark.

Finish	Trap	Names	Price	Time/Dis
1	1	BLACK TAXI	5/1	24.91
2	2	Greenlough Kew	7/2	1 1/2
3	4	Postle Supreme	5/1	2
4	6	Ardmayle Ace	6/1	HD
5	5	Cagey Luke	11/10F	3/4
6	3	Glory George	20/1	DIS

CHELTENHAM FESTIVAL SPRINT

LIKETHECLAPPERS, trained in Athenry, Co. Galway by Gerry Holian, lived up to his name by storming up the straight at Cheltenham to win the £2,500 Byrne Group Festival Sprint on the Thursday of the four-day National Hunt extravaganza.

What was once a novelty race is now firmly

The presentation after Fear Haribo's track record-breaking Scottish Derby win

established in the NGRC Calendar, and that was underlined by a quality entry received by Cheltenham organiser, Paul Lawrence.

The runners for the qualifying trials the Saturday before the Festival included a Derby finalist in Cleenas Lady and a Puppy Derby winner in Droopys Tops, as well as plenty of Irish interest, as one would expect at Cheltenham.

Sprint champion Mulcair Jo was one of the early stars, and ended the week by plundering the supporting Anglo-Irish Challenge, but it was Liketheclappers who overcame a slow start to storm to the front past halfway.

The July 2004 son of Daves Mentor and Josephines Fancy had competed in the previous year's Irish Laurels.

Winning breeder: Sean Dolan, Mannin, Co. Galway

Finish	Trap	Names	Price	Time/Dis
1	3	LIKETHECLAPPERS	6/4F	12.56
2	6	Slick Soviet	10/1	3/4
3	1	Iceman Vader	7/2	3/4
4	4	Droopys Tops	4/1	1
5	2	Nemos Record	5/1	NK
6	5	Droopys Ruby	9/1	1 1/2

REGAL SCOTTISH DERBY

FEAR HARIBO unleashed his blistering turn of early pace to set a new track record and improve trainer Charlie Lister's already brilliant record in the John R Weir Mercedes-Benz Scottish Derby final at a packed Shawfield.

Trained to a Gymcrack Puppy Championship victory by Carly Philpott and Darran Keefe in 2006, the Simon Wooder-owned runner put himself in pole position to become the eighth winner of the Scottish/English Derby double – and topped sponsor Blue Square's betting for Wimbledon immediately following his £20,000 triumph at the Glasgow venue.

A near track-record effort of 28.80sec in the first round – Farloe Verdict's best had stood at 28.79sec – was followed by defeat at the paws of the front-running Kylegrove Top in the semis, before a faster start from a slightly better draw in the final set up a great victory, back-to-back Scottish Derby wins for Simon Wooder, and a superb track record 28.76sec.

Mention should be made of the runner-up,

Groovy Stan, who never gave up after turning second and keeping up the gallop all the way to the line. From the same Paul Hennessy kennel that sent out Priceless Rebel to Scottish Derby glory a few years previously, the Irish raider was also earmarked for Wimbledon afterwards.

Winning breeder: Liam Dowling, Ballymacelligott, Co. Kerry

Finish	Trap	Names	Price	Time/Dis
1	5	FEAR HARIBO	10/11F	28.76TR
2	1	Groovy Stan	5/2	1 1/2
3	4	Greenwell Storm	6/1	1 3/4
4	3	Kylegrove Top	6/1	3/4
5	6	Manic Mile	10/1	1 1/4
6	2	Breeze Hill Juli	20/1	1

WILLIAM HILL BLUE RIBAND

ICEMAN VADER landed Lance and Pam Burford their biggest success and trainers – and owners – as Iceman Vader came up trumps in the £10,000 William Hill Blue Riband final at Hall Green.

The big ante-post punt in the event was Savana Highlands, who went off favourite in the decider. However, a tough draw proved his undoing in the final and Iceman Vader needed no second inviation.

Third in the Zigzag Puppy Championship at Coventry, he had then run third at Cheltenham.

Winning breeder: Alphonsus McDonald, Bagenalstown, Co. Carlow

Finish	Trap	Names	Price	Time/Dis
1	2	ICEMAN VADER	9/2	28.29
2	1	Fear Armani	7/1	2 1/2
3	4	Savana Highlands	7/4F	3/4
4	6	Dilemmas Flight	4/1	NK
5	3	Droopys Nelson	4/1	4 1/2
6	5	Oh His Nerves	20/1	SHD

LADBROKES SPRING FESTIVAL

CENTAUR TROOPER enjoyed a fantastic spring for connections when landing a big-race double in the Spring Trophy at Crayford before scoring in the £5,000 Ladbrokes Spring Festival 630 at the

Kent venue's sister track, Monmore.

Owned by the Centaur Greyhounds syndicate, the Terry Dartnall-trained bitch, an October 2004 daughter of Rapid Journey and Up In Lights, won heat and final easily of the 630m competition.

Winning breeder: Jimmy Fenwick, Morpeth, Northumberland

Finish	Trap	Names	Price	Time/Dis
1	2	CENTAUR TROOPER	7/4	38.07
2	5	Westmead Olivia	7/1	4 1/2
3	6	Westmead Aoifa	11/10F	SH
4	3	Colorado Lucy	20/1	3 1/4
5	1	Dark Hondo	7/1	1/2
6	6	Zigzag Dutchman	8/1	2 1/4

STUD BOOK TROPHY

FEAR ROBBEN starred in the British-bred only Stud Book Trophy to deny double Derby winner Westmead Hawk a glorious big-race triumph on his return to the track after injury.

Second in his heat, the Ian St Pier and Simon Wooder-owned runner had reached the Grand Prix in 2006 and that six-bend stamina always looked likely to see him prevail once he had hit the front past halfway.

Getting the run on 'The Hawk', Fear Robben won comfortably from his staying-on rival, who was then aimed at a Derby trial stakes at Wimbledon in a bid to rediscover past glories.

Winning breeder: Barry Bolton, Hitchin, Herts

Finish	Trap	Names	Price	Time/Dis
1	2	FEAR ROBBEN	7/1	28.72
2	6	Westmead Hawk	4/6F	2
3	4	Gee Vee	10/1	HD
4	3	Moyar Okee	14/1	1 1/4
5	1	Gotabetem	6/1	3 1/2
6	5	Funtime Chunky	3/1	3 1/2

GOLDEN CREST

RHYZOME WIZARD denied Blakes World the Portsmouth Golden Muzzle/Poole Golden Crest double when reeling in his rival late to claim the £3,000 final at the Dorset venue.

Graham Cleverly's runner, a standing dish at home track Swindon where he had also won the Pride Of The West, as well as producing track record runs over both the 480m and 509m trips, proved he could cut it elsewhere and struck gold at Poole with a typically strong-running effort.

Winning breeder: Stephen Cooney, Clonmel, Co. Tipperary

Finish	Trap	Names	Price	Time/Dis
1	6	RHYZOME WIZARD	3/1	26.61
2	4	Blakes World	13/8F	3/4
3	5	Swift Extort	28/1	1/2
4	1	Blonde Joey	7/2	1 3/4
5	3	Civil War	20/1	3 1/2
6	2	Rosmon Major	11/4	1

SENIORS DERBY

FARLOE HOBBS capped a glorious summer for Barrie Draper's team when winning the valuable Seniors Derby at Peterborough, leading early in the £5,000 final to strike gold.

Trouble behind saw the four-year-old race to a near-nine lengths win, to add to a stellar few weeks for the Sheffield-based handler after Farloe Hurricane's Gymcrack win.

As a younger dog, Farloe Hobbs contested the Derby in 2005 and also made the Ladbrokes 600 final during a fruitful Irish campaign in 2006.

However, the June 2003 three-quarter brother of the great Farloe Verdict, his Peterborough success came during a terrific run of form with race and stakes wins at Nottingham, Doncaster and Sheffield.

Winning breeder: Dessie Loughery, Limavady

Finish	Trap	Names	Price	Time/Dis
1	3	FARLOE HOBBS	5/2	25.98
2	1	Dark Davy	9/4F	8 3/4
3	6	Bea Twinks Chief	14/1	1/2
4	2	Local Call	4/1	1 1/2
5	5	Driving Up Henry	12/1	7
6	4	Rhincrew Stevie	11/4	DIS

NGRC STEWARDS CUP

MITZIE landed a surprise in the NGRC Stewards Cup final at Walthamstow, landing a local victory for Mick Puzey and owners Eddie and Maureen Jones.

In a hot race which featured the likes of big-race winners Jeddies Liberty and January Tiger, the latter the reigning Grand Prix champion, plus defending Stewards Cup champion Romford Car Two, Mitzie came from last to first in a scrappy affair.

However, the victory was fully deserved, and wasn't a complete surprise to connections, who were enjoying more success from the MInnies Sparkler dam-line, which has included champions such as Maxie Rumble, Keltie Sparkler, Jack Sparks and Manera Spark.

Winning breeder: Elizabeth Maher, Co. Tipperary

Finish	Trap	Names	Price	Time/Dis
1	3	MITZIE	7/1	40.02
2	4	Classy Star	8/1	1 1/4
3	2	Roswell Bluesky	10/1	NK
4	1	Romford Car Two	7/2	SH
5	5	January Tiger	7/4F	2 1/2
6	6	Jeddies Liberty	2/1	HD

EASTER CUP

TARBROOK TICO upset more fancied rivals, and one or two big names, to claim gold in the £5,000 Keith Johnson Easter Cup final at Perry Barr.

A cracking event, it ended with a very good final line-up including multiple big-race finalist Blackmagic Guy and Golden Jacket fourth Local Knowledge.

However, 16-1 chance Tarbrook Tico produced the goods when it mattered most to provide his trainer Mark Roberts with his biggest success to date, turning handy before powering to the front.

The September 2003 son of Honcho Classic and Tarbrook Buzz was winning his first open race of the year, but that mattered not to connections after this deserved success.

Winning breeder: Michael Purtill, Croom, Co. Limerick

Finish	Trap	Names	Price	Time/Dis
1	1	TARBROOK TICO	16/1	40.25
2	4	Blackmagic Guy	2/1JF	3 1/2
3	5	Hondo Blue	9/2	1/2
4	3	Local Knowledge	2/1JF	1 3/4
5	6	Kilmurry Lass	15/2	1 1/4
6	2	After Hondo	3/1	1 1/2

GORTON CUP

MANIC MILE helped his trainer land the decent race his efforts travelling up and down the country deserveD when winning the Gorton Cup at Belle Vue in March.

Graham Hutt, based in Kinross, Ayrshire, travels thousands of miles every year sending his greyhounds open racing, but boasted one of the best strike-rates of all during 2007.

Manic Mile, an August 2004 son of Pacific Mile and Cute Mandie, was sent off favourite in the final and deservedly landed the spoils at one of his favourite tracks, having also reached the Laurels final there in 2006.

Winning breeder: Alec Callachan, Wishaw, Lanarkshire

Finish	Trap	Names	Price	Time/Dis
1	4	MANIC MILE	6/4F	27.91
2	1	Blonde Sheriff	9/4	
3	3	Harbour Wind	5/1	3/4
4	2	Our Dog Bod	20/1	3 1/2
5	6	Knocklasheen Boy	12/1	3 3/4
6	5	Yorkshire	9/2	3/4

LADBROKE MIDLAND PUPPY DERBY

ROUGH RONALDINHO, later to be re-named Blonde Dino, emulated the two previous winners of the event – Ballymac Pires and Ballymac Charley – when racing through the Ladbrokes Midland Puppy Derby at Monmore unbeaten.

Owned by Mark Currell and trained by John Mullins, the April 2005 son of Daves Mentor and Charquest made his British debut in a trial stakes for the 480m youngsters' annual.

Making all then, he won his heat in a fastest-of-the-round 28.12sec before seeing off his semi-final and final opponents with a show of searing early pace.

His 28.07sec was the fastest in the competition.

Winning breeder: John McQuillan, Dunlay, Co. Antrim

Finish	Trap	Names	Price	Time/Dis
1	4	FARLOE HURRICANE	5/6F	28.31
2	3	Boherna On Air	11/4	2 1/4
3	6	Romeo Maldini	10/1	1
4	1	Droopys Robster	12/1	1
5	2	Bower Turbo	9/2	1/2
6	5	Westmead Meg	22/1	3/4

THE REGENCY

SPIRIDON LOUIS, laying the foundations for a great year for him and connections, completed an unbeaten run through the Coral Regency with a show-stopping performance to claim the £7,500 purse in front of the Sky cameras at Hove.

The Lorraine Sams-trained, Gail May-owned runner had grabbed the headlines the previous autumn with a track-record breaking run over Walthamstow's 640m.

And he was back to his very best with a sparkling off-the-pace run in the 695m decider, which had TV Trophy contender written all over him.

A litter brother of Oaks and Produce champion Dilemmas Flight and Racing Post Festival winner, Westmead Alec, the December 2004 son of Droopys Vieri and Early Flight (a litter sister of Westmead Hawk's sire, Sonic Flight) also continued the line of top-class winners of the Peterborough Puppy Cesarewitch, a roll of honour which includes Frisby Figo and Roxholme Girl.

Winning breeder: Nick Savva, Dunstable, Beds

Finish	Trap	Names	Price	Time/Dis
1	1	SPIRIDON LOUIS	6/4F	41.15
2	2	Westmead Sam	5/1	1 1/2
3	5	Droopys Riquelme	5/1	3 3/4
4	6	Free As Air	16/1	1/2
5	3	Stardome Girl	12/1	2 1/2
6	4	Go Princess	9/2	2 1/4

TOTESPORT GOLD COLLAR

VATICAN JINKY, named after the famous Celtic striker 'Jinky' Johnston, landed the major event his rich talent deserved when scoring for 'local' trainer Pat Rosney and Scottish owner Robert Ferrari in track record-breaking style in the Totesport Gold Collar over 590m at Belle Vue.

Flashing away from the boxes for the short run to the turn, the son of Hondo Black and Ladys Best Lass was always in control and had his owner in particular excited about having a St Leger entry with the December 04 whelp, a close-up runner-up in the 2006 Northern Puppy Derby.

The former Catford event is credited as a 'Classic' competition and Vatican Jinky's status as a Classic champion was achieved in runaway fashion to beat Thunderbird Two's previous best by five spots as he stopped the clock in 35.06sec and deservedly claim the headlines after a close call at Sunderland and in Nottingham's Puppy Classic (third).

Winning breeder: Rowley Dickinson, Northumberland

Finish	Trap	Names	Price	Time/Dis
1	3	VATICAN JINKY	9/2	35.06TR
2	4	Two Nicks	7/2	4 3/4
3	5	Boherash Patriot	9/2	NK
4	6	Cailins Pesto	12/1	1 3/4
5	1	Go Edie Honda	7/4F	1 3/4
6	2	Fear Robben	7/2	3 3/4

KENT DERBY

MOANING ZIZOU, one of two runners in the final for trainer Darren Whitton and principal owner Mitchell Nicolaou, scored a shock win in the John Smith's Kent Derby at Sittingbourne.

Lining up alongside kennelmate Debbies Choice in the final, both were hoping to make up for the disappointment suffered by the kennel in the Birmingham Cup at Perry Barr earlier in the year. But compensation now waited, with interest!

Landing his trainer his biggest win after leading at the bend, Moaning Zizou held off a spirited challenge up the run-in from Blonde Buzz with a victory which thrilled the family of both the owner and the trainer, Whitton being the grandson of Bryn Ford.

Winning breeder: Ian Lindsay, Co. Monaghan

Finish	Trap	Names	Price	Time/Dis
1	3	MOANING ZIZOU	20/1	29.62
2	2	Blonde Buzz	9/4	SH
3	4	Rough Gerrard	9/4	3 1/2
4	1	Directors Chair	4/1	1
5	5	Debbies Choice	2/1F	2
6	6	Rooster Nosey	16/1	HD

GRAPHITE PUPPY DERBY

CALZAGHE JOE, related to those champions Greenacre Lin and Big Freeze, upset the odds in the Graphite (UK) Puppy Derby final to make it another Walthamstow big-race success for Ted Soppitt.

Come the decider, Calzaghe Joe's kennelmate Droopys Obafemi was sent off favourite but took a tumble at the first bend, and it was the July 2005 son of Top Honcho and First To Return who emerged off the second in front and went on.

Opening Artist, who would later win his own Puppy Derby, this time at Wimbledon, ran on late for second after that first bend trouble.

Winning breeder: Ian Greaves, Co. Kildare

Finish	Trap	Names	Price	Time/Dis
1	4	CALZAGHE JOE	7/1	28.90
2	5	Opening Artist	4/1	2 1/2
3	6	Headford County	4/1	HD
4	2	Droopys Robster	3/1	1
5	1	July Captain	16/1	2 1/4
6	3	Droopys Obafemi	9/4F	DIS

LADBROKE MIDLAND GOLD CUP

BOHERNA ON AIR overcame a missed break to win the Ladbroke Midland Gold Cup as Barrie Draper's finally escaped from the shadow of his kennelmate Farloe Hurricane.

The August 2005 son of Kiwa Sweet Trey

and Free To Air had chased home the Gymcrack winner on a few occasions, but with Farloe Hurrican now aimed at the Select Stakes, it was Boher On Air's time to make hay.

Unleashing brilliant early speed in the heats and semis, he started a warm favourite for the final and looked to improve a record of never being out of the first two in eight races on these shores.

Just a half a length off the then track record in the semis with a stunning 27.86sec run, he came away moderately before forcing his way to the front between the first and second bends to go on to score in the £10,000 event for owner Anthony Rhodes.

Winning breeder: Liam Dwan, Holycross, Co. Tipperary

Finish	Trap	Names	Price	Time/Dis
1	3	BOHERNA ON AIR	4/7F	28.10
2	1	Iceman Vader	6/1	1
3	5	Pennys Shakira	12/1	5 1/2
4	2	Toledo Star	25/1	SH
5	6	Pilot Pretender	6/1	5 1/2
6	4	Venturemore	9/2	1/2

CARLING PUPPY CLASSIC

SIBSEY SHOWTIME made full use of a decent make-up to grab gold with a battling performance in the £7,500 Carling Puppy Classic final at Nottingham.

Ballymac Rita led early, but Sibsey Showtime, a September 2005 son of Hotshow Ben and Locnamon Mist was never too far off the pace, nosed in front off the second and gamely maintained the advantage of the way to the line.

Crapper bred the Category One winner having owned the dam Locnamon Mist and shared ownership in Sibsey Showtime with Derek Booth.

Winning breeder: Harry Crapper, Sheffield, South Yorskhire

Finish	Trap	Names	Price	Time/Dis
1	1	SIBSEY SHOWTIME	7/2	29.96
2	3	Ballymac Rita	11/4	HD
3	5	Opening Artist	11/4	2 1/4
4	2	Bawna Boy	2/1F	1
5	6	Farloe Tobias	6/1	3 3/4
NR		Stormy Scholes		

WILLIAM HILL PUPPY DERBY

OPENING ARTIST lunged for the line to deny Pea Ball in a thrilling Holsten Pils Puppy Derby final at Wimbledon, and with it the £6,000 prize.

Bernie Doyle's October 05 black son of Droopys Scolari had reached a number of finals, but struck gold in one for the Wimbledon handler. He had finished second to Meenala Cruiser in the Ritchie (UK) Puppy Cup final at Sunderland and to Calzaghe Joe in Walthamstow's Graphite (UK) Puppy Derby decider.

However, trailing the field early, the Lynn Canham-owned wide runer looked to have a mountain to climb before powering up the run-in to reel-in leader Ballymac Raymond and then Pea Ball.

Winning breeder: Michael Dunphy, Portlaw, Co. Waterford

Finish	Trap	Names	Price	Time/Dis
1	4	OPENING ARTIST	9/2	27.70
2	3	Pea Ball	3/1	SH
3	2	Fitzroy Sydney	20/1	SH
4	1	Ballymac Raymond	33/1	1/2
5	5	Droopys Mate	9/4	4 1/4
6	6	Droopys Hatton	2/1F	2 1/4

SUSSEX CUP

BARNFIELD ON AIR produced one of the performances of 2007 with an unbeaten run through the £10,000 Coral Sussex Cup at Hove, and setting a track record in the final.

Trained by Sam Poots and his assistant, Darran Keefe, the one-time Irish Puppy Derby finalist when known as On Air Always had impressed in the first round of the Derby before making a poor start in the second round, finding trouble and crashing out.

But those problems at the start were well and truly ironed out come Hove and some fast and faultless saw him start a short price in the final. Coming away, he soon led to win easily, taking seven spots off Ballybrazil Hero's previous best as he strode majestically clear to win by six-and-a-half lengths.

Afterwards, a campaign to mop up the middle distance competitions for the rest of the year was hatched for the February 2005 son of Pacific Mile and Always On Air.

Winning breeder: Liam Dwan, Holycross, Co. Tipperary

Finish	Trap	Names	Price	Time/Dis
1	4	BARNFIELD ON AIR	2/5F	29.20TR
2	5	Fear Me	7/1	6 1/2
3	3	Jazz Hurricane	8/1	1 1/2
4	2	Ballymac Weeshie	20/1	3/4
5	1	Lenson Earl	10/1	1 1/2
6	6	Brooklyn Bridge	12/1	1

WILLIAM HILL TV TROPHY

SPIRIDON LOUIS produced a storming back-straight surge to pass Wise Susie, and then hold that rival's spirited renewed challenge on the second lap, to win the William Hill TV Trophy final at Yarmouth.

The two-year-old littermate of Dilemmas Flight and Westmead Alec had been stepped up further in trip after winning the Regency at Hove and relished the opportunity by setting a new track record of 52.98sec in a trial stakes, bettering Change Guard's 20-year-old previous best.

Scoring well in his heat, Spiridon Louis and Wise Susie took advantage amongst the rest of the field in the final to have the rest between them off the second bend

In winning, the Lorraine Sams-trained, Gail May-owned runner bracketed himself with other Regency/TV Trophy double winners, including Scurlogue Champ, Killeacle Phoebe, Suncrest Sail and Shady Begonia.

Winning breeder: Nick Savva, Dunstable, Beds

Finish	Trap	Names	Price	Time/Dis
1	2	SPIRIDON LOUIS	4/7F	53.42
2	1	Wise Susie	28/1	1

3	6	Mitzie	18/1	6 1/4
4	3	Bubbly Kate	7/2	SH
5	5	Head Iton Jordan	4/1	2 1/2
6	4	Confident Foe	20/1	1 3/4

EAST ANGLIAN DERBY

ERIC CANTILLON wasted no time in sending out a Category One winner when the Bury St Edmonds-based owner-trainer, having had his licence for less than two years and his professional one for just three months, struck with Blackrose Mars in the 61st East Anglian Derby at Yarmouth.

Assisted at the kennels by wife Anja and daughter Shannah, plus Michelle Kemp, daughter of Yarmouth handler Hazel, Blackrose Mars first showed himself to be a talent when setting a track record at Harlow for the 592m trip, before reaching the Coventry Derby final.

Showing great speed in the Yarmouth decider, he led off the second after brushing aside fast-starting Hee Haws Cantona after kennelmates Blonde Buster and Black Taxi came together out of the boxes. Thereafter the August 04 son of Larkhill Jo and Christmas Holly went clear to win a shade comfortably.

The event had seen the 16-year-old track record of Dempsey Duke – ironically achieved in the 1991 final – finally broken, when defending champion Geordie Parker posted 27.52sec in the second round, before being crowded out in the semis.

Winning breeder: Christopher Holland, Co. Tipperary

Finish	Trap	Names	Price	Time/Dis
1	2	BLACKROSE MARS	11/2	27.71
2	5	Primitive Way	8/1	5 3/4
3	3	Black Taxi	25/1	1
4	1	Killer Keane	9/4	6
5	6	Hee Haws Cantona	6/1	SH
6	4	Blonde Buster	6/4F	3 1/2

LADBROKE STAYERS SUMMER CLASSIC

MONMORE's Ladbrokes Summer Festival is fast-becoming a must for open-race handlers, and betting shop punters alike, and Daytona Dandy produced the goods to win the showpiece prize in the £7,500 Ladbrokes Summer Stayers Classic final.

The Westmeads, Hawk and Aoifa, had won the previous two runnings of the 630m competition for Nick Savva, but this time is was the Yvonne Morris-trained son of Top Honcho and Datona Destiny who landed a surprise but deserved 20-1 success in the final.

Off the pace early, the March 2005 came through on the run-in to beat joint-favourites Head Iton Paddy and Shelbourne Laura.

The other finals were won by Chakalak Paris (bitches), Brooklyn Bridge (dogs) and Blonde Jet (sprint).

Winning breeder: David Eaton, Bolton, Lancashire

Finish	Trap	Names	Price	Time/Dis
1	2	DATONA DANDY	20/1	38.27
2	4	Head Iton Paddy	1/1JF	1
3	1	Shelbourne Laura	1/1JF	1
4	6	Coolanga Post	16/1	SH
5	3	Mill Lane Ebony	16/1	NK
NR		Elderberry Khan		

COVENTRY DERBY

ICEMAN ROSS landed the big-race final his consistent performances deserved when winning the Nigel Flowers & Glen Coulton Coventry Derby, and with it the £10,000 victor's cheque.

A beaten finalist in seven previous events, the Lance and Pam Burford-owned and trained runner tracked early-paced Blitz at the third bend before pulling clear off the last.

The success was appropriate given that it was Iceman Ross's 14th victory over course and distance, and his quickest, as connections mapped out a crack at the Select Stakes afterwards for the October 2004 son of Top Honcho and Dark Rose.

Winning breeder: Philomena Phelan, Co. Kilkenny

Finish	Trap	Names	Price	Time/Dis
1	6	Iceman Ross	6/4F	29.27
2	3	Blitz	13/2	3 3/4
3	5	Greenwell Flash	16/1	HD
4	2	Blackrose Mars	4/1	HD
5	1	Kaiser Chief	8/1	HD
6	4	Alibulk Rocket	9/4	DIS

TWO-YEAR-OLD PRODUCE STAKES

HEDSOR CHIPA became Reading trainer Keith Howard's second winner of the Two-Year-Old Produce Stakes at Swindon when making all in the £15,000 decider to repeat the feat of the kennel's Hedsor Rock in 1999.

The former Bristol-housed event was having its 61st running and, with no Nick Savva-trained runners in the original line-up, the British-bred event had an open look from the start.

Breeders Forum secretary Bob Gilling was appropriately represented by Saigon Hero, who went off favourite come on the final.

However, a faster start from the eventual winner saw the David Pearl part-owned son of Droopys Scolari and Hedsor Sheila, an August 2005 whelp, strike gold, completing a real home-bred success for Howard and assistant trainer Janet Bedwell.

The final had to be re-scheduled due to flooding, with a midweek final for the four-round event.

Winning breeder: Keith Howard, Maidenhead, Berks

Finish	Trap	Names	Price	Time/Dis
1	6	Hedsor Chipa	5/1	29.29
2	3	Saigon Hero	11/4	3 3/4
3	2	Bowmers Let Rip	14/1	1 3/4
4	5	Ziggys Boy	9/2	1 1/4
5	1	Fabulous Millie	2/1F	1 1/4
6	3	Callums Court	9/2	9

BETFAIR SCURRY GOLD CUP

HORSESHOE PING overcame a missed break to run through his field to claim the Betfair Scurry Gold Cup at Perry Barr, as the old sprinters' claim continued to reclaim his prestigious

place in the Calendar at its new home in Birmingham.

The Jim Reynolds-trained, John and Pam Desmond-owned runner had set a track record in the heats adding to his best figures over Walthamstow's 235m trip –and then ran away from his semi-final opponents, before making a real hash of the start in the £8,000 final.

However, it opened up nicely for the 2006 Trafalgar Cup champion and his speed took him to the front off the second and maintain his unbeaten run through the 275m competition.

Winning breeder: Alison Coxon, Co. Tipperary

Finish	Trap	Names	Price	Time/Dis
1	5	HORSESHOE PING	4/11F	16.19
2	1	Freight Train	9/2	1 1/2
3	6	Ladywell Trick	9/1	2 1/4
4	3	Pineapple Gene	8/1	DIS
5	2	Wheres Yer Man	8/1	DIS
NR		Oh His Nerves		

COORS PUPPY SILVER COLLAR

HARRY WILLIAMS, who had threatened to hang up his lead, was the toast of Sheffield and pledged to carry on sending out the winners after Stormy Scholes won the £5,000 Stones Puppy Silver Collar final.

Stormy Scholes, a September 2005 son of Droopys Scholes and Ludworth Josie, went to traps the 14-1 outsider for the Category Two final.

Turning handy, Stormy Scholes moved well down the back to take up the running past halfway to ultimately collect for Williams and owner Joss Barnfather.

Highlight of the supporting card was the record-breaking performance of Lunar Vacation in a 280-metre sprint contest.

Winning breeder: Dermot Fitzgerald, Glin, Co. Limerick

Finish	Trap	Names	Price	Time/Dis
1	4	STORMY SCHOLES	14/1	29.38
2	6	Farloe Spiderman	2/1	3 3/4)

3	3	Droopys Billy	5/4F	SH
4	1	Witton Chloe	6/1	4
5	2	Sibsey Showtime	8/1	2 1/4
6	5	Deanridge Newman	6/1	DIS

NORTHERN FLAT

BALLYMAC CHARLEY ran undefeated through the Ben Holmes Northern Flat Championship with a facile victory in the final of the Category Two event.

Owned by Nick Budimir and Harry Redknapp, he had won the Midland Puppy Derby as a pup and ran in both the 2006 and 2007 Derbys, reaching the semi-finals in the latter.

Off the track after the previous year's Classic, and then the Yarmouth Derby, he joined Charlie Lister afterwards who guided him, utimately, to Northern Flat success, the son of Daves Mentor and Ballymac Bargain leading up and making all .

Winning breeder: Liam Dowling, Ballymacelligott, Co. Kerry

Finish	Trap	Names	Price	Time/Dis
1	4	BALLYMAC CHARLEY	5/4F	27.70
2	2	Boherash Patriot	16/1	3
3	1	Killieford Brave	7/2	1/2
4	3	Pennys Shakira	8/1	3/4
5	5	Mattos	9/2	1/2
6	6	Rapidvite Liam	6/1	3

YORKSHIRE LEGER

LARKHILL BIRD successfully defended her Tetleys Yorkshire St Leger title at Doncaste.

Michael Walsh's bitch led off the second bend and was never threatened thereafter, winning by just under two lengths from staying-on Westmead Aoifa in 41.37sec, beating a high-class field in the process.

Winner of the Prestige, there had been close calls in the Cock O'The North and the Select Stayers when she was picked up by Spiridon Louis.

But flourishing on her return to Doncaster, the Australian-bred bitch produced arguably her best run of the year in the final.

Finish	Trap	Names	Price	Time/Dis
1	3	LARKHILL BIRD	9/2	41.37
2	4	Westmead Aoifa	9/4F	1 3/4
3	6	Butterbridge Ali	3/1	5
4	2	Romford Car Two	8/1	1
5	1	Cuil Magic	6/1	1 3/4
6	5	Shelbourne Rene	5/1	HD

WILLIAM HILL STEEL CITY CUP

BOHERNA ON AIR landed a second major success in a matter of weeks when winning the William Hill Steel City Cup final at Sheffield.

Already successful in the Ladbrokes Midland Gold Cup at Monmore, Barrie Draper's dog was continuing the form which saw him finish second to kennelmate Farloe Hurricane in the Gymcrack and a minor puppy stakes at Sheffield.

With that rival committed to a campaign including the Select Stakes, Boherna On Air made hay!

With the final reduced to a five-runner affair following the withdrawal of Pilot Pretender, Boherna On Air capped an unbeaten run through the £5,000 event for owner Anthony Rhodes by starting fast and just edging the equally well-away Rev Counter to the bend, with a searing burst of early pace. He then held that gallant rival well to win in a fast 29.19sec.

Winning breeder: Liam Dwan, Holycross, Co. Tipperary

Finish	Trap	Names	Price	Time/Dis
1	1	BOHERNA ON AIR	5/4JF	29.19
2	4	Rev Counter	20/1	1 1/4
3	2	Iceman Vader	5/1	1 1/4
4	3	Farloe Hobbs	7/1	HD
5	6	Iceman Ross	5/4JF	3/4
NR		Pilot Pretender		

READING MASTERS

BLITZ lived up to his name by blitzing his field in an eventful Reading Masters, scoring the biggest win of trainer Denis Stevenson's career, just a matter of months after he switched to becoming a licensed handler after huge experience on the independent circuit.

The £20,000 annual included a re-run this year after a semi-final was voided due to a hare malfunction. The five-dog semi (a tired Moaning Zizou was saved the prospect of a quick run) eventually went to Fear Haribo, and it was the back-to-form Scottish Derby winner, returned to the track after a blood disorder afflicted his English Derby effort, went off favourite in the Sunday final.

However, it was Blitz who paced up into the lead and was on his way to victory from Blonde Jeannnie. He had been running well again after a shoulder problem, a spell of the card which coincided with the trainer building new kennels. Second in the Coventry Summer Derby to Iceman Ross, he went one better at Reading for Stevenson and his fellow part-owner Janice Carter.

Winning breeder: Breda McCabe and John Murphy, Co.Wexford

Finish	Trap	Names	Price	Time/Dis
1	6	BLITZ	4/1	28.03
2	2	Blonde Jeannie	4/1	1 3/4
3	3	Fear Haribo	7/4F	1/2
4	5	Vipar Totti	8/1	2 1/2
5	1	Brickfield Class	7/2	1 1/2
6	4	Mulcair Jo	20/1	2 3/4

VICTOR CHANDLER GRAND PRIX

FOULDEN SPECIAL, owned by the Sugar Rush syndicate and trained by Hove handler Derek Knight, produced a startling late run to grab gold in a thrilling VCbet Grand Prix final at Walthamstow – a result that looked in doubt for three-quarters of the 640m trip!

Knight's dog had been unbeaten in five previous starts at the track, including the three preliminaries of the £15,000 event, and raced unbeaten through the competition by powering up the home-straight to deny Calzaghe Frisby and Fear Robben.

The last-named pair had dominated the race until the final strides. Calzaghe Frisby broke in front, before Fear Robben's middle pace took him to the head of affairs. When he began to tire off the last, Ted Soppitt's dog pounced, but could not hold the finish of the son of Smoking Baby, herself a marathon star, who was last at the fifth bend – but in front at the line.

Star of the undercard was undoubtedly Sussex Cup champion Barnfield On Air, who set new figures for the 475m trip when bolting home to reverse Select Stakes form with Cleenas Lady in 28.15sec, a stunning 27 spots off the previous best.

Winning breeder: Dave Wood, Berwick upon Tweed

Finish	Trap	Names	Price	Time/Dis
1	6	FOULDEN SPECIAL	1/1F	39.45
2	2	Calzaghe Frisby	7/1	HD
3	4	Fear Robben	2/1	NK
4	1	Shelbourne Laura	8/1	1 3/4
5	3	White Bomber	20/1	1/2
6	5	Shelbourne Ryan	25/1	2 1/2

WILLIAM HILL NORTHERN PUPPY DERBY

FARLOE REASON landed a first £8,000 Northern Puppy Derby victory for Charlie Lister when making all impressively in the William Hill-sponsored event at Sunderland.

The March 2006 whelp, from the first crop of Droopys Maldini progeny out of Farloe Oyster, had shown plenty of stamina in winning his three previous races but now upheld a 100 per cent record in all-the-way style for owner Ian Openshaw.

Suitably, the winning time was not only the fastest of the high-profile night, but also in the competition.

Winning breeder: Emmet Hazlett, Co. Derry

Finish	Trap	Names	Price	Time/Dis
1	2	FARLOE REASON	2/1	26.92
2	6	Westmead Keawn	6/4F	2 1/4
3	5	Fear Mambo	25/1	2 1/4
4	4	Barnfield Mike	8/1	4 1/4
5	1	Calzaghe Ted	5/2	5
6	3	Swift Sapphire	12/1	1 1/2

BREEDERS FORUM PRODUCE STAKES

FEEL FREE might have caused a shock for some punters, but his background always suggested a huge run in the competition and the Richard Baker-trained runner became a home-grown star as he won the British Breeders Forum Produce Stakes at Hall Green.

Baker had enjoyed great success with former open-race star and Walthamstow track-record holder Pennys Worth and now sent out the September 2005 son of Droopys Kewell and Road Princess for a 14-1 upset in the £15,000 final.

Toosey Blue, Hall Green's 480m track record holder, went off favourite but got caught up first-bend trouble as Feel Free slipped into an early advantage.

Baker won races the winner's dam, and was now watching her son race to glory.

Winning breeder: Richard Baker, Bletchingdon, Oxfordshire

Finish	Trap	Names	Price	Time/Dis
1	1	FEEL FREE	14/1	28.70
2	2	Witton Chloe	11/1	1 1/4
3	3	Wisdom Prevails	9/2	SH
4	4	Blonde Buzz	13/2	SH
5	6	Toosey Blue	4/6F	1
6	5	Bens Court	3/1	2

GLOBAL WINDOWS INVITATION

BLONDE JEANNIE continued her quite remarkable record at Sheffield by upsetting the odds in the Global Windows (formerly the Dransfield) Invitation, the famous four-runner showpiece at the Owlerton venue.

Blasting out of the boxes, the September 04 daughter of Daves Mentor and Easy And Breezy made it seven wins from seven at the south Yorkshire venue, which had included victory in the Yorkshire.

John Mullins' bitch had run well in the Derby having been off the track or some nine months with a serious muscle injury having starred in the 2006 Peterborough Puppy Derby.

Winning breeder: Ian Greaves,
Co. Kildare

Finish	Trap	Names	Price	Time/Dis
1	4	BLONDE JEANNIE	11/2	29.12
2	1	Vatican Jinky	11/4	NK
3	3	Boherna On Air	5/4F	3/4
4	6	Eye Onthe Veto	5/2	1 1/2

BETFRED LAURELS

KYLEGROVE TOP might have gone down as a fortuitous winner of the £10,000 Betfred Laurels on the night, but his previous top-class form, and that of his kennel, made the victory of the Julie Bateson-trained runner in the Belle Vue annual thoroughly deserved.

Barnfield On Air, who had broken his own track record in the semi-finals, went on a warm order but paced up into huge trouble after a moderate exit. While he managed to stay on his feet, he allowed the slow-starting Kylegrove Top to slip through on the rails, and away he went.

A Scottish Derby and St Mungo Cup finalist and winner of the Harry Holmes Memorial, the Howard Jenkinson and Jeff Kingsnorth-owned runner scored trainer Bateson's biggest win after a string of near-misses in big-race finals.

Winning breeder: Peter Burgon,
Co. Tipperary

Finish	Trap	Names	Price	Time/Dis
1	2	KYLEGROVE TOP	10/1	27.82
2	1	Barnfield On Air	2/7F	1 1/4
3	6	Droopys Wells	10/1	4 1/2
4	3	Highfield Hondo	16/1	1 1/4
5	5	Boherna On Air	7/1	3/4
6	6	Meenala Cruiser	16/1	1

THE ALL ENGLAND CUP

WRIGHT SIGNAL trapped in front of his rivals and was soon clear on his way to winning the William Hill All England Cup at Newcastle.

The Elaine Parker runner, a litter brother of Irish Derby Consolation winner, Farloe Black, won unchallenged in the end and helped connections, Kevin and Lynne Wright, to take the £10,000 first prize.

The event lost defending champion Geordie Parker at the first hurdle, and it was left to the March 2005 son son of Hondo Black and Farloe Signal to take advantage, bouncing back from defeat in the semis to put the Parker kennel, with Carly Philpott as assistant trainer, in line for possible qualification for the 2008 Trainers' Championship meeting.

Winning breeder: Dessie Loughery,
Limavady, Co. Derry

Finish	Trap	Names	Price	Time/Dis
1		WRIGHT SIGNAL	9/4	28.62
2		Rapidvite Liam	3/1	3 1/4
3		Leading Star	6/1	3 1/2
4		Droopys Tobey	5/4F	SH
5		Magna Action	8/1	2 1/4
NR		Greenfield Hero		

BLUE SQUARE 480 CUP

BARNFIELD ON AIR, winning in Britain for the 15th time in 23 starts, roared to success in the Blue Square 480 Cup final at Coventry to claim the third richest prize of the year in the £22,000 decider.

The Sam Poots-trained runner, a finalist in the 2006 Irish Puppy Derby when known as On Air Always, made it five track records in a handful of starts when setting new figures for the Brandon's track's four-bend trip in the second round, when reversing a first-round defeat at the paws of Fear Haribo.

Subsequently the middle seed was taken off Barnfield On Air and now, pitched inside the Scottish Derby champion in the final, was made a war favourite to lead up and make all, which he did.

With an eye on the Greyhound of the Year title, Poots and assistant trainer Darran Keefe targeted the Racing Post Festival afterwards, but the three Derby-bid in 2008 was still the major plan.

Winning breeder: Liam Dwan,
Hollycross, Co. Tipperary

Finish	Trap	Names	Price	Time/Dis
1	2	BARNFIELD ON AIR	1/3F	29.08

2	3	Fear Haribo	4/1	2 1/2
3	4	Toosey Blue	10/1	2
4	1	Larkhill Jim	40/1	1 3/4
5	5	Shelbourne Aston	33/1	1
6	6	Minnies Premier	25/1	2 1/4

THE BRIGHTON BELLE

JAZZ HURRICANE, runner-up the previous year, went one better when coming through in typically strong style to win the £2,500 Roy Pook Brighton Belle.

Showing great trackcraft and tenacity, the Derek Knight-owned and Steff Watson and Dave Abraham-owned runner, and a sister of Scurry champion Horseshoe Ping forced her way to the front at the third turn and go on after Shelbourne Poopa had led.

Knight then aimed her at the Oaks in which she finished third in 2006 before winning the Olympic at Hove and Circuit at Walthamstow.

Winning breeder: Alison Coxon, Co. Tipperary

Finish	Trap	Names	Price	Time/Dis
1	3	JAZZ HURRICANE	4/5F	30.33
2	6	Belindas Floss	5/2	2 3/4
3	5	Murlens Copper	12/1	1/2
4	1	Hope And Glory	5/1	3/4
5	4	San Suu Kyi	12/1	1/2
6	2	Shelbourne Poopa	10/1	SH

CORAL PUPPY CUP

WESTMEAD KEAWN came from off the pace in true Westmead style to win the Main Ring Bookmakers Puppy Cup at Romford.

Runner-up in the Northern Puppy Derby, he showed terrific back-straight pace to collar the leaders before running way to pocket the £8,000 prize for trainer Nick Savva and owner Bob Morton in a very decent 24.07sec.

On the night, Westmead Keawn's trackcraft drew comparison with his great half-brother Westmead Hawk, coming from the family that have supplied the previous three Derby champions.

Winning breeder: Nick Savva, Dunstable, Beds

Finish	Trap	Names	Price	Time/Dis
1	6	WESTMEAD KEAWN	11/8F	24.07
2	3	Droopys Geisha	25/1	2
3	4	Secretariat	7/1	1 1/4
4	2	Mustang Garcia	9/4	1
5	1	Black Ice Boss	9/2	2 1/4
6	5	Droopys Hamlet	20/1	1/2

GOLDEN MUZZLE

BLAKES WORLD became that rare breed of greyhound to successfully defend a major title when scoring a hugely popular win for 'evergreen' owner and trainer combination Roy Felmingham and Jo Burridge in the Portsouth Golden Muzzle.

The April 2004 son of Felmingham's TV Trophy winner Killeacle Phoebe and his own Derby finalist (2002) Blue Gooner, Blakes World had won his semi-final in good style and now, on a wet and miserable night on the south coast venue, warmed connections with a fast start and made all.

Winning breeder: Roy Felmingham, Meopham, Kent

Finish	Trap	Names	Price	Time/Dis
1	6	BLAKES WORLD	7/4F	26.86
2	2	Takemehomejoey	10/3	2 1/4
3	1	Eye For One	6/1	1 3/4
4	2	Full Bloom	9/2	2
5	3	Cobra	5/2	1 3/4
6	4	Bull Bull Barum	50/1	2 3/4

WILLIAM HILL LEGER

SPIRIDON LOUIS continued his amazing run of success in 2007 by successfully dropping down in distance to win the William Hill St Leger at Wimbledon.

Campaigned successfully over eight bends, six bends was the trip now for the Gail May-owned runner and a shrewd move paid-off with interest as he bounced back from semi-final defeat to strike with a fabulous run up the rail on the run for home in the decider after Lenson Joker and Directors Chair had a great battle for early supremacy.

In winning the £13,000 first prize, the Nick Savva-bred Spiridon Louis added a stayers'

Classic success to victories already achieved in the Regency, TV Trophy, Dorando Marathon and Select Stayers.

Winning breeder: Nick Savva, Dunstable, Beds

Finish	Trap	Names	Price	Time/Dis
1	3	SPIRIDON LOUIS	4/1	40.86
2	4	Lenson Joker	4/1	3/4
3	6	Westmead Aoifa	9/4F	3/4
4	2	Directors Chair	6/1	1 3/4
5	5	Local Knowledge	4/1	3/4
6	1	Iceman Brutus	7/1	3/4

BETFRED ECLIPSE

REV COUNTER landed trainer Chris Allsopp his biggest success of his training career when holding off Two Nicks to win the £8,000 Betfred Eclipse final.

Having run a terrific race in the Steel City Cup behind Boherna On Air, Rev Counter returned after a short break to tackle the prestigious Nottingham annual.

Owned by Richard Wheeler, his early pace took him to the front again in the final but having been caught in the two previous rounds he now held on, faster going on the night helping his ability to stay the trip more strongly.

Winning breeder: Martin Gleeson, Co. Kildare

Finish	Trap	Names	Price	Time/Dis
1	3	REV COUNTER	6/1	29.91
2	1	Two Nicks	5/4F	HD
3	6	Centaur Decree	5/1	3 1/4
4	4	Affleck Elite	9/2	2 1/4
5	2	Iceman Vader	4/1	HD
6	5	Cagey Luke	7/1	2 1/2

SUSSEX PUPPY TROPHY

WESTMEAD TINA, another top-class product from the Dunstable academy of Nick Savva, struck in the Coral Sussex Puppy Trophy for her trainer/breeder and owner Bob Morton.

Twelve months previously, the event had been won by another Savva-bred, Westmead Alec, that particular litter also including Dilemmas Flight and Spiridon Louis.

On the night, Westmead Tina was a comfortable victor, winning in a fastest-time-of-the-night 29.71sec to register a stakes win after finishing third in a Stow puppy event and reaching the semis of the Northern Puppy Derby.

She is from a repeat mating of Droopys Kewell and Mega Delight (January 2006), the litter including fellow winners Westmead Keawn, Kewell, Meg and Naomi. The previous batch famously includes 2007 Derby hero Westmead Lord.

Winning breeder: Nick Savva, Dunstable, Beds

Finish	Trap	Names	Price	Time/Dis
1	5	WESTMEAD TINA	2/1	29.71
2	3	Rough Rose	8/1	4 1/4
3	6	Ask The Question	4/5F	3/4
4	1	Lenas Adam	14/1	3 1/2
5	4	Rough Quest	12/1	SH
6	2	Hedgehog	50/1	4 1/2

2007 Trainers' Championship

Charlie Lister and his team celebrate their Betfair Trainers' Championship triumph

CHARLIE LISTER edged out Mark Wallis in a thrilling climax to the Betfair Trainers' Championship meeting at Hall Green in 2007.

Lister used the fixture to take the wraps off his Derby hotpots, with Geordie Parker and Fear Haribo both making their seasonal bows – in the case of the latter having his first run for the Newark team. And the quality of his team saw him begin an odds-on favourite to wear the the crown. However, Mark Wallis's team did not read the script.

As short as 1-16 in-running with the sponsors after landing three of the first four events via Geordie Parker, Fear Haribo and Shelbourne Rene, Lister was 13 points clear of his rivals. However, Wallis then hit back with Roswell Spaceman, Centaur Decree and Raging Jack and, going into the eighth and final race, Wallis led Lister by four points.

Wallis had Eye Onthe Veto running for him, but it was Lister's Zigzag Dutchy who produced one of the runs of his life to claim the title for Lister and his team.

The final points tally of the six competing trainers: Lister 55; Wallis 52; John Mullins 37; Brian Clemenson 31; Seamus Cahill 18; Ernie Gaskin 15.

480m

Finish	Greyhound	Trap	SP	Trainer	Time/Dis
1	Geordie Parker	5	8/13F	CL	28.50
2	Lady Sky	2	8/1	BC	2 1/2
3	Blonde Zak	4	20/1	JM	2 1/4
4	Fear Armani	1	9/4	MW	1 1/2
5	Rooster Nosey	6	20/1	SC	NK
6	Legal Major	3	14/1	EG	3 1/2

258m

Finish	Greyhound	Trap	SP	Trainer	Time/Dis
1	Roswell Spaceman	2	4/1	MW	15.51
2	Rhincrew Simba	3	7/4F	CL	1 1/2
3	Toosey Bill	5	6/1	JM	SH
4	Snazzy Time	1	8/1	SC	2 3/4
5	Johnny Liar	6	11/1	BC	2 1/4
6	Myella Honcho	4	3/1	EG	NK

480m

Finish	Greyhound	Trap	SP	Trainer	Time/Dis
1	Fear Haribo	4	4/11F	CL	28.23
2	Eye Onthe Gift	3	8/1	MW	6 1/2
3	Brookvill Genius	2	11/1	BC	1/2
4	Ross Fortune	1	20/1	SC	SH
5	Greenfield Hero	6	7/1	EG	3/4
6	Cagey Luke	5	11/1	JM	1 1/2

645m

Finish	Greyhound	Trap	SP	Trainer	Time/Dis
1	Shelbourne Rene	6	4/7F	CL	39.38
2	Junior Mechanic	5	10/1	JM	7 3/4
3	Coolanga Flyer	3	11/1	MW	2 1/4
4	Big Brett Coal	1	3/1	SC	HD
5	Bubbly Kate	2	9/1	BC	NK
6	Patch Of Blue	4	25/1	EG	5 1/4

480m

Finish	Greyhound	Trap	SP	Trainer	Time/Dis
1	Centaur Decree	5	5/2	MW	28.79
2	Toosey Blue	4	5/2	JM	2
3	Stormy Savanna	6	6/4F	CL	1/2
4	Erinaceous Rapid	3	14/1	EG	1 1/2
5	Flying Fancy	1	20/1	SC	2 1/2
6	Lifes Lukey	2	12/1	BC	1/2

480m

Finish	Greyhound	Trap	SP	Trainer	Time/Dis
1	Raging Jack	2	13/2	MW	28.32
2	Shelbourne Poopa 5	7/1	BC	3/4	
3	Fear Me	6	4/5F	CL	1 1/4
4	Ronnies Earner	1	3/1	EG	1 1/4
5	Blonde Jeannie	4	10/1	JM	5
6	Pork Pie	3	20/1	SC	2 1/2

645m

Finish	Greyhound	Trap	SP	Trainer	Time/Dis
1	Romford Car Two	2	5/2	JM	39.52
2	Blackmagic Guy	4	2/1F	MW	4 1/2
3	Droopys Riquelme	6	11/2	BC	4 1/4
4	Olynanoli	5	25/1	EG	1/2
5	Droopys Majella	3	8/1	SC	1
6	Miselar Custard	1	3/1	CL	HD

480m

Finish	Greyhound	Trap	SP	Trainer	Time/Dis
1	Zigzag Dutchy	4	3/1	CL	28.24
2	Coventry Bees	2	5/1	BC	2 1/4
3	Blonde Sheriff	1	6/1	JM	2 3/4
4	Eye Onthe Veto	6	11/4F	MW	2 1/4
5	Snazzy Rover	3	3/1	SC	3/4
6	Cobra Striking	5	6/1	EG	2 1/4

Trainers Championship Roll of Honour

2007 – Hall Green – Charlie Lister
2006 – Wimbledon – Mark Wallis
2005 – Perry Barr – Charlie Lister
2004 – Coventry Brian – Clemenson
2003 – Sittingbourne – Brian Clemenson
2002 – Hove Brian – Clemenson
2001 – Hove – Charlie Lister
2000 – Sittingbourne – Nick Savva
1999 – Walthamsdtow – Linda Jones
1998 – Sittingbourne – Ernie Gaskin
1997 – Walthamstow – Linda Mullins
1996 – Hackney – Ernie Gaskin
1995 – Wimbledon – John Coleman
1994 – Walthamstow – John Coleman
1993 – Walthamstow – Linda Mullins
1992 – Reading – John McGee
1991 – Reading – Linda Mullins
1990 – Hove – Bill Masters
1989 – Oxford – John McGee
1988 – Walthamstow – Ernie Gaskin
1987 – Wembley – Geoffrey De Mulder
1986 – Wembley – Ken Linzell
1985 – Walthamstow – Ken Linzell
1984 – White City – George Curtis
1983 – White City – Natalie Savva
1982 – White City – Adam Jackson
1981 – Perry Barr – Joe Cobbold
1980 – Crayford – Ted Dickson
1979 – Crayford – John Honeysett
1978 – Monmore – Ted Dickson
1977 – Newcastle – Natalie Savva and Geoffrey De Mulder

British Greyhound Racing Board Awards

Royal Lancaster Hotel, London, 21 January 2006

WESTMEAD HAWK became only the second greyhound to win back-to-back Greyhound of the Year awards when he helped trainer Nick Savva and owner Bob Morton almost sweep the board at the 2006 BGRB Awards at the Royal Lancaster Hotel, London, on the third Sunday in January, 2007.

In taking the top accolade, the dual Derby champion emulated the great Ballyregan Bob to be named the Greyhound Writers' Association ' top dog' once again, and for

good measure he also walked off with the Standard Distance award, and Best British-bred honour.

Morton and Savva returned to the podium for those trophies, while Savva himself also collected the Dam of Best British-bred award as Mega Delight, Hawk' s mother, also defended her own title. Morton then picked up the award for owner of the year.

Westmead Aoifa had already made it a good night for the Dunstable academy when picking up her ' Top Dog' award – the first

Sue and Bob Morton hold the Greyhound of the Year trophy with Nick Savva

Bob Betts receives his award from Roger Jackson, John Benbow and Mark Sullivan

and last time the honour would be bestowed on a greyhound – and for good measure later picked up the the Stayers' award.

The Raymond Gee-owned bitch missed the main autumn sweep of the big six-bend races due to seasonal rest, but was the epitome of consistency throughout the rest of the year with her biggest victory coming in the Ladbroke Summer Stayers' Classic at Monmore in June.

Top Sprinter was Ballymac Rooster, now trained by Ernie Gaskin junior for the Arch Enemies Syndicate but handled for the majority of 2006 by Carly Philpott, who sent him out to win the Betfair Scurry Gold Cup at Perry Barr in August following on from earlier victories in the Byrne Bros Cheltenham Festival Sprint and JP Doyle Gorton Cup at Belle Vue.

And there was a Philpott connection to the Marathon award as winner Roxholme Girl, owned and latterly-trained by Hayley Keightley, was in her charge when memorably landing the William Hill TV Trophy at Belle Vue in March with victories in heat and final

basically being the sum total of her marathon career, although she did also win the Totesport Gold Collar over 590m at the Manchester track later in the year.

Best Hurdler was William Hill Grand National champion Suit Man, trained by Bernie Doyle for the Ramat Racing Club, while the Charlie Lister-trained Clash Harmonica [owned by the Boys from Leicester Syndicate] was Best Newcomer following a debut year which saw him land Category One victories in the William Hill Laurels at Belle Vue and Betfred Eclipse at Nottingham as well as the Napoleons Casino Invitation at Sheffield.

Charlie Lister, who ran away with the points-based Trainers' Championship, also took the BGRB Trainer of the Year award.

Kennelhand of the Year went to Gemma Davidson from the John Davidson kennel at Crayford, former Sporting Life greyhound editor Bob Betts picked up his GWA' Services to Greyhound Racing' award, while Anne Shannon's dedicated welfare work was marked by the services to the Retired Greyhound Trust award.

2006 Roll of Honour

GREYHOUND OF THE YEAR
Westmead Hawk (bk d Sonic Flight-Mega Delight May 2003) Owned by Bob Morton, trained by Nick Savva

BEST SPRINTER
Ballymac Rooster (bd d Roanokee-Ballymac Pepes Sep 2003) Owned by the Arch Enemies Syndicate, trained by Carly Philpott

BEST STANDARD DISTANCE
Westmead Hawk (bk d Sonic Flight-Mega Delight May 2003) Owned by Bob Morton, trained by Nick Savva

BEST STAYER
Westmead Aoifa (bk b Larkhill Jo-Mega Delight Feb 2004) Owned by Ray David, trained by Nick Savva

BEST MARATHON
Roxholme Girl (bd b Pacific Mile-Gilded Choice Oct 2002) Owned by Hayley Keightley, trained by Carly Philpott/Hayley Keightley

BEST HURDLER
Suit Man (be d Droopys Kewell-Genuine Ginger Dec 2002) Owned by the Ramat Racing Club, trained by Bernie Doyle

BEST NEWCOMER
Clash Harmonica (bk d Fortune Mike-Clash Minnie Aug 2004) Owned by the Boys From Leicester Syndicate, trained by Charlie Lister

BEST BRITISH-BRED
Westmead Hawk (bk d Sonic Flight-Mega Delight May 2003) Owned by Bob Morton, trained by Nick Savva

DAM OF BEST BRITISH-BRED LITTER
Mega Delight (bd b Smooth Rumble-Knockeevan Joy Jun 1999) Owned by Bob Morton

OTHER NOMINATIONS
Sprint: Borna Miller, Centaur Striker, Driving Up Henry, Horseshoe Ping, Lenson Ace, Perrys Tango, Rhincrew Simba, Roxholme Freddie, Roxholme Ryan, Star Display, Ningbo Jack

Standard: Clash Harmonica, Cleenas Lady, Dilemmas Flight, Fear Me, Shelbourne Poopa, Geordie Parker, Westmead Joe

Stayers: Caloona Striker, Calzaghe Frisby, Daisyfield Seani, January Tiger, Ninja Blue, Westmead Olivia, Westmead Swift, Roxholme Girl, Greenacre Lin

Marathon: Countrywidecapel, Droopys Aoife, En It, Rosshill View, Star Of Dromin, Greenacre Lin

Hurdler: Baran Geronimo, Druids Mickey Jo, Jills Fault, Kaysers Hill, Ronnies Callum, Strong Flow, Taipan, Stradeen Ouzo, Thats The Bullet

British-bred: Dilemmas Flight, Fear Robben, Westmead Aoifa, Westmead Olivia, Westmead Joe, Geordie Parker

Dam: Caloona Move, Lydpal Louise.

Newcomer:Droopys Tops, Eye On the Veto, Fear Haribo, Fear Robben, Roswell Starship, Spiridon Louis, Dilemmas Flight, Calzaghe Frisby

Greyhound of the Year Roll of Honour

Year	Winner	Year	Winner
1970	Moordyke Spot	1988	Hit The Lid
1971	Dolores Rocket	1989	Waltham Abbey
1972	Patricias Hope	1990	Westmead Harry
1973	Case Money	1991	Bobs Regan
1974	Westpark Mustard	1992	Murlens Abbey
1975	Pineapple Grand	1993	Heavenly Lady
1976	Mutts Silver and Westmead Champ	1994	Westmead Chick
		1995	Staplers Jo
1977	Ballinska Band	1996	Spring Rose
1978	Lacca Champion	1997	Some Picture
1979	Desert Pilot and Kilmagoura Star	1998	Toms The Best
		1999	Chart King
1980	Sport Promoter	2000	Palace Issue
1981	Decoy Boom	2001	Rapid Ranger
1982	Lauries Panther	2002	Droopys Rhys
1983	Yankee Express	2003	Tims Crow
1984	Whisper Wishes	2004	Fire Height Dan
1985	Ballyregan Bob	2005	Westmead Hawk
1986	Ballyregan Bob	2006	Westmead Hawk
1987	Signal Spark		

Recent Winners of the Other Annual Awards

Greyhound Writers' Association

SERVICES TO GREYHOUND RACING

Bob Betts (2006), Pam Heasman (2005), David Hood (2004), Charlie Lister (2003), Bob Gilling (2002), Vinnie Jones/Ray White joint winners (2001), Linda Mullins (2000), Dave Lawrence (99), Gordon Bissett (98), Tom Smith (97), Florrie Tompsett (96), Theo Mentzis (95), Archie Newhouse (94), Lord Kimball (93), John Coleman (92), Roy Gibbons (91)

BEST BRITISH-BRED GREYHOUND

Westmead Hawk (2005), Robbie De Niro (2004), Blonde Ranger (2003), Shevchenko (2002), Sonic Flight (2001), Palace Issue (2000), Palace Issue (1999), Im Frankie (1998)

DAM OF BEST BRITISH-BRED LITTER

Mega Delight (2005), Whitefort Queen (2004) Grayslands Zoom (2003), Glencoe Star (2002), Hollinwood Major (2001), Celtic Lady (2000), Spenwood Magic (1999), Clear Issue (1998)Clear Issue (1998)

Dogs to Follow

BARNFIELD ON AIR
(Sam Poots)
Greyhound racing's four-bend superstar can
star again in 2008. His ferocious pace set up
five track records – he bettered his own at
Belle Vue – and a winter rest should see him
as fresh as paint come the spring when an
attack on the three Derbys will be launched
at Shawfield.

RIO QUANDO
(Danny Riordan)
Went close to Wimbledon record and not
disgraced on Racing Post Festival Grand
Finals' night at Walthamstow. Could be a
leading contender for the Classics from a
kennel that has supplied top-class
greyhounds in Rio Riccardo and Droopys
Corleone.

MUSTANG GARCIA
(Sam Poots)
From a kennel that has made giant strides in
2007, led by flag-bearer Barnfield On Air.
Boasts huge pace and will come on for
appearances in Romford Puppy Cup final and
Racing Post Festival second. Pall Mall looks
ideal.

FARLOE REASON
(Charlie Lister)
Ran unbeaten through the Northern Puppy
Derby. His defeat in the decider of Westmead
Keawn was later franked when that
greyhound won the Romford Puppy Cup.

BOHERBRADDA MAC
(Harry Williams)
Has good four-bend pace, and will have
gained confidence from sprint victory at
Newcastle towards back of year. On that
night he compared favourably time-wise with
leading sprinter Jetharts Here. Can win
plenty of races when stepped back up.

POND GALLILEO
(Harry Williams)
Kennel can have cracking 2008 and this
stayer can lead the way. Good enough so still
play a part over a stiff four bends, six bends
will bring out the best in him.

NINJA JAMIE
(Charlie Lister)
Thought to be just about as good as litter-
brother Farloe Reason. Injury setback caused
belated British debut, but trials and early race
experience augurs well.

BARNFIELD WOODY
(Sam Poots)
Ran well in the Racing Post Festival Maiden
and was a shade unlucky in the final. Can
come from off the pace or strike from the
front.

BALLYMAC UNDER
(Matthew Dartnall)
Early Reading and Coventry wins suggest
huge potential. A certain Patsy Byrne as
owner always catches the eye!

Sponsored by the BGRB

Previous Winners

Staged at Brough Park over 480m, and has been run over 500m, 507m, 484m, 550yds and originally 525yds. Was staged at Sunderland over 450m in 1995

2007	Wright Signal	9-4	E Parker, Sheffield	28.62
2006	Geordie Parker	EvsF	C Lister, Unattached	28.83
2005	Bell Devotion	5-2	C Lister, Unattached	28.29
2004	Tally Ho Shimmer	EvsF	J Little, Unattached	28.57
2003	Full Cigar	5-2	L McNair, Unattached	28.67
2002	Let It Slip	10-1	D Mullins, Romford	28.57
2001	Barney The Bold	2-1F	J Carmichael, Shawfield	28.63eqTR
2000	Toblermory Boy	1-2F	C Lister, Unattached	28.68
1999	Derbay Flyer	4-6F	C Lister, Unattached	28.97
1998	Stephens Hero	6-1	T Soppitt, Unattached	29.16
1997	Endon Tiger	4-6F	C Lister, Peterborough	29.10
1996	Greenwell Eagle	5-1	P Flaherty, Shawfield	28.97
1995	Just Right Jumbo	12-1	G Miller, Sunderland	27.94
1994	Moral Director	4-1	J Gibson, Belle Vue	28.97
1993	Toms Lodge	6-4F	N Johnson, Norton C.	29.20
1992	New Level	8-11F	H Williams, Unattached	28.73
1991	Monaree Tommy	3-1	J Copplestone, Portsmouth	30.75
1990	Alans Luck	4-1	R Andrews, Belle Vue	31.02
1989	Slippy Blue	11-4	K Linzell, Walthamstow	30.39
1988	Pond Hurricane	6-4Fl	H Williams, Brough P.	30.56
1987	Killouragh Chris	4-5F	P Beaumont, Sheffield	30.57
1986	Lavally Oak	8-11F	J Glass, Powderhall	30.39
1985	Moneypoint Coal	5-4F	S Graham, Ireland	30.08
1984	NOT RUN			
1983	Squire Cass	11-4	T Dartnall, Reading	30.15
1982	Long Spell	4-6F	J Booth, Unattached	30.92
1981	NOT RUN			
1980	Jon Barrie	5-2	R Andrews, Leeds	30.37
1979	Burniston Jet	5-1	R Hookway, Sheffield	29.45
1978	Champers Club	5-4F	S Milligan, Unattached	29.30
1977	Prince Hill	EvsF	J Kelly, Leeds	29.37
1976	Houghton Rip	2-1F	B Tompkins, Bletchley	29.93
1975	Show Man	4-5F	K Raggatt, Brough Park	29.21
1974	NOT RUN			
1973	Fly Dazzler	7-2	N Oliver, Brough Park	30.63
1972	Bright Tack	5-2	G Hodson, White City	30.20
1971	Spectre Jockey	4-5F	D Power, Unattached	30.54
1970	Allied Banker	3-1	M B Wilson, Unattached	30.64
1969	Jackpot Painter	5-1	M B Wilson, Unattached	30.54
1968	Pools Punter	20-1	J Brennan, Sheffield	30.57

1967	Home Grown	4-1	E Brennan, Sheffield	29.75
1966	Kilbeg Kuda	5-1	J Bassett, Unattached	29.40
1965	Booked Out	4-6F	E Adkins, Unattached	29.25
1964	Total Barber	20-1	A Prentice, Monmore	29.23
1963	Atomic Rake	20-1	R Singleton, Belle Vue	29.37
1962	West Bermuda	6-1	R Hookway, Sheffield	29.54
1961	Amys Pal	8-1	J Brennan, Sheffield	29.68
1960	Quare Flash	7-2	R Hookway, Sheffield	29.36
1959	Just Fame	3-1	T Johnston, Carntyne	29.51
1958	Simmer Down Pal	4-1	J Booth, Unattached	29.57
1957	NOT RUN			
1956	Paracelsus	5-1	N Collin, Unattached	29.30
1955	NOT RUN			
1954	Templenoe Rebel	5-1	D J Davis, Bristol	29.65
1953	Leafy Ash	6-4J	J Syder, Wembley	29.50
1952	Endless Gossip	4-11F	L Reynolds, Wembley	29.22
1951	Fancy Hero	10-3	H Harvey, Wembley	29.50
1950	Olivers Lad	7-1	P Brennan, Shawfield	29.60
1949	Intelligent Joe	9-4	L Reynolds, Wembley	29.58
1948	NOT RUN			
1947	NOT RUN			
1946	Monday's News	7-2	F G Farey, Unattached	29.55
1940-1945	NOT RUN			

THE ARC

Run at Walthamstow over 475m

2007	Too Risky	7-2	M Puzey, Walthamstow	28.70
2006	Milldean Billy	4-1	S Cahill, Walthamstow	29.19
2005	Fire Height Dan	5-2	M Puzey, Walthamstow	28.62
2004	Airtech Rapid	7-1	P Young, Walthamstow	29.21
2003	Hopeful Moment	7-2	E Gaskin, Walthamstow	28.92
2002	Vancouver Jet	3-1	L Jones, Walthamstow	28.94
2001	Scotts Kelly	9-4	J Mullins, Walthamstow	29.29
2000	Fat Boy Slim	15-8F	J Reynolds, Walthamstow	28.62
1999	El Hombre	7-2	L Mullins, Walthamstow	28.86
1998	Ceekay	10-1	L Mullins, Walthamstow	28.80
1997	Blue Murlen	13-8F	M Smith, Unattached	28.56
1996	Coom Cruiser	5-1	D Knight, Hove	28.92
1995	Westmead Merlin	EvsF	N Savva, Walthamstow	28.79
1994	Westmead Chick	8-1	N Savva, Hackney	28.73
1993	Bonney Seven	10-11F	J Coleman, Walthamstow	28.82
1992	Murlens Abbey	3-1	J Copplestone, Portsmouth	28.61
1991	Fires Of War	2-1	T Meek, Oxford	28.82
1990	Brownies Outlook	5-1	P Payne, Romford	28.94
1989	Kilcannon Bullet	33-1	J Coleman, Walthamstow	28.58
1988	Foretop	7-4F	K Linzell, Walthamstow	28.98
1987	Funny Oyster	9-2	J Sherry, Walthamstow	28.98

BALLYREGAN BOB MEMORIAL

Staged at Hove 695m

2006	Caloona Striker	EvsF	W Wrighting, Hove	41.72
2005	Caloona Striker	EvsF	W Wrighting, Hove	41.52
2004	Shebas Magic	2-5F	B Clemenson, Hove	42.02
2003	Special Trick	9-4F	L Jones	41.76
2002	Aughacasla Erin	25-1	K Tester	42.49
2001	Very Capable	3-1	T Lucas	41.50
2000	Palace Issue	1-4F	L Mullins	41.93
1999	Palace Issue	7-4	L Mullins	41.62
1998	Saleen Move	6-1	T Dartnall	42.49
1997	Musical Treat	6-1	B Clemenson	42.78
1996	Elbony Rose	3-1	N Savva	42.07
1995	Coolmona Road	11-10F	D Knight	42.06

740m

1994	Last Action	2-1	J Wileman	44.93

BLUE RIBAND

Staged at Hall Green from 1999 over 480m. Previously staged at Wembley over 490m

2007	Iceman Vader	4-1	L Burford, Coventry	28.56
2006	Westmead Joe	13-8F	N Savva, Henlow	28.58
2005	Tuttles Ronaldo	7-1	F Wright, Hall Green	28.26
2004	Droopys Oasis	5-4F	B Clemenson, Hove	28.28
2003	Farloe Verdict	5-2	C Lister, Unattached	28.09TR
2002	Hollinwood Wiz	8-1	M Clarke, Stainforth	28.45
2001	Hollinwood Chief	7-4F	M Clarke, Stainforth	28.51
2000	Vintage Cleaner	9-4	J McGee, Unattached	28.20TR
1999	Droopys Merson	EvsF	N Savva, Milton Keynes	28.53
1998	He Knows	11-4	B Draper, Sheffield	29.22
1997	Blue Murlen	2-7F	M Smith, Unattached	29.07
1996	Quick Tune	5-1	G Hodson, Hove	29.75
1995	Heres Seanie	2-7F	P Ryan, Perry Barr	28.85
1994	Ardilaun Bridge	11-10F	C Duggan, Walthamstow	29.03
1993	Hypnotic Stag	8-13F	J Coleman, Walthamstow	28.85
1992	Dempsey Duke	2-1JF	T Kibble, Bristol	28.87
1991	Wuncross Double	33-1	D Knight, Hove	29.02
1990	Westmead Harry	7-4F	N Savva, Milton Keynes	29.09
1989	Ring Slippy	3-1	D Millen, Canterbury	29.64
1988	Pike Alert	7-1	T Foster, Wimbledon	29.18
1987	Sambuca	16-1	G Smith, Hove	29.08
1986	Fearless Champ	8-11F	G De Mulder, Oxford	29.04
1985	Lulus Hero	3-1	G Smith, Hove	29.23
1984	Living Trail	50-1	J Honeysett, Wembley	29.69
1983	Cross Times	7-2	J Fisher, Reading	30.01
1982	Master Darby	7-2	J Fisher, Reading	29.88
1981	Arfur Mo	20-1	J Honeysett, Crayford	29.47

BRIGHTON BELLE

Bitches-only race at Hove over 515m from 1981, and previously 500m (1975-1980)

2007	Jazz Hurricane	4-5F	D.Knight, Hove	30.33
2006	Lady Sky	5-2	B Clemenson, Hove	29.81
2005	Shelbourne Nina	5-4F	B Clemenson, Hove	29.77
2004	Droopys Savanna	11-4F	B Clemenson, Hove	29.93
2003	Carn Breeze	3-1	C Lund, Stainforth	29.62
2002	Droopys Candice	3-1	G Sallis, Reading	29.85
2001	Senahel Ridge	3-1	O'McKenna, Wimbledon	29.97
2000	Danielles Minx	14-1	D Knight, Hove	30.03
1999	Im Okay	1-3F	B Draper, Sheffield	29.96
1998	She Can Boogie	3-1	B McBride, Harlow	30.43
1997	Droopys Trisha	3-1	C Duggan, Walthamstow	30.38
1996	Mountain Hope	6-1	R Young,Hove	30.22
1995	Sydney Miss	11-8F	B Masters, Hove	30.55
1994	Westmead Chick	4-7F	N Savva, Unattached	29.86
1993	Wexford Minx	6-1	D Knight, Hove	30.32
1992	Roving Trumpet	3-1	J Rouse, Hove	30.22
1991	Satharn Lady	7-4F	J Coleman, Walthamstow	30.01
1990	Westmead Chloe	7-1	N.Savva, Unattached	30.71
1989	Greenfield Madam	4-11F	P Coughlan, Crayford	30.22
1988	Coppertone	3-1	G Baggs, Walthamstow	30.21
1987	Westmead Move	1-4F	N Savva, Unattached	29.79
1986	Soft Lips	6-1	G Curtis, Hove	30.37
1985	Lisas Girl	15-8F	P Rees, Wimbledon	30.16
1984	Rushwee Pecos	5-2F	G Curtis, Hove	30.35
1983	Blue Total	8-1	N Gleeson, Wimbledon	30.45
1982	Sundridge Racing	EvsF	T Dennis, Southend	30.10
1981	Creepy Tulip	11-4	P Rees, Wimbledon	30.35
1980	Sunny Interval	6-1	P Rees, Wimbledon	29.56
1979	Masslock Lady	11-10F	G Curtis, Hove	29.14
1978	Loyal Katie	4-1	J Honeysett, Crayford	29.82

CESAREWITCH

Staged at Oxford over 645m from 2001. Previously staged over 718m at Catford (1995-2000); Belle Vue over 880 yards (1972-74), 815m (1975-84, and 1987) and 853m (1985-86, and 1988-94) and West Ham over 880yds, 600yds and 550yds (1928-1971)

2007	Dark Hondo	5-4F	P Foster, Swindon	39.80
2005	Zigzag Stewart	3-1	J McCombe, Belle Vue	39.61
2004	Solid Money	9-4	D Knight, Hove	39.56
2003	Maxie Rumble	EvsF	J Mullins, Walthamstow	39.62
2002	Cuba	4-5F	B Clemenson, Hove	40.18
2001	Solid Magic	11-10F	B Clemenson, Hove	39.72
2000	Lady Jean	11-8F	K Tester, Catford	45.63
1999	Bubbly Prince	4-6F	P Cusack, Crayford	45.90
1998	Fourth Ace	9-4	B Wileman, Perry Barr	47.01

Year	Greyhound	Odds	Trainer, Track	Time
1997	Tralee Crazy	1-2F	N Savva, Walthamstow	45.69
1996	Elbony Rose	11-10F	N Savva, Walthamstow	45.90
1995	Ballarue Minx	5-4	W Masters, Hove	45.98
1994	Sandollar Louie	10-1	K Connor, Canterbury	55.20
1993	Killenagh Dream	20-1	C Lister, Stainforth	55.21
1992	Zap	12-1	Honeyfield, Perry Barr	55.44
1991	Wayzgoose	20-1	D Hawkes, Walthamstow	55.30
1990	Carlsberg Champ	5-4F	B Silkman, Unattached	55.50
1989	Minnies Siren	6-4F	K Linzell, Walthamstow	56.03
1988	Pround To Run	7-1	H White, Canterbury	56.23
1987	Role Of Fame	1-7F	A Hitch, Wimbledon	52.41
1986	Yankee's Shadow	4-7F	G Curtis, Brighton	54.90
1985	Scurlogue Champ	1-3F	G Drake, Unattached	54.62
1984	Mobile Bank	7-4F	E Gaskin, Unattached	52.92
1983	Jo's Gamble	5-2	J Fisher, Reading	50.90
1982	Liga Lad	6-4JF	D Vass, Unattached	51.83
1981	Kinda Friendly	7-4F	E Gaskin, Unattached	52.68
1980	Linkside Liquor	3-1	G Bailey, Yarmouth	51.22
1979	Roystons Supreme	7-4	A Jackson, Wembley	51.47
1978	Sporting Blue	7-2	H Crapper, Sheffield	51.20
1977	Montreen	4-6F	E Bamford, Belle Vue	51.64
1976	Moy Summer	16-1	E Bamford, Belle Vue	51.32
1975	Silver Sceptre	4-1	R Young, Milton Keynes	52.31
1974	Westbrook Quinn	7-2	J E Coulter, Unattached	52.17
1973	Country Maiden	5-2	F Baldwin, Perry Barr	52.46
1972	Westmead Lane	11-4	N Savva, Unattached	51.65
1971	Whisper Billy	50-1	C Coyle, Unattached	33.45
1970	Gleneagle Comedy	10-1	R Hookay, Sheffield	33.25
1969	Cals Pick	6-4JF	H Harvey, Wembley	32.98
1968	Deen Valley	4-5F	P Keane, Clapton	33.29
1967	Silver Hope	2-1JF	P Keane, Clapton	32.99
1966	Rostown Victor	66-1	J Johnston, West Ham	34.06
1965	Lucky Montforte	5-1	J Bassett, Unattached	33.00
1964	Clifden Orbit	4-1	T Johnston, West Ham	33.08
1963	Jehu II	9-4	G Hodson, White City	33.15
1962	Dromin Glory	11-10F	J Bassett, Clapton	32.97
1961	Prairie Flash	9-4	H Harvey, Wembley	32.91
1960	Rostown Genius	2-1	J Pickering, White City	33.29
1959	Mile Bush Pride	2-7F	H Harvey, Wembley	32.66
1958	Pigalle Wonder	8-11F	J Syder, Wembley	33.06
1958	DH Rylane Pleasure	3-1	H Harvey, Wembley	33.06
1957	Scoutbush	7-4F	M Burls, Wembley	33.05
1956	Coming Champion	9-2	J Syder, Wembley	33.02
1955	Gulf Of Darien	4-6F	H Harvey, Wembley	32.99
1954	Matchlock	7-2	T Brennan, Sheffield	33.03
1953	Magourna Reject	1-4F	T Reilly, Walthamstow	33.24

1952	Shaggy Swank	5-1	T Lightfoot, Unattached	34.03
1951	Prionsa Luath	10-1F	M Burls, Wembley	33.77
1950	Quare Customer	11-10F	L Reynolds, Wembley	30.80
1949	Drumgoon Boy	4-9F	F Davis, Unattached	30.71
1948	Local Interprize	11-4F	S Biss, Clapton	30.88
1947	Red Tan	100-8	T Baldwin, Perry Barr	31.30
1946	Col Skookum	4-1	S Orton, Wimbledon	31.28
1945	Hurry Kitty	5-4F	W H Mill, Unattached	31.26
1939-1944	NOT RUN			
1938	Ballyjoker	3-1	S Orton, Wimbledon	34.02
1937	Jesmond Cutlet	11-4	D Hawkesley, West Ham	34.56
1936	Ataxy	2-1	L Reynolds, White City	31.24
1935	Grand Flight II	33-1	J Syder, Wembley	33.97
1934	Brilliant Bob	9-2	S Orton, Wimbledon	33.80
1933	Elsell	100-7	W R Dixon, White City	34.22
1932	Future Cutlet	2-7F	S Probert, Wembley	34.11
1931	Future Cutlet	10-11F	S Probert, Wembley	34.03
1930	Mick The Miller	1-7F	S Orton, Wimbledon	34.11
1929	Five Of Hearts	1-4F	T Cudmore, Wembley	24.82
1928	Dicks Son	6-4JF	W Fear, White City	34.38

CHAMPION HURDLE

460m Wimbledon

2007	Newlawn Berts	9-4f	P Cusack, Crayford	27.96
2006	Stradeen Ouzo	11-4	D Mullins, Romford	28.47
2005	Druids Mickey Jo	4-5F	S Cahill, Wimbledon	28.07
2004	Joe Bananas	6-4JF	N Colton, Oxford	28.23
2003	Farloe Browny	10-1	S Cahill, Wimbledon	28.09
2002	Top Jock	3-1	S Cahill, Wimbledon	28.70
2001	Born To Go	7-2	T Foster, Wimbledon	28.52
2000	Rackethall Rover	8-1	P Byrne, Wimbledon	28.27
1999	Monumental	25-1	T Foster, Wimbledon	28.49
1998	Strideaway Teddy	5-2	T Foster, Wimbledon	28.66
1997	Westmead Panda	3-1	N Savva, Walthamstow	28.19
1996	Glown Fox	6-4F	T Foster, Wimbledon	28.43
1995	Arrogant Prince	5-2	T Foster, Wimbledon	28.29
1994	Gis A Smile	1-1F	P Rees, Wimbledon	27.96

CHAMPION STAKES

Run at Romford over 575m

2007	Eye Onthe Veto	4-5F	M Wallis, Walthamstow	35.54
2006	Son Of Phoebe	6-4F	B Clemenson, Hove	35.49
2005	Denmarknick	9-4JF	P Rich, Romford	35.93
2004	Centour Para	5-1	B Clemenson, Hove	35.69
2003	Clover Top	11-8F	B Clemenson, Hove	35.34
2002	Cooly Cougar	3-1	B Clemenson, Hove	35.22

2001	El Othello	7-1	J McGee, Unattached	35.51
2000	Palace Issue	5-4F	L Mullins, Walthamstow	35.44
1999	Touchwood Gent	6-1	J Quinn, Romford	35.81
1998	Pottos Storm	11-1	D Mullins, Romford	35.12
1997	Elderberry Chick	2-5F	P Ryan, Unattached	34.86TR
1996	Lady Ellie	3-1	J Coleman, Walthamstow	35.19
1995	Westmead Merlin	4-9F	N Savva, Walthamstow	35.20
1994	Heres Seanie	6-4F	P Ryan, Perry Barr	35.22
1993	Westmead Surprise	3-1	N Savva, Unattached	36.05
1992	Chic Mona	11-4	E Gaskin, Walthamstow	35.58
1991	Sail Over	10-1	S Sykes, Wimbledon	35.28
1990	Sail Over	7-2	S Sykes, Wimbledon	36.06
1989	Sard	10-11F	J McGee, Canterbury	35.47
1988	Dads Flier	5-1	J Sherry, Walthamstow	35.79

CIRCUIT

Staged over 475m at Walthamstow

2007	Jazz Hurricane	EvsF	D Knight, Hove	28.69
2006	Cobra Striking	6-4F	E Gaskin, Walthamstow	28.92
2005	Kindred Rebel	7-1	M Puzey, Walthamstow	28.67
2004	Margan Bluebell	7-4	L Jones, Walthamstow	28.96
2003	Lozzas Dream	5-4F	D Knight, Hove	29.00
2002	Palacemews Lad	5-2	J Mullins, Walthamstow	29.02
2001	Blue Gooner	5-4F	J Mullins, Walthamstow	28.77
2000	Mumble Swerve	8-1	L Jones, Walthamstow	28.68
1999	Ceekay	5-2	L Mullins, Walthamstow	28.90
1998	Knockrour Casper	7-1	E Gaskin, Walthamstow	28.94
1997	Velvet Tom	5-2JF	D Firmager, Unattached	28.86
1996	Forward Venture	11-4	C Duggan, Walthamstow	28.70
1995	Countrywide Fox	4-5F	J Coleman, Walthamstow	29.00
1994	Connells Cross	7-1	E Gaskin, Walthamstow	28.55

Run at Belle Vue over 670m (647m to 2005)

COCK O' THE NORTH

2007	Charlies Dream	12-1	O Kueres, B Vue	40.60
2006	Roxholme Boy	EvsF	C Philpott, Coventry	40.77
2005	Droopys Sporty	8-1	B Draper, Sheffield	39.42
2004	Black Pear	11-8	W Wrighting, Hove	39.50
2003	Ali Qapu Oak	8-1	R Ward, Milton Keynes	39.68
2002	Illinois Icon	7-4F	J Mullins, Walthamstow	40.13
2001	Blackrock Issue	2-1	J Walton, Belle Vue	40.40
2000	Ruby Willows	9-2	P Stringer, Unattached	39.57
1999	Blind Joe	8-1	J Gibson, Belle Vue	40.69
1998	Millstream Lad	4-11F	A O'Flaherty	40.24
1997	Winetavern Tiger	9-4F	J Costello	40.61
1996	Thornfield Dino	4-1	A Coulton	40.32

| 1995 | Justright Melody | 3-1 | T Robinson | 40.38 |
| 1994 | Saints Charlie | 14-1 | P Branagh | 40.76 |

DORANDO MARATHON

Wimbledon 872m

2007	Charlies Dream	12-1	O Kueres, B Vue	40.60
2006	Call Girl	16-1	P Foster, Swindon	54.97
2005	Greenacre Lln	5-4F	B Clemenson, Hove	54.26
2004	Greenacre Lin	5-1	B Clemenson, Hove	54.86
2003	Ericas Equity	12-1	P Young, Walthamstow	55.47

Wimbledon 868m

2002	Lislevane Champ	16-1	J Reynolds, Walthamstow	55.46
2001	Cloheena Dingo	6-1	M Purdy, Reading	55.21
2000	Spenwood Gem	7-2	R Hough, Sheffield	55.31
1999	Jenilyn	12-1	R Foster, Wimbledon	55.56
1998	Marys Gem	5-1	M Lavender, Portsmouth	56.31
1997	Moanrue Slippy	5-4F	E Gaskin, Walthamstow	54.77
1996	Hillmount Gem	5-4F	D Vowles, Hackney	54.88
1995	Smart Decision	1-2F	E Gaskin, Walthamstow	55.24
1994	Smart Decision	1-5F	E Gaskin, Private	54.17
1993	Deenside Fire	11-8F	K Shearman, Private	55.00
1992	Lilac Wonder	2-1	P Stringer, Cradley	55.32
1991	Clonbrin Basket	1-1F	G Sharp, Walthamstow	54.93
1990	Citywide Suzy	1-8F	M Douglass, Private	55.63
1989	Sail On Valerie	11-4	E Gaskin, Walthamstow	55.00
1988	Kellymount Suzie	7-4F	D Platts, Canterbury	55.23
1987	Silver Mask	1-2F	B Masters, Hove	54.55
1986	Belladare	10-11F	L Simmons, Rye House	54.98
1985	Scurlogue Champ	1-10F	K Peckham, Ipswich	55.14

White City 962m

1984	Gala Special	2-1	B O'Connor, Walthamstow	60.40
1983	Sandy Lane	2-7F	G Curtis, Hove	60.08
1982	Jack O'Hearts	2-1	P Held, Ipswich	60.56
1981	Corboy Champion	6-4	G Curtis, Hove	60.09
1980	Keem Princess	10-11F	R Wilkes, Hall Green	59.98
1979	Portland Dusty	11-8F	F Melville, Harringay	59.81TR
1978	NOT RUN			
1977	Doverdale Lady	6-4JF	R Wood, Gloucester	60.07TR
1976	VOID			
1975	Hopeful Arkle	6-1	M Downes, Sheffield	60.25TR

EAST ANGLIAN DERBY

Originally run over 500 yards, it is now staged over 462m at Yarmouth

2007	Blackrose Mars	11-2	E Cantillon, Mildenhall	27.71
2006	Geordie Parker	EvsF	C Lister, Doncaster	27.94
2005	Fear No One	3-1	M Wallis, Walthamstow	28.73

2004	Fire Height Dan	9-4	M Puzey, Walthamstow	28.06
2003	Burberry Boy	EvsF	C Lister, Unattached	28.01
2002	Larkhill Bullet	6-4F	C Lister, Unattached	28.22
2001	Hanover Peer	16-1	R Pleasants, Yarmouth	28.48
2000	Courts Legal	15-8F	L Jones, Walthamstow	28.27
1999	Caseys Shadow	11-2	R Samson, Reading	27.93
1998	Ceekay	7-2	L Mullins, Walthamstow	28.27
1997	Terrydrum Kate	11-4	C Lister, Nottingham	28.28
1996	Blue Murlen	11-10F	J Harding, Yarmouth	28.10
1995	Dragon Prince	11-4	C Lister, Nottingham	28.56
1994	Franks Doll	5-1	J Scott, Unattached	29.38
1993	Just Right Kyle	10-11F	C Lister, Unattached	28.30
1992	Murlens Abbey	4-6F	J Copplestone, Portsmouth	28.19
1991	Dempsey Duke	7-4	T Kibble, Bristol	27.68
1990	Artie Joe	3-1	C Lister, Unattached	28.57
1989	Castleivy Mick	7-2	F Greenacre, Unattached	28.27
1988	Curryhills Gara	8-13F	E Gaskin, Unattached	28.35
1987	Money Matters	4-11F	G De Mulder, Unattached	28.27
1986	Short Answer	2-1	K Linzell, Walthamstow	28.34
1985	Ballygroman Jim	5-1	E Gaskin, Peterborough	28.51
1984	Blueberry Gold	9-1	I Parker, Peterborough	28.88
1983	Creamery Cross	5-4JF	A Briggs, Unattached	28.29
1982	Swift Rapier	6-4	B O'Connor, Walthamstow	28.24
1981	Swift Band	7-4	C Lister, Unattached	28.33
1980	Kilrickle Star	6-4F	N Simmons, Unattached	28.44
1979	Our Rufus	2-1	J Coleman, Walthamstow	28.44
1978	Our Rufus	7-2	J Coleman, Wembley	28.30
1977	Westmead Dance	EvsF	J Wells, Yarmouth	28.24
1976	Huberts Town	6-1	R Wilding, Bletchley	28.57
1975	Another Gear	2-1	R Wilding, Bletchley	28.36

FIRST RUN IN 1947

THE ECLIPSE

Staged at Nottingham over 500m

2007	Rev Counter	6-1	C Allsopp, Monmore	29.91
2006	Clash Harmonica	5-2	C Lister, Unattached	29.50
2005	Fear Me	4-5F	C Lister, Doncaster	29.47
2004	Ballybrazil Hero	3-1	B Clemenson, Hove	30.53
2003	Rockforest Pride	9-4	D Pruhs, Peterborough	30.49
2002	Texan Fox	7-2	J McGee Jnr, Unattached	29.74
2001	Bold Mossy	4-1	J Reynolds, WalthamStow	30.09
2000	Blue Tex	6-4JF	B Clemenson, Hove	30.03
1999	Mumble Swerve	7-2	L Jones, Walthamstow	30.52
1998	Laughta Man	7-2	B Mills, Perry Barr	30.21
1997	Larkhill Jo	EvsF	N Savva, Walthamstow	30.48
1996	Some Picture	3-1JF	C Lister, Nottingham	29.83

1995	Moyle Knight	9-4	D Pruhs, Peterborough	29.85
1994	Spit It Out	14-1	M Bacon, Perry Barr	29.80
1993	Tromora Mayor	20-1	H Johnson, Norton Canes	29.99
1992	New Level	9-4JF	H Williams, Sunderland	29.94
1991	Moyglare King	14-1	P McCombe, Belle Vue	30.47
1990	Bawnard It	12-1	J McGee, Hackney	30.69
1989	Westmead Harry	12-1	N Savva, Unattached	30.30
1988	Gulleen Wishes	5-2	D Conway, Swaffham	18.62
1987	Holiday Hope	2-1JF	P Ryan, Monmore	30.81
1986	NOT RUN			
1985	Parkers Gold	4-1	B Gaynor, Hall Green	28.73
1984	Tinahue Blond	7-1	B Gaynor, Coventry	28.67
1983	Ballyard McEnroe	3-1	B Gaynor, Coventry	28.83
1982	Ardralla Victor	7-4	M Buckland, Norton Canes	28.67
1981	Red Prim	9-4	Barratt, Cradley Heath	28.94
1980	Inca Boy	7-4F	L Pugh, Hall Green	28.42
1979	Sarahs Bunny	4-6F	G De Mulder, Hall Green	28.74

ESSEX VASE

Staged at Romford over 575m from 1994 and 1978-1989. Over 400m in 1990-1993; 600m (1975-1977); 650yds (1966-1974); 460yds (1949); 550yds (1940) and 460yds (1939)

2007	Eye On The Veto	4-9F	M Wallis, Walthamstow	35.30
2006	Eye Onthe Veto	4-5F	M Wallis, Walthamstow	35.99
2005	Eye Onthe Ball	16-1	P Young, Romford	36.26
2004	Loughteen Flyer	8-1	J Faint, Rye House	35.76
2003	Orient Ron	5-4F	B Clemenson, Hove	36.61
2002	Top Power	4-1	L Jones, Walthamstow	35.60
2001	Willowgrove Pal	2-1F	P Byrne, Wimbledon	36.06
2000	Ardera Laura	11-2	K Wyatt, Sittingbourne	35.98
1999	Honky Tonk Gal	8-1	L Jones, Romford	36.44
1998	El Loco	9-2	L Mullins, Walthamstow	35.77
1997	Lenson Billy	4-9F	N McEllistrim, Wimbledon	35.50
1996	El Tenor	4-1	L Mullins, Walthamstow	35.96
1995	NOT RUN			
1994	Lisa My Girl	EvsF	J Coleman, Walthamstow	35.69
1993	Up And Off	2-1F	E Gaskin, Walthamstow	24.70
1992	Frost Hill	5-1	L Mullins, Walthamstow	24.05
1991	Vics Snowdrop	5-1	P Rees, Wimbledon	24.34
1990	No Doubt	8-1	P Payne, Romford	24.02
1989	Poker Prince	8-1	P Rees, Wimbledon	35.44
1988	Double Bid	10-11F	P Rees, Wimbledon	35.27
1987	Silver Walk	5-1	E Gaskin, Unattached	35.56
1986	Rosehip Trish	11-10F	E Wiley, Hackney	35.49
1985	Ballyregan Bob	1-2F	G Curtis, Hove	35.15TR
1984	Wheelers Tory	4-1	P Wheeler, Unattached	35.45
1983	Winning Line	2-1F	B Foley, Unattached	35.36

1982	Glenmoy Raven	12-1	A Hitch, Unattached	36.03
1981	Shandy Edie	5-1	D Ingram-Seal, Unattached	35.48
1980	Taranaki	20-1	P Rich, Ramsgate	35.82
1979	Black Haven	6-1	P Payne, Romford	35.55
1978	Bermuda's Fun	4-1	K Usher, Romford	35.15TR
1977	Xmas Holiday	6-1	P Rees, Wimbledon	37.40
1976	Westmead Myra	7-4F	N Savva, Bletchley	36.69
1975	Handy High	11-10F	S Milligan, Unattached	36.62
1974	Cowpark Yank	5-2	T Duggan, Romford	36.70
1973	Kenneally Moor	4-1	S Orton, Wimbledon	36.91
1972	Fit Me In	8-1	J Singleton, Harringay	36.59
1971	Dolores Rocket	EvsF	White, Unattached	36.06TR
1970	Quail's Glory	8-1	E Parker, West Ham	36.38
1969	Tarry's Gay Lady	3-1	P Rees, Wimbledon	36.54
1968	Dick's Dilemma	3-1	G Hodson, White City	36.49
1967	Mel's Talent	11-10F	P Keane, Clapton	36.74
1966	Shamrock Clipper	4-5F	P Rees, Wimbledon	36.76
1950-1965	NOT RUN			
1949	Reynold's Maiden	EvsF	J Pinborough, Unattached	27.19
1948	Trev's Idol	9-1	F Trevillion, Unattached	26.26
1947	Humming Bee	4-6F	J Biss, Clapton	26.27
1946	Humming Bee	7-2	J Biss, Clapton	26.12
1941-1945	NOT RUN			
1940	Shamrock Peggy	7-2	C Crowley, Park Royal	32.75
1939	Happy Squire	4-1	S H Gray, Southend	27.75

FENGATE COLLAR

Staged at Peterborough over 420 metres

2007	Blonde Buster	6-4F	J Mullins, Unattached	25.61
2006	Bea Twinks Chief	10-1	C. Coulson	25.92
2005	Fear No One	8-11F	M Wallis, Walthamstow	25.74
2004	Ballydaniel Bozz	9-4	D Pruhs, Peterborough	26.46
2003	Bodell Honcho	8-1	H Kemp	25.64
2002	Pineapple Euro	1-1F	M Compton	25.45
2001	Midway Chance	3-1	G Drage	25.82
2000	Catunda Lord	6-1	D Pruhs, Peterborough	25.82
1999	Time N Tide	1-1F	L Jones	25.41
1998	Ballymacoda Sir	6-1	P Rich, Romford	25.79
1997	High Tech Lady	10/1	J March	25.78
1996	Spring Gamble	EvsF	D Pruhs, Peterborough	25.67
1995	Nikki Tanner	7-2	C Duggan	25.54

GOLD COLLAR

Staged at Belle Vue over 590m (465m in 2005 and 647m in 2004). Previously staged at Catford over 555m (1975-2003), 610yds (1972-1974), 570yds (1963-1971), 440yds (1936-1962), 540yds (1934-1935) and 400yds (1933)

2007	Vatican Jinky	9-2	P Rosney, Monmore	35.06TR
2006	Roxholme Girl	8-15F	C Philpott, Coventry	35.14
2005	Bat On	4-7F	C Lister, Unattached	27.34TR
2004	Roxholme Girl	4-6F	H Keightley, Unattached	39.01TR
2003	Toms Little Jo	3-1	G Baggs, Walthamstow	34.56
2002	Shevchenko	4-5F	S Cahill, Wimbledon	35.13
2001	Haughty Ted	2-1	D Luckhurst, Crayford	35.26
2000	Castlelyons Dani	5-4F	A Hitch, Wimbledon	35.04
1999	Rio Scorpio	12-1	D Riordan, Harlow	34.83
1998	Pure Patches	11-10F	D Luckhurst, Crayford	34.68
1997	Lenson Billy	1-2F	N McEllistrim, Wimbledon	35.02
1996	Homeside Knight	7-1	T Gates, Catford	34.80
1995	Alans Rose	11-10F	J Coleman, Walthamstow	34.61
1994	Pearls Girl	7-4JF	S Sykes, Wimbledon	34.82
1993	Ardcollum Hilda	5-4F	P Byrne, Wimbledon	34.84
1992	Westmead Surprise	6-4	N Savva, Milton Keynes	34.75
1991	Appleby Lisa	5-1	H Dodds, Norton Canes	34.67
1990	Dempseys Whisper	9-4F	P Byrne, Canterbury	34.84
1989	Burgess Ruby	11-8F	D Boyce, Hackney	34.72
1988	Sard	6-4	J McGee, Canterbury	34.61
1987	Half Awake	4-1	Barry Silkman, Unattached	34.90
1986	Westmead Move	11-4	N Savva, Unattached	34.80
1985	Black Whirl	5-1	T Gates, Unattached	34.99
1984	Wheelers Tory	11-4	P Wheeler, Unattched	35.05
1983	Rathduff Tad	7-1	T Dennis, Southend	35.13
1982	Donna's Dixie	13-8	H Kibble, Bristol	35.19
1981	Laughing Sam	4-1	B Goode, Hall Green	35.50
1980	Sport Promoter	8-15F	P Mullins, Cambridge	35.06
1979	Gay Flash	7-2	S R Milligan, Catford	35.08
1978	I'm A Smasher	7-1	J Coleman, Wembley	35.31
1977	Westmead Power	11-4	N Savva, Bletchley	34.98
1976	Westmead Champ	4-7F	P Heasman, Hackney	35.02
1975	Abbey Glade	11-4	G Curtis, Hove	34.97
1974	Leaders Champion	8-11F	D Geggus, Walthamstow	35.02
1973	Ramdeen Stuart	1-3F	N Oliver, Brough Park	35.04
1972	Rathmartin	7-4	C Orton, Wimbledon	35.36
1971	Down Your Way	5-2	H Warrell, Unattached	33.10
1970	Cameo Lawrence	8-1	A W Smith, Catford	33.84
1969	Surprising Fella	2-1J	A W Smith, Catford	33.40
1968	Shanes Rocket	7-2	S R Milligan, Unattached	33.39
1967	Stylish Lad	5-2	A W Smith, Catford	33.75
1966	Dark Symphony	100-8	P Collet, Unattached	33.21

1965	Friday Morning	11-10F	R Chamberlain, Unattached	33.73
1964	Mighty Wind	33-1	G Waterman, Wimb.	33.36
1963	Music Guest	5-2	T Johnston, West Ham	33.36
1962	Super Orange	4-1	P Heasman, Unattached	25.51
1961	Long Story	20-1	P R Rees, Unattached	25.69
1960	Catch Cold	8-1	D Hannafin, Wimbledon	25.56
1959	Dunstown Warrior	11-4	T Reilly, Walthamstow	25.77
1958	Five Up	6-4F	R Chamberlain, Unattached	25.43
1957	Silent Worship	4-11F	J Bassett, Unattached	25.50
1956	Ponsford	10-1	N Colin, Unattached	25.69
1955	Firgrove Slipper	7-2	J Syder, Wembley	26.35
1954	Ardskeagh Ville	9-4	D Barker, Catford	25.86
1953	Mushera Silver	13-2	I Gould, Unattached	25.70
1952	Hectic Birthday	10-1	B Melville, Wembley	25.41
1951	Loyal Accomplice	4-5F	T Reilly, Walthamstow	25.63
1950	Islandeady	8-1	H G Copsey, Unattached	26.07
1949	Local Interprize	6-4	S Biss, Clapton	25.88
1948	Local Interprize	8-13F	S Biss, Clapton	25.71
1947	Trevs Perfection	7-1	F Trevillion, Unattached	25.52
1946	King Silver	9-4	C Crowley, Clapton	25.88
1945	Ballyhennessy Seal	9-4	S Martin, Wimbledon	25.45
1944-1941	NOT RUN			
1940	Cash Balance	100-7	S Probert, Wembley	25.74
1939	Grosvenor Ferdinand	13-2	F S Rolfe, Unattached	25.92
1938	Junior Classic	11-8F	J Harmon, Wimbledon	25.77
1937	Avion Ballerino	6-1	J Hannafin, Wimbledon	25.87
1936	Fine Jubilee	4-5F	M Yate, Unattached	26.00
1935	Bosham	5-1	L Reynolds, White City	32.84
1934	Davesland	7-1	H Harvey, Harringay	32.70
1933	Wild Woolley	1-3F	J Rimmer, W. City (Man)	26.63

GOLDEN CREST

Staged at Poole over 450m

2007	Rhyzome Wizard	3-1	G Cleverley, Swindon	26.61
2006	Farloe Stormy	6-4F	P Foster	27.27
2005	Pennys Cadet	7-2	J Burridge	27.12
2004	Foxcover Jed	9-4JF	D Mann	27.39
2003	Palacemews Lad	8-1	J Mullins	27.03
2002	Blue Gooner	6-4	B Clemenson	26.90
2001	Docs Arizona	13-8JF	O McKenna	27.24
2000	Arleswood Spirit	9-4	O McKenna	27.30

GOLDEN JACKET

Run at Crayford from 1987 over 714m (540m in 1987). Previously staged at Monmore over 647m in 1986; Hall Green over 663 in 1985 and Harringay over 660m (1975-1984)

2007	Walk The Line	8-1	P Cusack, Crayford	46.00
2006	Greenacre Lin	4-1	B Clemenson, Hove	46.23
2005	Milldean Clarky	7-1	B O'Sullivan, Crayford	45.28
2004	Midway Tomsscout	12-1	H Chalkley, Henlow	44.72
2003	Centour Corker	11-8F	B Clemenson, Hove	44.74TR
2002	Sundar Storm	14-1	K Marlow, Romford	46.37
2001	Blues Best Tayla	7-4	P Young, Romford	45.19TR
2000	Knappogue Oak	3-1	K Bebbington, Monmore	45.37
1999	Gottabegood	11-2	P Garland, Sittingbourne	46.09
1998	El Onda	22-1	L Mullins, Walthamstow	46.36
1997	Broadacres Lad	7-1	T Dartnall, Wimbledon	46.08
1996	Coolmona Road	5-4F	D Knight, Hove	45.75
1995	Wexford Minx	13-8F	D Knight, Hove	45.67
1994	Wexford Minx	11-4JF	D Knight, Hove	45.83
1993	Heavenly Lady	2-5F	L Mullins, Walthamstow	45.33
1992	Bobs Regan	5-1	B Timcke, Unattached	46.10
1991	Bobs Regan	6-1	B Timcke, Unattached	47.00
1990	Chicita Banana	9-4	J McGee, Hackney	45.75
1989	Time Lord	10-1	H Dickson, Wembley	46.03
1988	Decoy Princess	7-2	T Lucas, Unattached	46.30
1987	Clover Park	10-1	J Gibbons, Crayford	35.40
1986	Glenowen Queen	5-2	D Hawkes, Walthamstow	40.92
1985	Keem Rocket	8-11F	A Meek, Swindon	41.67
1984	Amazing Man	5-2	D Knight, Hove	40.88
1983	Minnies Matador	4-1	P Milligan, Unattacged	40.69
1982	Try Travelscene	7-2	A J Mobley, Unattached	40.61
1981	Just It	7-2	T Duggan, Romford	40.67
1980	Brainy Prince	2-1JF	R Hayward, Coventry	40.63
1979	Westmead Bound	2-1	N Savva, Wembley	41.02
1978	Black Legend	7-4F	T Dickson, Slough	41.09
1977	Sindys Flame	11-10F	J Honeysett, Unattached	40.99
1976	Glin Bridge	9-4	G Curtis, Hove	40.59
1975	Nice One Cyril	11-4JF	C Coyle, Unattached	40.86

GOLDEN SPRINT

Run at Romford over 400m

2007	Black Taxi	5-1	J Mullins, Unattached	24.91
2006	Driving Up Henry	20-1	P Sallis, Hall Green	24.99
2005	Droopys Sammer	4-1	P Young, Romford	24.46
2004	Shes Our Star	10-1	P Young, Romford	24.34
2003	Tims Crow	2-1	P Rich, Romford	24.29
2002	Kinda Magic	11-10F	L Jones, Walthamstow	24.29
2001	Kinda Magic	2-1	L Jones, Walthamstow	24.18
2000	El Boss	11-4F	L Mullins, Walthamstow	24.28

1999	Spring Raider	5-2	J Brennan, Unattached	24.28
1998	Glenquin Blackie	7-4F	G De Mulder, Unattached	24.09
1997	King Oscar	4-5F	C Lister, Unattached	24.33
1996	Boys Dream	8-1	T Kibble, Bristol	24.39
1995	Countrywide Cub	2-1F	J Coleman, Walthamstow	24.44
1994	Witches Dean	4-1	P Rich, Romford	24.28
1993	Fast Copper	5-4F	J Copplestone, Reading	24.43
1992	Dealing Screen	9-4JF	K Linzell, Romford	24.90
1991	Murlens Lord	4-1	K Linzell, Romford	24.99
1990	Demesne Chance	9-4F	C Smith, Hove	24.56
1989	River Loch	3-1	L Mullins, Romford	24.32
1988	Minor Misfit	7-2	G Baggs, Walthamstow	24.20
1987	Aulton Henri	6-1	N McEllistrim, Wimbledon	24.27

GOODWOOD CUP

Staged at Walthamstow over 475m

2006	Lambstown Blue	11-4F	A Johnson, Unattached	28.72
2005	Abbot Pete	6-4F	M Puzey, Walthamstow	28.88
2004	Cocks Hero	9-4	C Lister	29.30
2003	Iceman Merlin	1-1F	T Lucas	28.75
2002	Count Sid Out	9-4	J Faint	28.67
2001	Whats Up Harry	11-4F	C Philpott	29.08
2000	El Mito	5-1	L Mullins	29.00
1999	Bossy Wade	2-1	L Mullins	29.08

GORTON CUP

Staged over 465m at Belle Vue

2007	Manic Mile	6-4F	G Hutt, Unattached	27.91
2006	Ballymac Rooster	7-4	C Philpott, Coventry	27.69
2005	Joes Gem	7-1	O Kueres	27.71
2004	Holdyoursilence	10-1	E McNair	27.72
2003	Lockup Firedice	8-1	J Mullins	27.87
2002	Pack Them In	5-6F	A Heyes	29.05
2001	Forans Field	9-2	B Draper	27.81
2000	Farloe Cobbler	1-1F	B Draper	28.02
1999	Thornfield Flash	5-4F	R Coulton	28.23
1998	Spoonbill Snowey	11-8F	M Bacon	28.59
1997	Aztec Travel	3-1	N Savva	28.36
1996	Burnpark Lord	7-4F	D Hopper	27.78
1995	White Ink	2-1F	J Gibson	28.31
1994	Just Right Kyle	2-1	C Lister	28.30

GRAND NATIONAL

Run at Wimbledon over 460mH from 1999. Previously staged at Hall Green over 474m (1985-1998) and White City over 500m (1975-1984) and 525 yards (1927-1974)

Year	Dog	Odds	Trainer	Time
2007	Jos Cigar	9-4	S Willey	28.07
2006	Suit Man	13-8F	B Doyle, Wimbledon	28.30
2005	Lethal Rumble	9-4F	M Wallis, Walthamstow	28.49
2004	Four Handed	6-4F	J Reynolds, Walthamstow	28.46
2003	Selby Ben	12-1	T Foster, Wimbledon	28.45
2002	Ballyvorda Class	7-4F	T Foster, Wimbledon	28.24
2001	Kish Jaguar	10-1	P Thompson, Crayford	28.60
2000	Tuttles Minister	7-2	T Foster, Wimbledon	28.36
1999	Pottos Storm	9-4CF	D Mullins, Romford	28.13DH
	Hello Buttons	9-4CF	L Mullins, Walthamstow	
1998	El Tenor	11-10F	L Mullins, Walthamstow	29.20
1997	Tarn Bay Flash	4-1	P McCombe, Belle Vue	29.07
1996	Dynamic Display	7-2	B O'Sullivan, Crayford	29.23
1995	Elegant Brandy	10-1	E Gaskin, Walthamstow	29.24
1994	Randy Savage	8-1	K Connor, Canterbury	29.50
1993	Arfur Daley	5-4F	B Meadows, Unattached	28.89
1992	Kildare Slippy	EvsF	P Hancox, Hall Green	28.52
1991	Ideal Man	3-1JF	J McGee, Peterborough	29.81
DH	Ballycarney Dell	14-1	A Gifkins, Yarmouth	29.81
1990	Gizmo Pasha	4-6F	L Mullins, Romford	29.62
1989	Lemon Chip	EvsF	P Rees, Wimbledon	29.84
1988	Breeks Rocket	5-1	D Luckhurst, Crayford	30.09
1987	Cavan Town	4-1	M Cumner, Maidstone	30.01
1986	Castlelyons Cash	5-4F	D Luckhurst, Unattached	29.51
1985	Seaman's Star	14-1	A E Boyce, Catford	30.08
1984	Kilcoe Foxy	4-5F	G Curtis, Hove	30.32
1983	Sir Winston	5-1	G Curtis, Hove	31.09
1982	Face The Mutt	11-10F	N McEllistrim, Wimbledon	30.71
1981	Bobcol	1-2F	N McEllistrim, Wimbledon	30.64
1980	Gilt Edge Flyer	4-5F	E Pateman, Unattached	30.22
1979	Topothetide	6-4F	T Lanceman, Southend	31.60
1978	Topothetide	8-11F	T Forster, Harringay	30.23
1977	Salerno	5-4F	J Coleman, Wembley	30.43
1976	Weston Pete	4-5F	C West, White City	30.60
1975	Pier Hero	EvsF	F Melville, Harringay	30.65
1974	Shanney's Darkie	10-1	C West, White City	29.43
1973	Killone Flash	5-2	R Singleton, White City	29.35
1972	Sherry's Prince	5-4F	C West, White City	29.80
1971	Sherry's Prince	1-3F	C West, West Ham	29.22
1970	Sherry's Prince	4-6F	J Shevlin, West Ham	30.02
1969	Tony's Friend	EvsF	R Singleton, White City	30.16
1968	Ballintore Tiger	1-3F	N Chambers, New Cross	29.50
1967	The Grange Santa	9-4F	N Gleeson, Wimbledon	29.72

Sponsored by the BGRB

1966	Halfpenny King	7-2	J Shevlin, New Cross	30.28
1965	I'm Crazy	11-4	R Singleton, White City	29.60
1964	Two Aces	10-11F	J Rimmer, Wembley	30.42
1963	Indoor Sport	4-5F	B O'Connor, Walthamstow	29.98
1962	Corsican Reward	9-4F	G Hodson, Unattached	30.15
1961	Ballinatona Special	6-4F	S Martin, Wimbledon	29.50
1960	Bruff Chariot	EvsF	J Jowett, Clapton	29.50
1959	Prince Poppit	3-1	D Hannafin, Wimbledon	30.10
1958	Fodda Champion	7-4F	J Jowett, Clapton	30.20
1957	Tanyard Tulip	2-1	H Harvey, Wembley	29.85
1956	Blue Sand	15-8F	K Appleton, West Ham	29.70
1955	Barrowside	1-3F	H Harvey, Wembley	29.43
1954	Prince Lawrence	10-1	J Pickering, White City	30.29
1953	Denver Berwick	10-11F	D Geggus, Walthamstow	30.26
1952	Whistling Laddie	20-1	S Martin, Wimbledon	30.13
1951	XPDNC	11-4JF	L Parry, White City	29.80
1950	Blossom Of Annagura	5-2	J Sherry, Ramsgate	29.97
1949	Blossom Of Annagura	8-1	J Sherry, Ramsgate	30.20
1948	Jove's Reason	2-1	K Appleton, Unattached	30.37
1947	Baytown Pigeon	25-1	P McEllistrim, Wimbledon	30.67
1946	Barry From Limerick	2-1	E Davidson, Unattached	30.61
1941-1945	NOT RUN			
1940	Juvenile Classic	EvsF	J Harmon, Wimbledon	30.23
1939	Valiant Bob	8-1	P Fortune, Wimbledon	30.50
1938	Juvenile Classic	2-1	J Harmon, Wimbledon	30.35
1937	Flying Wedge	EvsF	S Biss, West Ham	30.61
1936	Kilganny Bridge	3-1	P J Higgins, Clapton	30.70
1935	Quarter Cross	7-2	S Probert, Wembley	30.76
1934	Lemonition	11-4	D Costello, Wimbledon	30.84
1933	Scapegoat	6-1	A Jonas, White City	31.20
1932	Long Hop	3-1	I McCorkindale, Harringay	31.44
1931	Rule The Roost	5-2	J Harmon, White City	31.17
1930	Stylish Cutlet	11-4	J T Hutchinson, Wimbledon	30.94
1929	Levator	2-1	M Burls, Wembley	31.09
1928	Cormorant	4-1	S Probert, Wembley	31.16
1927	Bonzo	13-8F	J Buck, Belle Vue	31.42

Run at Wimbledon over 460mH from 1999. Previously staged at Hall Green over 474m (1985-1998) and White City over 500m (1975-1984) and 525 yards (1927-1974). In 1927 the event was run as the 'Champion Hurdle Race'. The first official Grand National was in 1928.

GRAND PRIX

Run over 640m at Walthamstow. Originally staged over 525 yards (1945-1958); then 500 yards (1960-1974), 700 yards (1966-73) and 640m from 1974.

2007	Foulden Special	EvsF	D Knight, Hove	39.45
2006	January Tiger	9-2	M Wallis, Walthamstow	39.47
2005	Clonbrin Show	5-2F	M Puzey, Walthamstow	39.55

2004	Ronnies Flight	11-8F	L Jones, Walthamstow	40.03
2003	Special Trick	4-1	L Jones, Walthamstow	40.05
2002	Sheriff Bow Wow	8-1	J Mullins, Walthamstow	40.05
2001	Slick Tom	9-2	O McKenna, Wimbledon	40.02
2000	Palace Issue	1-3F	L Mullins, Walthamstow	39.32
1999	Palace Issue	9-4F	L Mullins, Walthamstow	40.32
1998	Dans Sport	6-1	C Lister, Unattached	39.79
1997	El Grand Senor	12-1	L Mullins, Walthamstow	39.38
1996	Spring Rose	4-7F	C Lister, Nottingham	39.05
1995	Suncrest Sail	11-10F	C Lister, Unattached	39.62
1994	Redwood Girl	2-1	E Gaskin, Walthamstow	39.74
1993	Redwood Girl	5-1	E Gaskin, Walthamstow	39.89
1992	Westmead Darkie	2-1F	N Savva, Unattached	39.36
1991	Dempseys Whisper	2-1F	P Byrne, Wimbledon	39.20
1990	Dempseys Whisper	4-11F	P Byrne, Canterbury	39.07
1989	Waltham Abbey	2-1	E Gaskin, Unattached	39.91
1988	Digby Bridge	50-1	J Malcolm, Hall Green	40.14
1987	Olivers Wish	7-2	N Savva, Unattached	39.86
1986	Westmead Move	10-11F	N Savva, Unattached	39.35
1985	Slaneyside Gold	5-1	J Sherry, Walthamstow	40.00
1984	Sunrise Sonny	25-1	G Curtis, Brighton	40.00
1983	Flying Duke	4-1	P Coughlan, Crayford	40.49
1982	Huberts Shade	11-8F	A Jackson, Wembley	39.73
1981	Rathduff Solara	2-1JF	T Dennis, Southend	40.71
1980	Sport Promoter	2-1JF	P Mullins, Cambridge	40.17
1979	Frame That	11-2	E Dickson, Slough	39.57
1978	Paradise Spectre	3-1CF	P Mullins, Unattached	40.03
1977	Paradise Spectre	6-4F	P Mullins, Unattached	40.19
1976	Manderlay King	9-2	G De Mulder, Hall Green	40.21
1975	NOT RUN			
1974	Ballyglass Hope	7-1	D Thornton, Unattached	40.58
1973	Pendys Mermaid	11-8F	D Geggus, Walthamstow	40.65
1972	NOT RUN			
1971	Breach's Buzzard	4-5F	C McNally, Perry Barr	40.00
1970	Baton	9-4	J Durkin, Walthamstow	40.39
1969	Chame Sparrow	6-1	B O'Connor, Walthamstow	40.75
1968	Carmen John	10-1	J Mills, Unattached	41.16
1967	NOT RUN			
1966	Westpark Bison	8-11F	B O'Connor, Walthamstow	40.14
1965	NOT RUN			
1964	NOT RUN			
1963	Monday's Ranger	4-5F	T Reilly, Walthamstow	28.03
1962	NOT RUN			
1961	Clonalvy Romance	9-2	W Taylor, White City	28.57
1960	Dunstown Paddy	11-4	T Reilly, Walthamstow	28.26
1959	NOT RUN			

1958	Granthamian	EvsF	H Harvey, Wembley	29.98
1957	Kilcaskin Kern	8-11F	T W Dennis, Unattached	29.95
1956	Land Of Song	7-2	M Burls, Wembley	29.70
1955	Duet Leader	13-8F	T Reilly, Walthamstow	29.42
1954	Rushton Spot	100-30	F Johnson, Unattached	29.57
1953	NOT RUN			
1952	NOT RUN			
1951	Rushton Smutty	4-6F	F Johnson, Unattached	29.80
1950	Arrow Boy	5-1	H Harvey, Wembley	30.28
1949	Red Wind	10-11F	F Davis, Unattached	29.82
1948	Ruby Cut	11-4	J P Bott, Unattached	30.31
1947	Mondays News	2-1	S Orton, Wimbledon	30.41
1946	Tonycus	6-1	L Reynolds, Wembley	30.19
1945	Magic Bohemian	10-11F	L Reynolds, Wembley	30.05

GUYS AND DOLLS

Staged over 380m at Crayford

2007	Horseshoe Ping	EvsF	J Reynolds, Romford	23.14
2006	Letmekissya	6-4F	J Davidson, Crayford	23.47
2005	Thank You Madam	11-4	G Brabon	23.38
2004	Shes Our Star	9-4J	P Young	23.17
2003	Kingdom Club	5-1	P Cusack	23.01
2002	Knockevan Hollie	5-4F	P Young	23.22
2001	Lavender Prince	5-1	L Jones	23.65
2000	Haut Brion	2-1F	P Rich	23.79
1999	Chief Wigam	9-2	C Duggan	23.84
1998	Wildbriar Hare	11-4	T Dartnall	23.71
1997	Corpo Election	7-2	M Mulkerrin	23.76
1996	Clean Paws	9-2	King	23.57
1995	Reckless Champ	9-4F	L Sams	23.73
1994	Gun Fighter	8-1	B Masters	23.46

THE GYMCRACK

Staged at Hall Green over 480m

2007	Farloe Hurricane	5-6F	B Draper, Sheffield	28.31
2006	Fear Haribo	5-4F	C Philpott, Coventry	28.66
2005	Go Commando	11-4	M Wallis, Walthamstow	28.11
2004	Roman Road	7-4	A O'Flaherty, Unattached	28.69
2003	Moynies Cash	3-1	C Lister, Unattached	28.26
2002	Louis Saha	3-1	B Draper, Sheffield	28.26
2001	Reactabond Ace	EvsF	P Young, Romford	28.22
2000	Droopys Woods	2-1JF	P Young, Romford	28.34

JUVENILE CHAMPIONSHIP

Run at Wimbledon over 460m. Originally staged over 525yds (1963-1974)

| 2007 | 2 Express Ego | 6-4F | O McKenna, Ireland | 27.42 |

2006	6 Droopys Lomasi	25-1	S Dimmock, Peterborough	28.00
2005	4 Toms View	4-6F	P McComish, Nottingham	28.01
2004	2 Kinda Spooky	6-1	L Jones, Walthamstow	28.44
2003	6 On Line Deal	3-1	P Young, Romford	28.21
2002	6 Top Savings	4-5F	G Adam, Unattached	27.56
2001	6 Reactabond Rebel	3-1	P Young, Romford	28.05
2000	2 Knockanroe Rover	3-1	P Stringer, Unattached	27.84
1999	6 Im Okay	5-4F	B Draper, Sheffield	27.79
1998	2 Ground Zero	3-1	G DeMulder, Milton Keynes	27.95
1997	3 Black Gem Charm	5-4F	P Rees, Wimbledon	27.98
1996	6 Droopys Aldo	9-4JF	H Tasker, Perry Barr	28.35
1995	2 Bonmahon Darkie	11-10F	T Dartnall, Wimbledon	27.66
1994	6 Ayr Flyer	2-7F	D Wheatley, Nottingham	27.63
1993	3 Our Timmy	6-1	J Barrett, Cradley Heath	27.84
1992	6 Right Move	7-2	N Savva, Private	27.66
1991	4 Slaneyside Hare	7-4F	G Lightfoot, Norton Canes	27.76
1990	4 Druids Johno	6-4F	P Byrne, Canterbury	28.10
1989	5 Bimbo Bird	5-1	S Sykes, Wimbledon	28.03
1988	2 Wendys Dream	4-5F	T Foster, Wimbledon	27.77
1987	3 Spiral Darkie	10-1	G Baggs, Ramsgate	27.96
1986	6 Fearless Action	8-11F	G DeMulder, Oxford	27.64
1985	NOT RUN			
1984	2 Hong Kong Mike	6-4F	Andrews, Belle Vue	27.80
1983	6 Westmead Milos	3-1	Savva, Milton Keynes	27.73
1982	6 Mountkeefe Star	12-1	DeMulder, Coventry	27.86
1981	3 Kris Is Back	9-2	Johnston, Wembley	28.16
1980	2 Upland Tiger	1-2F	Curtis, Hove	27.48
1979	6 Sport Promoter	8-11F	Mullins, Cambridge	27.70
1978	2 Schofield Fish	10-1	Coker, Oxford	28.26
1977	2 Prince Hill	8-1	Kelly, Leeds	28.20
1976	5 Instant Gambler	9-4	Drinkwater, Bletchley	28.98
1975	1 Xmas Holiday	7-4F	Rees, Wimbledon	28.31
1974	3 Head The Poll	7-1	Rees, Wimbledon	28.56
1973	1 Myrtown	5-4F	Moore, Man W City	28.11
1972	4 Black Banjo	11-8F	O'Connor, Walthamstow	28.10
1971	2 Short Interview	10-1	Johnston, Wembley	27.98
1970	2 Dolores Rocket	7-2	White, Private	28.24
1969	5 Sovereign Mint	3-1	Collett, Private	28.21
1968	1 Mountleader Glen	100-7	Horsfall, Catford	28.53
1967	1 Fire Trap	5-1	McEvoy, Wimbledon	28.06
1966	6 Forward Flash	10-1	Brennan, Sheffield	28.50
1965	3 Morden Mist	4-6F	Orton, Wimbledon	29.08
1964	1 Hi Joe	4-7F	Collin, Private	28.65
1963	5 Pineapple Joe	5-4F	Hannifan Wimbledon	28.52

KENT DERBY

Year	Dog	Odds	Trainer	Time
2007	Moaning Zizou	20-1	D Whitton, Henlow	29.62
2006	Carlin Honcho	8-1	A Collett, Sittingbourne	29.38
2005	Manera Spark	10-11F	J Mullins, Walthamstow	29.34
2004	Manera Spark	4-1	J Mullins, Walthamstow	28.57
2003	Haughty Ted	8-11F	D Luckhurst, Crayford	28.80
2002	Willie Go Fa	7-2	B Clemenson, Hove	28.87
2001	Pinewood Blue	10-11	L Jones, Walthamstow	28.69
2000	Smoking Bullet	EvsF	D Knight, Hove	28.55

KENT ST LEGER

Run at Crayford over 714m from 1996. Originally staged at Ramsgate

Year	Dog	Odds	Trainer	Time
2007	Princessmonalulu	6-4F	B Clemenson, Hove	46.70
2006	Dods Delight	9-4	S Walsh Harlow	46.12
2005	Return To Suir	12-1	J Carter, Crayford	46.02
2004	Droopys Savanna	7-4F	B Clemenson, Hove	45.84
2003	Latin Beauty	5-4F	C Miller, Sittingbourne	45.21
2002	Countrywidekaren	EvsF	P Young, Romford	45.56
2001	Moreton Jazz	16-1	J Spracklen, Unattached	46.07
2000	Pearl Barley	3-1	R Joyce, Henlow	47.12
1999	Phils Ann Marie	8-1	P Young, Romford	46.28
1998	Droopys Paul	4-5F	L Mullins, Walthamstow	46.37
1997	Bubbly Boy	6-4JF	L Jones, Walthamstow	46.56
1996	Musical Treat	9-4F	B Clemenson, Hove	46.06
1995	Decoy Cheetah	4-1	P Cobbold, Private	39.92

THE LAURELS

Run over 470 at Belle Vue (465m from 1998 to 2005). Originally staged at Wimbledon over 500 yards (1930-1974) and 460m 1975-1997)

Year	Dog	Odds	Trainer	Time
2007	Kylegrove Top	10-1	J Bateson, Unattached	27.82
2006	Clash Harmonica	3-1	C Lister, Unattached	27.88
2005	Blonde Boss (T4)	5-2	C Lister, Doncaster	27.86
2004	Ningbo Jack	4-1	C Lister, Unattached	27.60
2003	Knockeevan Magic	11-10F	P Rich, Romford	28.25
2002	Full Cigar	11-4	E McNair, Unattached	27.94
2001	Pack Them In	6-4F	A Heyes, Belle Vue	27.55
2000	Courts Legal	7-4F	L Jones, Walthamstow	27.86
1999	Derbay Flyer	10-11F	C Lister, Unattached	27.80
1998	Ardant Jimmy	10-1	S Ralph, Monmore	28.05
1997	El Premier	4-7F	L Mullins, Walthamstow	27.36
1996	El Grand Senor	9-4J	L Mullins, Walthamstow	27.52
1995	Demesne Bear	14-1	P Payne, Romford	27.94
1994	Deenside Dean	5-2	T Dartnall, Wimbledon	27.97
1993	Slipaway Jaydee	9-4	J McGee, Reading	27.61
1992	Balligari	6-4	N Savva, Unattached	27.37
1991	Glengar Ranger	6-4J	J Fletcher, Canterbury	27.47

Year	Dog	Odds	Trainer	Time
1990	Concentration	4-7F	G McKenna, Ireland	27.75
1989	Parquet Pal	9-4	A Hitch, Wimbledon	27.68
1988	Comeragh Boy	6-4F	E Gaskin, Unattached	27.86
1987	Flashy Sir	11-4	N Savva, Milton Keynes	27.52
1986	Mollifrend Lucky	4-6F	C Packham, Reading	27.48
1985	Ballygroman Jim	7-4F	E Gaskin, Unattached	27.68
1984	Amenhotep	7-1	L Mullins, Crayford	27.82
1983	Darkie Fli	2-1F	F Stevens, Cambridge	27.87
1982	Lauries Panther	9-2	T Duggan, Romford	27.79
1981	Echo Spark	5-1	J Cobbold, Ipswich	27.84
1980	Flying Pursuit	6-4F	J Gibbons, Crayford	27.89
1979	Another Spatter	7-2	J Pickering, White City	27.75
1978	Jet Control	9-2	B Gaynor, Perry Barr	27.45
1977	Greenfield Fox	4-5F	T Dickson, Slough	27.26
1976	Xmas Holiday	3-1	P C Rees, Wimbledon	27.66
1975	Pineapple Grand	3-1	F Baldwin, Perry Barr	27.77
1974	Over Protected	7-4	J Coleman, Wembley	28.00
1973	Black Banjo	5-2CF	B O'Connor, Walthamstow	27.93
1972	Cricket Bunny	10-3	J Booth, Unattached	28.11
1971	Black Andrew	11-2	R Singleton, White City	27.96
1970	Sole Aim	6-4F	D Geggus, Walthamstow	28.04
1969	Ardrine Flame	8-1	J Kinsley, Wembley	27.96
1968	Ambiguous	8-1	P McEvoy, Wimbledon	28.10
1967	Carry On Oregon	8-13F	C Orton, Wimbledon	27.89
1966	Super Fame	9-4	N Gleeson, Wimbledon	28.05
1965	Conna Count	11-2	P McEvoy, Wimbledon	28.13
1964	Conna Count	100-7	D Hannifin, Wimbledon	28.08
1963	Dalcassian Son	7-2	A Hiscock, Belle Vue	28.08
1962	Tuturama	4-6F	M Sanderson, Unattached	27.83
1961	Clonalvy Pride	2-1JF	H Harvey, Wembley	27.66
1960	Dunstown Paddy	5-1	T Reilly, Walthamstow	28.02
1959	Mighty Hassan	5-1	H Harvey, Wembley	28.01
1958	Granthamian	10-1	H Harvey, Wembley	28.57
1957	Ford Spartan	2-7F	D Hannifin, Wimbledon	27.89
1956	Duet Leader	EvsF	T Reilly, Walthamstow	28.13
1955	Duet Leader	7-4	T Reilly, Walthamstow	28.25
1954	Coolkill Chieftain	1-2F	H Harvey, Wembley	28.05
1953	Polonius	7-2	T Reilly, Walthamstow	28.04
1952	Endless Gossip	2-11F	L Reynolds, Wembley	27.96
1951	Ballylanigan Tanist	8-11F	L Reynolds, Wembley	28.37
1950	Ballymac Ball	15-8	S Martin, Wimbledon	28.19
1949	Ballymac Ball	4-5F	S Martin, Wimbledon	28.61
1948	Good Worker	5-2	J Daley, Ramsgate	28.49
1947	Rimmells Black	8-1	S Biss, Clapton	28.77
1946	Shannon Shore	7-1	L Reynolds, Wembley	28.26
1945	Burhill Moon	1-3F	S Orton, Wimbledon	28.42

138

1941-1944	NOT RUN			
1940	April Burglar	100-8	K Appleton, West Ham	28.56
1939	Musical Duke	EvsF	C Crowley, Park Royal	28.42
1938	Ballyhennessy Sandills	11-8F	S Orton, Wimbledon	28.50
1937	Ballyhennessy Sandills	4-5F	S Orton, Wimbledon	28.25
1936	Top Of The Carlow Road	5-2	S Orton, Wimbledon	28.39
1935	Kitshine	3-1	A Callanan, Wembley	29.05
1934	Brilliant Bob	7-1	S Orton, Wimbledon	28.46
1933	Wild Woolley	10-3	J Campbell, Belle Vue	28.80
1932	Beef Cutlet	4-6F	J Hegarty, W. City (Cardiff)	28.47
1931	Future Cutlet	2-5F	S Probert, Wembley	28.52
1930	Kilbrean Boy	10-1	S Orton, Wimbledon	29.20

LADBROKE HURDLE

Staged at Walthamstow over 475m hurdles

2007	Snazzy Time	5-2CF	S Cahill, Walthamstow	29.50
2006	Ronnies Callum (T2)	1-2F	M Wallis, Walthamstow	29.21
2005	Oklahoma Jo	7-1	T Foster	29.37
2004	Box Office Magic	4-1	T Taylor	29.83
2003	Germain	3-1	J Mullins	29.62
2002	Opus Joe	7-1	P Thompson	29.66
2001	Ballmac Keano	5-2JF	N McEllistrim	29.19
2000	Funcheon Oscar	7-2	M Mavrias	30.14
1999	Ballinabola Gale	1-2F	J Foster	29.24
1998	Stradeen Ranger	2-1	G Baggs	29.41
1997	Clear Prospect	7-1	L Mullins	29.05

THE MASTERS

Run at Reading over 465m

2007	Blitz	4-1	D Stevenson, Unattached	28.03
2006	Farloe Rio	5-2	P Hennessy, Ireland	28.13
2005	Killeigh Grand	EvsF	C Lister, Unattached	28.09
2004	Droopys Chester	7-1	C Philpott, Unattached	27.92
2003	Blonde Ranger	6-1	J Mullins, Walthamstow	28.00
2002	Aranock Lance	7-1	P Young, Romford	27.95
2001	Marshals June	11-4	R Stiles, Reading	27.99
2000	Jicky	11-2	B Clemenson, Hove	28.16
1999	Torbal Piper	14-1	A Meek, Hall Green	28.15
1998	You Will Call	5-1	J Burridge, Poole	27.90
1997	Night Trooper	6-1	N Adams, Rye House	27.86
1996	Doyougetit	2-5F	A Meek, Hall Green	27.99
1995	Longvalley Manor	9-2	J Coleman, Walthamstow	28.35
1994	Druids Elprado	11-8F	J McGee, Reading	27.99
1993	Im His	5-4F	E Jordan, Hove	28.09
1992	Dempsey Duke	9-4	T Kibble, Bristol	28.09

MIDLAND FLAT

Run at Hall Green over 892m from 2005. Previously staged over 480m

2006	Rosshill View (T1)	4-5F	C Allsopp, Monmore	55.72
2005	Lig Do Scith	5-4	J Kavanagh, Ireland	55.98
2004	NOT RUN			
2003	Lodgeview Flash	11-4	D Talbot, Unattached	28.91
2002	Aranock Lance	10-1	P Young, Romford	28.69
2001	Ballydaly Score	9-4	J Mullins, Walthamstow	28.54
2000	Wise Emerald	4-1	C Lister, Unattached	28.31
1999	Westmead Striker	5-1	C Liser, Unattached	28.46

MIDLAND GOLD CUP

Staged at Monmore over 480m. Previously over 484m (1994-95)

2007	Boherna On Air	4-7F	B Draper, Sheffield	28.10
2006	Westmead Joe (T4)	6-4	N Savva, Henlow	27.89
2005	Loughteen Bandit	6-1	M Harris, Monmore	27.92
2004	Elderberry Veron	5-2	P Cowdrill, Monmore	28.21
2003	Farloe Brazil	9-2	C Lister, Unattached	28.12
2002	Lodgeview Chance	10-1	D Talbot, Kinsley	28.89
2001	Potto Knows	4-1	D Mullins, Romford	28.51
2000	Fervent Flash	4-1	T Meek, Hall Green	28.59
1999	Crack Off	2-1F	B Clemenson, Hove	28.13
1998	Black Buster	9-2	I Williams, Perry Barr	28.13
1997	Toms The Best	2-1	N Savva, Walthamstow	28.21
1996	Chairman	6-4F	J Gibson, Belle Vue	29.22
1995	Westmead Chick	4-6F	N Savva, Walthamstow	29.09
1994	Droopys Craig	5-2	H Tasker, Unattached	29.31

MIDLAND OAKS

Run at Hall Green over 474m until 1996, then 663m (1997-98) and now over 480m

2006	Larkhill Bird (T3)	4-1	M Walsh, Pelaw Grange	28.43
2005	Shelbourne Nina (T6)	1-3F	B Clemenson, Hove	28.80
2004	Whiteoak Jane			28.74
2003	Yorkys Girl			28.40
2002	Tullerboy Lass			28.43
2001	Call Me Baby			28.54
2000	Kaaman Linda			28.78
1999	Alannas Spark			29.22
1998	Impulsive One			41.43
1997	El Ektra			41.30
1996	Briar Maid			28.66
1995	Bettys Wish			28.46
1994	Active Summer			

MIDLAND PUPPY DERBY

Run at Monmore over 460m from 1997. Previously staged over 484m

2007	Blonde Dino (ex Rough Ronaldinho)	EvsF	J Mullins, Unattached	28.07
2006	Ballymac Charley (T2)	7-4F	C Philpott, Coventry	28.41
2005	Ballymac Pires	3-1	C Philpott, Coventry	27.82TR
2004	Dairyland Sue	5-4F	P Rosney, Monmore	28.27
2003	Knock Split	5-4F	B Draper, Sheffield	28.70
2002	Droopys Hewitt	8-1	N Savva, Unattached	28.74
2001	Micks Best Hero	4-6F	B.Clemenson, Hove	28.42
2000	Rio Riccardo	11-10F	D Riordan, Unattached	28.60
1999	Active Jack	7-1	P Walden, Oxford	28.53
1998	Eleets Noir Boyy	7-1	J Coxon, Monmore	28.55
1997	Elliots Gift	6-1	N Chambers, Nottingham	27.40
1996	Eleets Noir Bill	7-4	M Barlow, Hall Green	29.92
1995	Staplers Jo	5-2	N Savva, Walthamstow	29.72
1994	Mr Tan	6-1	D Catchpole, Unattached	30.06

NATIONAL SPRINT

Run at Nottingham over 300m

2006	Centaur Striker	14-1	C Lister, Unattached	17.82
2005	Clounlaheen	6-1	M Hurst, Unattached	17.74
2004	Ningbo Jack	2-1	C Lister, Unattached	17.78
2003	Louisville	6-1	J Mullins, Walthamstow	17.74
2002	Very Hot	4-1	H Crapper, Sheffield	18.08
2001	Nervous Paddy	10-11F	C Evans, Unattached	17.81TR
2000	Elliots Pride	9-1	M Burt, Monmore	17.95
1999	Gulleen Slaney	EvsF	C Lister, Unattached	18.07

NORTHERN PUPPY DERBY

Staged at Sunderland over 450m

2007	Farloe Reason	2-1	C Lister, Unattached	26.92
2006	Droopys Mcandrew	9-4	T Soppitt, Unattached	27.24
2005	Calzaghe Boyo	5-2	T Soppitt, Unattached	26.90
2004	Toms View	9-4	P Rutherford, Brough Park	26.82
2003	Dairyland Sue	5-2	P Rosney, Monmore	27.14
2002	Lodgeview Blue	7-2	D Talbot, Kinsley	27.21
2001	Farloe Chief	6-4F	O Kueres, Belle Vue	27.36
2000	Harsu Super	4-5F	J McGee, Unattached	27.51
1999	Knockeevan Star	4-6F	M Bacon, Belle Vue	27.53
1998	Tracys Glory	9-4	P Ryan, Unattached	27.13
1997	Knockeevan Dan	2-5F	G Calvert, Sunderland	27.54
1996	El Premier	5-2	L Mullins, Walthamstow	27.34
1995	Droopys Aldo	3-1	H Tasker, Perry Barr	27.36
1994	Justright Melody	1-2F	T Robinson, Unattached	27.47

1993	Farloe Bid	8-1	S Richards, Powderhall	27.82
1992	Listen To Dan	4-1	T Meek, Oxford	27.55
1991	Right Move	3-1	N Savva, Milton Keynes	27.61

NORTHERN FLAT

Run over 465m at Belle Vue

2007	Ballymac Charley	5-4F	C Lister, Unattached	27.70
2006	Giddy Kipper	25-1	J McCombe, Belle Vue	27.70
2005	Phone For Who	3-1	G Hutt, Unattached	27.95
2004	Tarn Bay Jet	7-1	J McCombe	27.74
2003	One Yard	4-7F	A Johnson	27.74
2002	Cool Scenario	5-2CF	B Draper	28.03
2001	Carhumore Cross	4-1	N Savva	27.65
2000	El Dante	8-1	L Mullins	28.00
1999	Killaree George	8-1	D Hopper	28.43
1998	Ratsastory	5-2	P Ryan	28.09
1997	Brannigans Gig	7-1	C Lister	28.00
1996	Rainstorm	7-1	G DeMulder	28.10
1995	Countrywide Cub	6-4F	J Coleman	28.66
1994	Gold Doon	6-1	A Palmer	28.02
1993	Toms Lodge	8-13F	T Johnson	27.59

THE OAKS

Run at Wimbledon from 1988 over 480m. Originally staged at White City over 500yds (1927) and 525yds (1928-1958), and Harringay over 525yds (1959-1974) and 475m (1975-1987)

2006	Dilemmas Flight	7-1	N Savva, Henlow	28.96
2005	Droopys Stacey (T1)	4-6F	I Reilly, Ireland	29.10
2004	Tidyplayroom	5-1	D Knight, Hove	29.27
2003	Cooly Pantera	11-8F	B Clemenson, Hove	29.18
2002	Purley Queen	8-1	N McEllistrim, Wimbledon	29.14
2001	Talktothehand	6-4JF	J Gibson, Belle Vue	29.06
2000	Ragga Juju	7-1	J Page, Milton Keynes	29.29
1999	Spring Time	4-9F	G Watson, Ireland	28.97
1998	Sarah Dee	6-4F	N Savva, Walthamstow	28.82
1997	Flashy Get	14-1	E Gaskin, Walthamstow	28.75
1996	Annies Bullet	7-4JF	N Savva, Walthamstow	28.76
1995	Sadlers Return	3-1	E Gaskin, Walthamstow	28.76
1994	Westmead Chick	8-11F	N Savva, Walthamstow	28.60
1993	Pearls Girl	8-11F	S Sykes, Wimbledon	28.55
1992	Skelligs Smurf	11-8F	R Gilling, Reading	29.71
1991	Simple Trend	2-1F	E Gaskin, Walthamstow	29.06
1990	Liberal Girl	5-1	D Knight, Hove	28.95
1989	Nice And Lovely	9-4	D Tidswell, Unattached	29.02
1988	Wendys Dream	4-5F	T Foster, Wimbledon	28.81
1987	Lucky Empress	2-1	A Briggs, Unattached	28.43
1986	Sullane Princess	20-1	P Payne, Romford	28.79

1985	Spiral Super	10-11F	G Curtis, Brighton	28.57
1984	Sandy Sally	9-2	J Coker, Milton Keynes	28.69
1983	Major Grove	6-1	E Pateman, Wimbledon	28.59
1982	Duchess Of Avon	EvsF	A Jackson, Wembley	28.72
1981	Thanet Princess	11-2	D Hawkes, Walthamstow	28.82
1980	Devilish Dolores	20-1	E Gaskin, Unattached	28.72
1979	Sunny Interval	12-1	P C Rees, Wimbledon	28.77
1978	Kilmagoura Mist	10-1	T Johnston, Wembley	28.55
1977	Switch Off	6-4F	J Singleton, Harringay	28.69
1976	Ballinderry Moth	4-6F	B O'Connor, Walthamstow	28.60
1975	Pineapple Grand	8-11F	E Baldwin, Perry Barr	28.85
1974	Lady Devine	3-1	S Ryall, Wembley	28.76
1973	Miss Ross	8-1	T Johnston, Wembley	28.63
1972	Decimal Queen	6-4F	F G Hawkins, Unattached	28.60
1971	Short Cake	5-1	D Geggus, Walthamstow	28.98
1970	Perth Pat	13-8F	J Morgan, Unattached	28.81
1969	Shady Bracelet	7-4F	P Collett, Unattached	28.63
1968	Shady Parachute	1-2F	P R Rees, Wimbledon	29.38
1967	Solerina	12-1	J Thistleton, Catford	29.50
1966	Merry Emblem	7-4	E Bruton, Ireland	29.58
1965	Marjone	4-1	P O'Toole, Ireland	29.37
1964	Cranog Bet	4-9F	P R Rees, Unattached	29.02
1963	Cranog Bet	7-2	P R Rees, Unattached	29.31
1962	Ballinasloe Blondie	1-2F	H Harvey, Wembley	29.68
1961	Ballinasloe Blondie	2-7F	H Harvey, Wembley	29.58
1960	Wheatfield Countess	5-4F	S Martin, Wimbledon	29.33
1959	Gurteen Scamp	11-2	G Waterman, Wimbledon	29.90
1958	Antartica	7-2	J Jowett, Clapton	29.13
1957	Dark Rose	4-6F	W G Brown, Unattached	29.02
1956	First But Last	2-7F	H Harvey, Wembley	29.08
1955	Lizette	6-4	H Harvey, Wembley	29.52
1954	Ashcott Winsome	16-1	H Hayes, White City	29.39
1953	Lizette	6-4F	P Fortune, Wimbledon	29.18
1952	Flo's Pet	8-1	P Fortune, Wimbledon	29.60
1952	Monachdy Girlie	10-1	J Jowett, Clapton	29.60
1951	Ballinasloe Mona	6-4F	H Harvey, Wembley	29.28
1950	Caledonian Faith	8-1	A Mountfield, Unattached	29.62
1949	Still Drifting	11-2	S Probert, Wembley	29.48
1948	Night Breeze	4-1	S Biss, Clapton	29.19
1947	Rio Cepretta	6-5F	S Biss, Clapton	29.42
1946	Dumbles Maid	13-8	S Biss, Clapton	29.42
1945	Prancing Kitty	13-8	P Fortune, Wimbledon	29.54
1939-1944	NOT RUN			
1938	Quarter Day	4-5F	J Harmon, Wimbledon	29.49
1937	Brave Queen	4-9F	S Biss, West Ham	29.62
1936	Genial Radiance	4-6F	A G Hiscock, Belle Vue	29.86

1935	Kitshine	11-2	A F Callanan, Wembley	30.12
1934	Gallant Ruth	10-11F	H Buck, Harringay	30.22
1933	Queen Of The Suir	2-5F	S Biss, West Ham	30.23
1932	Queen Of The Suir	9-4	S Biss, West Ham	30.89
1931	Drizzle	4-6F	H N Woolner, White City	30.00
1930	Faithful Kitty	4-6F	P McEllistrim, Wimbledon	30.02
1929	Bewitching Eve	3-1	R Cooper, Hall Green	30.33
1928	Moselle	1-2F	J Quinn, Unattached	30.50
1927	Three Of Spades	5-1	S Jennings, Harringay	29.96

THE OLYMPIC

Staged at Hove over 515m

2007	Jazz Hurricane	7-4F	D Knight, Hove	29.84
2006	Son Of Phoebe	2-1J	B Clemenson, Hove	29.75
2005	Droopys Oasis	9-2	B Clemenson, Hove	29.86
2004	Orient Ron	11-8F	B Clemenson, Hove	29.68
2003	Droopys Oasis	5-1	B Clemenson, Hove	29.86
2002	Cuba	8-1	B Clemenson, Hove	29.83
2001	Solid Magic	6-4F	B Clemenson, Hove	29.93
2000	Smoking Wardy	5-4F	D Knight, Hove	29.90
1999	Principal Meteor	11-4	D Knight, Hove	30.13
1998	Xamax Na Cap	8-1	E Gaskin, Walthamstow	30.71
1997	Astrosyn Eureka	7-4F	D Knight, Hove	30.05
1996	Hart To Mine	1-1F	B Clemenson, Hove	30.05
1995	Sir Frederick	5-4F	D Knight, Hove	29.99
1994	Westmead Chick	6-4F	N Savva	30.55
1993	Hypnotic Stag	4-7F	J Coleman, Walthamstow	29.74
1992	Satharn Lady	3-1	J Coleman, Walthamstow	30.08
1991	Shanavulin Bingo	7-4	E Gaskin, Walthamstow	30.40
1990	Labana Mathew	2-5F	G DeMulder	30.04
1989	White Island	8-1	B Masters, Hove	30.30
1988	John Doe	4-1	B Masters, Hove	30.14
1987	House Hunter	3-1	G Smith, Hove	30.14
1986	House Hunter	3-1	G Smith, Hove	30.06
1985	Ballyregan Bob	2-5F	G Curtis, Hove	30.04
1984	Westmead Milos	15-8JF	N Savva	30.20
1983	Huberts Shade	8-1	A Jackson	30.33
1982	Glen Miner	15-8	P Rich	29.62TR
1981	Corrakelly Air	5-1	C Coyle	30.86
	Greenane Metro	13-8F	A Hitch	DH

OXFORDSHIRE GOLD CUP

500 metres

1980	Young Breeze	11-4	J Coker	29.03
2007	Mahers Boy	9-4F	E Parker, Sheffield	26.54
2006	Two Cool Cats	10-1	A Heyes, Bellevue	26.76

2005	Roswell Spaceman	7-2	M Wallis, Walthamstow	26.74
2004	Fire Height Dan		M Puzey, Walthamstow	
2003	Knockeevan Magic		P Rich, Romford	
2002	Bomber Graham		J Gibson, Belle Vue	
2001	El Ronan		C Lister, Unattached	
2000	El Boss		L Mullins, Walthamstow	
1999	Crack Off		B Clemenson, Hove	
1998	Reactabond Gold		P Young, Harlow	
1997	Silver Circle		A Heyes, Private	
1996	Clean Paws		King, Peterborough	
1995	Self Made		Massey, Oxford	
1994	Freds Flyer		B Masters, Hove	
1992	Lackabane Tap		Goodwin, Private	
1991	Seafield Quest		Westwood, Peterborough	
1990	Kilcurley Coal		McGee, Hackney	
1989	Castleivy Mick		Greenacre, Private	
1988	Money Matters		G De Mulder, Hall Green	
1987	Fairway Wink		Gaynor, Hall Green	
1986	Cannonroe		Bass, Private	
1985	Nippy Law		G De Mulder, Oxford	

THE PALL MALL

Run at Oxford over 450m since 1988. Previously staged at Harringay over 475m

2007	Ballymac Charley	3-1	C Lister, Unattached	26.75
2006	Seomra Rock (T1)	7-2	E Gaskin, Walthamstow	27.14
2005	Lisnafulla Flash	2-1JF	E Gaskin, Walthamstow	26.63
2004	Tims Crow	EvsF	P Rich, Romford	26.90
2003	Cooly Cheetah	4-1	B Clemenson, Hove	27.09
2002	Windgap Java	4-1	C Miller, Sittingbourne	27.03
2001	Kinda Magic	5-1	L Jones, Walthamstow	27.06
2000	El Boss	4-1	L Mullins, Walthamstow	26.87
1999	Leitrim Charm	8-1	B Clemenson, Hove	26.94
1998	Black Buster	11-2	I Williams, Perry Barr	26.70
1997	Night Trooper	11-10F	N Adams, Rye House	27.19
1996	Highview Pet	3-1	L Mullins, Walthamstow	27.21
1995	Longvalley Manor	6-1	J Coleman, Walthamstow	27.36
1994	Lassa Java	5-2	A Meek, Hall Green	27.17
1993	Sullane Castle	4-9F	N Saunders, Belle Vue	27.13
1992	Deanpark Atom	5-1	A Meek, Oxford	27.27
1991	Clonlusk Villa	11-4	H Dickson, Wembley	27.19
1990	Noelles Turbo	7-2	P Rich, Ramsgate	27.15
1989	Fearless Ace	4-1	T Mentzis, Milton Keynes	26.80TR
1988	Fearless Ace	5-4F	G De Mulder, Norton Canes	26.96
1987	Forest Fawn	7-1	A Hill, Unattached	29.06
1986	Tico	7-4F	A Hitch, Slough	28.45
1985	Hongkong Mike	11-10F	R Andrews, Belle Vue	28.35

Year	Dog	Odds	Trainer	Time
1984	Game Ball	11-10F	J Fisher, Reading	28.23
1983	Yankee Express	4-5F	G Curtis, Hove	28.55
1982	Sugarville Jet	8-1	J Honeysett, Crayford	28.58
1981	Creamery Pat	7-1	R Chamberlain, Unattached	28.62
1980	Lift Coming	3-1JF	D Hawkes, Walthamstow	28.94
1979	Sampsons Pal	7-2	P Mullins, Unattached	28.91
1978	Ballinderry Moth	10-3	B O'Connor, Walthamstow	28.80
1977	Greenfield Fox	11-4	E Dickson, Slough	28.71
1976	Gin And Jass	3-1	W Drinkwater, Rye House	28.81
1975	My Dowry	4-1	P Heasman, Unattached	29.11
1974	Blackwater Champ	7-1	P Payne, Unattached	28.53
1973	Carraig Shane	EvsF	J Lancashire, Unattached	28.57
1972	Forest Noble	16-1	P McEvoy, Wimbledon	28.85
1971	Camira Story	5-1	A Jackson, Clapton	28.88
1970	Moordyke Spot	4-6F	S Martin, Wimbledon	28.74
1969	Bread Soda	20-1	W Wilson, Sheffield	28.80
1968	Local Motive	15-2S	J Kinsley, Wembley	28.86
1967	Castle Fame	6-1	J Pickering, White City	29.48
1966	Dusty Trail	2-5F	S R Milligan, Unatt.	29.40
1965	Clonmannon Flash	2-5F	R Hookway, Sheffield	29.41
1964	Poor Linda	5-2	G Waterman, Wimbledon	29.70
1963	Cahara Rover	6-4F	G De Mulder, Unattached	29.74
1962	Hurry On King	5-2	T Johnston, West Ham	29.67
1961	Jockeys Glen	6-4	M Sanderson, Unattached	29.15
1960	Clonalvy Pride	10-3	H Harvey, Wembley	30.18
1959	Mile Bush Pride	1-5F	H Harvey, Wembley	29.26
1958	Pigalle Wonder	11-10F	J Syder, Wembley	29.03
1957	Clara Prince	6-5F	P McEvoy, Clapton	29.44
1956	Silent Worship	5-1	J Bassett, Monmore	29.42
1955	Duet Leader	8-13F	T Reilly, Walthamstow	29.42
1954	Rushton Mac	EvsF	F Johnson, Unattached	30.24
1953	Home Luck	5-1	S Martin, Wimbledon	29.49
1952	Marsh Harrier	11-10F	W H Mills, Unattached	29.82
1951	Westbourne	10-1	N Merchant, Unattached	29.97
1950	Ballycurreen Garrett	7-4	H Harvey, Wembley	30.02
1949	Drumgoon Boy	EvsF	F Davis, Unattached	29.71
1948	Night Breeze	10-3	S Biss, Clapton	30.03
1947	Monday's News	4-6F	S Orton, Wimbledon	30.10
1946	Dante II	11-2	W France, Harringay	30.36
1945	Shannon Shore	7-2	L Reynolds, Wembley	29.80
1939-1944	NOT RUN			
1938	Roeside Creamery	4-5F	A R Harmon, Stamford Bridge	30.43
1937	Golden Safegaurd	7-2	H Harvey, Harringay	30.22
1936	Safe Rock	Evs F	F Wilson, Rochester	31.01
1935	Shove Ha'penny	7-4F	C W Ashley, Stamford Bridge	30.97

PETERBOROUGH DERBY

Staged at Peterborough over 420m

Year	Dog	Odds	Trainer	Time
2007	Blonde Buster	4-1	J Mullins, Unattached	25.36
2006	Seomra Rock (T3)	7-2	E Gaskin, Walthamstow	25.77
2005	Fear No One	4-7F	M Wallis, Walthamstow	25.57
2004	Run On Trooper	6-1	M Mavrias, Sittingbourne	25.73
2003	Tims Crow	4-5F	P Rich, Romford	25.59
2002	Letter Slippy	2-1	P Byrne, Wimbledon	25.57
2001	Kinda Magic	3-1	L Jones, Walthamstow	25.52
2000	Reactabond Rebel	11-10F	P Young, Romford	25.78
1999	NOT RUN			
1998	Spoonbill Snowey	4-6F	M Bacon, Perry Barr	25.20
1997	Dynamic Fair	7-2	P Byrne, Wimbledon	25.45
1996	Dynamic Fair	6-1	P Byrne, Wimbledon	25.46
1995	Gold Buster	5-1	N Saunders, Belle Vue	25.81
1994	Highway Leader	7-4JF	M Bacon, Perry Barr	25.47
1993	Gentle Warning	3-1	J McGee, Reading	25.76
1992	Pineapple Magic	4-5F	M Compton, Unattached	25.80
1991	Chief Canary	5-2	K Marlow, Milton Keynes	25.77
1990	Bolt Home	5-1	E Gaskin, Unattached	26.02
1989	Sky Jack	6-1	D Pruhs, Peterborough	26.62
1988	Lissadell Tiger	4-6F	E Gaskin, Unattached	25.80
1987	Quick Judgement	7-1	L Pruhs, Peterborough	26.61
1986	Stylish Start	5-2F	Mrs Talmage, Unattached	26.28
1985	Decoy Tulip	14-1	P Cobbold, Unattached	26.12
1984	Decoy Moon	4-1	P Cobbold, Unattached	25.92
1983	Dutch Jet	10-1	Mrs Talmage, Rye House	26.11

PETERBOROUGH PUPPY DERBY

Run at Peterborough over 420m

Year	Dog	Odds	Trainer	Time
2007	Westmead Prince	4-5F	N Savva, Henlow	25.29
2006	Too Risky	6-4	M Puzey, Walthamstow	25.66
2005	Fear No One	5-4F	M Wallis, Walthamstow	25.41
2004	Fire Height Dan	4-5F	M Puzey, Walthamstow	25.46
2003	Slinky	6-1	P Young, Romford	25.89
2002	Bocelli	13-2	D Luckhurst, Crayford	25.41
2001	Reactabond Ace	6-1	P Young, Romford	25.72
2000	Reactabond Rebel	11-10F	P Young, Romford	25.49
1999	NOT RUN			
1998	Del Piero			25.60
1997	Lenson Billy			25.41
1996	Spring Gamble			25.41
1995	Slick Mick			25.74
1994	Pams Silver			25.58
1993	Sure Fantasy			25.83
1992	Bagshot Boozer			25.90

PRODUCE STAKES

Run over 480m at Hall Green. Originally staged at Harringay over 475 (1983-1987), before switching to Wembley over 490m (1988-1992)

2007	Feel Free	14-1	R Baker, Coventry	28.70
2006	Dilemmas Flight	9-4	N Savva, Henlow	28.29
2005	Westmead Hawk	4-11F	N Savva, Henlow	28.44
2004	Paint Spot	4-6F	V Green, Nottingham	28.91
2003	Perchancetodream	4-5F	D Steels, Peterborough	28.65
2002	Abbeyfeale Ebony	5-4F	R Samson, Unattached	28.72
2001	Willie Go Fa	7-1	B Clemenson, Hove	28.54
2000	Hes Nobody Fools	7-4F	P Ruddick, Poole	28.36
1999	Back Seat Billy	6-5F	J Coleman, Walthamstow	28.95
1998	Wrestin Cool	4-1	J Page, Milton Keynes	28.71
1997	Hedsor Kurt	7-4F	K Howard, Reading	28.53
1996	Batsford Blade	5-1	D Mann, Swindon	28.69
1995	Staplers Jo	1-5F	N Savva, Walthamstow	28.49
1994	Westmead Merlin	11-8F	N Savva, Walthamstow	28.33
1993	Magical Piper	9-4JF	L Mullins, Walthamstow	28.91
1992	Westmead Spirit	3-1	N Savva, Unattached	29.39
1991	El Tigre	2-1JF	D Knight, Hove	29.52
1990	Phantom Flash	1-2F	N Savva, Milton Keynes	28.94
1989	Cannongrand	7-1	M Bass, Henlow	29.08
1988	Decoy Regan Lass	11-4	Lucas, Unattached	29.21
1987	Able Sam	5-2	S Houlker, Norton Canes	28.56
1986	Westmead Cannon	10-11F	N Savva, Milton Keynes	28.53
1985	Fearless Champ	8-11F	G De Mulder, Oxford	28.64
1984	Queen Lisa	13-2	E Pateman, Wimbledon	28.72
1983	Glatton Grange	8-11F	K Linzell, Walthamstow	28.68

PUPPY CLASSIC

Staged at Nottingham over 500m

2007	Sibsey Showtime	7-2	H Crapper, Sheffield	29.96
2006	Fear Robben	6-4F	M Wallis, Walthamstow	30.19
2005	Ronnies Champion	9-4	M Wallis, Walthamstow	30.01
2004	Ballymac Niloc	6-4F	C Philpott, Coventry	30.37
2003	Droopys Shearer	2-9F	T Soppitt, Unattached	29.47
2002	Jurassic Jack	7-4F	T Meek, Hall Green	30.24
2001	Top Savings	2-1	G Adam, Peterborough	29.67TR
2000	Westmead Woofa	4-5F	N Savva, Unattached	29.87TR
1999	Kit Kat Kid	10-11F	C Lister, Unattached	30.56
1998	Sarah Dee	9-1	N Savva, Milton Keynes	30.58
1997	Jaspers Boy	11-10F	D Pruhs, Peterborough	30.17
1996	Buchari	14-1	T Meek, Hall Green	30.29
1995	Elliots Gem	7-1	N Chambers, Nottingham	30.09

PUPPY CUP

Staged at Romford over 400m

Year	Dog	Odds	Trainer/Owner	Time
2007	Westmead Keawn	11-8F	N Savva, Henlow	24.07
2006	Roswell Starship	7-4	M Wallis, Walthamstow	24.36
2005	Fear Assasin	9-2	M Wallis, Walthamstow	24.74
2004	Vamoose	10-1	D Mullins, Romford	24.40
2003	Living Jewel	14-1	D Mullins, Romford	24.55
2002	Knockeevan Magic	5-4F	P Rich, Romford	24.70
2001	Droopys Survivor	50-1	P Young, Romford	24.73
2000	Polar King	15-8F	E Gaskin, Walthamstow	24.42
1999	Droopys Rivero	6-1	N Chambers, Nottingham	24.61
1998	Bunker Buster	11-8F	K Linzell, Romford	24.43
1997	Ballyard Recruit	7-2	C Lister, Unattached	24.89
1996	Kalko	EvsF	T Dennis, Romford	24.33
1995	Teds Move	16-1	M Thomas, Reading	24.84
1994	Welfare Panther	7-2	R Wheeler, Unattached	24.17
1993	Chakalak Zeus	7-1	K Linzell, Romford	24.47
1992	Bonney Seven	10-11F	J Coleman, Walthamstow	24.77
1991	Taringa Bay	EvsF	E Jordan, Hove	24.89
1990	Dempsey Duke	8-1	T Kibble, Bristol	24.55
1989	Kylehill Zig	5-2	P Milligan, Catford	24.79
1988	Brownies Outlook	10-11F	P Payne, Romford	24.44
1987	Curryhills Gara	4-11F	E Gaskin, Private	24.23
1986	Rhincrew Whisper	14-1	J Wood, Private	24.61
1985	Cannonroe	6-4F	N Savva, Milton Keynes	24.31
1984	Hong Kong Mike	4-9F	R Andrews, Belle Vue	24.31
1983	Blue Style	3-1	J Honeysett, Wembley	24.02TR
1982	Creamery Cross	5-2JF	A Briggs, Private	24.48
1981	Seaway Lady	9-4F	P Milligan, Private	24.72
1980	Coolmakee Hero	7-4	T Foster, Harringay	24.45
1979	Sport Promoter	5-2	P Mullins, Cambridge	24.13
1978	Scholfied Fish	5-1	J Coker, Oxford	24.69
1977	Gan On Smokey	8-1	R Singleton, White City	26.25
1976	Lyons Skipper	5-2	C Orton, Wimbledon	26.54
1975	Xmas Holiday	10/-11F	P Rees, Wimbledon	25.48

PUPPY DERBY

Staged over 460m at Wimbledon

Year	Dog	Odds	Trainer/Owner	Time
2007	Opening Artist	9-2	B Doyle, Wimbledon	27.70
2006	Droopys Tops	3-1	C Lund, Unattached	27.57
2005	Droopys Lomasi	12-1	S Dimmock, Milton Keynes	27.79
2004	Olybean	11-10F	E Gaskin, Walthamstow	27.47
2003	Kinda Spooky	8-1	L Jones, Walthamstow	27.51
2002	On Line Deal	5-1	P Young, Romford	27.96
2001	Bringinthemoney	25-1	P Thompson, Crayford	28.00
2000	Navigation Lad	6-4JF	P McComish, Unattached	27.69

1999	Micks Lotto	2-7F	P Byrne, Wimbledon	27.49
1998	Sarah Dee	11-8F	N Savva, Milton Keynes	27.73
1997	Lenson Hero	5-1	N McEllistrim, Wimbledon	27.97
1996	Black Gem Charm	7-1	P Rees, Wimbledon	27.74
1995	Corpo Election	1-4F	W Wilson, Sittingbourne	27.56
1994	Bonmahon Darkie	2-1F	T Dartnall, Wimbledon	27.70
1993	Lughill Slippy	11-4	A Meek, Oxford	27.99
1992	Bixby	7-2	W Black, Reading	28.04
1991	Right Move	14-1	N Savva, Milton Keynes	28.25
1990	Murlens Support	1-2F	A Meek, Oxford	28.50
1989	Newry Flash	4-1	A Hitch, Wimbledon	27.97
1988	Spring Band	3-1	S Sykes, Wimbledon	28.13
1987	Debby Hero	12-1	D Kinchett, Wimbledon	27.99
1986	Spiral Darkie	9-2	G Baggs, Ramsgate	27.70
1985	Fearless Swift	4-5F	G De Mulder, Oxford	27.67
1984	Ben's Champion	4-6F	E Pateman, Wimbledon	27.61
1983	Rhincrew Moth	1-3F	Gwynne, Ipswich	27.53
1982	Mountleader Mint	2-1F	T Duggan, Romford	27.82
1981	Special Account	7-2	Mrs N Savva, Cambridge	27.79
1980	Desmond's Fancy	7-1	H Coker, Oxford	28.22
1979	Price Wise	12-1	E Baldwin, Perry Barr	27.70
1978	Purdy's Pursuit	20-1	P Rees Jnr, Wimbledon	27.83
1977	Ruakura's Mutt	9-4	C Coyle, Unattached	27.65
1976	Carhurmore Speech	1-2F	L White, Unattached	28.17
1975	Knockrour Bank	11-10F	J Coleman, Wembley	27.72
1974	Tory Mor	3-1	S R Milligan, Unattached	28.40
1973	Handy High	4-5F	S R Milligan, Unattached	28.17
1972	Seaman's Pride	5-2F	S R Milligan, Unattached	27.78
1971	Tawny Satin	9-2	T Johnston, Wembley	28.22
1970	Crefogue Flash		S Mitchell, Belle Vue	27.99
1969	Sherwood Glen		J Booth, Unattached	28.27
1968	Winter Hope	4-7F	D Dare, Unattached	28.53
1967	Breach's Bill	5-4F	Mrs Pattinson, Unattached	28.10
1966	Wattlehurst Rogue	5-2	J Jowett, Clapton	28.58
1965	Morden Mist		C Orton, Wimbledon	28.27
1964	Bad Trick		F Curtis, Portsmouth	28.46
1963	Pineapple Joe		D Hannafin, Wimbledon	27.95
1962	Cloudbank		D Geggus, Walthamstow	27.96
1961	Dancing Point		C Orton, Wimbledon	28.35
1960	Oregon Prince		P Rees, Unattached	28.59
1959	Violet's Duke		B O'Connor, Walthamstow	28.04
1958	Varra Black Nose		D Hannafin, Wimbledon	28.08
1957	Sean's Pal		T Reilly, Walthamstow	28.21
1956	Ford Spartan		D Hannafin, Wimbledon	28.02
1955	Glacier Metal		P Fortune, Wimbledon	28.74
1954	Gulf of Darien		H Harvey, Wembley	28.31

1953	Lancelot	P Fortune, Wimbledon	28.96
1952	Lizette	P Fortune, Wimbledon	28.75
1951	Moreton Ann	H Harvey, Wembley	28.59
1950	Rushton Smutty	H Harvey, Wembley	28.96
1949	Ballycurreen Garrett	H Harvey, Wembley	29.21
1948	Saft Alex	F Toseland, Perry Barr	28.72
1947	Mad Birthday	S J Biss, Clapton	28.56
1946	Castletown Tiptoes	S J Orton, Wimbledon	29.20
1945	Lee Ripple	S J Biss, Clapton	28.81
1944	Prancing Kitty	W Weaver, Catford	29.20
1943	Allardstown Playboy	S J Biss, Unattached	29.32
1942	Clow's Top	S Jennings, Wembley	28.99
1941	Laughing Lieutenant	H Hayes, White City	29.41
1940	Grosvenor Flexion	J Harman, Wimbledon	29.45
1939	Keel Border	J Harmon, Wimbledon	29.08
1938	Grosvenor Ferdinand	S Rolfe, Unattached	29.04
1937	Junior Classic	J Harmon, Wimbledon	28.86
1936	Berwick Law	L Parry, Powderhall	29.63
1935	Flying Joule	Mrs M Yate, Unattached	29.26
1934	Maiden's Delight	Miss Young, Unattached	28.87
1934	DH Tosto	S Orton, Wimbledon	28.87
1933	Denham Robin	Mrs Westerley, Unattached	29.31
1932	Mikado Beauty	J P Syder, Wembley	29.81
1931	Lavaka	J Hannafin, Wimbledon	30.00
1930	Mountain Loafer	P McEllistrim, Wimbledon	30.00
1929	So Green	J P Syder, Wembley	30.73

THE REGENCY

Staged over 695m at Hove. Run over 515m for puppies 2004-2005. Previously staged over 695m for all-aged dogs (1996-2003), and before then 740m (1981-95), 680m (1978-79), 670m (1975-77) and 725yds (1968-74). Originally over 525yds

2007	Spiridon Louis	6-4F	L Sams, Unattached	41.15
2006	Caloona Striker (T2)	4-7F	W Wrighting, Hove	40.82
2005	Jordans Glory	3-1CF	A Ingram, Romford	30.00
2004	Normandy Boy	3-1	M Collins, Hove	29.95
2003	Soviet Gypsy	3-1	E Gaskin, Wathamstow	41.32
2002	Dunbarton Cross	9-2	W Wrighting, Hove	41.20
2001	Killeacle Phoebe	6-4JF	B Clemenson, Hove	41.28
2000	Solid Magic	4-7F	B Clemenson, Hove	41.76
1999	Knappogue Oak	8-15F	K Bebbington	41.60
1998	Honest Lord	4-1	L Gifkins, Unattached	41.27
1997	Million Percent	10-11F	B Clemenson, Hove	41.69
1996	Restless Lass	7-4F	B Clemenson, Hove	42.40
1995	Suncrest Sail	1-20F	C Lister, Unattached	44.26
1994	Decoy Cougar	6-4F	T Cobbold, Unattached	45.00
1993	Trans Domino	6-4F	M Thomas, Reading	44.44

1992	Integrity Boy	4-1	D Knight, Hove	44.74
1991	Bobs Regan	6-4F	B Timcke, Unattached	45.05
1990	Sail On Valerie	2-1JF	E Gaskin, Unattached	44.45
1989	Manx Sky	5-4F	E Gaskin, Unattached	44.98
1988	Silver Mask	3-1	W Masters, Hove	46.07
1987	Yankees Shadow	1-2F	W Masters, Hove	45.28
1986	Yankees Shadow	8-1	G Curtis, Hove	46.03
1985	Scurlogue Champ	8-15F	K Peckham, Ipswich	45.20
1984	Mac's Jeanie	9-2	G Smith, Hove	45.41
1983	Aquila Bay	6-1	C Barwick, Unattached	47.41
1982	Paradise Lost	20-1	G Smith, Hove	44.65TR
1981	Fluffylugs	25-1	G Smith, Hove	46.84
1980	Garbally Magpie	5-2	E Gaskin, Unattached	43.78
1979	Jingling Star	5-2	G Smith, Hove	40.62
1978	Ballinamona Sam	11-8F	J Horsfall, Catford	41.74
1977	Bonzo	9-2	G Curtis, Hove	40.03
1976	Westmead Champ	13-8	P Heasman, Hackney	39.78TR
1975	Glin Bridge	1-2F	G Curtis, Hove	40.19
1974	Chain Gang	5-2	F Melville, Harringay	40.05
1973	Pepper Joe	10-11F	C Coyle, Unattached	40.81
1972	Adamstown Lane	4-1	G Hodson, White City	40.82
1971	Specfire	4-5F	P McEvoy, Wimbledon	40.88
1970	Glory Crazy	11-4	P Rees, Wimbledon	40.88
1969	Shady Begonia	1-2F	N Oliver, Brough Park	40.51
1968	Steer Me Home	9-2	N Gleeson, Wimbledon	41.35
1967	Ever Work	2-1	G Curtis, Hove	40.95
1966	Ardvullen	15-8F	E Eade, Unattached	40.71
1965	Warley	13-8	D Plowden, Unattached	28.86
1964	Chittering Cheapjack	EvsF	A Jackson, Clapton	29.32
1963	Tripaway	8-1	V Pateman, Unattached	28.81
1962	Royal Ace	16-1	D Hannafin, Wimbledon	29.63
1961	Luxury Liner	2-5F	G Smith, Hove	29.65
1960	Mr Watt	3-1	G Smith, Hove	29.60
1959	Ford Scud	7-2	W Taylor, White City	29.98
1958	Entre Nous	9-2	R A Chamberlain, Unattached	
1957	Highwood Sovereign	4-5F	L Reynolds, Wembley	29.14
1956	Barnaby Rudge	11-2	G Smith, Hove	29.39
1955	Kensington Bramble	4-1	M D Phipps, Unattached	29.46
1954	Box Hedge	3-1	G Smith, Hove	29.57
1953	Kensington Perfection	5-2	W Higgins, Oxford	29.56
1952	Ranjies Humoresque	8-1	J O'Hea, Park Royal	29.45
1951	Gay Rimmell	14-1	H Bullock, West Ham	30.04
1950	Kennel Sport	3-1	H Buck, White City	29.39
1949	Kings Signature	4-1	R G Mackay, Hove	29.49
1948	Bunnys Hoard	4-1	G J Smith, Unattached	29.83

THE SCOTTISH DERBY

Staged over 480m at Shawfield (switched to Powderhall 1987-88).
Previously held at Carntyne from inception to 1968

Year	Dog	Odds	Trainer	Time
2007	Fear Haribo	10-11F	C Lister, Unattached	28.76TR
2006	Fear Me (T3)	7-4JF	C Lister, Doncaster	29.21
2005	Droopys Marco	4-1	F Black, Ireland	29.05
2004	Farloe Verdict	11-4	C Lister, Unattached	28.79TR
2003	Micks Mystic	4-6F	C Lister, Unattached	29.07
2002	Priceless Rebel	5-2	P Hennessy, Ireland	29.08
2001	Sonic Flight	5-4	N Savva, Unattached	29.19
2000	Knockeevan Star	3-1	T Flaherty, Unattached	29.19
1999	Chart King	4-5F	R Hewitt, Ireland	28.98
1998	Larkhill Jo	5-4F	N Savva, Milton Keynes	29.01
1997	Some Picture	EvsF	C Lister, Nottingham	29.02
1996	Burnpark Lord	5-2	D Hopper, Sheffield	29.32
1995	Solar Symphony	5-2JF	S Ray, Stainforth	28.97
1994	Droopys Sandy	EvsF	F Murray, Ireland	29.39
1993	New Level	3-1	H Williams, Sunderland	30.22
1992	Glideaway Sam	25-1	M Compton, Norton Canes	30.26
1991	Phantom Flash	1-4F	P Byrne, Wimbledon	29.77
1990	Westmead Harry	5-4F	N Savva, Milton Keynes	29.62
1989	Airmount Grand	EvsF	G Kiely, Ireland	30.03
1988	Killouragh Chris	6-4F	P Beaumont, Sheffield	28.65
1987	Princes Pal	EvsF	H Travers, Ireland	27.58
1986	NOT RUN			
1985	Smokey Pete	7-2	K Linzell, Walthamstow	30.29
1984	NOT RUN			
1983	On Spec	2-1	H Crapper, Sheffield	30.50
1982	Special Account	EvsF	N Savva, Milton Keynes	29.99
1981	Marbella Sky	12-1	R Andrews, Belle Vue	30.66
1980	Decoy Sovereign	4-1	J Cobbold, Ipswich	30.68
1979	Greenville Boy	6-4F	P Mullins, Cambridge	30.49
1978	Pat Seamur	11-4	G De Mulder, Hall Green	30.52
1977	Amber Sky	6-4F	P Beaumont, Unattached	29.08
1976	Flip Your Top	11-10F	R Young, Unattached	30.56
1975	Dromlara Master	7-1	B Gaynor, Perry Barr	29.30
1974	Cosha Orchis	12-1	J Meechan, Shawfield	29.20
1973	Dashalong Chief	11-2	A Jackson, White City	29.60
1972	Patricias Hope	9-2	A Jackson, Clapton	29.22
1971	NOT RUN			
1970	Brilane Clipper	9-4F	J Kelly, Leeds	29.46
1969	NOT RUN			
1968	Lisamote Precept	5-1	J Kelly, Leeds	28.93
1967	Hi Ho Silver	5-2	N Oliver, Brough Park	28.90
1966	Dusty Trail	4-5F	S R Milligan, Unattached	28.59
1965	Clonmannon Flash	2-1F	R Hookway, Sheffield	29.00

1964	Hi Imperial	20-1	T Johnston, Carntyne	29.13
1963	We'll See	4-6F	T Johnston, Carntyne	28.91
1962	Dromin Glory	4-1	J Bassett, Clapton	29.09
1961	Hey There Merry	12-1	H Spencer, Portsmouth	29.11
1960	Rostown Genius	5-4F	J Pickering, White City	28.92
1959	Mile Bush Pride	2-7F	H Harvey, Wembley	29.41
1958	Just Fame	4-1	T Johnston, Carntyne	29.36
1957	Ballypatrick	7-1	C Beaumont, Belle Vue	29.53
1956	Quick Surprise	EvsF	J Mullins, Portsmouth	29.44
1955	NOT RUN			
1954	Rushton Mac	5-2	F Johnson, Unattached	29.20
1953	NOT RUN			
1952	NOT RUN			
1951	Rushton Smutty	9-4	F Johnson, Unattached	29.08
1950	Behattans Choice	4-6F	M Buris, Wembley	29.35
1949	NOT RUN			
1948	Western Post	8-1	F Davis, Unattached	29.45
1947	Trev's Perfection	9-4F	F Trevillion, Unattached	29.25
1946	Lattin Pearl	11-10F	M Gemmell, Shawfield	29.53
1945	Monday's Son	5-2JF	P Moores, South Shields	29.19
1944	Gladstone Brigadier	2-1F	K Newham, Warrington	29.55
1943	Bilting Hawk	9-4	C Askey, Catford	29.25
1942	Ballycurreen Soldier	EvsF	M Conroy, Carntyne	29.94
1941	Lights O'London	EvsF	J Harmon, Wimbledon	29.75
1940	Ballycurreen Soldier	4-5F	M Conroy, Carntyne	29.65
1939	Misty Law II	5-1	J Anderson, Powderhall	29.60
1938	Roeside Scottie	EvsF	M Downey, Unattached	29.53
1937	Jesmond Cutlet	2-1JF	D Hawkesley, Catford	29.83
1936	Diamond Glory	EvsF	B Melville, Unattached	29.99
1935	Olive's Best	4-7F	A Callanan, Wembley	30.16
1934	Olive's Best	7-4JF	A Callanan, Wembley	29.90
1933	SLD	4-9F	JW Tallantire, Powderhall	30.30
1932	Laverock	8-1	White City, Glasgow	30.10
1931	Sister Olive	5-1	White City, Glasgow	30.65
1930	Captured Half	1-5F	S Biss, West Ham	30.30
1929	Clevaralitz	3-1	F Mulliner, Wembley	30.87
1928	Glinger Bank	100-6	J Snowball, Powderhall	30.39

SCURRY GOLD CUP

Staged at Perry Barr over 275m. Previously held at Catford (385m) from 1987 to 2002, Slough (434m/475yds) from 1974 to 1984 and Clapton (400yds) from 1928 to 1973

2007	Horseshoe Ping	4-11F	J Reynolds, Romford	16.19
2006	Ballymac Rooster	7-4	C Philpott, Coventry	16.08
2005	Laser Beam	EvsF	H Williams, Unattached	16.06
2004	NOT RUN			
2003	NOT RUN			
2002	Letter Slippy	5-2	P Byrne, Wimbledon	23.73

2001	Kalooki Jet	7-4JF	S Spiers, Catford	23.90
2000	El Boss	5-4F	L Mullins, Walthamstow	23.65
1999	Lissenair Luke	3-1JF	C Lister, Unattached	23.49
1998	Im Frankie	9-1	M Puzey, Walthamstow	24.40
1997	Shoreham Beach	10-1	D Stinchcombe, Reading	23.78
1996	Come On Royal	4-1	B McIntosh, Canterbury	23.58
1995	Demesne Bear	10-11F	P Payne, Romford	23.68
1994	Rabatino	7-2	J McGee, Canterbury	23.57
1993	Kind Of Magic	5-1	L Miller, Oxford	23.82
1992	Glengar Desire	5-1	J Fletcher, Canterbury	23.96
1991	Portrun Flier	2-1F	P Milligan, Catford	23.43
1990	Ready Rubbed	5-1	J McGee, Hackney	23.76
1989	Nans Brute	16-1	W Masters, Hove	23.59
1988	Farncombe Black	8-13F	E Gaskin, Unattached	23.56
1987	Rapid Mover	EvsF	F Wiseman, Unattached	23.62
1986	Mollifrend Lucky	5-4F	C Packham, Reading	26.62
1985	Daley's Gold	4-5F	J Fisher, Reading	27.23
1984	Yankee Express	11-10F	G Curtis, Hove	27.03
1983	Yankee Express	8-11F	G Curtis, Hove	26.84
1982	Yankee Express	5-2	G Curtis, Hove	27.19
1981	Longcross Smokey	5-1	P C Rees, Wimbledon	27.17
1980	Willing Slave	2-1	E Dickson, Slough	27.11
1979	Northway Point	20-1	G Morrow, Cambridge	27.20
1978	Greenfield Fox	5-2	E Dickson, Slough	27.00
1977	Wired To Moon	4-1	G Curtis, Hove	26.63
1976	Xmas Holiday	11-10F	P Rees, Wimbledon	26.67
1975	Longnor Lad	4-1	B Parsons, Hall Green	26.77
1974	Westmead Valley	11-10F	H McEntyre, Bletchley	26.24
1973	Casa Miel	7-2	J Pickering, White City	22.83
1972	Cricket Bunny	6-1	J Booth, Unattached	22.77
1971	Don't Gambol	4-11F	P McEvoy, Wimbledon	22.73
1970	Don't Gambol	3-1	P McEvoy, Wimbledon	22.48
1969	Ace Of Trumps	EvsF	J Coleman, Romford	22.85
1968	Foyle Tonic	15-8F	P Keane, Clapton	22.59
1967	Carry On Oregon	1-2F	C Orton, Wimbledon	22.62
1966	Geddy's Blaze	9-2	T Gudgin, Clapton	22.79
1965	After You	7-1	J Bassett, Clapton	22.47
1964	Salthill Sand	100-6	J Bassett, Clapton	22.72
1963	Lucky Joan II	3-1	J Bassett, Clapton	22.70
1962	Hi Darkie	6-4F	R J Wilkes, Unattached	22.95
1961	Palm's Printer	10-11F	G C Doyle, Clapton	22.63
1960	Gorey Airways	5-4F	J Jowett, Clapton	22.48
1959	Gorey Airways	9-4	J Jowett, Clapton	22.95
1958	Beware Champ	8-11F	G Waterman, Wimbledon	22.71
1957	Lisbrook Chieftain	6-1	M Holland, Unattached	23.09
1956	Belinga's Customer	100-3	B Melville, Wembley	22.92
1955	Chance Me Paddy	2-1F	J Linney, Catford	22.85

1954	Demon King	4-9F	H Harvey, Wembley	22.84
1953	Rolling Mike	5-2Jf	J Jowett, Clapton	22.77
1952	Monachdy Girlie	4-1	J Jowett, Clapton	23.08
1951	Defence Leader	4-1	J Mills, Unattached	22.99
1950	Gortnagory	3-1	H Merchant, Unattached	23.47
1949	Burndennet Brook	5-2	L Reynolds, Wembley	23.48
1948	Local Interprize	5-4F	S Biss, Clapton	23.04
1947	Rimmell's Black	EvsF	S Biss, Clapton	23.48
1946	Mischievous Manhattan	5-4F	P Fortune, Wimbledon	23.40
1945	Country Life	10-1	P McEllistrim, Wimbledon	23.50
1940-44	NOT RUN			
1939	Silver Wire	9-4F	T Green, Derby	23.53
1938	Orluck's Best	11-8F	C W Ashley, Harringay	23.24
1937	Hexham Bridge	3-1	T Cowell, Southend	23.37
1936	Mitzvah	5-2F	A Callanan, Wembley	23.29
1935	Jack's Joke	10-11F	H Champion, Catford	23.15
1934	Brilliant Bob	9-4F	S Orton, Wimbledon	23.47
1933	Creamery Border	13-8	A Callanan, Wembley	23.61
1932	Experts Boast	4-6F	S Jennings, Wembley	23.61
1931	Brave Enough	7-1	H Buck, Harringay	23.62
1930	Barlock	100-7	J Kennedy, Harringay	24.19
1929	Loose Card	100-7	J Madden, W. City (Man)	24.13
1928	Cruseline Boy	4-7F	P McEllistrim, Wimbledon	24.91

SHEFFIELD INVITATIONAL

Four-runner invitation staged over 500m at Sheffield. Run as the Global Windows Invitation in 2007

2007	Blonde Jeannie	11-2	J Mullins, Unattached	29.12
2006	Clash Harmonica	5-4	C Lister, Unattached	28.97
2005	NOT RUN			
2004	Velvet Rebel	4-6F	C Lister, Unattached	29.70
2003	Toms Little Jo	9-2	G Baggs, Walthamstow	29.38
2002	McCarthys Duke	5-4F	B O'Sullivan, Crayford	29.67
2001	Magna Mint	7-1	B Draper, Sheffield	29.41
	Top Savings	EvsF	G Adam, Unattached	DH
2000	Droopys Honcho	10-1	P Young, Romford	29.58
1999	Frisby Flashing	4-1	H Crapper, Sheffield	29.74
1998	Plasterscene Gem	11-8F	E Parker, Sheffield	29.00
1997	He Knows	6-4F	B Draper, Sheffield	29.16

THE SELECT STAKES

Run at Nottingham (500m) from 1997. Previously staged at Wembley (490m)

2007	Cleenas Lady	5-1	T Dartnall, Reading	29.69
2006	Cleenas Lady (T3)	9-2	T Dartnall, Reading	29.61
2005	Roxholme Girl	8-1	H Keightley, Unattached	29.84
2004	Dairyland Sue	25-1	P Rosney, Monmore	29.74
2003	Droopys Shearer	2-1	T Soppitt, Unattached	29.85
2002	Droopys Rhys	6-4F	T Soppitt, Unattached	30.42

2001	Sonic Flight	4-11F	N Savva, Unattached	30.26
2000	Rackethall Jet	7-1	P Byrne, Wimbledon	30.45
1999	Jaspers Boy	11-10F	D Pruhs, Peterborough	30.00
1998	Jaspers Boy	6-4F	D Pruhs, Peterborough	30.29
1997	Larkhill Jo	2-1F	N Savva, Walthamstow	30.19
1996	Some Picture	9-4F	C Lister, Unattached	28.91
1995	Courier Kid	9-2	J Coleman, Walthamstow	29.25
1994	Snow Flash	6-1	C Dolby, Wembley	29.71
1993	Simply Free	7-1	C Lister, Unattached	29.16
1992	Pineapple Lemon	7-4	Compton, Unattached	29.35
1991	Summerhill Super	7-4JF	J Copplestone, Portsmouth	29.19
1990	Westmead Harry	3-1	N Savva, Unattached	29.30
1989	Yes Speedy	2-1	J McGee, Unattached	28.84
1988	Curryhills Gara	11-8F	E Gaskin, Unattached	29.10
1987	Stouke Whisper	4-1	J Honeysett, Wembley	29.48
1986	Fearless Action	4-5F	G De Mulder, Oxford	28.96
1985	Ballintubber One	9-2	K Linzell, Walthamstow	28.96
1984	Living Trail	66-1	J Honeysett, Wembley	29.32
1983	Whisper Wishes	5-2	J Holt, Slough	29.30
1982	Brief Candle	7-4	P Hancox, Perry Barr	29.13
1981	Greenane Metro	7-2	A Hitch, Unattached	29.47
1980	Desert Pilot	EvsF	G De Mulder, Hall Green	29.21
1979	Desert Pilot	4-6F	G De Mulder, Hall Green	29.46
1978	Dale Lad	3-1	G De Mulder, Hall Green	29.95
1977	Huberts Shade	13-8F	T Reilly, Walthamstow	29.32
1976	Mutts Silver	29.22	P Press, Wimbledon	29.22
1975	Tory Mor	4-1	S R Milligan, Unattached	29.21
1974	Acomb Dot	29.20	J Malcolm, Hall Green	29.20
1973	Say Little	7-4F	C McNally, Perry Barr	29.64
1972	Westmead County	9-4F	N Savva, Unattached	29.23
1971	Supreme Fun	5-2	S Ryall, Unattached	29.19
1970	Kilronane Jet	7-1	T Johnston, Wembley	29.07
1969	Valiant Ray	29.02	K O'Neill, Walthamstow	29.02
1968	Butchers Tec	9-2	B Melville, Wembley	29.31
1967	Carry On Oregon	13-8	S Orton, Wimbledon	29.15
1966	Dusty Trail	4-5F	S R Milligan, Unattached	29.20
1965	Geddy's Empress	11-2	W Kelly, Clapton	29.02
1964	Pineapple Joe	3-1	D Hannafin, Wimbledon	28.93
1963	Lucky Boy Boy	3-1F	J Bassett, Clapton	29.30
1962	Dromin Glory	4-1	J Bassett, Clapton	29.23
1961	Oregon Prince	2-5F	P Rees, Unattached	29.29
1960	Clonalvy Pride	11-8F	H Harvey, Wembley	29.02
1959	Mile Bush Pride	2-5F	H Harvey, Wembley	29.11
1958	Mile Bush Pride	5-2	H Harvey, Wembley	29.12
1957	Ford Spartan	9-4	D Hannafin, Wimbledon	29.18
1956	Duet Leader	11-4	T Reilly, Walthamstow	29.26
1955	Duet Leader	5-4JF	T Reilly, Walthamstow	29.77

1954	Rushton Mac	10-1	F Johnson, Unattached	29.34
1953	Endless Gossip	5-1	L Reynolds, Wembley	29.68
1952	Ballylanigan Tanist	11-8	L Reynolds, Wembley	29.23

THE SPRINGBOK

Run at Wimbledon over 460mH

2007	Blackmagic Jamie	8-1	E Gaskin, Walthamstow	28.82
2006	Kaysers Hill (T3)	6-4F	T Foster, Wimbledon	28.61
2005	Druids Mickey Jo	8-13F	S Cahill, Wimbledon	28.14
2004	Farloe Chinook	20-1	M Locke, Wimbledon	29.23
2003	Deep Sensation	3-1JF	J Reynolds, Walthamstow	28.41
2002	Opus Joe	7-4	P Thompson, Crayford	28.51
2001	Rossa Ranger	EvsF	J Counsell, Unattached	28.92
2000	Lenson Eddie	8-13F	R Peacock, Wimbledon	28.70
1999	Ballinabola Gale	EvsF	J Foster, Catford	28.11
1998	Frisco Sir	3-1	R Peacock, Wimbledon	28.05
1997	Simon Simon	5-1	G Baggs, Walthamstow	28.21
1996	Colorado Joker	4-1	P Rees, Wimbledon	28.32
1995	Arrogant Prince	7/4JF	T Foster, Wimbledon	28.35
1994	Avoid The Rush	7-2	B Doyle, Oxford	29.44
1993	Arfur Daley	3-1	B Meadows, Oxford	27.80TR
1992	Double Rock	25-1	P Rees, Wimbledon	28.62
1991	Fennessys Gold	5-1	R Peacock, Catford	28.41
1990	Ranger Supreme	5-4F	N McEllistrim, Wimbledon	28.80
1989	Lemon Chip	6-1	P Rees, Wimbledon	28.87
1988	Skyline Prince	5-2	D Kinchett, Wimbledon	28.59
1987	Lemon Yachtsman	7-2	P Rees, Wimbledon	28.36
1986	Raffles Nitespot	5-1	L Mullins, Harringay	28.59
1985	Knight Of Raft	8-11F	N McEllistrim, Wimbledon	28.65
1984	Scarcely Unknown	6-4F	D Knight, Hove	30.69
1983	Space Top	5-1	P Hancox, Perry Barr	31.94
1982	Democracy	6-1	P Mullins, Cambridge	31.41
1981	Clashing Ash	6-1	P Rees, Wimbledon	30.57
1980	Bobcol	2-1	N McEllistrim, Wimbledon	31.17
1979	Westmead Manor	6-4	N Savva, Unattached	31.28
1978	Super Hunter	8-15F	P Rees, Wimbledon	30.47
1977	Autumn Groves	9-4	F Melville, Harringay	31.31
1976	Stuart Captain	2-1F	J Coleman, Wembley	30.70
1975	Ashgrove Road	9-2	P McEvoy, Wimbledon	31.51
1974	Weston Pete	2-1	C West, White City	32.04
1973	Killone Flash	9-2	Singleton, White City	31.53
1972	Jacks Ship	11/10F	B Burls, Wembley	32.16
1970	Bawnies Rocket	2-1	P Rees, Wimbledon	31.86
1971	Ragtime	5-4F	J Coleman, Wembley	32.10
1969	Happy Harry	7-4	P Rees, Wimbledon	31.92
1968	Haydens Star	6/1	N Gleeson, Wimbledon	31.60

STEEL CITY CUP

Run over 500m (550yds 1970-1974)

2007	Boherna On Air	5-4JF	B Draper, Sheffield	29.19
2006	Womble	25-1	B Rumney, Sheffield	29.39
2005	Bell Legend	8-15F	M Wallis, Walthamstow	29.81
2004	Rhincrew Santini	9-4	E Parker, Sheffield	29.49
2003	Starofthebill	12-1	J Houfton, Sheffield	29.60
2002	Droopys Rhys	5-6F	T Soppitt, Unattached	29.26
2001	Jerrys Surprise	7-1	B Picton, Perry Barr	29.38
2000	Farloe Cobbler	7-4F	B Draper, Sheffield	29.43
1999	Knockanroe Rover	2-1JF	P Stringer, Unattached	29.35
1998	Anhid Knight	9-4	D Conway, Sheffield	29.68
1997	Frisby Free	14-1	G De Mulder, Hall Green	29.77
1996	Andys Surprise	7-2	D Conway, Unattached	29.47
1995	Justright Melody	7-4F	T Robinson, Unattached	29.36
1994	Anhid Blaze	6-1	D Conway, Unattached	29.45
1993	Gulleen Cove	8-1	D Conway, Unattached	29.53
1992	Gulleen Cove	14-1	D Conway, Unattached	29.92
1991	Woodhill Echo	2-1F	D Milligan, Unattached	29.59
1990	Kilcannon Bullet	8-11F	J Coleman, Walthamstow	29.56
1989	Nip And Tuck	3-1	D Hopper, Sheffield	29.75
1988	Lyons Turbo	5-6F	C Lister, Unattached	30.29
1987	Hollyhill Way	4-1	M Buckland, Hall Green	30.29
1986	Well Rigged	5-4F	R Hayward, Nottingham	30.59
1984-1985	NOT RUN			
1983	Caribbean Spice	6-4F	P Beaumont, Sheffield	30.29
1982	Fire Dragon	EvsF	J Booth, Unattached	30.14
1981	NOT RUN			
1980	Desert Pilot	2-13F	G De Mulder, Unattached	29.38TR
1979	Burniston Jet	3-1	R Hookway, Sheffield	29.99
1978	Westmead Manor	5-1	N Savva, Bletchley	30.08
1977	Gan On Paddy	4-5F	P Milligan, Unattached	29.58
1976	Tilbrook Herald	7-4	B Tompkins, Bletchley	29.21
1975	Company Cash	11-4	J Kelly, Leeds	29.65
1974	Gone The Time	4-1	J Kelly, Leeds	30.26
1973	Priory Hi	4-7F	R P Andrews, Unattached	30.42
1972	Kudas Honour	7-4JF	J Brennan, Sheffield	29.88TR
1971	Toremore Flash	9-4	J Brennan, Sheffield	31.20
1970	Westpark Toots	—	T Michell, Belle Vue	30.66

THE ST LEGER

Run over 668 metres at Wimbledon (from 2003). Previously staged over 660m (1999-2002) and at Wembley over 655m (1975-1998) and 700 yards (1928-1974)

2007	Spiridon Louis	4-1	L Sams, Unattached	40.86
2006	Ninja Blue	11-4	C Lister, Unattached	41.52
2005	Greenacre Lin	7-4JF	B Clemenson, Hove	41.16

Year	Dog	Odds	Trainer/Owner	Time
2004	Roxholme Girl	3-1	H Keightley, Unattached	41.32
2003	Shelbourne Star	4-7F	B Clemenson, Hove	41.21
2002	Alibulk Lad	10-1	D Steels, Peterborough	40.95
2001	Frisby Folly	3-1	H Crapper, Sheffield	40.74
2000	Palace Issue	1-2F	L Mullins, Walthamstow	40.74
1999	Dilemmas Lad	5-1	N Savva, Milton Keynes	40.56
1998	Droopys Pacino	4-1	T Bullen, Unattached	39.67
1997	Tralee Crazy	4-1	N Savva, Walthamstow	39.41
1996	Spring Rose	2-5F	C Lister, Nottingham	39.29
1995	Kens Dilemma	2-1F	T Mentzis, Rye House	39.80
1994	Ballarue Minx	7-2	W Masters, Hove	39.65
1993	Galleydown Boy	13-2	J Copplestone, Reading	40.06
1992	Airmount Flash	3-1	J Gibson, Belle Vue	39.81
1991	Temps Perdu	9-4	A Hill, Unattached	40.18
1990	Match Point	7-1	T Kibble, Bristol	l39.92
1989	Manx Marajax	33-1	N Saunders, Belle Vue	39.87
1988	Exile Energy	9-2	G Baggs, Walthamstow	39.76
1987	Life Policy	12-1	R Young, Brighton	39.96
1986	Lone Wolf	9-2	G Curtis, Brighton	39.99
1985	Jet Circle	11-4	T Dickson, Wembley	40.14
1984	Gizzajob	33-1	J Coleman, Romford	40.28
1983	Easy And Slow	5-2	A Jackson, Wembley	40.37
1982	Huberts Shade	13-2	A Jackson, Wembley	39.83
1981	Fox Watch	5-2JF	Mrs J Holt, Unattached	40.17
1980	Fair Reward	5-2	R V Young, Unattached	40.46
1979	Kilmagoura Mist	9-2	T Johnston, Wembley	40.04
1978	Westmead Power	4-5F	N Savva, Coventry	39.67
1977	Stormy Spirit	10-1	J Pickering, White City	40.22
1976	Westmead Champ	9-4	P Heasman, Hackney	39.90
1975	Tartan Khan	7-2	G Lynds, Bletchley	39.45
1974	Cute Caddie	4-1	D Kinchett, White City	41.17
1973	Case Money	6-4JF	E Parker, Harringay	39.89
1972	Ramdeen Stuart	2-1	N Oliver, Brough Park	39.82
1971	Dolores Rocket	1-2F	H White, Unattached	40.03
1970	Spotted Rory	2-1	P McEllistrim, Wimbledon	40.28
1969	Crefogue Dancer	8-1	M Burls, Wembley	39.65
1968	Forward King	9-4	J Brennan, Owlerton	39.98
1967	O'Hara's Rebel	6-1	M Burls, Wembley	39.54
1966	Summer Guest	11-8F	W France, Harringay	40.03
1965	Greenane Flash	2-1	J J Quinn, Perry Barr	40.13
1964	Lucky Hi There	1-2F	J Jowett, Clapton	39.90
1963	Friendly Lass	2-1	T W Dennis, Unattached	40.15
1962	Powerstown Prospect	8-1	B Melville, Harringay	40.62
1961	Clonalvy Pride	4-7F	H Harvey, Wembley	39.64
1960	Jungle Man	2-1	H Tasker, Unattached	39.93
1959	Wincot Clifford	5-4F	F J Toseland, Perry Barr	40.25

160

1958	Barry's Prince	4-1	H Harvey, Wembley	40.01
1957	Duke Of Alva	4-6F	H C Myles, Coventry	39.97
1956	Jakfigaralt	7-2	J Booth, Unattached	40.50
1955	Title Role	4-1	H Harvey, Wembley	40.78
1954	Pancho Villa	EvsF	H Harvey, Wembley	40.99
1953	Magourna Reject	7-4F	T Reilly, Walthamstow	39.88
1952	Funny Worker	6-1	M Burls, Wembley	40.50
1951	Black Mire	2-1	J Toseland, Perry Barr	40.19
1950	Fawn Mack	11-10F	G Curtis, Park Royal	40.56
1949	Lovely Rio	7-1	H Harvey, Wembley	40.77
1948	Streets After Midnight	5-2	L Parry, White City	40.40
1947	Dante II	2-9F	M Burls, Wembley	39.70
1946	Bohernagraga Boy	EvsF	J Syder, Wembley	39.92
1945	Robeen Printer	2-5F	G McKay, Coventry	40.03
1940-44	NOT RUN			
1939	Gayhunter	7-4	E L Wright, Harringay	41.79
1938	Greta's Rosary	7-4JF	E L Wright, Harringay	40.82
1937	Grosvenor Bob	1-2F	J Syder, Wembley	41.13
1936	Ataxy	6-4	L Reynolds, White City	40.39
1935	Satan's Baby	10-11F	L Parry, White City	40.95
1934	Bosham	13-8	L Reynolds, White City	41.17
1933	The Daw	6-4F	S Probert, Wembley	41.24
1932	Fret Not	7-2	L Reynolds, White City	41.35
1931	Mick The Miller	EvsF	S Orton, Wimbledon	41.31
1930	Maiden's Boy	4-9F	S Young, Unattached	41.48
1929	Loughnagare	4-9F	P McEllistrim, Wimbledon	42.76
1928	Burletta	5-2	F Mulliner, Wembley	41.91

SUMMER CLASSIC

Staged at Monmore over 630m (run over 684m in 2003)

2007	Datona Dandy	20-1	Y Morris, Doncaster	38.27
2006	Westmead Aoifa (T4)	EvsF	N Savva, Henlow	37.62
2005	Westmead Hawk	10-11F	N Savva	37.08TR
2004	Marmions	5-4F	P Young	37.93
2003	Centour Corker	4-5F	B Clemenson	40.60TR
2002	Glencoes Tom	9-4CF	D Steels	37.59

SUSSEX PUPPY TROPHY

Staged at Hove over 515 metres

2007	Westmead Tina	2-1	N Savva, Henlow	29.71
2006	Westmead Alec	9-4	W Wrighting, Hove	30.05
2005	Powerfast Rapid	9-2	C Miller, Sittingbourne	
2004	Dawnski Gypsy	9-2	P Young, Romford	
2003	NOT RUN			
2002	Young Deal	8-1	P Young, Romford	
2001	Santovita	12-1	O McKenna	

2000	Micks Best Hero	2-5F	B Clemenson
1999	Fat Boy Slim	5-4F	J Reynolds
1998	Dukes Again	7-1	M Puzey
1997	Metric Puma	4-5F	C Lister
1996	Kalko	6-4F	T Dennis
1995	Phardy	5-4F	R Steele
1994	Dennys Bar	4-6F	M Cantrell
1993	NOT RUN		
1992	Hypnotic Stag	7-4	J Coleman
1991	Handsome Henry	1-1F	J Honeysett
1990	Curryhills Brock	10-11F	E Gaskin
1989	Slippy Blue	1-6F	K Linzell
1988	Prideview Lady	15-8JF	M Puzey
1987	Ramtogue Dasher	13-8	P Hancox
1986	Hymenstown Wish	6-4	B Foley

TRAFALGAR CUP

Run at Oxford over 450 metres from 1999. Previously staged at Wembley over 490m (1975-1998) and 525 yards (1929-1974)

2007	Westcountry Lady	7-1	Jo Burridge, Poole	27.14
2006	Horseshoe Ping	3-1	J Reynolds, Romford	26.86
2005	Camp Bugler	5-2	B Draper, Sheffield	26.72
2004	Kegans Choice	5-1	B Clemenson, Hove	27.41
2003	Money Sweeper	6-1	J March, Peterborough	27.23
2002	Cooly Cougar	9-4F	B Clemenson, Hove	26.87
2001	Greenacre Belle	3-1	R Peacock, Wimbledon	27.13
2000	Droopys Mint	6-1	T Soppitt, Unattached	27.06
1999	Sensational	5-2	J Reynolds, Walthamstow	27.15
1998	El Cantor	4-1	L Mullins, Walthamstow	29.30
1997	Ground Zero	2-9F	G De Mulder, Perry Barr	28.85
1996	Listen To This	6-4JF	C Duggan, Walthamstow	29.35
1995	Clear Prospect	20-1	L Mullins, Walthamstow	29.58
1994	Trade Exchange	7-4F	K Taylor, Unattached	29.16
1993	Affadown Tony	7-2	N Adams, Canterbury	29.48
1992	Gara Paint	7-2	N McEllistrim, Wimbledon	29.30
1991	Claymor Spot	2-1	R Gilling, Reading	29.32
1990	Madison Supreme	7-2	B Silkman, Unattached	29.36
1989	Saucy Ben	7-1	T Foster, Wimbledon	29.99
1988	Alley Bally	7-2	T Dartnall, Wembley	28.96
1987	Fearless Ace	7-2	G De Mulder, Unattached	29.06
1986	Trans Brandy	16-1	E Gaskin, Unattached	29.70
1985	Ticketys Gift	10-11F	G De Mulder, Oxford	29.36
1984	Debbies Time	2-1F	P Hancox, Hall Green	29.34
1983	Glenamona	9-2	M Buckland, Cradley Heath	29.52
1982	Mt Keeffe Star	7-1	G De Mulder, Coventry	29.35
1981	Careless Dragon	11-8F	J Morgan, Oxford	29.24

1980	Sailor May	10-11F	D Kinchett, White City	29.45
1979	Trinas Girl	3-1	E Wearing, Bletchley	29.53
1978	Offshore Diver	12-1	C Coyle, Unattached	29.32
1977	Homely Girl	3-1	G De Mulder, Hall Green	29.30
1976	Hunsdon Pride	11-2	D Geggus, Walthamstow	29.33
1975	The Snow Queen	6-4F	Ryall, Wembley	29.34
1974	Pineapple Grand	1-5F	F Baldwin, Perry Barr	29.08
1973	Coin Case	1-5F	Smoothy, Clapton	29.55
1972	Stow Welcome	2-1JF	B O'Connor, Walthamstow	29.44
1971	Todos Imp	14-1	D Geggus, Walthamstow	29.56
1970	Todos Kingpin	10-1	Durkin, Walthamstow	29.67
1969	Sherwood Glen	5-4	Booth, Unattached	29.47
1968	Active Host	2-1	P McEvoy, Wimbledon	29.73
1967	King Cheatha	16-1	B O'Connor, Walthamstow	29.94
1966	Lucky Me	5-1	T Reilly, Walthamstow	29.33

TV TROPHY

Yarmouth 843m

| 2007 | Spiridon Louis | 4-7F | L Sams, Unattached | 53.42 |

Belle Vue 878m

| 2006 | Roxholme Girl (T2) | 4-5F | C Philpott, Coventry | 55.86 |

Wimbledon 868m

2005	Ericas Equity	5-4F	P Young, Romford	55.75
2004	Double Take	11-10F	A Heyes, Belle Vue	55.22
2003	Ericas Equity	6-4	P Young, Romford	54.62
2002	Serious Dog	4-1	P Young, Romford	55.14
2001	Killeacle Phoebe	EvsF	B Clemenson, Hove	54.27
2000	Sexy Delight	9-4F	C Lister, Unattached	54.51
1999	Hollinwood Poppy	10-1	M Clarke, Stainforth	54.89
1998	Note Book	5-1	G Adams, Peterborough	54.75

Hall Green 815m

| 1997 | Thornfield Pride | 12-1 | R Morris, Unattached | 52.17 |

Wimbledon 820m

| 1997 | Moanrue Slippy | 5-1 | K Rockman, Harlow | 51.35 |

Walthamstow 820m

| 1996 | Suncrest Sail | 7-2 | C Lister, Nottingham | 51.75 |

Oxford 845m

| 1995 | Last Action | 10-11F | J Wileman, Monmore | 53.68 |

Sunderland 827

| 1994 | Jubilee Rebecca | 2-1 | G Rooks, Brough Park | 53.13 |

Wimbledon 820m

| **1993** | **Heavenly Lady** | **6-1** | **L Mullins, Walthamstow** | **51.40** |

Belle Vue 855m

| 1992 | Fortunate Man | 6-4F | G Fell, Unattached | 55.70 |

Monmore 815m

| 1991 | Jennys Wish | 12-1 | E Jordan, Hove | 52.44 |

Walthamstow 820m

1990	Shropshire Lass	11-4	R Hubble, Unattached	52.48

Catford 850m

1989	Proud To Run	4-5F	H White, Canterbury	55.25

Hall Green 815 m

1988	Minnies Siren	16-1	T Duggan, Hackney	52.50

Oxford 845m

1987	Glenowen Queen	7-1	D Hawkes, Walthamstow	53.37

Brough Park 825m

1986	Scurlogue Champ	2-5F	K Peckham, Ipswich	52.65

Monmore 815m

1985	Scurlogue Champ	1-5F	K Peckham, Ipswich	51.64

Wimbledon 820m

1984	Weston Prelude	4-1	A Hitch, Oxford	52.14

Walthamstow 820m

1983	Sandy Lane	7-4	G Curtis, Hove	52.43

Belle Vue 815m

1982	Alfa My Son	9-2	L Steed, Cambridge	52.41

Perry Barr 830m

1981	Decoy Boom	7-4F	J Cobbold, Ipswich	54.27

Wembley 850m

1980	Tread Fast	12-1	G Sharp, Walthamstow	53.20

Hall Green 815m

1979	Weston Blaze	5-1	R A Young, Bletchley	53.16

Walthamstow 820

1978	Westown Adam	11-4	N Savva, Bletchley	52.27

Walthamstow 820

1977	Montreen	13-2	H Bamford, Belle Vue	52.40

Belle Vue 815m

1976	Aughadonagh Jock	12-1	B Jay, Perry Barr	52.77

Monmore 815m

1975	Lizzies Girl	7-4JF	E F Williams, Unattached	52.16

White City 880 yards

1974	Stage Box	16-1	N Savva, Bletchley	51.75

Wimbledon 880 yards

1973	Leading Pride	2-1F	G Curtis, Hove	51.16
1972	NOT RUN			
1971	NOT RUN			

White City, Manchester 880 yards

1970	Hi Diddle	10-1	P Heasman, Unattached	51.95

White City 880 yards

1969	Cash For Dan	5-4F	B Parsons, Nottingham	49.44

Romford 880 yards

1968	Shady Begonia	2-1F	N Oliver, Brough Park	50.53

Hove 880 yards

1967	Spectre II	EvsF	J Hookway, Sheffield	50.09

Walthamstow 880 yards				
1966	Bedford	20-1	R G Thomson, Romford	52.46
Wimbledon 880 yards				
1965	Lucky Hi There	13-8F	J Jowett, Clapton	51.35
Powderhall 880 yards				
1964	Hillstride	6-4F	T J Perry, Unattached	51.37
Wimbledon 880 yards				
1963	Curraheen Bride	4-1	W Kelly, Clapton	52.32
Wembley 880 yards				
1962	Avis	8-13F	J Rimmer, Wembley	51.30
Belle Vue 880 yards				
1961	Chantilly Lace	3-1	J Clubb, Unattached	52.38
Harringay 880 yards				
1960	Crazy Paving	100-7	C Payne, Unattached	51.22
West Ham 700 yards				
1959	Don't Divulge	5-1	L Reynolds, Wembley	38.72
Wimbledon 500 yards				
1958	Town Prince	20-1	L Reynolds, Wembley	28.14

WILLIAM HILL GOLD CUP

Run at Sunderland over 450 metres

2006	6 Paramount Silver	3-1	P Liddle, Sheffield	26.99
2005	6 Elwick Review	7-1	D Wilkinson, Unattached	27.39
2004	4 Airtech Rapid	6-4F	P Young, Romford	27.49
2003	6 Cool Scenario	7-4F	B Draper, Sheffield	27.24
2002	4 El Ronan	9-4F	C Lister, Unattached	27.47
2001	2 Deerfield Felix	9-4	O McKenna, Wimbledon	27.38
2000	5 Concorde Rascal	12-1	P Young, Romford	27.30

VASE

Run over 540m at Crayford

2007	Fear Martina	2-1JF	S Willey, Unattached	33.75
2006	Xamax Johndee	6-1	J Davidson, Crayford	33.87
2005	Merton Flower	4-5F	P Garland	33.68
2004	Topmeup	3-1JF	P Garland	33.89
2003	Droopys Regina	6-1	G Sallis	33.63
2002	Top Power	5-4F	L Jones	33.93
2001	Little Vintage	11-4	L Jones	33.77
2000	Baby Courtney	5-4F	L Lawrence	34.47
1999	Lake Shadow	7-4	D Luckhurst	34.64
1998	Rio Shadow	5-4F	D Riordan	34.45
1997	El Tenor	10-11F	L Mullins	33.83
1996	El Tenor	7-4F	L Mullins	33.81
1995	Heaven Sent	4-1	P Rich	34.05

Irish Review

by Ian Fortune

The presentation after Tyrur Rhino's Irish Derby success – on a rare Friday night

You could term 2007 a year of firsts in Irish greyhound racing. On the track we had the first ever Derby success for our leading owner/trainer combination of P.J. Fahy and Paul Hennessy, while there was also the first ever Classic success for 23-year-old trainer Pat Guilfoyle. Catunda Harry also became the first greyhound in Ireland to break the magical 28-second barrier when posting 27.99 around Limerick.

But, then, we also had the firsts off the track. For instance, in mid-November the new Irish Greyhound Board website was launched and, within days, live streaming of racing started from Dublin and Cork with linked online betting.

As one would expect of such an ambitious undertaking, there were some early glitches but the take-up was extremely encouraging. Within the first five days more than 500 accounts were registered and activated and the money started to roll into the tote pools.

This is the commencement of an exciting new era for Irish greyhound racing, but a close watch will be kept on attendance trends to see if the new facility has a damaging effect on the numbers paying through the turnstiles.

Talking of turnstiles they are expected to click merrily at Dundalk where we have entered the exciting new era of integrated greyhound and horseracing programmes.

The first of these was run on December 5 when a greyhound card followed on immediately from a horseracing card, but in 2008 it is hoped that the two forms of racing will intermingle in the same card.

Yes, these are certainly exciting times, but as always the happenings on the track were where the real headlines were made.

The Fahy/ Hennessy team came up with a fabulous one-two in the Paddypower.com Irish Derby, but for the Gowran-based trainer there

> *Tyrur Rhino, who had improved with each and every round, was only a late entry as both his owner and trainer felt that it might be too soon for him. It is remarkable how such decisions can change lives. Just ask P.J. Fahy and Paul Hennessy.*

was the added thrill of handling the great Ardkill Jamie.

Not only was Jamie the star of the tracks during the year, but as we pen these words, he is burning up the track as he undergoes schooling behind the inside lure for an ambitious challenge for the Derby Lane Million in Florida in February/ March next.

As with any year the feature was the Paddypower.com Derby and the record books will forever state that Tyrur Rhino was the 76th Irish Derby winner. But for once the biggest night in Irish greyhound racing was on a Friday.

Yes, we did say Friday!

Due to a clash with a European Cup qualifier, pressure from RTE saw the IGB change the date of the Derby to fall a day earlier. The move seemed insane and the attendance reflected the mood in Irish greyhound circles. A much smaller crowd made their way to the famous Ringsend venue, but those present will remember the celebrations for the rest of their days.

From the outset, the 2007 Derby was destined to leave a mark. There were a huge number of superb performances, many of the usual shocks, while the competition also had more plot twists than a Stephen King novel.

The early rounds saw the likes of Farloe Black, All Heart, Ardkill Jamie, Si Senor, Nawhobberthadda, Groovy Stan and the defending champion Razldazl Billy impress. Things had started to take shape by the quarter-final stage, however, and a Paul Hennessy-trained victory seemed ever more likely once Razldazl Billy was unluckily knocked out.

By now it was the emerging names that started to make their presence known. Kennel companions Tyrur Rhino and Tyrur Laurel recorded a 62-1 double for Paul Hennessy in the semi-finals, while Ardkill Jamie also qualified. If Hennessy was to win a first Irish Derby, this was his chance.

Although the crowd on Derby final night was down on previous years, the atmosphere was electric. The action in the betting ring was as always frenetic as the money flooded for Ardkill Jamie, who was to start a clear favourite at 5-4. Tyrur Laurel started 7-2 second choice in the betting ahead of Groovy Stan at 4-1, Express Ego at 9-2, while So Determined was the rank outsider at 16-1. Despite winning his semi-final, Tyrur Rhino started a 10-1 chance.

It was soon evident that 10-1 was overly generous about Tyrur Rhino. The son of the brilliant Tyrur Ted shot from trap five to dispute the early lead. Ardkill Jamie had also been fast into stride, but he failed to clear Express Ego and when the latter cut the turn, the favourite was left short of room and checked wide.

This effectively ended his chance. Instead Tyrur Rhino and Express Ego disputed the lead, but Tyrur Rhino had the better momentum on the outside and he edged to the front before the second bend. By now Tyrur Laurel had moved third and was soon challenging for second with Express Ego.

The race was on, but pole position lay firmly with Tyrur Rhino. Express Ego and Tyrur Laurel both tried in vain to reel in the leader, but he wasn't to be denied. Displaying real determination, Tyrur Rhino galloped strongly up the home-straight to deny the brave Tyrur Laurel by a length-and-a-half in a fast 29.73sec.

Not only had Paul Hennessy and P.J. Fahy won the Derby, but they were also responsible for the runner-up.

In victory Tyrur Rhino had become the third champion in four years to win at odds of 10-1. Incredible scenes followed as what seemed like half the population of Galway poured onto the track to congratulate P.J. Fahy.

It later transpired the Tyrur Rhino, who had improved with each and every round, was only a late entry as both his owner and trainer felt that it might be too soon for him. It is remarkable how such decisions can change lives. Just ask P.J. Fahy and Paul Hennessy.

Of course, it had already been a magnificent year for Hennessy, mainly due to the exploits of Ardkill Jamie. The 2006 Laurels champion had an even better 2007. His year got off to a flying start in the Donal Reilly Auctioneers Easter Cup.

As the second most valuable stake on the calendar, it was fitting that it featured many of Ireland's top names and the likes of Razldazl Billy, Jaxerback, Holborn Post, Loyal Honcho, Astronomic and Ballyhoe Marble made it a competition to remember.

Come the night of the decider, Razldazl Billy was the 7-4 favourite, with Loyal Honcho at 3-1 and Ardkill Jamie at 4-1. All three were to play their part in making this perhaps the most memorable race of 2007.

Rank outsider Aries Son set the pace to the turn, but he was joined down the back by Razldazl Billy who soon took over. By now Ardkill Jamie was closing and he moved second before the third turn at which point he was forced to check slightly. Razldazl Billy turned for home with a two-length lead, but Ardkill Jamie wasn't finished with yet.

In a driving finish, and to an incredible ovation, Ardkill Jamie got up to snatch victory by a head in a sensational 28.30sec.

Ardkill Jamie's next outing came in the Ladbrokes 600 and, while he was caught in the opening round by Greenwell Storm, he always seemed to have an edge in the competition. There was no sign of Razldazl Billy on this occasion, although Si Senor made sure the brilliant blue stayed on his toes.

The pair met three times in the competition with Ardkill Jamie emerging on top on all three occasions, most notably in the decider when leading from start to finish to beat Si Senor by three-parts-of-a-length in 32.58sec.

Jamie then had a break, but his spell on the sidelines seemed to take a bit of the edge off and he failed to make the final of the Boylesports Champion Stakes and another clash with his great rival, Razldazl Billy.

Many will believe it was no harm as on this occasion, Razldazl Billy may have been unbeatable. If his defeat behind Ardkill Jamie in the Easter Cup was the race of the year, then Razldazl Billy's display in winning the Champion Stakes was perhaps the performance of the year.

Coming from fifth spot on the turn, the brilliant son of Brett Lee shot past a number of top-class rivals down the back-straight before showing magical trackcraft to shoot through on the inside at the third turn. From there Razldazl Billy went on to beat Tyrur Bertie by two lengths in 29.72sec. It was a truly awesome run from an awesome greyhound.

While the well-established Razldazl Billy and Ardkill Jamie were dominating the headlines in the first half of the year, a young greyhound by the name of Catunda Harry was starting to make ripples. After making a real impression in his early starts around Shelbourne Park he was then sent to Limerick for the Golden Muzzle.

The fact that he went unbeaten through the stake is hardly surprising, but he did create history by becoming the first greyhound in Ireland to dip under the magical 28 second barrier. To prove that this was no fluke, the Owen McKenna-trained superstar ended the year with a real flourish.

First he captured the Cashmans Laurels at Curraheen Park. His task was made easier after Droopys Robinho was withdrawn after picking up an injury in the days leading up to the decider, but it is doubtful whether he could have done anything to stop Catunda Harry. The son of Elite State was in superlative form on the big night and, leading before the turn, he went on to beat Derby runner-up Tyrur Laurel by two-and-a-half lengths in a brilliant 28.18sec.

There was no resting on his 'Laurels', however. A fortnight later Catunda Harry took his place in the semi-finals of the Gain Waterford Masters, winning in 29.41sec before going one spot faster in the final when coming home six lengths clear of Click Click in 29.40sec.

Of course, Owen McKenna had earlier tasted classic victory with Lughill Jo in the Kerry Agri-Business Irish St Leger at Limerick.

The enigmatic blue made steady progress through the stake before pouncing with a brilliant display in the decider. Leading from trap-rise, the result was never in doubt and Lughill Jo came home two-and-a-half lengths clear of Tyrur Rocky in a near-record 29.37sec.

Pat Buckley also tasted big-race success in Mullingar's sole classic, the Irish Cesarewitch.

After sending out Droopy Armani to claim the runner-up spot the previous year, it must have been hugely gratifying for Buckley to go one better with Micks Savings.

The sleek black was simply untouchable in the competition. He was never headed in the competition and turned the decider into an exhibition as the powerful son of Top Savings made every inch to beat Florys Attraction by five lengths in a track record-breaking 32.92sec.

Incidentally, Droopys Ike, a kennel companion to Micks Savings, finished third before going on to provide Buckley with further Classic glory.

After the Cesarewitch, Droopys Ike was switched to six bends and he made an immediate impact, winning the Barrys Tea 750 at Cork before hitting Harold's Cross for a crack at the sole six-bend Classic, the Corn Cuchulainn.

It was at Harold's Cross that Droopys Ike really came into his own. Going unbeaten through the competition, the talented son of Droopys Vieri came from way off the pace to claim a length success over Bombersgoinghome in the decider.

On the opposite end of the scale are the sprinters and Johnny Gatillo upset some of the big guns when claiming Ireland's premier sprinting competition, the Bar One Racing Irish Sprint Cup at Dundalk.

Despite a series of impressive performances, the Martin Lanney-trained Johnny Gatillo was sent to traps a 7-1 chance in the decider, but he belied his odds, leading on the turn before going on to stop the clock in 21.26sec.

Other big winners worth a mention were Ballyhoe Marble, who started the year off with a bang in the Tote Gold Cup, and Green Heat who starred in the final of the Connolly's Red Mills Produce Stakes, but it is fitting that we finish the review of 2007 by mentioning Ms Firecracker's Sporting Press Irish Oaks victory.

In this day and age the greyhound game needs to encourage young people to get involved and stay involved in the industry and Ms Firecracker's victory did just that.

The daughter of Magical Captain was bred, reared and expertly handled throughout her racing career by Pat Guilfoyle, who at only 23 years of age is clearly a young man with an exceptional future.

After Ms Firecracker led from the start to beat Alexandrova by a half a length in 28.54 sec, her young handler spoke so eloquently about the importance of encouraging young people into the industry and it was immediately evident that he was speaking the truth.

Let us hope that more young people will follow in his footsteps in 2008.

IRISH LAURELS

Run over 525 yards at Cork

2007	Catunda Harry	28.18
2006	Ardkill Jamie	28.35
2005	Tyrur Ted	28.33
2004	Boherduff Light	28.14
2003	Nikita Billie	28.34
2002	Rummy Lad	28.33
2001	Sonic Flight	28.41
2000	Barefoot Ridge	28.69
1999	Lumber Boss	29.42
1998	Mr Pickwick	29.29
1997	Mr Pickwick	29.16
1996	Deerfield Bypass	29.12
1995	Standard Image	29.04
1994	Clounmellane Oak	29.44
1993	Lisglass Lass	28.97
1992	Market Rascal	29.58
1991	Terrydrum Tico	28.86
1990	Adraville Bridge	28.78
1989	Airmount Grand	28.78
1988	Odell King	28.98
1987	Yellow Bud	29.28
1986	Big Oran	-
1985	Follow a Star	29.42
1984	Rugged Mick	29.09
1983	Back Garden	29.66
1982	The Stranger	28.95
1981	Knockeen Master	29.50
1980	Knockrour Slave	29.00
1979	Knockrour Slave	29.45
1978	Knockrour Girl	29.40
1977	Ashleigh Honour	29.15
1976	Nameless Star	29.30
1975	Moonshine Bandit	29.30
1974	Silent Thought	29.50
1973	Kilbracken Style	29.10
1972	Dublin Eily	29.70
1971	Ivy Hall Flash	29.15
1970	Gabriel Boy	29.25
1969	Skipping Tim	29.50
1968	Flaming King	29.25
1967	Philotimo	29.65
1966	Westpark Ash	29.40
1965	Boro Parachute	29.60
1964	Tanyard Heather	29.20
1963	Powerstown Proper	29.75
1962	Dark Baby	29.40
1961	Round Tower Rose	29.80
1960	Last Lap	28.15
1959	Celbridge Chance	28.50
1958	Brook Prancer	28.43
1957	Kilcasey Streak	28.80
1956	Rather Grand	29.00
1955	Spanish Battleship	28.35
1954	Come On Bella	28.90
1953	Templenoe Rebel	28.55
1952	Tragumna Dasher	28.70
1951	Knockrour Favourite	28.55

CESAREWITCH

Run over 549m at Mullingar from 2001, previously staged at Navan

2007	Micks Savings	32.92TR
2006	Holborn Major	33.26
2005	Make All	32.79
2004	Karma Knight	33.12
2003	Droopys Gloria	33.58
2002	Mega Delight	33.10
2001	Ormond Park	33.45
1999	Not Run	
1998	Bonus Prince	33.48
1997	Bonus Prince	33.04
1996	Bonus Prince	33.16
1995	Roan Hurricane	33.08
1994	Roan Hurricane	32.80
1993	Ratify	32.68
1992	Gunboat Jeff	33.32
1991	Big Cloud	33.18
1990	Fly Cruiser	33.40
1989	Gourmet Manor	33.12
1988	Keystone Prince	33.60
1987	Oughter Brigg	33.08
1986	Cranley Special	33.12
1985	Sharons Postman	33.56
1984	Summerhill Sport	33.44
1983	Curryhills Sailor	34.16
1982	Debbycot Lad	32.94
1981	Murrays Mixture	33.54
1980	Rahan Ship	33.68
1979	Lomans Lad	33.90
1978	Gullion Lad	33.76

Year	Winner	Time
1977	First Debenture	33.70
1976	Murray's Turn	33.46
1975	Ballybeg Prim	33.30
1974	Ballinatin Boy	34.06
1973	Rita's Choice	33.04
1972	Itsachampion	33.48
1971	Rapid Maxi	33.22
1970	Postal Vote	33.08
1969	April Flower	33.32
1968	Young Ferranti	33.88
1967	Yanka Boy	33.38
1966	Pendant	33.59
1965	Butterfly Billy	33.26
1964	High Note	33.30
1963	Mothel Chief	33.71
1962	Harem Queen	34.35
1961	Perrys Orchard	34.00
1960	Pocked Glass	33.85

CHAMPION STAKES

Run over 503m at Shelbourne (staged at Lifford 2001)

Year	Winner	Time
2007	Razldazl Billy	29.72
2006	Large Mac	29.76
2005	Droopys Maldini	29.43
2004	Never Give Up	29.90
2003	World Class	30.50
2002	Longvalley Tina	30.15
2001	Glencloy Swift	29.09
2000	Lemon Ralph	30.08
1999	Mr Bozz	30.42
1998	Deep Decision	30.31
1997	Airmount Rogue	30.44
1996	Mountleader Peer	30.58
1995	Dew Reward	30.61
1994	Velvet Rocket	30.39
1993	Trade Union	30.59
1992	Within the Law	30.64
1991	Ardfert Mick	30.43
1990	Fly Cruiser	30.35
1989	Manorville Magic	30.34
1988	Randy	30.42
1987	Lisroe Pride	30.85
1986	Storm Villa	30.45

COX CUP

Run over 503m at Newbridge

Year	Winner	Time
2007	Tyrur Lee	29.96
2006	Droopys Electric	30.05
2005	Disguised	29.96
2004	Top Boe	29.89
2003	Simply Vintage	30.08
2002	Flashing Moment	30.06
2001	Word of God	30.09
2000	Lemon Sash	30.12
1999	Everton Hero	30.10
1998	Sineads Slaney	30.20
1997	Sir Grand	29.98
1996	Summerhill King	28.96
1995	Love Another	28.92
1994	Valais Express	28.96
1993	Kenmare Gem	28.90
1992	Lodgefield Gold	28.90
1991	Ardfert Mick	29.00
1990	Loum Lord	29.32
1986-89	NOT RUN	
1985	Cast No Stones	29.16
1984	Wise Band	29.20
1983	Celbridge Rose	29.28
1982	Cool Countess	29.30
1981	Mistress Post	29.82
1980	Brindle Choice	29.98
1979	Blushing Spy	29.78
1978	Point Duty	30.02
1977	Master Kim	29.51
1976	Stop It	29.26
1975	Newpark Twilight	29.72
1974	Nelsons Belle	29.64
1973	Pearl Ring	29.56
1972	Ashley Park	29.56

EASTER CUP

Run over 480m at Shelbourne Park

Year	Winner	Time
2007	Ardkill Jamie	28.30
2006	Ahane Lad	28.21
2005	Mineola Farloe	28.39
2004	Premier Fantasy	28.08
2003	Mobhi Gamble	28.47
2002	Late Late Show	28.74
2001	Late Late Show	28.60
2000	Mr Bozz	28.94

1999	Chart King	28.40
1998	Mr Pickwick	28.91
1997	Park Jewel	29.27
1996	Ballyduag Manx	29.23
1995	Lacken Prince	29.38
1994	Valais Express	29.13
1993	Jacks Well	29.54
1992	Farloe Melody	28.95
1991	Farloe Melody	29.53
1990	Lassana Champ	29.34
1989	Annagh Bar	29.61
1988	Joannes Nine	29.65
1987	Spartafitz	29.36
1986	Baby Doll	29.37
1985	Oran Express	29.67
1984	Spartacus	29.22
1983	Wicklow Sands	29.64
1982	Speedy Wonder	29.40
1981	Murrays Mixture	29.15
1980	Indian Joe	29.16
1979	Shady Bunch	29.42
1978	Rokeel Light	29.50
1977	Weight In First	29.58
1976	Cindys Spec	29.20
1975	Tantallons Flyer	29.60
1974	Aquaduct Rosie	29.52
1973	Newpark Arle	29.40
1972	Catsrock Daisy	29.01
1971	Postal Vote	29.36
1970	Monalee Gambler	29.52
1969	Move Gas	30.29
1968	Itsamint	29.63
1967	Tinys Tidy Town	29.59
1966	Clomoney Grand	29.50
1965	The Grand Time	29.50
1964	Ballet Dante	30.27
1963	General Courtnowski	29.98
1962	The Grand Canal	29.93
1961	Tinys Trousseau	29.66
1960	Springvalley Grand	29.92
1959	War Dance	29.76
1958	Sharavogue	29.96
1957	Doon Marshall	30.41
1956	Baytown Duel	29.67
1955	Spanish Battleship	29.72
1954	Spanish Battleship	30.17

1953	NOT RUN	-
1952	Wee Chap	30.12
1951	Clogher Mcgrath	30.03
1950	Sandown Champion	29.85
1949	Flash Prince	29.85
1948	Castlecoman	29.90
1947	Patsys Record	30.15
1946	Astra	30.40
1945	Astra	29.86
1944	Empor Lassie	30.35
1943	Monarch Of The Glen	30.43
1942	Wayside Clover	30.39
1941	Prince Norroy	30.32

LADBROKE 600

Run at Shelbourne Park (600yds)

2007	Ardkill Jamie	32.68
2006	Tyrur Ted	32.48
2005	Satellite Flight	32.52
2004	Awesome Impact	32.44
2003	The Other Master	32.81
2002	Haliska Vienna	32.69
2001	Late Late Show	32.20
2000	Joannestown Cash	32.49
1999	Frisby Flashing	32.83
1998	Real Branch	33.22
1997	Spiral Nikita	33.35
1996	Brickfield Blaze	33.45
1995	Druids Omega	33.61
1994	Tip Top	33.16
1993	Castleland Dream	33.40
1992	Trudys Fox	33.61
1991	Fly Cruiser	33.31
1990	Colorado Holly	33.56
1989	Gourmet Major	33.45
1988	Manorville Major	33.32
1987	Murlens Slippy	33.50
1986	Oughter Brigg	33.76
1985	Lispopple Story	33.73
1984	Killowna Gem	33.23
1983	Debbycot Lad	33.50
1982	Millbowe Sam	33.73
1981	Macintosh Mentor	33.78
1980	Ballarat Prince	33.54
1979	Tough Decison	33.72
1978	Ivy Hall Solo	33.47

1977	Heres Tat	33.26
1976	Ballybeg Prim	34.05
1975	Ballybeg Prim	33.40
1974	Tommy Astaire	33.56
1973	Case Money	33.68
1972	Itsachampion	33.45
1971	Postal Vote	33.27
1970	Mic Mac	33.65
1969	Itsamint	33.69
1968	Russian Gun	33.48
1967	Limits Crackers	33.50
1966	Vals Prince	33.30
1965	Faithful Hope	33.51
1964	Cranog Bet	33.60

NATIONAL SPRINT

Run at Ballyskeagh from 1999.
Previously staged at Dunmore

2002	Fast Gladiator	20.28
2002	Fast Gladiator	20.28
2001	Fact File	20.06
2000	Knockeevan Star	20.14
1999	Quarter to Five	20.24
1996	Old Kingdom	23.42
1995	Analysis	23.39
1993	Ballyfolion Shy	23.16
1988	Lisnakill Carmel	23.44
1987	Oran Flash	23.72
1986	Autumn Magic	23.53
1985	Arties Rover	23.79
1984	Market Major	23.78
1983	I'm Slippy	23.50
1982	Otago	23.56
1981	Noble Legion	23.78
1980	Blue Train	—
1979	La Cosa Nostra	23.83
1978	Noble Brigg	23.76
1977	Land Power	23.97
1976	Thurles Yard	24.04
1975	Rapid Roger	—
1974	Empty Pride	24.05
1973	Get the Point	23.87
1972	Clashing	23.72
1971	Benbradagh Luck	23.74
1970	Gaultier Swank	24.00
1968	Newhill Printer	24.10

1967	Mullaghroe Hiker	23.72
1966	Hairdresser	23.89
1965	Bauhus	23.73
1964	Dorade	24.08
1963	Melody Wonder	24.17
1962	Tanyard Chief	23.96
1961	Highland Fame	24.22
1960	Skips Choice	23.92
1959	Clougherevan Boy	23.84
1958	Obedias Son	23.89
1957	Coalfield Here	24.04
1956	Keep Moving	23.65
1955	Claremont John	23.77
1954	Hi There	24.51
1953	Mushera Shaggy	23.99
1952	Kilrid Blackbird	23.90
1951	Mad Companion	23.88
1950	Sandown Champion	23.88
1949	Burndennet Brook	23.99
1948	Leamas Sport	24.66
1947	Fair Moving	24.32
1946	Count Lally	24.56
1945	Oranmore Bandit	24.08
1944	Mad Tanist	24.11
1943	Fair Mistress	24.03

THE OAKS

Run at Shelbourne Park over 525 yards
from 1993 and 1977-78.
Staged at Harolds Cross 1970-76, and
1979-92

2007	Miss Firecracker	28.54
2006	Shelbourne Becky	28.58
2005	Grayslands Pixie	28.78
2004	Legal Moment	28.59
2003	Axle Grease	28.64
2002	Lifes Beauty	28.70
2001	Marinas Tina	28.60
2000	Marinas Tina	28.56
1999	Borna Survivor	28.67
1998	April Surprise	28.95
1997	Borna Best	28.86
1996	Fossabeg Maid	29.51
1995	Cool Survivor	29.35
1994	Shimmering Wings	29.23
1993	Libertys Echo	29.48

1992	Old Spinster	29.42
1991	Gentle Soda	29.12
1990	Bornacurra Liz	29.10
1989	Picture Card	29.40
1988	Tracey Budd	29.26
1987	Yale Princess	29.42
1986	Meadowbank Tip	29.34
1985	Airmount Jewel	29.06
1984	Burnpark Sally	28.92
1983	Quick Suzy	29.38
1982	My Last Hope	29.32
1981	Claremount Mary	29.52
1980	Strange Legend	29.24
1979	Nameless Pixie	29.34
1978	Hail Fun	29.40
1977	Snow Maiden	29.09
1976	Clashing Daisy	29.64
1975	Main Avenue	28.98
1974	Fur Collar	29.40
1973	Romping to Work	29.20
1972	Brandon Velvet	29.45
1971	Blissful Pride	29.30
1970	Rosmore Robin	29.60
1969	Itsamint	29.35
1968	Orwell Parade	29.96
1967	Kevinsfort Queen	29.79
1966	Hairdresser	29.40
1965	Drumsough Princes	29.76
1964	Knock Her	29.98
1963	Cherry Express	29.87
1962	Purty Good	29.78
1961	Just Sherry	29.95
1960	Tristam	30.03
1959	Last Landing	30.09
1958	Ballet Festival	29.73
1957	Gallant Maid	30.02
1956	Baytown Duel	29.99
1955	Prairie Peg	29.55
1954	Wild Iris	30.04
1953	Peaceful Lady	30.11
1952	Peaceful Lady	29.95
1951	Glenco Pearl	30.23
1950	Celtic Gem	30.00
1949	Coolkill Darkie	30.36
1948	Lovely Lousia	29.90
1947	Belle O' Manhattan	30.46

1946	Cold Christmas	29.86
1945	Paladins Charm	30.70
1944	My Little Daisy	30.08
1943	Mad Printer	30.05
1942	Fair Mistress	30.10
1939	Janetta Hunloke	30.47
1938	Gentle Sally Again	30.13
1937	Godivas Turn	30.61
1936	Chicken Sandwich	30.73
1935	The Fenian Bride	30.73
1934	Chocolate Kid	31.18
1933	Loophole	30.55
1932	Queen of the Suir	31.80

PRODUCE STAKES

Run at Clonmel over 525 yards (staged at Thurles 1999-2002)

2007	Green Heat	28.78
2006	Eskimo Jack	28.54
2005	Roisins Dessie	28.82
2004	Geldrops Touch	28.56
2003	Clashduff Fun	28.79
2002	Give N Go	29.19
2001	Droopys Kewell	28.95
2000	Moyne Rebel	28.70
1999	Borna Survivor	29.15
1998	Maestro Mike	28.84
1997	Clashaphuca	28.68
1996	Shanless Slippy	29.24
1995	Airmount Coal	29.31
1994	Come On Ranger	28.82
1993	Rhincrew Sean	28.64
1992	Glenmoira	29.21
1991	Live Contender	28.90
1990	Adraville Bridge	29.14
1989	Arrancourt Duke	28.46
1988	Dangerous Bridge	28.94
1987	Droopys Jaguar	29.44
1986	Dilly Dont Dally	29.52
1985	Kansas Rebel	29.58
1984	Spring Play	29.28
1983	Game Ball	29.26
1982	Badge of Hickory	29.70
1981	Calandra Champ	29.66
1980	Flying Marble	30.02
1979	Hume Highway	30.16

1978	Always Kelly	30.34
1977	Greenane Decca	29.68
1976	Cill Dubh Darkey	29.64
1975	Kaiser Bill	29.64
1974	Quote Me	29.64
1973	Big Kuda	29.98
1972	Rathokelly Gem	30.05
1971	Westpark Anti	30.18
1970	Gentle Lady	29.90
1969	Right O Myross	29.90
1968	Sallys Chance	29.85
1967	Whiteleas Gift	29.90
1966	Happy Thadie	29.70
1965	Kileden Guest	29.76
1964	Mothel Chief	29.70
1963	Piper Apache	29.85
1962	Rattle the Kee	29.45
1961	Kileden General	29.55
1960	Springvalley Grand	29.95
1959	Toast the Champ	29.95
1958	Summerhill Reject	30.20
1957	The Grand Fire	29.45
1949	Esso Major	30.15
1948	Something Short	29.90
1947	Priceless Border	29.54
1946	Crissie Tanist	30.40
1945	Victory Star	30.45
1944	Lottys Gay Boy	30.35
1943	Britannias Son	30.30
1941	Botleys Best	29.95
1940	Landys Style	30.30
1939	Sporting Fancy	30.20

PUPPY DERBY

Run at Harold's Cross over 525 yards. First run in 1943

2007	Royal Treason	29.12
2006	Oran Majestic	28.71
2005	Greenwell Storm	28.46
2004	Droopys Brooklyn	29.17
2003	Droopys Cahill	28.56
2002	Fortune Mike	28.40
2001	Rutland Budgie	28.34
2000	Droopys Vieri	28.36
1999	Cool Performance	28.50
1998	Prince of Tinrah	28.50

1997	Treasury Tag	29.05
1996	Rantogue Pride	29.04
1995	Airmount Rogue	28.94
1994	Glasskenny Echo	28.80
1993	Supplement	29.28
1992	Barefoot Racer	29.06
1991	Polnoon Chief	28.98
1990	Summerhill Super	29.18
1989	Crossford Dana	29.32
1988	Airmount Grand	29.26
1987	Make History	29.38
1986	Dream of Kerry	29.88
1985	Burnpark Black	29.32
1984	Summerhill Jet	29.24
1983	Lauragh Six	29.04
1982	Aulton Villa	29.30
1981	Greenwood Robic	29.82
1980	Killahora Cha	29.42
1979	Tivoli Cant	29.88
1978	Greenhill Paddy	29.40
1977	Hammond	29.46
1976	Glen Rock	29.08
1975	Elsinor Silver	29.40
1974	Shamrock Point	29.48
1973	Blessington Boy	29.68
1972	Clane Royal	30.20
1971	Luminous Lady	29.70
1970	Hey Dizzy	29.74
1969	Ballad	29.64
1968	Always Keen	29.75
1967	Quarrymount Prim	29.70
1966	Little Kate	30.17
1965	Prince of Roses	29.40
1964	Wonder Guest	29.96
1963	Fleadh Music	29.40
1962	Kudas Tiger	29.55
1961	Wild Spark	29.75
1960	King Niall	30.68
1959	Choc Ice	29.80

IRISH ST LEGER

Run over 550 yards at Limerick

2007	Lughill Jo	29.37
2006	Indesacjack	29.66
2005	Redbarn Panther	29.72
2004	Never Give Up	29.88

Year	Dog	Time
2003	Mountleader Rolf	30.01
2002	Larking About	29.73
2001	Droopys Kewell	30.37
2000	Extra Dividend	29.79
1999	Frisby Flashing	29.64
1998	Deerfield Sunset	30.03
1997	Fire Fly	30.36
1996	Airmount Rogue	29.89
1995	Batties Spirit	30.42
1994	Kilvil Skinner	30.84
1993	Barefoot Marty	30.54
1992	Barefoot Dash	30.40
1991	Castleland Dream	30.22
1990	Alans Judy	30.42
1989	Dereen Star	30.24
1988	Local Kate	31.04
1987	Randy	30.23
1986	Storm Villa	30.65
1985	Ballintubber One	30.42
1984	Morans Beef	30.06
1983	The Stranger	31.04
1982	Supreme Tiger	30.44
1981	Oran Jack	30.60
1980	Rahan Ship	30.72
1979	Airmount Champ	31.20
1978	Rhu	31.44
1977	Red Rasper	31.15
1976	Nameless Star	30.62
1975	Ballybeg Prim	30.44
1974	Lively Band	31.20
1973	Romping to Work	31.04
1972	Time Up Please	31.05
1971	Time Up Please	30.56
1970	Mark Anthony	31.02
1969	Own Pride	30.95
1968	Pools Punter	30.88
1967	Yanka Boy	30.77
1966	Movealong Santa	30.92
1965	Lovely Chieftain	30.92
1964	Brook Jockey	31.66
1963	General Courtnowski	31.12
1962	Appollo Again	31.26
1961	Jerrys Clipper	31.10
1960	Swanlands Best	31.60
1959	Ocean Swell	31.18
1958	Firgrove Snowman	31.28
1957	Kilcaskin Kern	31.05
1956	Prince of Bermuda	30.66
1955	Doonmore Dreamer	30.98
1954	Mount Nagle Surprise	31.10
1953	Gortaleen	31.26
1952	Silver Earl	31.25
1951	Ellas Ivy	31.08
1950	Maddest Daughter	31.55
1949	Ballybeg Surprise	31.45
1948	Beau Lion	31.52
1947	Pouleen Boy	31.48
1946	Star Point	31.55
1945	Dark Shadow	31.37
1944	No Relation	31.48
1943	Monarch of the Glen	31.48
1942	Monarch of the Glen	31.28
1941	NOT RUN	
1940	Cherrygrove Cross	31.82
1939	Negros Crown	31.77
1938	Abbeylara	31.61
1937	Cheers for Ballyduff	31.42
1936	Moresby	31.68
1935	Carras Son	31.82
1934	Chicken Sandwich	31.59
1933	Brilliant Bob	31.53
1932	Castle Eve	32.08

TIPPERARY CUP

Run at Thurles over 525 yards (550 yards 1964 to 2002)

Year	Dog	Time
2007	Comeonthecats	28.88
2006	Gifted Sir	28.69
2005	Broadacres Tommy	28.59
2004	Weatherman	28.64
2003	Killahara Dream	28.52
2002	Anchorage	30.25
2001	Matts Picture	30.42
2000	Always Sorry	29.11
1999	Brownside Darkie	30.29
1998	She Will Survive	30.50
1997	Airmount Ranger	30.72
1996	Emly Express	30.18
1995	Glenlara Ash	30.62
1994	Viscount Hustle	30.66
1993	Billy George	30.72
1992	Kilcloney Chief	30.48

1991	Coalbrook Tiger	30.44
1990	More Miles	30.86
1989	Manx Star	31.58
1988	Yellow Bud	30.84
1987	Lisadell Ranger	30.66
1986	Inchons Best	30.68
1985	Sybil Don	30.16
1984	The Other Duke	29.28
1983	Sailing Weather	29.20
1982	Shinrone Jet	29.42
1981	Bally Echo	29.72
1980	Carrick Chance	29.50
1979	Racing Prince	29.54
1978	Laundry Basket	29.68
1977	Linda's Champion	29.44
1976	Stop It	29.38
1975	Peruvian Style	29.48
1974	Millers Express	29.90
1973	Caultown Rose	29.50
1972	Westpark Ceylon	29.80
1971	Bold Invader	29.28
1970	Paddock Judge	29.85
1969	Clonsherry	29.80
1968	Roundtower Ville	29.45
1967	Gortkelly Hope	30.05
1966	Movealong Santa	30.10
1965	Knocklate	30.10
1964	Good Brandy	29.55
1963	April Twilight	29.85

PADDY POWER IRISH DERBY

Run over 550 yards at Shelbourne Park (525yds to 1985)

2007	Tyrur Rhino	29.73sec
2006	Razldazl Billy	29.49sec
2005	He Said So	29.66sec
2004	Like A Shot	29.87sec
2003	Climate Control	29.71sec
2002	Bypass Byway	29.42sec
2001	Cool Performance	29.68sec
2000	Judical Pride	29.68sec
1999	Spring Time	30.00sec
1998	Eyeman	30.09sec
1997	Toms The Best	30.09sec
1996	Tina Marina	30.20sec
1995	Batties Rocket	30.19sec
1994	Joyful Tidings	30.35sec
1993	Daleys Dennis	30.30sec
1992	Manx Treasure	30.53sec
1991	Ardfert Mick	30.18sec
1990	The Other Toss	30.14sec
1989	Manorville Magic	30.53sec
1988	Make History	30.26sec
1987	Rathgallen Tady	30.49sec
1986	Kyle Jack	30.41sec
1985	Tubbercurry Lad	29.14sec
1984	Dipmac	29.15sec
1983	Belvedere Bran	29.65sec
1982	Cooladine Super	29.34sec
1981	Bold Work	29.32sec
1980	Suir Miller	29.18sec
1979	Penny County	29.28sec
1978	Pampered Rover	29.23sec
1977	Lindas Champion	29.52sec
1976	Tain Mor	29.35sec
1975	Shifting Shadow	29.35sec
1974	Lively Band	29.11sec
1973	Bashful Man	28.82sec
1972	Catsrock Daisy	29.20sec
1971	Sole Aim	29.12sec
1970	Monalee Pride	29.28sec
1969	Own Pride (HX)	29.20sec
1968	Yellow Printer	29.11sec
1967	Russian Gun (HX)	29.44sec
1966	Always Proud	29.44sec
1965	Ballyowen Chief (HX)	29.42sec
1964	Wonder Valley	29.30sec
1963	Drumahiskey Venture (HX)	29.60sec
1962	Shanes Legacy	29.58sec
1961	Chieftains Guest (HX)	29.45sec
1960	Perrys Apple	29.55sec
1959	Sir Frederick (HX)	29.30sec
1958	Colonel Perry	29.79sec
1957	Hopeful Cutlet (HX)	29.60sec
1956	Keep Moving	29.18sec
1955	Spanish Battleship (HX)	29.53sec
1954	Spanish Battleship	29.64sec
1953	Spanish Battleship (HX)	29.78sec
1952	Rough Waters	29.95sec
1951	Carmodys Tanist (HX)	29.64sec
1950	Crossmolina Rambler	29.70sec

1949	Spanish Lad (HX)	29.87sec
1948	Western Post	29.90sec
1947	Daring Flash (HX)	30.04sec
1946	Steve	30.20sec
1945	Lilac Luck (HX)	30.12sec
1944	Clonbonny (HX)	30.53sec
1943	Famous Knight (HX)	30.26sec
1942	Uacteriainn Riac (CRK)	30.22sec
1941	Brave Damsel	30.64sec
1940	Tanist	29.82sec

1939	Marching Thro Georgia (LMK)	30.05sec
1938	Abbeylara (HX)	30.09sec
1937	Muinessa	30.83sec
1936	Minstrel Rover (HX)	30.48sec
1935	Roving Yank	30.18sec
1934	Frisco Hobo (HX)	30.45sec
1933	Monologue	30.52sec
1932	Guidless Joe	30.36sec

NGRC TRACKS

Shawfield

Newcastle
Sunderland
Pelaw Grange

Hull
Kinsley
Belle Vue • Stainforth
Sheffield

Nottingham

Monmore

Peterborough
Yarmouth
Perry Barr
Hall Green • Mildenhall
Coventry
Henlow

Oxford
Rye House
Walthamstow
Harlow
Romford
Swindon
Wimbledon
Reading
Crayford
Sittingbourne

Poole
Portsmouth
Hove

NGRC Tracks and Statistics

British Greyhound Racing Board

Address: Kirkmanshulme Lane, Gorton, Manchester, M18 7BA

Phone: 0161 223 8000 (General); 0870 840 7504 (Racing Office); 0870 840 7550 (Restaurant reservations);

Fax: 0870 840 7525

How to get there

Road: Follow signs to City Centre, then take A57 signs for Hyde and Sheffield. Belle Vue is signposted 10 minutes drive from City Centre. 3 miles

Rail: To Picadilly Manchester or Victoria. 10 minutes drive from each. Piccadilly, 3 miles; Victoria, 3 1/2 miles

Website: www.bellevuestadium.co.uk and lovethedogs.co.uk

Racing Manager: Bob Rowe

General Manager: Mick Hardy

Race days: Tuesday, Thursday, Friday, Saturday

Trials: Every Tuesday (before racing), Wednesday (day), Thursday (before racing), Friday (before racing)

Hare type: Swaffham

Distance to the first bend: 105m

Track Records:

237m	Little Flash	14.02sec	
260m	Quick Bozz	15.23sec	(8/11/05)
	Hackman	15.23sec	(18/6/06)
260mH	Blonde Chief	15.76sec	(26/02/06)
470m	Barnfield On Air	27.20sec	(04/10/07)
470mH	Emerson Squire	28.46sec	(16/04/06)
590m	Thunderbird Two	35.11sec	(13/11/05)
670m	Roxholme Boy	40.54sec	(20/7/06)
878m	Roxholme Girl	54.33sec	(18/3/06)

Major Events: Betfred Laurels, Wafcol Cock O'The North, J P Doyle Gorton Cup, Ben Holmes Northern Flat, Colin Harney Northern Oaks, Keith Swain Manchester Puppy Cup, Totesport Gold Collar

Trainers: Helen Adamson, Joy Andrews, Ronald Barber, Martin Cutler, Richard Fielding, Jimmy Gibson, Paul Gregson, Darren Hampson, Beverley Heaton, Andy Heyes, Otto Kueres, June McCombe, Nigel Saunders, Ron Smith, John Walton.

Address: Coventry Stadium, Rugby Road, Brandon, Coventry, CV8 3GJ
Phone: 02476 542395 (General) 02476 541155 (Racing Office)
Fax: 02476 541144

How to get there

Road: M6 Junction 2. Take the A46 to Coventry. Go across two roundabouts. At third one, with TGI Friday on the right, turn left into Rugby Road. Coventry Stadium half a mile on left

Website: www.coventrygreyhounds.com
Email: info@coventrygreyhounds.com
General Manager: Malcolm Francis/Avtar Sandhu
Head of Racing: Simon Harris
Race days: Wednesday, Friday, Saturday, Sunday

Trials: Tuesday and before racing, except Sunday
Hare type: Sealey
Distance to first bend (standard trip): 93m

Track Records:

280m	Ningbo Jack	16.63sec	(18/7/04)
480m	Barnfield On Air	28.85sec	(31/10/07)
625m	Well Tutored	38.96sec	(23/12/06)
680m	Tinrah Lad	42.48sec	(29/1/06)
880m	Head Iton Jordan	56.63sec	(22/7/07)
1,025m	Swift Demand	67.55sec	(17/06/07)
1,080m	Zuzus Petal	70.77sec	(23/12/05)

Major events: Tom Fruit St Leger, Nigel Flowers Coventry Summer Derby, Emerald Cup, Zigzag Kennels Puppy Cup, Blue Square, Blue Square 480, Mark Hill Marathon, SD British Sprint

CRAYFORD

Address: Ladbroke Stadium, Stadium Way, Crayford, Kent
Phone: 01322 557836 (general/Restaurant); 01322 522262 (racing office)
Fax: 01322 559394
How to get there
Road: M25 – Junction 1. Take A2 and follow signs to Crayford. Track is on large one-way system in town centre
Bus: 96 (red) 480 (green)
Rail: British Rail Crayford station is adjacent to course
Website: www.crayford.com
Email: crayford@formnet.org
Racing Manager: Danny Rayment
General Manager: Barry Stanton
Race days: Monday, Tuesday (BAGS), Thursday (BAGS), Saturday (BAGS and evening)

Trials: Before racing and Wednesday
Hare type: Outside Swaffham
Distance to first bend (380m): 77m
Track Records:

380m	Kingdom Club	23.01sec	(27/09/03)
380H	Rossa Ranger	23.36sec	(15/4/02)
540m	Sunshine Sophie	33.13sec	(28/2/04)
540H	Selby Ben	33.68sec	(26/5/03)
714m	Double Take	44.57sec	(21/02/04)
874m	Clonbrin Black	56.15sec	(10/93)
1048m	Stansted Flyer	69.93sec	(9/96)

Major Events: John Smiths Kent St Leger, Ladbroke Golden Jacket, Guys & Dolls, Tony Morris & John Humphreys Vase, Flying Four
Trainers: Jean Carter, Pat Cusack, John Davidson, Steve Gammon, Arun Green, Julie Luckhurst, Barry O'Sullivan, Ian Stevens, Pat Thompson and Paul Tompsett.

DONCASTER

Address: Meadow Court Stadium, Station Road, Stainforth, near Doncaster, S Yorks, DN7 5HS

Phone: 01302 351639 (restaurant); 01302 351204 (racing office), 01302 351650 (fax)

How to get there

Road: J4 off M18, follow signs towards Hatfield; stadium situated opposite Hatfield and Stainforth station (over bridge)

Rail: Hatfield & Stainforth station (local line serving Doncaster-Rotherham-Sheffield). Doncaster mainline approx 8 miles

Website: www.meadowcourtstadium.co.uk

Racing Manager: Stephen Gray

General Manager: Robert Watson

Race Days: Tuesday, Friday, Saturday

Trials: Before Racing

Track Records:

275m	Glendon Jack	16.63sec	
480m	Farloe Verdict	28.94sec	(13/7/04)
483m	Yorkshire	29.07sec	(2/8/05)
661m	Frisby Figo	41.00sec	(1/9/04)
	Black Pear	41.00	(4/9/04)
709m	Frisby Figo	43.93sec	(1/5/05)
910m	Ericas Equity	58.08sec	(10/9/04)

HALL GREEN

Address: York Road, Hall Green, Birmingham, B28 8LQ
Phone: 0121 777 1181 (General); 0870 840 7371 (Racing Office); 0870 840 8502 (Restaurant)
Fax: 0870 840 7390

How to get there

Road: 4 miles south of Birmingham city centre, off A34 into Fox Hollies Road and then York Road (400 yards).
Bus: 6, 31
Rail: Main line to New Street. Local trains to Hall Green station
Website: www.hallgreenstadium.co.uk
Racing Manager: Robert Coulthard
General Manager: Stephen Rea
Race days: Tuesday, Wednesday (BAGS), Friday (BAGS and evening), Saturday
Trials: Before racing and Wednesday (after BAGS) and fortnightly Thursdays

Hare type: Swaffham McGee
Distance to first bend (standard): 82m

Track Records:

258m	Lunar Vacation	15.30sec
480m	Farloe Verdict	28.09sec
480H	Kildare Slippy	28.52sec
645m	Palace Issue	39.01sec
645H	Go Dutch	40.70sec
670m	Fearless Lsynx	40.44sec
820m	Kilpipe Bib	51.71sec
892m	Head Iton Jordan	55.34sec

Major Events: William Hill Blue Riband, Skybet Gymcrack, Breeders Forum Produce Stakes, Prestige
Trainers: Sandy Baker, Gary Bakewell, Mark Barlow, Stuart Buckland, Nick Colton, Bob Hall, Allan Jenkins, John Pearce, Paula Simmons, Barbara Smith, Jenny Walters, Paul Sallis, Paul White

HARLOW

Address: Barclay Entertainment Ltd., The Pinnacles, Roydon Road, Harlow, Essex, CM19 5DY
Phone: 01279 426 804 (General), 01279 639248 (Racing office)
Fax: 01279 444182
Email: info@harlowgreyhounds.com
Website: www.harlowgreyhounds.co.uk

How to get there

Road: From M11 take A414. Signs to 'Industrial area', later 'Pinnacles'; follow through several roundabouts until reaching 'Gates Ford Motors' site (on left) on roundabout. Take first exit off roundabout and continue. Pass 'drivethrough' McDonalds on left, Burger King on right, keep going, pass railway station, rugby ground and golf course, then up a hill and track is on the right hand side.

Rail: Harlow Town (BR). Taxi to stadium
Racing Manager: Mark Schellenberg
General Manager: Gavin Patmore
Race days: Wednesday, Friday, Saturday
Trials: Tuesday (am)
Hare type: Bramich
Distance to first bend: 80m

Track Records:

238m	Nellie Thursby	14.73sec	
415m	Barton Wade	25.50sec	
415H	Bossy Pallashell	26.20sec	
	Inkspot	26.20sec	
592m	Treasured Manx	37.13sec	
	Decoy Cheetah	37.13sec	
592H	Blackrose Mars	37.11sec	
769m	Snappy Girl	49.43sec	(31/5/06)
964m	Countrywidecapel	62.98sec	(8/02/06)

Major Events: £500 Competition every week, 415m & 592m
Alternatively

HENLOW

Address: Henlow Greyhound Stadium,
Bedford Road, Lower Stondon, Bedfordshire,
SG16 6EA
Phone: 01462 851850
Fax: 01462 815593
Email: henlow@formnet.org
Website: www.henlow-racing-ltd.co.uk

How to get there

Road: From A1 and M1, take Luton turn off
to Hitchin. From Hitchin, take A600 towards
Bedford for about six miles. Follow signs for
RAF Henlow, track is on this road, on the left
and opposite Henlow Camp.
Rail: Hitchin Station then 10 minute taxi ride
Racing Manager: Paul Mellor
General Manager: Keith Woolsey
Race days: Monday, Friday, Saturday
Trials: Tuesday night
Hare type: Swaffham
Distance to first bend (standard trip):
60m
Track Records:

250m	Quivers Ace	14.92sec	(7/6/07)
277m	Second Option	16.67sec	(1/9/07)
460m	Fear Khan	27.28	(22/9/05)
550m	Questhouse Ellie	33.10sec	(24/4/06)
660m	Spankee Moved	42.46sec	(25/10/07)
692m	Lobo	40.21sec	(15/10/99)
870m	Betathan Pebbles	54.95sec	(30/10/05)

Major Events: Bedfordshire Derby

Address: Nevill Road, Hove, Sussex, BN3 7BZ

Phone: 01273 204601 (General), 01273 223805 (Racing Office), 08457 023952 (Restaurant)

How to get there

Road: From London, M23 to A23 (virtually motorway throughout), big new roundabout with Q8 garage on the right. Take the road up the hill so garage remains on the right.Top of hill, go straight on at next round-about, following signs for Hove. Take second turning on left, stadium is 200 yards on left.

Rail: Nearest station Hove (on Victoria – Littlehampton Main Line) taxi 5 mins, or Brighton, taxi 10 mins.

Website: www.www.brightondogs.co.uk
Email: hove.stadium@coral.co.uk
Racing Manager: Peter Miller
General Manager: Simon Horton
Race days: Tuesday, Wednesday (BAGS), Thursday, Saturday, Sunday (BAGS)
Trials: Monday

Hare type: 80m
Distance to first bend: 80m
Outside Swaffham
Track Records:

285m	Tims Crow	16.05sec	(22/5/03)
475m	Swift Star	27.47sec	(01/05/02)
	Cash The Deal	27.47sec	(26/07/03)
515m	Barnfield On Air	29.20sec	(31/07/07)
515H	Greenacre George	30.08sec	(01/08/02)
695m	Caloona Striker	40.73sec	(21/06/05)
740m	Form Of Magic	43.59sec	(30/03//5)
930m	Greenacre Lin	56.20sec	(08/06/04)

Major Events: Courage Olympic, The Regency, Coral Brighton Belle, Sussex Cup, Anna Derkson Sussex Puppy Trophy, Ballyregan Bob Memorial

Trainers: Colin Barwick, Brian Clemenson, Maria Collins, John Gammon, Claude Gardiner, Derek Knight, Tony Lucas, Wendy Short, Ken Tester, Roy Towner, Doreen Walsh and Wayne Wrighting

HULL

Address: Boulevard Stadium, Hull
Phone: 01482 215013
How to get there
Follow M62 into Hull then take A63 into the centre. Go past the cinema and bowling alley and take the next exit signposted 'Local Traffic Infirmary'. At the roundabout turn left into Hessle Road, then right into Boulevard. The stadium is off Massey Close (off Selby Street).

Email: hulldogs@bluebottle.com
Racing Manager: Mick Smith
Race days: Thursday and Saturday
Distances: 270m, 460m, 655m
Run to first bend: 106m
Hare type: Fannons waffham
Major Events: Summer Derby

KINSLEY

Address: 96 Wakefield Road, Kinsley, Near Pontefract, West Yorkshire, WF9 5EH
Phone: 01977 610946 or 01977 625124
Fax: 01977 625335
How to get there
The stadium is situated south east of Wakefield, a few miles from the stately home and grounds of Nostell Priory
Website: www.kinsleydogs.co.uk
Email: kinsley@formnet.org
Racing Manager: Craig Hunt

General Manager: John Curran
Race days: Tuesday, Friday, Saturday and Sunday afternoon (BAGS)
Trials: Before Racing
Hare type: outside swaffham
Track Records:

Distance	Dog	Time	Date
270m	Farloe Kinrush	16.05sec	(16/7/2005)
	Ballyneale Cash	16.05sec	(8/7/06)
465m	Drumwood Rebel	27.61sec	(26/11/2005)
655m	Welers Pet	40.26sec	(6/09/2005)
850m	Top Plan	53.18sec	(7/11/2004)

MILDENHALL

Address: Hayland Drove, West Row, Mildenhall, Suffolk, IP28 8QU.
Phone: 01638 711777
How to get there
Road: A11 to Barton Mills roundabout, take Mildenhall exit (A1101). Follow A1101 to mini-roundabout, go straight across (signed West Row). Follow road until reaching T-junction, turn left then first right. Stadium is approximately 1.25 miles on left.
Rail: Nearest station is Ely.

Racing Manager: Mike Hill
General Manager: Carl Harris
Website: www.mildenhallstadium.com
Race Days: Monday, Friday
Trials: Wednesday
Track Records:

220m	Lots Of Jolly	(26/10/93)	13.39sec
375m	Flashy Beo	(11/10/96)	22.88sec
545m	Much Approved	(18/5/04)	33.74sec
700m	Trade Link	(04/10/99)	44.44sec
870m	Barwise Smiler	(28/9/98)	56.15sec
1025m	Dusty Image	(16/11/94)	67.49sec

Address: Monmore Green, Sutherland Avenue, Wolverhampton.

Phone: 01902 456663 (racing office); 01902 452648 (restaurant)

Fax: 01902 456912

How to get there

Road: M6 take exit 10 (A454) Wolverhampton Road, which bypasses Willenhall and continue to the junction with Stow Heath Lane. Stadium is behind Wolverhampton wholesale vegetable market off that road

Rail: Wolverhampton Station, buses and taxis available to track

Website: www.monmoredogs.co.uk

Email: monmoregreen@ladbrokes.co.uk

Racing Manager: Jim Woods

General Manager: Richard Brankley

Race Days: Monday (BAGS), Thursday, Friday (BAGS), Saturday (BAGS November to January)

Trials: Tuesday (not last Tuesday of month)

Hare type: Outside Swaffham

Distance to first bend (standard trip): 60.9m

Track Records:

210m	Cry Havoc	12.64sec	(20/3/97)
264m	Jetharts Here	14.95sec	(8/9/07)
416m	Funtime Chunky	24.33sec	(24/8/07)
480mH	Caspers Gallileo	28.78sec	(26/5/03)
480m	Blonde Dino	27.81sec	(9/9/07)
630m	Iceman Brutus	37.07sec	(20/8/07)
684m	Centour Corker	40.60sec	(29/5/03)
835m	Head Iton Tonge	51.60sec	(21/6/07)
880m	Thornfield Poppy	54.79sec	(19/7/97)
900m	Ladys Storm	57.03sec	(9/7/98)
1104m	Travel Now	72.66sec	(25/3/00)

Major Events: Ladbrokes Midland Puppy Derby, Ladbrokes Summer Classic, Ladbrokes Midland Gold Cup, Ladbrokes Christmas Festival, Peter John Chinn Memorial

Trainers: Chris Allsopp, Melvin Baker, Ken Bebbington, Peter Billingham, Martin Burt, Pat Cowdrill, Michael Harris, Kevin Meakin, Karen Prince and Barry Riddiford

Address: The Fossway, Newcastle-Upon-Tyne, NE6 2XJ
Phone: 0191 265 2665/5305 (Racing Office), 0191 210 5300 (General)
Fax: 0191 210 5306
How to get there
Road: from Newcastle city centre, follow A193 towards Wallsend for two miles.
Rail: Main Line Station in city centre, then take Metro to Chillingham Rd (five mins walk from track)
Website: www.broughparkdogs.co.uk
Senior Racing Manager: Iain Hillis
Racing Manager: Peter Douglas
Operations Manager: Terry Meynell
Race days: Tuesday, Wednesday, Thursday, Saturday (BAGS and evening)
Trials: Before racing and after racing on Wednesdays, Fridays during BEGS season
Hare type: Swaffham

Distance to the first bend: 81m
Track Records:

290m	Gateman	16.84sec
480m	Droopys Shearer	27.90sec
480H	Ballyhane Rio	30.10sec
500m	Tally Ho Shimmer	29.52sec
500H	Kildare Slippy	31.06sec
640m	Calzaghe Frisby	38.61sec
670m	Fortune Jim	40.84sec
706m	Hesley Gale	42.83sec
825m	Greenacre Lin	50.44sec
895m	Give Her Time	56.67sec

Major Events: William Hill All England Cup, William Hill Northumberland Plate
Trainers: Caroline Allen, Andrew Bell, Paul Buckland, Deborah Calvert, Barry Clements, Lesley Eagleton, Thomas Edgar, Jimmy Fenwick, Graham Jones, Glenn Lynas, Peter McLaughlin, Stuart Ray, Paul Rutherford, Brian Stirling, Amanda Varley, John Walton, Pamela Weir

Address: Colwick Park, Nottingham, NG2 4BE

Phone: 0115 910 3333 (General); 0115 910 3331 (Racing Office)

Fax: 0115 910 3336

How to get there

Road: Adjacent to horse racecourse in Colwick district of Nottingham, near to Nottingham Forest and Notts County football grounds and Trent Bridge. Follow AA signs to racecourse, just off A612.

Rail: Two miles from BR Midland Station. Taxi to stadium costs around £4

Bus: Number 44 from city centre

Website: www.nottinghamdogs.com

Email: info@nottinghamdogs.com

General Manager: Rachel Corden

Racing Manager: Peter Robinson

Race Days: Monday, Tuesday (BAGS), Friday, Saturday

Trials: Before Racing

Hare type: Outside Swaffham

Distance to first bend (500m): 85m

Track Records:

305m Against The Lead 17.51sec
(21/8/06) Ningbo Jack 17.51sec (21/8/06)
480m Lively Arthur 28.59sec (21/8/07)
500m Shelbourne Rene 29.29sec (18/9/06)
680m Wentworth Which 41.36sec (9/7/07)
730m Blonde Pearl 44.19sec (20/02/06)
885m Lisnakill Cathal 55.68sec (27/7/04)
905m Ziggy Girl 57.76sec (12/01/04)
925m Seathwaite Robby 58.13sec (20/11/06)

Major Events: Betfred Select Stakes, Betfred Superstayers Select Stakes, Betfred Eclipse, Stadium Bookmakers National Sprint, Carling Puppy Classic

Trainers: Alan Bodell, David Bull, Malcolm Cooper, Krys Gebski, Val Green, Peter Harnden, Terry Munslow, Sylvia Oakes, Alan Winsper, Ken Perrin, Sheila Poole, Ian Pooley, Margaret Roberts, Elaine Saville, Charlie Savory, Brian Thompson, Paula Timmins and Laurence Tuffin

OXFORD

Address: Sandy Lane, Cowley, Oxford, OX4 6LJ

Phone: 01865 778222 (general); 0870 8408903 (restaurant)

How to get there

Road: two miles south of town on the B480. Off the Oxford ring road at the Rover Works

Bus: Frequent bus and taxi service to Blackbird Leys Estate

Rail: 3 miles from Oxford Station – on main line from Paddington Station

Website: www.lovethedogs.co.uk

Racing Manager: Gary Baiden

General Manager: Maureen Ridley

Race Days: Tuesday (plus BAGS), Friday, Saturday, Sunday (BAGS)

Trials: Monday

Hare type: Swaffham

Track Records:

250m	Ballymac Gloria	14.88sec	(14/3/06)
450m	Paramount Silver	26.37sec	(1/5/05)
450H	Druids Mickey Jo	27.12sec	(5/4/05)
595m	Little Honcho	36.18sec	(5/2/05)
645m	Black Pear	39.36sec	(5/8/04)
645H	Bozy Blue Blaze	40.94sec	(6/2/01)
845m	Tralee Crazy	52.16sec	(22/3/98)
1040m	Honeygar Bell	67.63sec	(14/11/89)

Major Events: Mike Alan Trafalgar Cup, RD Racing Gold Cup, William Hill Pall Mall, William Hill Cesarewitch, Oxfordshire Trophy

Trainers: Terry Atkins, Ron Bicknell, Paul Clarke, Paddy Curtin, Robert Hannon, Gilly Hepden, Angie Kibble, Terry Kibble, Tony Magnasco, Maurice Massey, Jim Morgan, Michael Peterson, Alan Stevens, Gloria Stringer, Ian Wills

PELAW GRANGE

Address: Pelaw Grange Stadium
Drum Road, Chester-le-Street, Co. Durham,
DH3 2AF.
Tel: (0191) 4102141,
Racing Office (0191) 492 9870 ,
Bookings & Restaurant (0191) 492 9872.
Fax: (0191) 4102235.
How to get there: Pelaw Grange is about 1
mile from the A1M, halfway between
Durham City and Newcastle Upon Tyne.
Leave the A1Motorway at junction 63,
Chester-le-Street (just North of Durham
City/South of Washington Services). Follow
the A693 towards Stanley, then the A167
towards Birtley. Pelaw Grange Stadium is sit-
uated in the Drum Industrial Estate, just
before Birtley.
General Manager: Jeff McKenna

Racing Manager: Graeme Henigan
Web: www.pelawgrange.co.uk
Email: admin@pelawgrange.co.uk.
Race Nights: Monday, Thursday at 7.45pm
and Saturday at 7.30p.m.
Admission: Adults £5.00, OAP FREE,
Children £2.00, Under 5yrs FREE.
Trials: Before racing on Monday, Thursday &
Saturday at 6.30p.m.
Schooling Trial Tuesday 11.00am
Distances: 260m, 435m, 605m, 780m &
955m.
Track circumference: 345m.
Track Records:

260m	Stouke Society	04.02.06	15.52
435m	Maglass Legend	10.09.07	25.35sec
605m	Zigzag Kit	26.12.05	36.84sec
780m	Vegas Showgirl	26.12.05	48.92sec

PERRY BARR

Address: Perry Barr Greyhound Racing Club, Aldridge Road, Perry Barr, Birmingham B42 2ET

Tel: Stadium 0870 840 7410
Reservations 0870 840 7411
Racing Office 0870 754 7812/7813/7810

How to get there

Road: From Birmingham, leave on A324 for the Bull Ring, join the A34 and then take the A453 under fly-over, stadium is 100 yards on left. From M6/M5, turn off towards city centre at Junction 6 of M6, follow A34 and fork left at Perry Barr onto A453 (Albridge Road). Large free parking at the stadium.

Website: ww.lovethedogs.co.uk

Email: Stadium – carolchown-smith@gralimited.co.uk,
Reservations – pbreserve@gralimited.co.uk,
Racing Office – perrybarr@clara.co.uk

Racing Manager: Gary Woodward

Deputy Racing Manager: Martin Seal

General Manager: Carol Chown-Smith

Race Days: Wednesday (BAGS) Thursday, Friday, Saturday, Sunday (BAGS)

Trials: Tuesday

Hare type: Outside Swaffham

Distance to first bend (standard): 45m

Track Records:

275m	Horseshoe Ping	15.81sec
460m	Velvet Spark	27.67sec
480m	Raging Jack	28.13sec
	Zigzag Dutchman	28.13sec
480m	Taipan	28.87sec
500m	Toms Lodge	29.94sec
660m	Jack Spark	39.98sec
660m	Selby Ben	41.73sec
710m	Swift Jade	43.01sec
895m	Spenwood Wizard	56.97sec
915m	Head Iton Jordan	56.75sec

Major Events: Keith Johnson Easter Cup, Birmingham Cup, Betfair Scurry Cup

Trainers: Kath Babe, Paul Barrett, Mark Beet, George Bradnock, Lynn Cook, George Corbett, Kevin Davis, Stanley Deeley, Stephen Donnelly, David Freeman, Frederick Gilbert Elaine Gordon, Alex Grewcock, David Hunt Lynn Johnson, Mary Kimberley, John Lambe Paul Meek, Sandra Ralph, Julie Ridley, Geoffrey Rocke, William Russell, Joseph Scanlon, Paul Slater, Neil Slowley, Robert Stanton, Alec Stone, Kirsty Turner, Ian Walker, Susan Whitehouse, Margaret Williams

PETERBOROUGH

Address: Fengate Stadium, First Drove, Fengate, Peterborough, Cambridgeshire
Phone: 01733 296930 (General); 01733 296939 (Restaurant)
Fax: 01733 296932
How to get there
Road: Half a mile on east side of city centre. Off A1 and A47, turn off at Fengate, off ring road and follow Fengate Stadium signs
Rail: One mile from Peterborough (Kings Cross and Edinburgh Lines)
Website:
www.peterboroughgreyhounds.com
Email:
info@peterboroughgreyhounds.com
Racing Manager: Martin Race
Deputy Racing Manager: Paul Miller
General Manager: Rob and Richard Perkins

Race Days: Tuesday, Wednesday, Friday, Saturday
Trials: Monday, Thursday. Kennelling 9.45am to 10.15am, trials start 11am. No evening trials
Hare type: Outside Swaffham
Distance to first bend (420m): 70m
Track Records:

235m	Mount Royal Fox	14.31sec	(19/2/95)
420m	Highway Leader	25.15sec	(30/7/94)
420H	Im Henry	25.85sec	(17/5/97)
605m	Glencoes Tom	37.11sec	(9/4/02)
790m	Greenacre Lin	49.61sec	(14/5/05)
975m	Lenas Cadet	63.30sec	(19/11/88)

Major Events: Peterborough Puppy Derby, Peterborough Derby, Alan Speechley Fengate Collar, Puppy Cesarewitch, Peterborough Cesarewitch, Veterans' Derby, Peterborough Marathon

Charity No. 269668

Faithful, good-natured male WLTM like-minded family to share his zest for life. Loves animals, children and enjoys most sports.

If only we could give each of our retired greyhounds their own personal ad. But as the RGT re-homes around three thousand dogs a year, it's just not possible.

We always need more people to adopt our dogs, so perhaps you could help? Retired greyhounds are gentle, intelligent animals who have devoted their early years to racing and now need some TLC in a loving family home.

They ask very little in return: regular walks and meals, the odd cuddle and maybe a warm basket by a cosy fire. So if you're looking for a devoted companion to share happy times, look no further. Simply send the coupon, log onto our website or phone us on: **0870 444 0673**

POOLE

Address: Wimborne Road, Poole, Dorset, BH15 2BP
Phone: 01202 685107 (Racing Office); 01202 677449 (General)
Fax: 01202 677980
How to get there
Road: From London, M3 then M27 and then signposts to Poole town centre. Dolphin shopping centre is adjacent to track
Rail: Main line Waterloo to Poole, station is 500 yards from track.
Website: www.stadiauk.com
Email: info@poolegreyhounds.com, info@stadiauk.com

Racing Manager: David Lawrence
General Manager: Shaun Spencer-Perkins
Race Days: Tuesday, Friday, Saturday
Trials: Monday
Track Records:

250m	Louisville	14.96sec	(7/2/04)
450m	Rosmon Ranger	26.45sec	
640m	El Onda	38.96sec	(9/5/98)
840m	Blonde Pearl	52.06sec	(15/11/97)

Major Events: Golden Crest, Jem Racing Super Paws

Address: Target Road, Portsmouth, PO2 8QU

Phone: 02392 663232 (Racing Office); 02392 698000 (General)

How to get there

Road: Entering Portsmouth on the M275, the stadium can be seen on the left. Approaching the flyover, take the slip road and first left at the roundabout under the flyover. Follow signs for approx half a mile, stadium is on the left

Rail: Portsmouth and Southsea Station. Taxi 5 minutes.

Email: ericgraham@gralimited.co.uk

Website: www.portsmouthstadium.co.uk

Racing Manager: Paul Clark

General Manager: Eric Graham

Race Days: Tuesday, Friday, Saturday

Trials: Before Racing

Hare type: Outside Swaffham

Distance to the first bend (430m): 85m

Track Records:

246m	Soho Square	15.27sec	(4/8/06)
430m	Blakes World	26.15sec	
601m	Bills Paid	37.51sec	(2/6/06)
784m	Active Pearl	50.43sec	(4/8/06)
955m	Zuzus Petal	62.18sec	(2/6/06)

Major Events: Golden Muzzle (October)

READING

Address: Stadia UK (Reading) Ltd., A33 Relief Road, Berkshire RG2 0JL
Phone: 0118 975 0746, 0118 986 3161 (Racing Office)
Fax: 0118 9313264
How to get there
Road: Junction 11 off M4, Reading Central (3 mins from M4 on A33)
Rail: To Reading Station, 5 mins taxi ride
Website: www.stadiauk.com
Email: readingdogs@bluebottle.com
Racing Manager: Ian Sillence
General Manager: Martyn Dore
Race Days: Tuesday, Thursday, Saturday

Trials: Friday
Track Records:

275m	Greenfield Box	16.32sec	(23/10/82)
465m	Blue Murlen	27.56sec	(28/4/97)
465H	Druids Mickey Jo	28.40sec	(22/9/95)
660m	Double Take	40.50sec	(14/12/03)
660H	Gold Splash	41.95sec	(24/4/93)
850m	Greenacre Lin	53.26sec	(16/9/04)
1045m	Souda Bay	67.58sec	(3/5/98)

Major Events: Reading Masters, Hunt Cup

Address: London Road, Romford, Essex
Phone: 01708 762345 (racing office),
01708 725213 (restaurant)
Website:
www.romfordgreyhoundstadium.co.uk
Email: romford.stadium@galacoral.com
How to get there
Road: Stadium situated in main Ilford to
Romford road (A118)
Bus: No 86.
Rail: Romford main line from London
Liverpool Street, then taxi five minutes
Racing Manager: Peter O'Dowd
General Manager: Cathy Johnston
Race Days: Monday, Wednesday, Thursday
(BAGS), Friday, Saturday (BAGS and evening)
Trials: Tuesday
Hare type: Outside Swaffham

Distance to first bend: 80m
Track Records:

Distance	Name	Time
225m	Louisville	13.37sec
400m	Sandwichsunshine	23.58sec
400H	Sizzlers Bossman	24.15sec
575m	Solid Money	34.78sec
575H	El Tenor	35.53sec
715m	Scurlogue Champ	44.18sec
750m	Killeacle Phoebe	46.64sec
925m	Salina	59.13sec
1110m	Cregagh Prince	72.59sec

Major Events: Coral Golden Sprint, Coral
Essex Vase, Coral Champion Stakes, Coral
Romford Puppy Cup, Coral Gold Vase
Trainers: Maxine Locke, Maggie Lucas,
Alison Ingram, Ernie Gaskin, David Mullins,
Peter Payne, Jim Reynolds, Martyn Wiley and
Paul Young

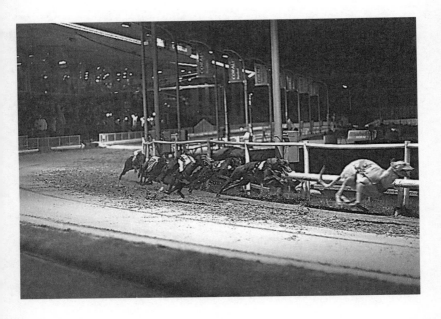

SHAWFIELD

Address: Rutherglen, Glasgow
Phone: 0141 647 4121 (Racing Office and Restaurant)
Fax: 0141 6477265
Email: racing@shawfieldgreyhounds.com
Website: www.shawfieldgreyhounds.com
How to get there
Road: South side of Glasgow, 3 miles off A74
Rail: Rutherglen Station 1/2 mile, Dalmarnock underground 1/2 mile
Air: Glasgow Airport 8 miles
Race Days: Tuesday, Thursday, Friday, Saturday

Racing manager: William Reid
Trials: Wednesday
Hare type: Outside Swaffham
Distance to first bend (480m): 70m
Track Records:

300m	Ravage Again	17.35sec	(7/4/90)
450m	Fairhill Boy	26.85sec	(27/10/89)
480m	Fear Haribo	28.76sec	
500m	Droopys Sandy	29.39sec	(21/5/94)
500H	Face The Mutt	31.07sec	(22/5/82)
670m	Crack Of The Ash	40.50sec	(11/9/93)
730m	Decoy Princess	45.09sec	(16/8/88)
882m	Rosemoor Flower	56.55sec	(13/4/02)
932m	Silken Dancer	59.35sec	(2/9/93)

Major Events: Scottish Derby, St Mungo Cup

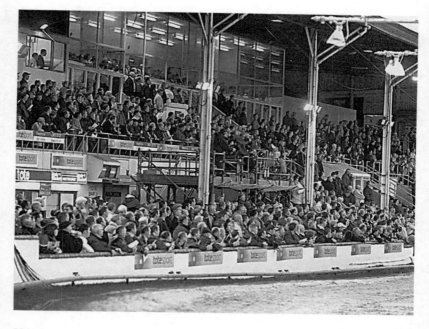

Address: Sheffield Sports Stadium, Penistone Road, Sheffield S6 2D
Phone: 0114 234 3074 (General) 0114 385 5888 (Racing Office), 0114 2888300 (Retired Greyhounds).
Fax: 01142 333 631

How to get there

Road: From M1 South, Junction 36, follow A61. Penistone Road is on A61.
Rail: To Midland Station, then a five-minute cab ride.
Bus: 10-minute bus journey. Number of buses available very frequent. Bus station at side of train station.
Email: racingoffice@owlertonstadium.co.uk, inquiries@owlertonstadium.co.uk, info@owlertonstadium.co.uk
Website: www.owlertonstadium.co.uk, www.sheffieldretiredgreyhounds.co.uk
Director of Racing: David Baldwin
Racing Manager: David Perry
General Manager: John Gilburn
Race Days: Monday (BAGS), Tuesday, Thursday (BAGS), Friday, Saturday

Trials: Wednesday
Hare type: Outside Swaffham
Distance to first bend (standard): 60m
Track Records:

280m Flat	Lunar Vacation	15.94sec	23/7/2007
362m Flat	Farloe Bubble	20.82sec	04/10/1997
480m Flat	Reggies Hero	28.90sec	14/11/1997
500m Flat	Farloe Hobbs	28.90sec	21/9/2006
500m Hurdle;	Jills Fault	29.65sec	06/11/2007
660m Flat	Larkhill Bird	39.39sec	10/12/2006
720m Flat	Swift Ninja	42.80sec	03/11/2007
800m Flat	Hollinwood Poppy	48.25sec	27/12/2000
915m Flat	Hollinwood Poppy	56.25sec	04/07/2000
934m Flat	Seathwaite Robby	57.87sec	05/09/2006

Major Events: William Hill Steel City Cup, Global Windows Invitation, Global Windows Queen Mother Cup, Nigel Troth Yorkshire Oaks, Harry Holmes Memorial, Napoleons Invitation, Coors Brewers Puppy Silver Collar
Trainers: Harry Crapper, Barrie Draper, John Davy, Jane Houfton, Ron Hough, Paul Liddle, Norma Melbourne, Michael O'Donnell, Tony McKenna, Elaine Parker, Jamie Smith Philip Stamp, Lisa Stephenson, Louise Taylorson, Mona Wainwright, Russell Warren

SITTINGBOURNE

Address: Central Park Stadium, Church Road, Eurolink, Sittingbourne, Kent ME10 3SB

Phone: 01795 438438 (Racing office); 01795 475547 (General)

Fax: 01795 430337

How to get there

Road: Take M20 to Junction 7 or M2 to Junction 5. From M20: Head north to roundabout at Junction 5 of the M2. Here, turn off for Sittingbourne on A249 (Sheerness Road). Take second turn-off (signposted Sittingbourne Industry). B2006 to Sittingbourne, straight across first roundabout, following signs to Town Centre and Industry. Right at next roundabout 'Town Centre and Other Industry'. Straight across the next roundabout, pass Swale Motors on the right. At next roundabout, straight across to T-Junction. Left here and follow signs to Central Park Stadium.

Email: mail@sittingbournegreyhounds.co.uk

Website: www.sittingbournegreyhounds.co.uk

Racing Manager: Jess Packer

General Manager: Roger Cearns

Race Days: Thursday (BEGS), Friday, Saturday (BEGS) and occasional Sundays

Trials: Tuesday

Hare Type: Outside Swaffham

Distance to first bend (480m): 83m

Track Records:

Distance	Greyhound	Time
265m	Fast Ranger	16.20sec
450m	Jims Havana	27.35sec
473m	Droopys Vieri	28.53sec
473H	Ballymac Keano	29.30sec
480m	Lenson Joker	28.92sec
480m	Castledale Lad	29.71sec
500m	Lenson Express	30.31sec
642m	Lobo	39.96sec
708m	Sumi Girl	44.32sec
893m	Omega Wink	57.44sec
916m	Ericas Equity	58.09sec
943m	Omega Wink	60.69sec

Major Events: Kent Derby, Silver Salver

SUNDERLAND

Address: Newcastle Road, Sunderland, Tyne And Wear, SR5 1RP
Phone: 0191 568 6200 (General); 0191 568 6223 (Racing Office)
Fax: 0191 568 6237
How to get there
Road: A19 to Testo's roundabout, then take the A184. Track is about two miles on left.
Bus: 310 and 319 from Sunderland pass stadium
Rail: To East Boldon station. Track is 5-minute taxi ride.
Email: inquiries@sunderlanddogs.com, sunderland@formnet.org
Website: www.sunderlanddogs.com
Racing Manager: Jimmy Nunn

General Manager: Ian Walton
Race Days: Wednesday, Friday, Saturday, Tuesday (BAGS), Thursday (BAGS)
Trials: Before Racing
Hare type: Swaffham McKee
Distance to first bend (standard trip): 93m
Track Records:

261m	Ballymac Rooster	15.54sec	(10/10/06)
450m	Roxholme Silks	26.65sec	(8/12/04)
640m	Autumn Tiger	38.97sec	(22/10/95)
828m	Shes The Deal	51.98sec	(14/12/04)

Major Events: William Hill Puppy Derby, William Hill Gold Cup

SWINDON

Address: Swindon Stadium, Lady Lane, Blunsdon, Wiltshire, SN25 4DN
Phone: 01793 721253 (General)
How to get there
Road: Junction 15 off M4, Swindon East, take A419 towards Cirencester for approx. 4 miles to Lady Lane on left at traffic lights
Rail: Paddington to Swindon, approx. one hour. 10min taxi ride to track.
Website: www.stadiauk.com
General Manager: Chris Lowe
Racing Manager: Clive Oseman and Dave Stowe

Race Days: Monday (am), Wednesday (pm), Friday (afternoon and pm), Saturday
Trials: Tuesday
Track Records:

285m	Leaders Highway	16.23sec	(10/6/98)
	Everton Cheetah	16.23sec	(12/3/03)
460m	Pindi Express	27.33sec	(11/2/04)
480m	Rhyzome Wizard	28.44sec	(10/7/06)
480H	Greenacre George	28.93sec	(3/9/02)
509m	Rhyzome Wizard	29.73sec	(26/8/06)
685m	Shelbourne Star	40.94sec	(11/2/04)
737m	Streaky Luvs Men	45.11sec	(11/7/03)

Major Events: British Two-Year-Old Produce Stakes, Pride Of The West

WALTHAMSTOW

Address: 300 Chingford Road, London E4 8SJ

Phone: 020 8498 3311/020 8498 3300 (General); 020 8498 3333 (Restaurant)

Fax: 020 8523 2747

How to get there

Road: Crooked Billet roundabout exit from North Circular Road (A406). Track is opposite Sainsbury's, five minutes from end of M11 (from which take A406 west). A12 link to M11, giving fast road to A102M (Blackwall Tunnel)

Bus: Frequent buses from Walthamstow Central (alight directly opposite stadium)

Rail: Walthamstow Central (Victoria Line or BR), taxi or bus 1.5 miles to stadium. South Woodford (Central line), taxi to stadium

Website: www.wsgreyhound.co.uk

Email: mail@wsgreyhound.co.uk

Racing Manager: Chris Page

Race Days: Monday (BAGS), Tuesday, Thursday, Friday (BAGS), Saturday

Trials: Wednesday

Hare type: Outside Swaffham

Distance to first bend (475m): 100m

Track Records:

235m	Horseshoe Ping	14.14sec	(16/9/06)
430m	Thank You Madam	25.71sec	(20/8/2005)
475m	Barnfield On Air	28.15sec	(4/9/2007)
475H	Blue Meadow Lad	28.75sec	(30/6/2005)
640m	Spiridon Louis	39.19sec	(07/11/2006)
640m	Sizzlers Bossman	39.78sec	(9/7/2005)
835m	Bubblu Kate	52.19sec	(4/9/2007)
880m	Ebony Ocean	55.53sec	(4/9/2007)
1045m	Betathan Pebbles	67.50sec	(15/10/2005)

Major Events: Ladbrokes Circuit, Ladbrokes Arc, The Test, Ocean Trailers Puppy Stakes, Graphite UK Puppy Derby, Victor Chandler Grand Prix, Racing Post Festival

Trainers: Gary Baggs, Seamus Cahill, John Coleman, Paul Garland, Ernie Gaskin, Dickie Hawkes, Kelly Mullins, Mark Wallis, Mick Puzey, Peter Rich, Graham Sharp and John Sherry

WIMBLEDON

Address: Plough Lane, Wimbledon, London SW17 0BL
Phone: 0208 946 8000 (General); 0870 840 8905 (Reservations)
How to get there
Road: From A219 turn left into Alexandra Road and across traffic lights into Plough Lane. Stadium is on your left
Bus: 44, 77, 220, 280 (156 from Wimbledon).
Rail: Tooting Broadway (Northern Line); Wimbledon (District Line); Earlsfield (Waterloo Line); Haydons Road (Holborn Viaduct Line except Saturday, use London Bridge)
Email: wmreserve@gralimited.co.uk
wimbledon.racingoffice@virgin.net
Website: www.wimbledonstadium.co.uk
Racing Manager: Gary Matthews
General Manager: Darren Kennedy
Race Days: Tuesday, Friday, Saturday

Trials: Wednesday
Hare type: Outside Swaffham
Distance to first bend (460): 95m
Track Records:

256m	Setemup Joe	15.24sec
256mH	Limited Blue	15.82sec
276m	Lunar Vacation	16.25sec
460m	Droopys Shearer	27.32sec
	Zigzag Dutchy	27.32sec
460H	Arfur Daley	27.80sec
480m	Greenane Squire	28.21sec
668m	Black Pear	40.51sec
668mH	Sizzlers Bossman	41.68sec
688m	Caloona Striker	41.77sec
872m	Greenacre Lin	54.26sec

Major Events: Blue Square Greyhound Derby, St Leger, Oaks, Grand National, Springbok, Racing Post Juvenile, Puppy Derby
Trainers: Bernie Doyle, Norah McEllistrim, Andrew Peacock, Phil Rees, John Simpson, Tony Taylor, Jason Foster

Address: Yarmouth Road, Caister On Sea, Norfolk, NR30 5TE

Phone: 01493 720343 (Restaurant and Executive Lounges), 01493 378168 (Racing Office)

Fax: 01493 721200

How to get there

Road: from London M11/A11 becomes A47 from Norwich or use A12 via Ipswich. Follow signs to Caister-on-Sea from Great Yarmouth. Once in Great Yarmouth follow BROWN Tourist signs. The stadium is on the left as you leave Great Yarmouth on the A149 heading to Caister-on-Sea.

Bus: Blue bus no.8 from Great Yarmouth

Rail: BR to Norwich, links with Yarmouth. Then cab to stadium, one mile

Website: www.yarmouthstadium.co.uk

Racing Manager: Nigel Long

General Manager: Nigel Bray

Promotions Manager: Justin Franklin

Race Days: Wednesday, Friday and Saturday, first race 7.30pm; plus Boxing Day morning, first race 10.30am

Trials: Thursday mornings and limited number before racing

Hare type: Swaffham

Distance to first bend (462m): 86m

Track Records:

277m	Beardys Robbie	16.46sec
462m	Geordie Parker	27.52sec
659m	Rackethall Holly	40.71sec
843m	Spiridon Louis	52.98sec
1041m	Some Moth	68.81

Major Events: 61st East Anglian Derby run in September 2007, plus the Pepsi Sprint and Derby Purse. John Smith's East Anglian Challenge (August), The Fosters Cup (462m graded handicap), 49th Yarmouth Championship (graded), Yarmouth Home-finders Veterans Race for five years and over (graded) on Boxing Day

Irish Tracks

CLONMEL

Address: Davis Road, Clonmel, Co. Tipperary
Phone: (00353) 052 83334/052 83333 **Fax:** (00353) 052 80091
Race nights: Thursday, Sunday
Track Records:

300y	Rising Fire	24-08-06	16.01
525y	Charity Jack	05-03-06	28.36
550y	Off The Fags	06-02-07	29.81
550y	Leahs Boss	08-07-07	29.81
575y	Lucky Lindsay	23-08-07	31.05
750y	Musical Beauty	29-10-06	41.49
790y	Lady Norma	22-08-04	44.72
1015y	Original Charm	27-07-03	58.15

CORK

Address: Curraheen Park, Curraheen, Co. Cork
Phone: (00353) 021 454 3095 **Fax:** (00353) 021 4543011
Race Nights: Wednesday, Thursday, Saturday
Track Records:

330y	Paulo Coelho	17-03-04	17.40
525y	Ardkill Jamie	23-09-06	28.03
525y	Droopys Robinho	29-09-07	28.03
550y	Goldstar Lee	10-13-06	29.42
575y	Nikita Billie	12-07-03	30.62
750y	Heart Rumble	31-06-05	41.30
810y	Shelbourne Kay	11-6-05	46.18
525yH	Bay Star	21-10-06	28.99

DERRY

Address: Derry Greyhound Stadium, Brandywell Grounds, Co. Derry
Telephone: 048 71265461
Race nights: Monday, Thursday
Track Records:

300y	Pipers Gold	22-09-89	16.43
500y	Cavies Cruncher	31-10-03	27.78
525y	Lignamonagh Bray	11-07-03	28.90
600y	Star Model	24-11-03	33.79
720y	Farloe Frown	16-07-01	41.01

DUNDALK

Address: Dundalk Stadium, Racecourse Road, Dundalk, Co. Louth
Phone: (00353) 042 933 4438 **Fax:** (00353) 042 933 2611
Race Nights: Thursday, Friday, Saturday
Track Records:

350yds	Mulcair Jo	12-07-06	18.71
400yds	Gingko	21-07-07	20.95
525yds	Open Door	12-07-07	28.39
550yds	Si Senor	12-07-07	29.47
575yds	Lunar Boy	04-09-04	31.45
600yds	Fairly Smart	21-10-06	32.82
620yds	Dromana Blue	30-03-07	33.51
670yds	Prince Monalulu	04-02-05	36.47
900yds	Shelbourne Kay	15-08-06	50.14

ENNISCORTHY

Address: Enniscorthy Greyhound Racing Co. Ltd. Show Grounds, Enniscorthy, Co. Wexford
Telephone: (00353) 054 33172 Fax: (00353) 054 34941
Race nights: Monday, Thursday
Track Records:

350 yds.	MONTOS MARK	07-Sep-97	18.50
525 yds.	WHITEFORT BOMBER	30-Sep-07	28.57
550 yds.	LARGE MAC	22-Jun-06	29.83
575 yds.	BALLYGANNON STAR	07-Jun-07	31.22
600 yds.	SMOOTH RHYTHM	27-Jul-06	32.59
750 yds.	wilcos mate	29-Oct-06	42.24
830 yds.	five gold bars	08-Mar-07	47.32

GALWAY

Address: College Road, Co. Galway, Co. Galway
Telephone: (00353) 091 562273 Fax: (00353) 091 562025
Race nights: Thursday, Friday, Saturday
Track Records:

325yds	DROOPYS MARCO	28-Jul-04	17.37
525yds.	HILLCROFT JOSIE	28-Jul-07	28.34
550yds.	HANDY PRINCESS	10-Mar-07	29.66
575yds.	ILLTELLYOUTHIS	08-Sep-07	31.43
700yds.	tyrur rachel	30-Jul-07	38.69
810yds.	IFLOOKSCOULDKILL	04-Aug-07	45.09
525yds.H	TOP LARK	23-Jul-04	29.34

HAROLD'S CROSS

Address: Dublin Greyhound and Sports Assoc. Harolds Cross, Dublin 6W
Telephone: (00353) 01 4971081 **Fax:** (00353) 01 4910111
Email: hospitalityhrxtrack@eircom.net
Racing Manager: Eamon Mackey
Race Nights: Monday, Tuesday, Friday
Track Records:

325yds	Staley Vegas	02-09-05	17.16
525yds	Airport Express	21-09-01	28.15
550yds	Quattro Power	06-07-01	29.65
570yds	Analyse	15-12-06	31.01
575yds	Serene Rumble	24-11-02	30.83
750yds	Roxholme Girl	24-06-05	41.45
810yds	Recovery Mission	17-10-03	45.35
1010yds	Air Force Honcho	03-12-04	57.88
1010 yds	DEBIDEE LANE	23-Dec-05	57.68
525 ydsH	JIMMY THE LAD	01-Oct-04	29.18
570 ydsH	DRUIDS FORREST	26-May-06	32.66

KILKENNY

Address: St James Park, Co. Kilkenny
Telephone: (00353) 056 7721214 **Fax:** (00353) 056 7762388
Race Nights: Wednesday, Friday
Track Records:

300y	Honchos Pearl (asb)	15-06-05	16.08
525y	Boherduff Light	10-09-04	28.49
700y	Smooth Slippy	25-06-04	40.33
745y	Kilcloney Wine	20-06-04	42.98
970y	Hulkster	18-06-06	56.88
525H	Comans Joe	24-06-07	29.56
	Bally Euro	16-04-04	29.10

LIFFORD

Address: Lifford Racing Company Ltd., Lifford, Co. Donegal
Telephone: (00353) 074 9141083 **Fax:** (00353) 074 9142596
Website: www.liffordgreyhounds.com
Race Nights: Friday, Saturday, Sunday
Track Records:

350y	Royal Delight	01-07-07	18.39
525y	Farloe Bond	25-08-02	28.45
550y	Farloe Black	28-10-07	29.39
575y	Line Of Fire	07-10-07	31.05
600y	Always A Rumble	21-09-03	32.50
750y	Droopys Quiff	07-10-07	41.56
820y	Recovery Mission	11-09-03	45.74
525H	Setanta	08-08-04	29.48
550H	Lemon Rambo	28-11-04	30.81

LIMERICK

Address: Market Fields, Co. Limerick
Telephone: (00353) 061 214604 **Fax:** (00353) 061 214611
Racing Manager: Gus Ryan
Race Nights: Monday, Thursday, Saturday
Track Records:

300y	Silkey Joe	15-01-05	16.06
525y	Catunda Harry	17-06-07	27.99
550y	Hondo Dingle	02-06-07	29.32
700y	Hondo Dingle	25-09-06	38.62
750y	Nobodywantsme	09-07-05	41.53
525H	Lemon Rambo	09-10-04	28.91

LONGFORD

Address: Park Road, Co. Longford
Telephone: (00353) 043 42018
Racing Manager: Sean Fogarty
Race Nights: Monday, Friday
Track Records:

330y	Gingko	13-07-07	17.35
525y	Dustin Fox	14-07-06	28.15
550y	Break The Clock	01-08-03	29.78
570y	Dundrum Prince	5-04-05	30.74
805y	Bluetoon Solo	05-12-03	45.10

MULLINGAR

Address: Ballinderry, Mullingar, Co. Westmeath
Telephone: (00353) 044 48348 **Fax:** (00353) 044 42362
Website: www.mullingargreyhoundstadium.ie
General Manager: Patrick Flynn
Race Nights: Thursday, Saturday
Track Records:

3400y	Kilmalady Boy	31-07-03	21.17
525y	Unsinkable Girl	02-10-99	28.88
550y	Forsale Or Rent	01-09-07	30.59
600y	Micks Savings	15-04-07	32.92
805y	Bombersgoinghome	09-09-07	46.22
525H	Mexico	10-09-05	29.70

NEWBRIDGE

Address: Newbridge, Co. Kildare,
Phone: (00353) 045 446658 **Fax:** (00353) 045 431385
Email: racing@newbridgegreyhoundstadium.ie
Racing Manager: Phillip Mullaney
Race Nights: Friday, Saturday
Track records:

325y	Kafima	14-10-05	17.37
525y	Hillcroft Josie	19-10-07	28.39
550y	Top Boe	02-07-04	29.62
575y	Wilcos Mate	14-07-06	31.12
750y	Hulkster	05-11-05	41.85
845y	Marshalls Trigger	30-12-04	47.68
525H	Frightened Pig	09-07-04	29.14

SHELBOURNE

Address: Shelbourne Greyhound Stadium, Shelbourne Park, Dublin 4
Telephone: (00353) 01 6683502 **Fax:** (00353) 01 6683503
Email: info@shelbournepark.ie or hospitality @shelbournepark.ie
Managing Director: Paddy Ryan
Racing Manager: Declan Carey
Race Nights: Wednesday, Thursday, Saturday
Track Records:

350y	Sycamore Dan	18-09-04	18.41
525y	Premier Fantasy	10-04-04	28.08
550y	Bypass Byway	14-09-02	29.42
575y	Ronans Delight	16-10-04	31.04
600y	Late Late Show	09-06-01	32.20
750y	Making Merry	15-09-01	41.59
850y	Hulkster	30-07-05	47.81
1025y	Let Us Know	16-03-02	58.87
525H	Secondrate Champ	16-04-05	28.73

THURLES

Address: Townparks, Thurles, Co. Tipperary
Telephone: (00353) 0504 21003 **Fax:** (00353) 0504 26009
General Manager: Sandra Peavoy
Racing Manager: Paul Hayes
Race Days: Tuesday, Saturday
Track records:

330y	Quarter To Five	11-05-99	17.64
	Pretty Smokey	27-05-01	17.64
360y	Rambling Jack	29-07-06	19.01
525y	Digital	16-07-05	28.11
550y	Moyne Rebel	16-09-00	29.99
570y	Ronans Delight	11-12-04	30.98
600y	O Learys Peggy	17-09-05	32.70
750y	O Learys Peggy	03-06-06	42.09
840y	Debidee Lane	28-01-06	46.81
525H	Goofys Lofty	29-05-04	29.51

TRALEE

Address: Kingdom Greyhound Stadium, Oakview Park, Tralee, Co. Kerry
Telephone: (00353) 066 7124033 **Fax:** (00353) 066 7125416
Email: kingdom-stadium@esatclear.ie
Racing Manager: Kieran Casey
General Manager: John Ward
Race Nights: Tuesday, Friday, Saturday
Track Records:

3325y	Pineapple Mandy	23-04-99	17.46
500y	Scarty Lad	04-05-07	27.14
525y	Deerfield Mover	14-09-04	28.14
550y	Goldstar Premier	20-05-05	29.64
570y	Three Bells Hell	17-06-03	30.88
750y	Iflookscouldkill	21-07-07	41.79
525H	Queen Christine	04-06-05	29.21

WATERFORD

Address: Kilcohan Park, Co. Waterford
Phone: (00353) 051 874531
Restaurant: (00353) 1890 730730
Fax: (00353) 051 874235
Racing Manager: Eamon Mackey
General Manager: Orla Strumble
Race Nights: Friday, Saturday
Track Records:

300y	Montos Mark	04-11-06	15.91
500y	Ardfert Billy	28-05-05	26.95
525y	Lolos Choice	27-09-05	28.09
550y	Ardfert Billy	22-10-05	29.20
730y	Making Merry	18-08-01	40.05
790y	Making Merry	25-08-01	43.20
525H	Secondrate Champ	02-04-05	28.67

YOUGHAL

Address: Youghal, Co. Cork
Tel: (00353) 024 92305/92355 **Fax:** (00353) 024 91967
Email: ygltrack@indigo.ie
Racing Manager: Pat Herbert
Race Nights: Tuesday, Friday
Track Records:

325y	Sycamore Dan	17-10-03	17.37
525y	Boherduff Light	25-06-04	28.61
550y	Clover Hare	13-09-02	29.92
700y	Tinas Girl	19-08-03	38.79
790y	Shining Rumble	13-07-04	44.76

FOR ALL THE LATEST INFORMATION ON GREYHOUND RACING IN IRELAND www.igb.ie

WEBSITE DIRECTORY

OFFICIAL 'VIRAL' GAME
Doggles www.racedoggles.com

GOVERNING & ADMINISTRATIVE BODIES
British Greyhound Racing Board (for NGRC form and results) www.thedogs.co.uk
British Greyhound Racing Fund www.bgrf.org.uk
Irish Racing Board (for Irish form and results) www.igb.ie
National Coursing Club www.nationalcoursingclub.org
National Greyhound Racing Club www.ngrc.org.uk

OWNERS
Hove owners forum discussion and advance cards www.hovedogs.co.uk
Oxford Owners Association www.oxforddowners.fsnet.co.uk
Romford Greyhound Owners Association www.rgoa.co.uk
Wimbledon owners htpp//groups.msn.com/wgoa

TRAINERS
Trainers' Association www.greyhoundtrainersassociation.co.uk
Trainers directory www.greyhoundtrainers.com

TRACKS
Belle Vue www.lovethedogs.co.uk
Brough Park www.broughparkdogs.co.uk
Coventry www.coventrygreyhounds.com
Crayford www.crayford.com
Hall Green www.lovethedogs.co.uk
Henlow www.henlowdogs.co.uk
Hove www. brightonandhovegreyhound stadium.co.uk
Kinsley www.kinsleydogs.co.uk
Lifford www.liffordgreyhounds.com
Monmore www.monmoredogs.co.uk

Nottingham www.nottinghamdogs.com
Oxford www.lovethedogs.co.uk
Pelaw Grange www.pelawgrange.co.uk
Poole www.poolegreyhounds.com
Portsmouth www.lovethedogs.co.uk
Romford www.romfordgreyhound stadium.co.uk
Sheffield www.owlertonstadium.co.uk
Shelbourne www.shelbournepark.com
Stain www.greyhoundstadium.fsnet.co.uk
Sunderland www.sunderlanddogs.com
Swindon ww.swindongreyhounds.com
Walthamstow ww.wsgreyhound.co.uk
Wimbledon www.lovethedogs.co.uk
Yarmouth www.yarmouthstadium.co.uk

WELFARE
Greyhounds' Voice www.thegreyhoundsvoice.org (email: greyhounds voice@btinternet.com)
Catford Retired Greyhound Trust (still open) www.rgtcatford.co.uk
Retired greyhound database http://www.bgrd.co.uk for registered organisations
Greyhounds R Us (based in Swindon) www.greyhounds-r-us.co.uk
Greyhound home-finding (Essex) www.greyhoundrescueuk.co.uk
Home Straight (Essex) www.home-straight.fsnet.co.uk
Kamascave www.kamascave.com
Monmore Retired Greyhounds www.greyhoundhomefinders.co.uk www.rgtmonmore.co.uk
Perry Barr www.rgtperrybarr.org.uk
Retired Greyhounds www.retiredgreyhounds.co.uk
Romford www.rgoa.co.uk
Sheffield Homefinding Scheme www.sheffieldretiredgreyhounds.co.uk

Sittingbourne
www.rgtsittingbourne.co.uk
Walthamstow Homefinding Scheme
http://homepage.ntlworld.com/greyhounds
Wimbledon Greyhound Welfare
http://www.hershamhounds.org
RGT Homefinding Kennels
www.rgtcroftview.co.uk

PHOTOGRAPHY/VIDEOS
Flame Photos www.flamephotos.co.uk
Steve Nash photography
www.steve-nash.co.uk
Vincent Video www.greyhoundvideos.co.uk

INTERNET BOOKMAKERS
Coral www.coral.co.uk
Ladbrokes www.ladbrokes.co.uk
Sporting Options
www.sportingoptions.co.uk
William Hill www.williamhill.co.uk
UkBetting www.ukbetting.com

INTERNET BET EXCHANGES
Betfair www.betfair.com

KENNELS/STUDS/SALES
Ardrine Kennels www.racing-world .com
/ardrinekennels
Alison Ingram www.bersheda.co.uk
Barry O'Sullivan
www.oakracingkennels.btinternet.co.uk
Beechfield Kennels (Carly Philpott)
www.beechfieldracing.co.uk
Bodell Kennels www.bodellkennels.com
Chris Haywood
www.greyhoundkennels.com
David Egan www.oakviewfarm.co.uk
Elbony Kennels
www.elbonykennels.com
Riverstown www.riverstown.mysite.
wanadoo-members.co.uk
Jimmy Fenwick
www.northumbriagreyhounds.com
Paul Garland
www.paulgarlandgreyhoundkennels.com

Ian Greaves
www.iangreavesgreyhounds.com
Greyhound Sales
www.greyhoundsales.co.uk
Hollyoak Greyhounds
www.hollyoakgreyhounds.com
Ivydene Kennels (Attwaters)
www.caloona.co.uk
Mount Cashel Kennels
www.irishgreyhoundstud.com
Newlawn Kennels
www.newlawnkennels.com
Newpark Stud www.newparkstud.com
Peter Payne www.ppayne.50megs.com
Patsy Cusack
www.patsycusackgreyhounds.com
Rosewood Kennels (Gary Baggs)
www.rosewoodracing.com
Pat Thompson
www.nestledown.20m.com
Questhouse Kennels
www.questhousekennels.com
Mark Wallis
markwallisgreyhounds.com
Westmead Merlin site
www.westmeadmerlin.com

PUBLICATIONS
Greyhound Star www.greyhoundstar.com
Racing Post www.racingpost.co.uk
Sporting Press www.sportingpress.ie

SYNDICATES
Abacus Racing www.rockysracers.co.uk
Jimmi in Boys www.jimmyin.mysite.
wanadoo-members.co.uk
Sparca Racing
www.sparca-racing.co.uk
Top Aim Racing www.topaimracing.mysite.
wanadoo-members.co.uk

MESSAGE BOARD
Global Greyhounds
www.globalgreyhounds.com

MISCELLANEOUS
Tote betting
www.24dogs.com
Breeding Database
www.greyhound-data.com
Irish Greyhound Farm
www.irishgreyhoundfarm.com
Stud Directory
www.greyhounds-racing.co.uk
Trap6 www.trap6.com
Greyhound artist
www.davidfrenchgreyhounds.co.uk
Uk Greyhounds
www.clix.to/ukgreyhound

Please forward amendments to
greyhounds@racingpost.co.uk

Trainers

ABBOTT Sonya Mary (Mrs)
Address: Itchen Farm,
Otterbourne Road,
Compton, Winchester, Hampshire
SO21 2BD
Tel: 07940 646542
(Attached to: Reading Stadium)

ABEL Taryn Louise (Miss)
Address: Diglake Kennels,
Diglake House, Harridge Lane,
Scarisbrick, Ormskirk,
Lancashire L40 8HD
Tel: 01704 841527
(Attached to: Doncaster Stadium)

ACOTT David
Address: 35 Prince Edward
Avenue, Rhyl,
Clwyd LL18 4PT
Tel: 01745 334 323
(Attached to: Kinsley Stadium)

ADAM Thomas Reid
Address: 3 Cedar Place,
Blantyre, Glasgow G72 9QQ
Tel: 01698 828 097
(Attached to: Shawfield Stadium)

ADAMS Adam Robert
Address: 99 Woodlands Way,
Birmingham B37 6RN
Tel: 0121 788 2923
(Unattached)

ADAMS Janice Mary (Mrs)
Address: The Bungalow,
Haggs Lane, Willerby
Hull, North Humberside
HU10 6EG
Tel: 01482 671 221
(Attached to: Hull Stadium)

ADAMS Peter
Address: 45 Glentyan Avenue,
Kilbarchan, Johnstone,
Renfrewshire PA10 2JU
Tel: 01505 702 226
(Attached to: Shawfield Stadium)

ADAMS William Thomas
Address: Inglenook Kennels,
Honiley Avenue, Wickford, Essex
SS12 9JE Tel: 07786 036955
(Unattached)

ADAMSON Helen (Miss)
Address: Lower Barn Farm,
Castle Hill Road, Hindley, Wigan,
Lancashire WN2 4BY
Tel: 01942 522020
(Attached to: Belle Vue Stadium)

ADAWAY David John
Address: Long Acre,
Bimbury Lane, Detling,
Maidstone, Kent ME14 3HY
Tel: 01622 736 233
(Unattached)

AGNEW Adam
Address: 5 Castlehill Crescent,
Hamilton, Lanarkshire ML3 7TZ
Tel: 01698 305965
(Unattached)

AITKEN Thomas George
Address: Magpie Kennels,
Magpie Nest, Little Warley,
Brentwood, Essex CM13 3DT
Tel: 07960 622343
(Attached to: Mildenhall)

AITKEN Wendy Jean (Miss)
Address: 144 Lismore Avenue,
Kirkcaldy, Fife KY2 6DH
Tel: 01592 265 028
(Attached to: Shawfield)

ALDEN Maximillian Frederick
Address: Kelva, Gate End Bridge,
Parson Drove, Wisbech,
Cambridgeshire PE13 4LH
Tel: 01945 700858
(Attached to: Peterborough)

ALEXENDER Giovanni
Address: 28 The Crescent,
Chester Le Street, County
Durham DH2 2DU
Tel: 07958 109 166
(Attached to: Pelaw Grange)

ALI Afzal
Address: 20 Mentmore Close,
High Wycombe,
Buckinghamshire HP12 4LX
Tel: 01494 510 786
(Attached to: Reading)

ALLDER Reginald Ernest
Address: Dead Queen Farm,
1 Stoke Road, Newton
Longville, Milton Keynes,
Buckinghamshire MK17 0BQ
Tel: 01908 379398
(Unattached)

ALLEN David John
Address: 21 Southview Road,
Hockley, Essex SS5 5DY
Tel: 01702 202 895
(Unattached)

ALLISON Michael John
Address: 25 Thornham Drive,
Bolton, Lancashire BL1 7RE
Tel: 01204 307117
(Attached to: Kinsley)

ALLISON Paul Royston
Address: School Bungalow,
Middleton Crescent,
Norwich, Norfolk NR5 0PX
Tel: 01603 594898
(Attached to: Yarmouth)

ALLSOP Keith Rowland
Address: The Stables, Little
Belvoir Stud, Nottingham Road,
Little Belvoir, Melton Mowbray,
Leicestershire LE14 3JD
Tel: 01664 822 954
(Unattached)

ALLSOPP Christopher
Address: Unit 5/6 West View,
Wall Hill Road, Corley, Coventry,
West Midlands CV7 8AD
Tel: 01676540302
(Attached to: Monmore Green)

ANDERSON Anita Jayne
Anderson (Miss)
Address: 1 White Gate Cottages,
Ivetsey Bank, Wheaton Aston,
Stafford, Staffordshire
ST19 9QT
Tel: 01785 840 652
(Unattached)

ANDERSON Leslie Robert
Address: Watermill Farm,
Diddlington, Thetford, Norfolk
Tel: 0777 6283015
(Attached to: Mildenhall)

ANDREAS George
Address: Yasso Greyhound
Kennels, Nestledown Greyhound
Complex, Eastbourne Road,
Blindley Heath, Lingfield,
Surrey RH7 6LG
Tel: 07984 633220
(Attached to: Sittingbourne)

ANDREW Edward Joseph
Address: Winterhaven,
12 Carfin Road, Motherwell,
Lanarkshire ML1 5AB
Tel: 01698 290208
(Attached to: Shawfield)

ANDREWS Craig Leonard
4 Sycamore Drive, Whitby,
Ellesmere Port, Merseyside
CH66 2PN
Tel: 01513 552 513
(Attached to: Coventry)

ANDREWS Joy (Miss)
Address: Thornfield, Liverpool
New Road, Much Hoole, Preston,
Lancashire PR4 4RL
Tel: 01772 617421
(Attached to: Belle Vue)

APPLETON Armine Anthony
Address: Wood View, Tower
Road, Fleggburgh, Great
Yarmouth, Norfolk NR29 3AU
Tel: 01493 368110
(Unattached)

ARBON Owen
Address: 22 Malvern Road,
Peterborough,
Cambridgeshire PE4 7TU
Tel: 01733 320286
(Attached to: Peterborough)

ARCHER Roger Charles
Address: Furzehill Kennels,
Legbourne Road
Louth, Lincolnshire LN11 8LQ
Tel: 01507 606 946
(Attached to: Hull)

ARMITAGE Craig David
Address: 56 Smithy Wood Lane,
Dodworth, Barnsley, South
Yorkshire S75 3NJ
Tel: 01226 244914
(Attached to: Kinsley)

ARMITAGE Frank
Address: 38 Littleworth Lane,
Monk Bretton, Barnsley, South
Yorkshire S71 2JR
Tel: 01226 218045
(Attached to: Hull)

ARMSTRONG Alan
Address: Drumbeg Kennels,
Blackridge, Bathgate, West
Lothian EH48 3AG
Tel: 01501 753224
(Attached to: Shawfield)

ASH Monty
Address: Mayfield,
Church Lane, Betley, Crewe,
Cheshire CW3 9AX
Tel: 01270 820568
(Unattached)

ASHPOLE Barry William
Address: 8 Wootton Green,
Wootton, Bedford,
Bedfordshire MK43 9EE
Tel: 01234 767509
(Attached to: Henlow)

ATKINS Derrick John
Address: Raceover, Dog Drove
South, Holbeach Drove,
Spalding, Lincolnshire
PE12 0SD
Tel: 01406 330873
(Attached to: Henlow)

ATKINS Donna Elaine (Mrs)
Address: 24 Chestnut Crescent,
Whittlesey, Peterborough,
Cambridgeshire PE7 1TW
Tel: 01733 767825
(Attached to: Peterborough)

ATKINS Terence
Address: Sunnymeads Kennels,
Dedworth Road, Windsor,
Berkshire SL4 4LH
Tel: 01753 868801
(Attached to: Oxford)

ATKINSON Jodie (Miss)
Address: 38 Tudor Road,
Hinckley, Leicestershire
LE10 0EQ
Tel: 07765 305730
(Unattached)

ATKINSON Trevor Robert David
Address: 47 High Street, Sutton,
Sandy, Bedfordshire SG19 2NF
Tel: 01767 260590
(Attached to: Henlow)

ATTWATER Harry Richard
Address: Ivydene, Vaggs Lane,
Hordle, Lymington,
Hampshire SO41 0FP
Tel: 01425 616648
(Attached to: Poole)

AUSTIN Barry
Address: Forest Lodge Kennels,
Forest Road, Quinton,
Northampton,
Northamptonshire NN7 2EQ
Tel: 01604 862239
(Unattached)

AXFORD Frederick
Address: Redwing Kennels,
Redwing Farm, Lantern Lane,
Stevenage, Hertfordshire
SG2 0NU
Tel: 01462 451500
(Attached to: Henlow)

AYLWARD Ian Thomas
Address: Baliff Racing Kennels,
Westfield Lodge, Sleaford Road,
Heckington, Sleaford,
Lincolnshire NG34 9QN
Tel: 01529 460922
(Attached to: Coventry)

BABE Kathleen Geraldine (Miss)
Address: Old Covert Bungalow,
Weston, Underwood, Ashbourne,
Derbyshire DE6 4PJ
Tel: 01773 550054
(Attached to: Perry Barr)

BACKHURST Malcolm Geoffrey
Address: Strawberry Farm,
Glaziers Lane, Normandy,
Guildford, Surrey GU3 2DF
Tel: 01483 811534
(Attached to: Reading)

BAGGS Gary
Address: Rosewood Kennels,
Sawyers Green Farm,
Langley Park Road, Slough,
Berkshire SL3 6DD
Tel: 01753 547895
(Attached to: Walthamstow)

BAILEY Margaret (Miss)
Address: 324 Hall Road,
Norwich, Norfolk NR4 6NE
Tel: 07769 965216
(Attached to: Yarmouth)

BAILEY Peter
Address: Horsalls, Stede Hill,
Harrietsham, Maidstone, Kent
ME17 1NT
Tel: 01622 859304
(Attached to: Sittingbourne)

BAKER Alexander Groat
Address: Harriotts Hayes Farm,
Harriotts Hayes Road, Codsall
Wood, Wolverhampton
West Midlands WV8 1RQ
Tel: 01902374064
(Attached to: Hall Green)

BAKER Melvin Thomas
Address: Rycot Kennel,
Colton Road, Rugeley
Staffordshire WS15 3HE
Tel: 01889 574854
(Attached to: Monmore Green)

BAKER Richard Arthur
Address: Wood View, Mill Lane,
Elsfield, Oxford
Oxfordshire OX3 0QD
Tel: 07880 534993
(Attached to: Coventry)

BAKEWELL Dennis Walter
Address: 33 Regent Street,
Bedworth, Warwickshire
CV12 9BN
Tel: 02476 310599
(Unattached)

BAKEWELL Gary James
Address: The Elms Kennels,
Withybrook Road,
Bulkington, Bedworth,
Warwickshire CV12 9JW
Tel: 02476 314634
(Attached to: Hall Green)

BALLARD Scott John
Address: 8 Gisleham Road,
Carlton Colville, Lowestoft,
Suffolk NR33 8DF
Tel: 01502 582468
(Unattached)

BALLENTINE Gerald Bernard
Address: West View Kennels,
Wall Hill Road, Corley, Coventry,
West Midlands CV7 8AD
Tel: 01676 54 23 38
(Attached to: Hall Green)

BALLERINO Juan
Address: 22 Rutherwyk
Road,Chertsey, Surrey KT16 9JF
Tel: 01932 569430
(Attached to: Reading)

BALLS John Leslie
Address: Summer Lodge, Church
Lane, Tydd St. Giles, Wisbech,
Cambridgeshire PE13 5LG
Tel: 01945 870386
(Attached to: Peterborough)

BALLS Robert Charles
Address: Valley Farmhouse,
Church Road, Hedenham,
Bungay, Suffolk NR35 2LF
Tel: 01508 482685
(Attached to: Yarmouth)

BAMBER James William
Address: Rose Grove, Hugh Barn
Lane, New Longton, Preston,
Lancashire PR4 4SQ
Tel: 01772 615685
(Unattached)

BANDURAK Michaelo Andre
Address: Old Yells Farm, Hilton
Lane, Essington, Wolverhampton,
West Midlands WV11 2AU
Tel: 01922 701031
(Unattached)

BANKS John
Address: 25 Cowper Road,
Mexborough, South Yorkshire
S64 0LQ
Tel: 07970 541199
(Attached to: Hull)

BARBER Ronald
Address: The Kennels, Southport
Road, Scarisbrick, Ormskirk,
Lancashire L40 8HE
Tel: 01695 570138
(Attached to: Belle Vue)

BARLOW Mark Antony
Address: The Kennels, No 1
Barn, Stourbridge Road,
Wombourne, Wolverhampton,
West Midlands WV5 0JN
Tel: 01902 324565
(Attached to: Hall Green)

BARLOW Phil
Address: 31 Sunnyhill Crescent,
Wrenthorpe, Wakefield, West
Yorkshire WF2 0PR
Tel: 07789 513 740
(Unattached)

BARNARD Irene Joan (Mrs)
Address: The Homestead, Low
Road, West Caister, Great
Yarmouth, Norfolk NR30 5SP
Tel: 01493 721227
(Attached to: Yarmouth)

BARNETT Geoffrey Gordon
Address: Blythe House Farm,
Leek Road, Weston Coyney,
Stoke On Trent ST3 5BD
Tel: 01782 599651
(Attached to: Doncaster)

BARRETT Derek Ailwyn
Address: Glebe Farm,
Holt Road, Horsford, Norwich
Norfolk NR10 3AG
Tel: 01603 898263
(Unattached)

BARRETT Paul James
Address: Village Farm,
Coventry Road, Elmdon,
Birmingham B26 3QS
Tel: 0121 782 4952
(Attached to: Perry Barr)

BARRON Keith
Address: 13 Myrtle Road,
Palmers Green,
London N13 5QX
Tel: 020 8245 9214
(Attached to: Reading)

BARTLEY Patrick James
Address: 41 Croyland Green,
Leicester, Leicestershire
LE5 2LD
Tel: 01162 417 955
(Unattached)

BARTON Frederick
Address: 71 Pontefract Road,
Barnsley, South Yorkshire
S71 1HA
Tel: 01226 212847
(Unattached)

BARWICK Colin Eric
Address: Shimeon, Park Lane,
Maplehurst, Horsham, West
Sussex RH13 6LL
Tel: 01403 891528
(Attached to: Brighton & Hove)

BATEMAN Berenice Winsome
June (Mrs)
Address: Novedene, Hovefields
Avenue, Wickford,
Essex SS12 9JA
Tel: 07999 865243
(Unattached)

BATES Roger Arthur
Address: 19 Northgate Close,
Kidderminster, Worcestershire
DY11 6JW
Tel: 01562 750 526
(Unattached)

BATESON Julie (Mrs)
Address: 59 Lythe Fell Avenue,
Halton, Lancaster,
Lancashire LA2 6NL
Tel: 01524 811 428
(Unattached)

BAXTER David
Address: Gannow House,
Gannow Lane, Burnley,
Lancashire BB12 6JJ
Tel: 01282 426243
(Attached to: Doncaster)

BEACH Ian Patrick
Address: 130 St. Georges Road,
Hull, North Humberside HU3 3QE
Tel: 01482 228083
(Attached to: Hull)

BEALE Alan
Address: 6 Lydgate Lane,
Wolsingham, Bishop Auckland,
County Durham DL13 3LF
Tel: 01388 526908
(Attached to: Pelaw Grange)

BEALE Alec Henry
Address: Catford Stadium
kennels, Layhams Road, Keston,
Kent BR2 6AR
Tel: 01959 576 986
(Attached to: Sittingbourne)

BEARD Valerie Joy (Mrs)
Address: Brickyard Kennels,
Hall End Road, Wootton,
Bedfordshire MK43 9HJ
Tel: 01234 852648
(Attached to: Henlow)

BEAT James
Address: Sunny Cottage, Trent
Lane, North Clifton, Newark,
Nottinghamshire NG23 7AT
Tel: 01777 228 046
(Attached to: Doncaster)

BEATTIE Daniel
Address: Moorfoot Cottage,
Dalblair, Near Logan, Cumnock,
Ayrshire KA18 3JA
Tel: 01290 429566
(Attached to: Shawfield)

BEAUMONT Terence Frank
Address: 37 Ketts Hill, Necton,
Swaffham, Norfolk PE37 8HX
Tel: 01760 723484
Yarmouth)

BEBBINGTON Kenneth Marshall
Address: White House, Moss
Lane, Minshull Vernon, Crewe,
Cheshire CW1 4RJ
Tel: 01270 522278
(Attached to: Monmore Green)

BEDFORD Troy
Address: 2 Rockley Cottages,
Stony Houghton, Mansfield,
Nottinghamshire NG19 8TS
Tel: 01623 819755
(Attached to: Doncaster)

BEECH David George
Address: 15 The Croft,
Measham, Swadlincote,
Derbyshire DE12 7NL
Tel: 01530 272025
(Attached to: Coventry)

BEET Mark Anthony
Address: 90 Rowden Drive,
Birmingham
B23 5UH
Tel: 07939 723 018
(Attached to: Perry Barr)

BELL Andrew Robinson
Address: Greensfield Moor Farm,
Alnwick, Northumberland NE66
2HH Tel: 01665 603 891
(Attached to: Newcastle)

BELL Charles Anthony
Address: 117 Church Balk,
Edenthorpe, Doncaster, South
Yorkshire DN3 2PR
Tel: 01302 888737
(Attached to: Kinsley)

BELL Elizabeth Yvonne (Mrs)
Address: 1 Bishops Close
Cottages, Whitworth,
Spennymoor, County Durham
DL16 7QR
Tel: 01388 815 113
(Attached to: Sunderland)

BELLIS Alan
Address: 8 Hooten Lane,
Leigh, Lancashire LN7 3BS
Tel: 01942 517127
(Attached to: Pelaw Grange)

BENFOLD Paul
Address: 9 Roseberry Street,
Beamish, Stanley, County
Durham DH9 0QR
Tel: 01913 702 501
(Attached to: Pelaw Grange)

BENNETT Brian Andrew
Address: 182 Whitehouse Road,
Edinburgh EH4 6DB
Tel: 0131 339 2203
(Unattached)

BENNETT Michael Charles
Address: 14 Newport Road,
Hemsby, Great Yarmouth,
Norfolk NR29 4NN
Tel: 01493 384 019
(Attached to: Yarmouth)

BENNETT Robert Frederick
Address: The Granary, Fogget
Farm, Dipton Mill, Hexham,
Northumberland NE46 1YB
Tel: 01434 601598
(Attached to: Pelaw Grange)

BENTHAM Stephen
Address: 2 North Crescent,
Choppington, Northumberland
NE62 5JH
Tel: 01670 854 027
(Attached to: Pelaw Grange)

BENTLEY Andrew John
Address: 3 The Court,
Off Halifax Road, Hightown,
Liversedge, West Yorkshire
WF15 6NA
Tel: 01274 876826
(Attached to: Kinsley)

BENTLEY John Keith
Address: Green Acre Farm, Hop
Hills Lane, Dunscroft, Doncaster,
South Yorkshire DN7 4JX
Tel: 01302 841652
(Attached to: Hull)

BENTLEY Keith Joseph
Address: 28 Doncaster Road,
Askern, Doncaster, South
Yorkshire DN6 0AL
Tel: 01302 707 635
(Attached to: Kinsley)

BERRY Kenneth Anthony
Address: Manor Farm,
Easterfields, East Malling,
Kent ME19 6BE
Tel: 01732 849402
(Unattached)

BERWICK Bruno
Address: Glendon Kennels, Ferry
Bank Farm, Northampton Road,
Orlingbury, Kettering,
Northamptonshire NN14 1JF
Tel: 07930 641138
(Attached to: Henlow)

BERWICK Kevin
Address: The Old Nursery,
Stamford Road, Morcott,
Oakham, Leicestershire
LE15 9DU
Tel: 07761 727995
(Unattached)

BEUMER Johanna Liseta (Miss)
Address: Whittingham Kennels,
6 Claverhambury, Galley Hill,
Waltham Abbey, Essex EN9 2BL
Tel: 01992 893 734
(Unattached)

BEVAN Quentin Paul
Address: Downfield Farm,
The Pry, Purton, Swindon,
Wiltshire SN5 4JP
Tel: 01793 770917
(Attached to: Swindon)

BICKNELL Ronald
Address: South Lodge,
Ford Lane, Iver,
Buckinghamshire SL0 9LL
Tel: 01753 653 580
(Attached to: Oxford)

BILLINGHAM Peter Arnold
Address: Church Cottage Farm,
Smestow, Swindon, Dudley,
West Midlands DY3 4PH
Tel: 01902 892 151
(Attached to: Monmore Green)

BINDING Kenneth William
Address: 183 Old Road, Neath,
West Glamorgan SA11 2ER
Tel: 01639 773 709
(Attached to: Reading)

BIRCH Barrie Peter
Address: Keepers Cottage,
Back Lane, Weeton, Preston,
Lancashire PR4 3HS
Tel: 01253 836485
(Unattached)

BIRCHNALL Dennis
Address: 6 Oakmere Close,
Shiney Row, Houghton Le
Spring, Tyne and Wear DH4 7NF
Tel: 0191 385 2471
(Attached to: Pelaw Grange)

BIRTLES Gary
Address: 50 Tombridge
Crescent, Kinsley, Pontefract,
West Yorkshire WF9 5HD
Tel: 01977 618 322
(Attached to: Kinsley)

BITTLESTONE Stephen
Address: 19 Shellbark,
Houghton Le Spring,
Tyne and Wear DH4 7TD
Tel: 01913 853 447
(Attached to: Pelaw Grange)

BLABY Martin Rowland
Address: 107 Kitchener
Crescent, Waterloo Estate,
Poole, Dorset BH17 7HY
Tel: 01202 696360
(Attached to: Poole)

BLACK Neil Sinclair
Address: Killieford Kennels,
Craig Farm, Laurieston,
Castle Douglas,
Kirkcudbrightshire DG7 2NA
Tel: 01644 450 267
(Unattached)

BLACK William John
Address: Horseshoe Paddock,
Old Odiham Road, Alton,
Hampshire GU34 4BU
Tel: 01420 544085
(Attached to: Portsmouth)

BLACKBIRD Karolyn (Mrs)
Address: 10 Balmoral Road,
Ferryhill, County Durham
DL17 8QF
Tel: 01740 653 304
(Attached to: Pelaw Grange)

BLACKBURN Elizabeth Ann (Mrs)
Address: 15 Cathcart Close,
Whitley, Goole, North
Humberside DN14 0JE
Tel: 01977 662345
(Attached to: Kinsley)

BLAIR Francis William
Address: 1 Golfhill Road,
Wishaw, Lanarkshire ML2 7RW
Tel: 01698 373504
(Unattached)

BLAKE Gary Leslie
Address: Cottesloe Farm,
Cublington Road, Wing, Leighton
Buzzard, Bedfordshire LU7 0LB
Tel: 07984 423641
(Unattached)

BLANCHARD Eve Romayne (Mrs)
Address: Old Rectory Garden,
Church Road, Shillingstone,
Blandford Forum, Dorset
DT11 0SL
Tel: 01258 860410
(Attached to: Poole)

BLINKHORN Alan
Address: 68 Edwinstowe Road,
Ansdell, Lytham St. Annes,
Lancashire FY8 4BG
Tel: 01253 733573
(Unattached)

BLOOMFIELD Christopher
Address: 223 High Newham
Road, Stockton-on-Tees,
Cleveland TS19 8NG
Tel: 01642 613 807
(Attached to: Pelaw Grange)

BLOOMFIELD Jason
Address: 1 Queens Bank,
Crowland, Peterborough,
Cambridgeshire PE6 0JR
Tel: 07808 572616
(Attached to: Peterborough)

BLUNT Philip Steven
Address: 25 Eastfield Road,
Wolverhampton,
West Midlands WV1 2RG
Tel: 07930 613 231
(Attached to: Coventry)

BODELL Alan Terence
Address: The Old Stables, Rear
of 194 Burton Road, Annswell,
Ashby-de-la-Zouch,
Leicestershire LE65 2LH
Tel: 07973 833643
(Attached to: Nottingham)

BODILY Jodie Marie (Miss)
Address: Unit 2 Summer Lane
Kennels, Summer Lane,
Carbrooke, Thetford,
Norfolk IP25 6TR
Tel: 077482 98229
(Attached to: Mildenhall)

BOLAND Allan Edward
Address: 44 Calder Avenue,
Royston, Barnsley, South
Yorkshire S71 4AS
Tel: 01484 280 237
(Unattached)

BOLTON Barry Michael
Address: 9 Hanscombe End
Road, Shillington, Hitchin,
Hertfordshire SG5 3NA
Tel: 01462 711035
(Attached to: Henlow)

BOND Mr Roger
Address: Keepers Cottage,
Angram, York, North Yorkshire
YO23 3PA
Tel: 1904 738229
(Attached to: Doncaster)

BOOSEY Robert Carlo
Address: 13 Inglefield Road,
Fobbing, Stanford-le-Hope,
Essex SS17 9HW
Tel: 01268 551441
(Attached to: Harlow)

BOOTH Brian
Address: Rosedale Kennels,
Avago Greyhounds,
Rusham Road, Shatterling,
Canterbury, Kent CT3 1JL
Tel: 01227 722847
(Attached to: Sittingbourne)

BOOTH Victoria Elizabeth (Miss)
Address: 28 Taranis Close,
Wavendon Gate, Milton Keynes,
Buckinghamshire MK7 7SJ
Tel: 01908 587450
(Attached to: Henlow)

BORRELLI Emanuel
Address: 6 Lando Road, Burry
Port, Dyfed SA16 0UR
Tel: 01792 881705
(Attached to: Reading)

BOTHWAY Robert Nigel
Address: The Grange, Whipps
Lane, Fundenhall, Norwich,
Norfolk NR16 1DT
Tel: 01508 489217
(Attached to: Yarmouth)

BOUGHTON David Andrew
Address: Blean View, Junction
Road, Herne Bay, Kent CT6 7SE
Tel: 01227 363111
(Unattached)

BOWMAN Barry John
Address: 4 Billing Close,
Norwich, Norfolk NR6 7EL
Tel: 01603 487308
(Attached to: Yarmouth)

BRADBURY Wendy (Mrs)
Address: 22 Milcroft Crescent,
Hatfield, Doncaster, South
Yorkshire DN7 6LA
Tel: 01302 841 484
(Attached to: Doncaster)

BRADMAN Nicholas Derek
Address: Sandhouse Farm,
Messingham Common,
Susworth, Scunthorpe, South
Humberside DN17 3AU
Tel: 07939 135258
(Attached to: Hull)

BRADNOCK George Ephraim
Henry
Address: 66 Arden Road, Saltley,
Birmingham B8 1DY
Tel: 0121 608 0817
(Attached to: Perry Barr)

BRAIN Richard Verdun
Address: Oakfield,
Golden Cross, Hailsham,
East Sussex BN27 4AN
Tel: 01825 873476
(Attached to: Reading)

BRAITHWAITE Paul Anthony
Address: 30 Queens Road,
Peterborough, Cambridgeshire
PE2 8BP
Tel: 01733 319952
(Attached to: Peterborough)

BRANNAN James
Address: 95 Torbothie Road,
Shotts, Lanarkshire ML7 5NE
Tel: 01501 822871
(Unattached)

BRANNIGAN Anthony Gerald
Address: 128 Shepherds House,
Ashley Road, Newmarket,
Suffolk CB8 8DZ
Tel: 01638 668791
(Attached to: Mildenhall)

BRASS Janet (Mrs)
Address: 27 Salisbury Terrace,
Darlington, County Durham
DL3 6PA
Tel: 01325 360197
(Attached to: Pelaw Grange)

BREARLEY Lara Kay (Mrs)
8 Holway Court, Holway Road,
Holywell, Clwyd CH8 7DR
Tel: 01352 719 019
(Attached to: Coventry)

BREWER Paul Leslie
Address: 59 White Edge Moor,
Liden, Swindon, Wiltshire
SN3 6LZ
Tel: 01793 527795
(Unattached)

BRIGGS Allen Harry
Address: The Hollies,
36 Whitehall Lane, Buckhurst
Hill, Essex IG9 5JG
Tel: 020 8504 4199
(Unattached)

BRIGHTON Derek Henry
Address: Highland Farm,
Ilketshall St. Margaret, Bungay,
Suffolk NR35 1NB
Tel: 01986 781461
(Unattached)

BRISTOW Julia Ann (Miss)
Address: Caravan, Fen Lane,
Stilton, Peterborough,
Cambridgeshire PE7 3SA
Tel: 01733 241378
(Attached to: Henlow)

BROOKS Christopher Patrick
3Address: 5 Britten Road,
Lowestoft, Suffolk NR33 9BW
Tel: 01502 583669
(Attached to: Yarmouth)

BROOME Philip Gordon
Address: 250 March Road,
Whittlesey, Peterborough,
Cambridgeshire PE7 2DE
Tel: 01733 840578
(Attached to: Peterborough)

BROTHERTON Robert
Address: 19 Auriel Avenue,
Dagenham, Essex RM10 8BS
Tel: 0208 595 1362
(Unattached)

BROUGH William Norman
Address: The Bungalow,
101 Front Street, Frosterley,
Bishop Auckland. County
Durham DL13 2RH
Tel: 01388 527662
(Unattached)

BROWN Andrea Jean (Mrs)
Address: The Kennels, Mill
Street, Stanton St. John, Oxford,
Oxfordshire OX33 1HJ
Tel: 01865 351 710
(Attached to: Reading)

BROWN Bernard
Address: 1 Beda Hill,
Blaydon-on-Tyne,
Tyne and Wear NE21 4BD
Tel: 0191 440 1583
(Attached to: Pelaw Grange)

BROWN Ian Harold
Address: 2 Broadside, Decoy
Road, Ormesby, Great Yarmouth,
Norfolk NR29 3LX
Tel: 01493 731589
(Attached to: Yarmouth)

BROWN Jerome James
Address: Park Lane, Whitehall,
Commercial Road, Dereham,
Norfolk NR19 1AE
Tel: 01362 851518
(Attached to: Mildenhall)

BROWN Mervyn John
Address: Redhills Farm,
Twyford, Shaftesbury,
Dorset SP7 0JD
Tel: 01747 812 655
(Attached to: Poole)

BROWNLIE Ian
Address: 2 Stanmore Crescent,
Lanark, Lanarkshire ML11 7DF
Tel: 01555 666251
(Unattached)

BRYANT Ralph Paul
Address: 42 Hempstead Road,
Hempstead, Gillingham,
Kent ME7 3RF
Tel: 01634 364227
(Attached to: Harlow)

BRYSON John Andrew
Address: 6 Cove Place,
Gretna, Dumfriesshire
DG16 5BU
Tel: 01461 338198
(Unattached)

BUCKLAND Paul
Address: 8 Fenwick Stead
Cottages, Belford,
Northumberland NE70 7PL
Tel: 07944133347
(Attached to: Newcastle)

BUCKLAND Stuart Maurice
Address: Watford Gap Cottage,
Watford Gap Road, Lichfield,
Staffordshire WS14 0QG
Tel: 0121 308 2112
(Attached to: Hall Green)

BUCKLEY Eamon
Address: 16 Meadway, Seven
Kings, Ilford, Essex IG3 9BG
Tel: 020 8599 4599
(Attached to: Harlow)

BUGDEN William Harry George
Address: 1 Mons Way, Bromley,
Kent BR2 8EX
Tel: 020 8462 5492
(Unattached)

BULL David Cyril
Address: Beechwood Farm,
Scotter Common, Gainsborough,
Lincolnshire DN21 3JF
Tel: 01724 763290
(Attached to: Nottingham)

BULLEN Anthony Reginald
Address: 346 White Hart Lane,
Tottenham, London N17 8LN
Tel: 020 8885 4688
(Unattached)

BURCHELL Anthony Donald
Address: Eton Bury Farm House,
Stotfold Road, Arlesey,
Bedfordshire SG15 6XB
Tel: 07786 777390
(Attached to: Henlow)

BURFORD Lance
Address: Monkspath Cottage,
Trysull Road, Wombourne,
Wolverhampton, West Midlands
WV5 8DQ
Tel: 01902 892 839
(Attached to: Coventry)

BURNS James Stewart
Address: 43 Brown Street,
Greenock, Renfrewshire
PA15 2DG
Tel: 01475 710696
(Attached to: Shawfield)

BURNS John
Address: 32 Park Avenue,
Thornaby, Stockton-on-Tees,
Cleveland TS17 7JN
Tel: 01642 649445
(Attached to: Pelaw Grange)

BURRIDGE Josephine Margaret
(Mrs)
Address: Kerstins, Tarrant
Launceston, Blandford Forum,
Dorset DT11 8BY
Tel: 01258 830261
(Attached to: Poole)

BURT Martin John
Address: West View Kennels,
Wall Hill Road, Corley, Coventry,
West Midlands CV7 8AD
Tel: 01676 540600
(Attached to: Monmore Green)

BUTCHER Ernest George
Address: The Small Holding,
Wood Lane, Woodcote, Reading
Berkshire RG8 0PU
Tel: 01491 680 594
(Attached to: Reading)

BUTLER Douglas Brandon
Address: 18 Avon Close,
Wrexham, Clwyd LL12 7US
Tel: 01978 363068
(Unattached)

BUTLER Raymond William
Address: Foxdene, Rumstead
Lane, Stockbury, Sittingbourne
Kent ME9 7RT
Tel: 01622 880001
(Attached to: Sittingbourne)

BUZZARD Christopher Gordon
Address: 122 Hawthorn Way,
Shepperton, Middlesex
TW17 8QD
Tel: 01932 765 504
(Unattached)

CAHILL Kenneth
Address: 23 Hempbridge Close,
Selby, North Yorkshire YO8 4XJ
Tel: 01757 701 164
(Attached to: Kinsley)

CAHILL Seamus Augustine ,
Address: Catford Racing
Kennels, Layhams Road, Keston,
Kent BR2 6AR
Tel: 01959 576777
(Attached to: Walthamstow)

CAILE Stephen
Address: High Jobs Hill House,
Helmington Row, Crook, County
Durham DL15 0SF
Tel: 01388 764 971
(Attached to: Pelaw Grange)

CALVERT Debbie (Miss)
Address: Drover House Farm,
Satley, Bishop Auckland, County
Durham DL13 4JG
Tel: 07727 686917
(Attached to: Newcastle)

CALVERT Julie (Mrs)
Address: Sedgeletch Farm,
Fencehouses, Houghton Le
Spring, Tyne and Wear DH4 5PN
Tel: 0191 385 4041
(Attached to: Sunderland)

CAMERON Alexander
Address: West Cairns,
Kirknewton, Midlothian EH27
8DH Tel: 01506 881 401
(Unattached)

CAMPBELL James Graham
Address: Railway Kennels,
Larbert, Stirlingshire FK5 3NN
Tel: 07963 046 481
(Unattached)

CAMPBELL John
Address: 32 Gladys Avenue,
Cowplain, Waterlooville,
Hampshire PO8 8HT
Tel: 02392 250664
(Attached to: Portsmouth)

CANNING Harold Harris
Address: 3 Smeaton Road,
Upton, Pontefract, West Yorkshire
WF9 1EY Tel: 01977 608220
(Attached to: Kinsley)

CANTILLON Eric Joseph
Address: Oak View, Herringswell
Manor Stud, Tuddenham Road,
Herringswell, Bury St. Edmunds,
Suffolk IP28 6SW
Tel: 01638 552594
(Attached to: Mildenhall)

CARLEY Bruce (Snr)
Address: Roxton Hill House,
Roxton Road, Great Barford,
Bedford, Bedfordshire MK44 3LJ
Tel: 01234 871 453
(Unattached)

CARMICHAEL Gary
Address: Liberton Greyhound
Kennels, 4 Stanedykehead,
Edinburgh EH16 6YE
Tel: 01316662264
(Attached to: Shawfield)

CARNE Alan John
Address: 147 Honey Lane,
Waltham Abbey, Essex EN9 3AX
Tel: 01992 764 779
(Unattached)

CARR Nicola Louise
Address: Elizabeth Cottage,
Crown Lane, Tendring, Clacton-
on-Sea, Essex CO16 0BH
Tel: 01255 831275
(Attached to: Yarmouth)

CARR Peter Ronald
Address: Hopeville, New Road,
Little Burstead, Billericay,
Essex CM12 9TS
Tel: 01268 545903
(Unattached)

CARRINGTON Steven Brian
Address: Haggswood Greyhound
Kennels, Station Road,
Stainforth, Doncaster,
South Yorkshire DN7 5HS
Tel: 077404 167 34
(Attached to: Kinsley)

CARSON William
Address: 7 Park Avenue,
Dennyloanhead, Bonnybridge,
Stirlingshire FK4 1SB
Tel: 01324 811873
(Unattached)

CARTE David Frank
Address: Shair Lane Kennels,
Shair Lane, Great Bentley,
Colchester, Essex CO7 8QT
Tel: 1206 251203
(Attached to: Henlow)

CARTER Jean Mary (Mrs)
Address: Well House, Hertford
Road, Tonwell, Ware,
Hertfordshire SG12 0EZ
Tel: 01920 462684
(Attached to: Crayford)

CARTER John George
Address: 33 Colescliffe Road,
Scarborough, North Yorkshire
YO12 6SA
Tel: 07778 315 491
(Attached to: Hull)

CARTER Royce
Address: Chips Farm, Southport
Road, Scarisbrick, Ormskirk,
Lancashire L40 8HE
Tel: 07743 158887
(Unattached)

CARTER Sandra Elizabeth (Mrs)
Address: 6 Lye Green Cottages,
Lycrome Road, Chesham,
Buckinghamshire HP5 3LD
Tel: 01494 786 562
(Attached to: Henlow)

CASH Frank Darley
Address: The Kestrels, Boston
Road, Heckington, Sleaford,
Lincolnshire NG34 9JF
Tel: 01529 460761
(Unattached)

COLIN Christopher Michael
Address: Cashmore, 317
Gateford Road, Worksop,
Nottinghamshire S81 7BH
Tel: 01909 530187
(Attached to: Kinsley)

CHALKLEY Alfred
Address: 100 Kettering Road,
Weldon, Corby,
Northamptonshire NN17 3JG
Tel: 01536 202913
(Attached to: Peterborough)

CHALKLEY Henry
Address: Swanbridge Farm,
Midway Kennels, Long Drove,
Parson Drove, Wisbech,
Cambridgeshire PE13 4JT
Tel: 01945 700612
(Attached to: Henlow)

CHAMBERS Terrence
Address: 91 Arnold Crescent,
Mexborough, South Yorkshire
S64 9JR
Tel: 01709327753
(Attached to: Doncaster)

CHAPMAN Eric John
Address: The Stables, Sheep Dip
Lane, Princethorpe, Rugby,
Warwickshire CV23 9SP
Tel: 01926 633 360
(Attached to: Coventry)

CHAPMAN Kenneth George
Address: 34 Barnard Avenue,
Whitefield, Manchester M45 6TY
Tel: 0161 773 8322
(Unattached)

CHEETHAM Lucille (Mrs)
Address: 45 Keycol Hill, Bobbing,
Sittingbourne, Kent ME9 8LZ
Tel: 01795 842182
(Attached to: Sittingbourne)

CHESHIRE Jane (Mrs)
Address: Lower Farm,
Picket Twenty, Andover,
Hampshire SP11 6LF
Tel: 01264 353384
(Attached to: Poole)

CHILDS Dean
Address: 3 Ockendon Kennels,
Ockendon Road, Upminster,
Essex RM14 3PT
Tel: 0772 942 5787
(Unattached)

CHRISTIE Joyce (Miss)
Address: 23 Rodney Road,
Twickenham, Middlesex
TW2 7AW
Tel: 0208 274 0170
(Attached to: Reading)

CHRISTIE Richard
Address: 13 Newton Road,
Bedford, Bedfordshire
MK42 9NA
Tel: 01234 405625
(Attached to: Henlow)

CLAPP Cindy Anne (Mrs)
Address: The Meads Common,
Mead Lane, Hambrook,
Bristol, Avon BS16 1QQ
Tel: 01179 567548
(Attached to: Swindon)

CLARE Michael
Address: The Old Monastery,
The Moor, Reepham, Norwich,
Norfolk NR10 4NL
Tel: 01603 871014
(Attached to: Yarmouth)

CLARK James Galloway
Address: 280 Carlisle Road,
Kirkmuirhill, Lanark, Lanarkshire
ML11 9RA
Tel: 01555 893 913
(Attached to: Shawfield)

CLARK Sally Ann (Miss)
Address: 93a Regent Road,
Brightlingsea, Colchester,
Essex CO7 0NW
Tel: 01206 307500
(Unattached)

CLARK Thomas Wythe
Address: 187 Abbeygreen Road,
Lesmahagow, Lanark,
Lanarkshire ML11 0AL
Tel: 07788982207
(Attached to: Shawfield)

CLARKE David John
Address: 9 Fairview Road, North
Walsham,   Norfolk NR28 9HR
Tel: 01692 406905
(Attached to: Yarmouth)

CLARKE James
Address: 15 Bank Street,
Brimington, Chesterfield,
Derbyshire S43 1LZ
Tel: 01246 237627
(Attached to: Doncaster)

CLARKE Michael Geoffrey
Address: Hollinwood Farm,
Hollinwood Lane, Calverton,
Nottingham, Nottinghamshire
NG14 6NQ
Tel: 01159 652688
(Attached to: Doncaster)

CLARKE Paul
Address: Family Farm House,
Weston-on-the-Green, Bicester,
Oxfordshire OX25 3QQ
Tel: 07789 466948
(Attached to: Oxford)

CLAYTON John Alan
Address: 4 The Close, Kippax,
Leeds, West Yorkshire LS25 7NB
Tel: 0113 286 6347
(Unattached

CLEMENSON Brian Adrian
Address: Rowfold Greyhound
Kennels, Coneyhurst Road,
Billingshurst, West Sussex
RH14 9DF
Tel: 01403 786610
(Attached to: Brighton & Hove)

CLEMENTS Barry David
Address: Folly Farm, Crane Row
Lane, Hamsterley, Bishop
Auckland, County Durham
(Attached to: DL13 3QU
Tel: 07833 323783
Newcastle)

CLEMENTS Thomas Hugh
Address: 49 Kelso Drive, East
Kilbride, Glasgow G74 4DA
Tel: 01355 265 253
(Attached to: Shawfield)

CLEVERLEY Graham
Address: 13 Hillview Mobile
Home Park, Potters Hill, Felton,
Bristol, Avon BS40 9XE
Tel: 01275 474630
(Attached to: Poole)

CLIFFE Michael Leonard
Address: Cranberry Cottage,
Wrenbury Heath, Wrenbury,
Nantwich, Cheshire CW5 8EF
Tel: 01270 780605
(Unattached)

COBB Sandra Eve (Mrs)
Address: Clarks Farm, Wash
Lane, Little Totham, Maldon,
Essex CM9 8LX
Tel: 01621 788 315
(Unattached)

COBBOLD William David
Address: 34 Fallowfield Walk,
Bury St. Edmunds, Suffolk
IP33 2QS
Tel: 01284 705237
(Attached to: Mildenhall)

COCK Pamela Patricia (Mrs)
Address: The Homestead, 11
Long Lane, Feltwell, Thetford,
Norfolk IP26 4BJ
Tel: 01842 828619
(Attached to: Mildenhall)

COGAN Stuart Roger
Address: Limekiln Kennels,
Charterhouse-on-Mendip,
Blagdon, Bristol,
Avon BS40 7XW
Tel: 07765 260900
(Attached to: Swindon)

COLEMAN Barbara (Mrs)
Address: Kildara Kennels,
Odiham Lane, Ewshot, Farnham,
Surrey GU10 5AE
Tel: 01252 850 384
(Attached to: Reading)

COLEMAN Frank
Address: 21 Musgrave Road,
Bradford, West Yorkshire
BD2 3JX
Tel: 01274 404 497
(Attached to: Kinsley)

COLEMAN John Joseph
Address: 4 Claverhambury
Kennels, Galley Hill, Waltham
Abbey, Essex EN9 2BL
Tel: 01992 899195
(Attached to: Walthamstow)

COLK Terence Melvin
Address: The Bungalow,
Shoulder of Mutton, Snarehill,
Thetford, Norfolk IP24 2SN
Tel: 01842 766 365
(Attached to: Mildenhall)

COLLETT Anthony Martin Peter
Address: Kennel 1, Croft View
Kennels, White Horse Lane,
Meopham, Gravesend,
Kent DA13 0UE
Tel: 01474 813 511
(Attached to: Sittingbourne)

COLLINGWOOD William
Address: 4 Park Grove,
Washington, Tyne and Wear
NE37 2QU Tel: 0191 4179256
(Attached to: Pelaw Grange)

COLLINS Joseph Patrick
Address: Gramercie, Mooredges,
Thorne, Doncaster, South
Yorkshire DN8 5SE
Tel: 01405 816148
(Attached to: Doncaster)

COLLINS Maria Cecilia
Bernadette (Miss)
Address: Croft Handy Kennels,
51a Lonesome Lane, Reigate,
Surrey RH2 7QT
Tel: 01737 249022
(Attached to: Brighton & Hove)

COLTMAN Dean David
Address: Patches Farm,
Galley Hill, Waltham Abbey,
Essex EN9 2AG
Tel: 07739 908 798
(Attached to: Mildenhall)

COLTON Nicholas
Address: Greenacres,
49 Puxley Road, Deanshanger,
Milton Keynes, Buckinghamshire
MK19 6LR
Tel: 01908 263211
(Attached to: Hall Green)

CONWAY Graham
Address: 9 Millcroft,
Stainforth, Doncaster, South
Yorkshire DN7 5NN
Tel: 01302 843182
(Unattached)

COOK Gavin
Address: 12 Dene Avenue,
Peterlee, County Durham
SR8 3NL
Tel: 0191 527 3201
(Attached to: Pelaw Grange)

COOK Lynn (Miss)
Address: The Kennels, Shelt Hill,
Woodborough, Nottingham,
Nottinghamshire NG14 6DG
Tel: 01159 664029
(Attached to: Perry Barr)

COOKE Peter Alan
Address: Cookes Kennels,
54 Sedge Fen, Lakenheath,
Brandon, Suffolk IP27 9LH
Tel: 01353 675248
(Attached to: Mildenhall)

COOPER David
Address: 39 Chatsworth
Crescent, Doncaster,
South Yorkshire DN5 9JU
Tel: 01302 787977
(Attached to: Doncaster)

COOPER Malcolm
Address: 90 Spring Lane,
Swannington, Coalville,
Leicestershire LE67 8QQ
Tel: 01530 458614
(Attached to: Nottingham)

COOPER Paul
Address: 21 Hillcrest View,
Maerdy, Ferndale, Mid
Glamorgan CF43 4TR
Tel: 01443 732 914
(Unattached)

CORBETT George
Address: 82 Stechford Road,
Hodge Hill, Birmingham
B34 6BH
Tel: 0121 783 3766
(Attached to: Perry Barr)

CORNER Royston Keith
Address: 47 Great Back Lane,
Debenham, Stowmarket,
Suffolk IP14 6PZ
Tel: 01728 860640
(Attached to: Yarmouth)

CORRIGAN Susan Ann (Mrs)
Address: Orton Croft,
Great North Road, Haddon,
Peterborough, Cambridgeshire
PE7 3TN
Tel: 01733 244413
(Attached to: Peterborough)

COTTEE Frederick
Address: Woodside, Colchester
Road, Tiptree, Colchester,
Essex CO5 0EU
Tel: 01621 815348
(Attached to: Harlow)

COULSON Colin Alfred
Address: 270 Elm Low Road,
Wisbech, Cambridgeshire
PE14 0DF
Tel: 01945 466823
(Attached to: Peterborough)

COULSON Mark
Address: 449 New Cross Row,
Wingate, County Durham
TS28 5BB
Tel: 01429 838 174
(Attached to: Pelaw Grange)

COULTER Edmund
Address: 15 Bosmore Road,
Luton, Bedfordshire LU3 2TR
Tel: 01582 502 427
(Attached to: Henlow)

COULTON Ronald
Address: 25 Moss Lea, Tarleton,
Preston, Lancashire PR4 6BH
Tel: 01772 816430
(Unattached)

COUNSELL John William
Address: Black Hall Farm,
Temple Road, Isleham, Ely,
Cambridgeshire CB7 5RF
Tel: 01353 720154
(Attached to: Mildenhall)

COUSEN Sydney Arnold
Address: 188 Valletts Lane,
Bolton, Lancashire BL1 6DY
Tel: 01204 494244
(Unattached)

COWDRILL Patricia Irene (Mrs)
Address: Shaw Cottage,
Shaw Lane, Shifnal,
Shropshire TF11 9PN
Tel: 07958 684437
(Attached to: Monmore Green)

COWELL Darren Nichol
Address: 60 Durham Road,
Stanley, County Durham
DH9 6QX
Tel: 01207 234 060
(Attached to: Pelaw Grange)

COWIE Alwyne
Address: 15 Northside Cottage,
Wilks Hill, Quebec, Durham,
County Durham DH7 9RX
Tel: 07808 653 980
(Attached to: Pelaw Grange)

COWLE George Frederick
Address: 12 Drummond Ride,
Tring, Hertfordshire HP23 5DE
Tel: 01442 826260
(Unattached)

COX David Christopher
Address: 450 Birmingham Road,
Great Barr, Birmingham B43 7AJ
Tel: 0121 357 3810
(Attached to: Henlow)

COX Dennis Charles
Address: 100 Birdsfoot Lane,
Luton, Bedfordshire LU3 2DH
Tel: 01582 654552
(Attached to: Henlow)

COX Nigel Nicholas
Address: The Old Waterworks,
Kingsdon, Somerton, Somerset
TA11 7HU
Tel: 01458 223718
(Unattached)

CRAIG Grant
Address: 116 Rullion Road,
Penicuik, Midlothian EH26 9HT
Tel: 01968 673237
(Unattached)

CRANE Donald Leonard
Address: Northbox Kennels, 2
Warwick Road, Kibworth,
Leicester, Leicestershire LE8 0JF
Tel: 0116 279 269
(Attached to: Peterborough)

CRANFIELD Lionel Steve
Address: 2 White Barn Cottages,
Clacton Road, Elmstead,
Colchester, Essex CO7 7DB
Tel: 01206 561194
(Attached to: Yarmouth)

CRAPPER Harry
Address: Commonside Farm,
Main Road, Renishaw, Sheffield,
South Yorkshire S21 3UW
Tel: 01246 434475
(Attached to: Sheffield)

CRASKE Jane Elise (Mrs)
Address: Hartwood, Middletons
Field, Eccles-on-Sea, Norwich,
Norfolk NR12 0SS
Tel: 01692 598427
(Attached to: Yarmouth)

CRAWFORD Colin
Address: 1 Thornlea Avenue,
Hollinwood, Oldham,
Lancashire OL8 3PX
Tel: 0161 681 5368
(Attached to: Doncaster)

CRAWLEY Peter John
Address: Old Park Farm,
Cublington Road, Wing, Leighton
Buzzard, Bedfordshire LU7 0LB
Tel: 077986 12621
(Attached to: Henlow)

CRECKENDON Robert Charles
Address: Ivy House, Greens
Lane, Tilney All Saints, King's
Lynn, Norfolk PE34 4RR
Tel: 01553 829 466
(Attached to: Peterborough)

CREW Keith George
Address: 162 Ladysmith Road,
Enfield, Middlesex EN1 3AB
Tel: 020 8363 3924
(Unattached)

CRITCHLEY William Stuart
Address: 22 Grove Road,
Stockingford, Nuneaton,
Warwickshire CV10 8JR
Tel: 02476 343425
(Attached to: Coventry)

CROFT Kathleen Mary (Mrs)
Address: 2 Cherry Holt Road,
Bourne, Lincolnshire PE10 9LA
Tel: 01778 424090
(Attached to: Henlow)

CRONIN Christopher Neil
Address: Lynton Kennels,
Lower Dunton Road, Dunton,
Brentwood, Essex CM13 3SP
Tel: 01268 545925
(Unattached)

CROOKES Derek
Address: 14 Tombridge
Crescent, Kinsley, Pontefract,
West Yorkshire WF9 5HA
Tel: 01977 616 635
(Attached to: Kinsley)

CROSS Pamela Ivy
Address: The Bungalow, Drury
Square, Beeston, King's Lynn,
Norfolk PE32 2NA
Tel: 01328 701493
(Attached to: Yarmouth)

CROSSE Peter
Address: 71 Woodhead Road,
Tintwistle, Glossop, Derbyshire
SK13 1JX
Tel: 01457 867554
(Attached to: Doncaster)

CROSSLAND John
Address: 2 California Gardens,
Barnsley, South Yorkshire
S70 1YW
Tel: 01226 239578
(Attached to: Doncaster)

CROW Edward John
Address: 1 Castle View,
Godstone Hill, Godstone,
Surrey RH9 8DH
Tel: 01883 744623
(Attached to: Reading)

CROWE Christine (Mrs)
Address: 127 Upwell Road,
March, Cambridgeshire
PE15 0DE
Tel: 01354 659191
(Unattached)

CROWE Eric George
Address: 11 West End Road,
Saxlingham Thorpe, Norwich,
Norfolk NR15 1UE
Tel: 01508 470190
(Attached to: Yarmouth)

CROWE Francis Edward
Address: 7 Clydesdale Avenue,
Wishaw, Lanarkshire ML2 0AX
Tel: 01698 357956
(Attached to: Shawfield)

CROWSON Paul
Address: Newsham Far, March
Road, Guyhirn, Wisbech,
Cambridgeshire PE13 4DD
Tel: 07860 591568
(Unattached)

CRYAN Peter James
Address: 19 Keyworth Place,
Sheffield, South Yorkshire
S13 7GX
Tel: 01142 696 200
(Unattached)

CULL Simon John
Address: Cherry Tree, High Side,
Wisbech St. Mary, Wisbech,
Cambridgeshire PE13 4SA
Tel: 01945 410624
(Attached to: Peterborough)

Sponsored by the BGRB

CUMNER Marilyn Ann (Mrs)
Address: Unit 4, Nestledown
Kennels, Blindley Heath, Nr
Lingfield, Surrey RH5 6LJ
Tel: 01342 836 014
(Attached to: Sittingbourne)

CURRAN Julie Mary (Mrs)
Address: 43a Neville Road,
Luton, Bedfordshire
LU3 2JG
Tel: 01582 502972
(Attached to: Henlow)

CURRY Jonathan
Address: 223 Big Barn Lane,
Mansfield, Nottinghamshire
NG18 3LB
Tel: 01623 487 805
(Attached to: Doncaster)

CURTIN Denis Michael
Address: 22 Devonshire Drive,
Greenwich, London SE10 8JZ
Tel: 020 8691 2285
(Attached to: Reading)

CURTIN Patrick Andrew
Address: Village Farm,
Gaydon, Warwick,
Warwickshire CV35 0HF
Tel: 07795 097574
(Attached to: Oxford)

CUSACK Patrick Joseph
Address: 1 Ockendon Kennels,
Ockendon Road, Upminster,
Essex RM14 3PT
Tel: 01708 224134
(Attached to: Crayford)

CUSWORTH Allen
Address: 188 Tombridge
Crescent, Kinsley, Pontefract,
West Yorkshire WF9 5HG
Tel: 01977 618393
(Attached to: Kinsley)

CUTLER Martin
Address: Whinmoor Grange,
York Road, Leeds,
West Yorkshire LS14 3AD
Tel: 01132 735791
(Attached to: Belle Vue)

DAGLEY Michael Alan
Address: Lily Cottage, Main
Street, Reedness, Goole, North
Humberside DN14 8HG
Tel: 01405 704 858
(Attached to: Kinsley)

DALBY Tyrone Roy
Address: 18 Friar Way, Boston,
Lincolnshire PE21 9ER
Tel: 01205 360686
(Unattached)

DALE Albert Edward
Address: 93 Campbell Road,
Ipswich, Suffolk IP3 9RE
Tel: 01473 710189
(Attached to: Mildenhall)

DALEY Morris Graham
Address: 7 Priory Avenue,
Harefield, Uxbridge,
Middlesex UB9 6AP
Tel: 01895 821815
(Attached to: Henlow)

DALY James
Address: Woodlands,
Hethel Road, Wreningham,
Norwich, Norfolk NR16 1BB
Tel: 07916 268858
(Attached to: Yarmouth)

DANIELS Malcolm
Address: Quernhow Cafe & Park,
Great North Road, Sinderby,
Thirsk, North Yorkshire
YO7 4LG
Tel: 01845 567221
(Attached to: Hull)

DARLER John
Address: Shimmering Kennels,
100 Undley Common,
Lakenheath, Brandon,
Suffolk IP27 9BY
Tel: 07786 874162
(Attached to: Henlow)

DARNELL June (Mrs)
Address: Chestnut Tree Farm,
First Drove, Burwell, Cambridge,
Cambridgeshire CB5 0BH
Tel: 01638 742958
(Attached to: Mildenhall)

DAVIDSON Gemma Louise (Miss)
Address: Yewtree Farm,
Copthorne Road, Felbridge,
East Grinstead, West Sussex
RH19 2QQ
Tel: 01342 328 258
(Attached to: Crayford)

DAVIES John
Address: Roman Kennels,
Roman Road, Wheatley, Oxford,
Oxfordshire OX33 1UU
Tel: 07946 849577
(Attached to: Reading)

DAVIES Michael John
Address: 40 Twelfth Avenue,
Merthyr Tydfil, Mid Glamorgan
CF47 9TB
Tel: 01685 375 906
(Attached to: Reading)

DAVIS Kevin Alan
Address: 78 Greencroft,
Lichfield, Staffordshire
WS13 7JF
Tel: 01543 268513
(Attached to: Perry Barr)

DAVY Beverley Eirwen (Mrs)
Address: Ty Mawr Farm, Cefn-Y-
Crib, Crumlin, Newport, Gwent
NP11 5BN Tel: 01495 248715
(Attached to: Swindon)

DAVY John David
Address: Station House,
Crossmoor Bank, Swinefleet,
Goole, North Humberside
DN14 8DR
Tel: 07768 084748
(Attached to: Sheffield)

DAWE David James
Address: Glenfield Farm,
Plucknett, Crewkerne,
Somerset TA18 7NZ
Tel: 07776 008041
(Attached to: Poole)

DAWSON Keith
Address: The Cottage, Pigot
Lane, Framingham Pigot,
Norwich, Norfolk NR14 7PY
Tel: 01508 494560
(Attached to: Yarmouth)

DEAKIN Kevin Roy
Address: 3 Tadmore Close,
Bilston, West Midlands
WV14 0JA
Tel: 01902 448 830
(Attached to: Coventry)

DEAKIN Simon Wayne
Address: The Barn, Barton Farm,
Icknield Street, Rowley Green,
Worcestershire B48 7EW
Tel: 0776 665616
(Attached to: Hall Green)

DEAL Steve Peter
Address: 2 Woollards Gardens,
Long Melford, Sudbury,
Suffolk CO10 9EJ
Tel: 07854 334 417
(Unattached)

DEBENHAM Peter Geoffrey
Address: Brands Farm, Brands
Lane, Felthorpe, Norwich,
Norfolk NR10 4EA
Tel: 01603 627971
(Attached to: Yarmouth)

DEELEY Stanley
Address: Tythe Barn Farm,
Tythebarn Lane, Shirley, Solihull,
West Midlands B90 1PH
Tel: 07931 925 467
(Attached to: Perry Barr)

DENBY Barry
Address: Penniment Lodge
Farm, Penniment Lane,
Mansfield, Nottinghamshire
NG19 6PH
Tel: 01623 634260
(Attached to: Coventry)

DENNING James Charles
Address: 18 Little Park,
Andover, Hampshire SP11 7AX
Tel: 01264 711020
(Attached to: Portsmouth)

DENNIS Maria Toni (Miss)
Address: Fallowfield Kennels,
Grays Avenue, Langdon Hills,
Basildon, Essex SS16 5LP
Tel: 01268 542061
(Unattached)

DERSLEY Julie Doreen (Mrs)
Address: 26 The Crescent,
Wicken, Ely, Cambridgeshire
CB7 5XN
Tel: 01353 624278
(Unattached)

DERWIN Patrick John
Address: Croft Farm, Aston
Common, Aston, Sheffield,
South Yorkshire S26 2AE
Tel: 01909 563812
(Attached to: Kinsley)

DESMOND John Robert
The Horsehoe Inn,
Mildenhall, Marlborough,
Wiltshire SN8 2LR
Tel: 01672 514980
(Unattached)

DICKINSON Linda (Miss)
Address: 22 Northall Close,
Eaton Bray, Dunstable,
Bedfordshire LU6 2EB
Tel: 01525 222248
(Attached to: Henlow)

DILGER Roger Norman
Address: 1 Alderman Road,
Ipswich, Suffolk IP1 2DU
Tel: 01473 402194
(Unattached)

DIMMOCK Heather Jean (Miss)
Address: Ivy Cottage Farm,
Grafton Regis, Towcester,
Northamptonshire NN12 7SP
Tel: 01908 542 328
(Attached to: Peterborough)

DIX Ronald Eric
Address: 2 Limekiln Cottages,
Charterhouse-on-Mendip,
Blagdon, Bristol, Somerset
BS40 7XW
Tel: 01761 462040
(Attached to: Swindon)

DIXON Andrew
Address: 31 South Market
Street, Hetton-le-Hole, Houghton
Le Spring, Tyne and Wear
DH5 9DP
Tel: 0191 526 1408
(Attached to: Pelaw Grange)

DIXON David
Address: Keepers Cottage,
Stanhope, Bishop Auckland,
County Durham DL13 2EZ
Tel: 01386 528 366
(Attached to: Pelaw Grange)

DIXON Jack
Address: 46 Wistow Road,
Selby, North Yorkshire YO8 3LY
Tel: 01757 704611
(Attached to: Doncaster)

Sponsored by the BGRB

DIXON Sydney
Address: 44 Taff Road, Caldicot,
Gwent NP26 4PY
Tel: 01291 422623
(Unattached)

DOBBIE James
Address: 47 Sandaig Road,
Barlanark, Glasgow G33 4TA
Tel: 0141 573 1808
(Attached to: Shawfield)

DOBBIN Hugh Bernard
Address: 241 Overdown Road,
Tilehurst, Reading, Berkshire
RG31 6NX
01189 674270
(Unattached)

DOBSON Kenneth
Address: Blue House Farm,
Hartlepool Road, Newton Bewley,
Billingham, Cleveland
TS22 5PQ
Tel: 07840 935765
(Attached to: Pelaw Grange)

DODD David Andrew
Address: Old Coach House,
Peatons Lane, Lytchett
Matravers, Poole, Dorset
BH16 6HW
Tel: 01929 459309
(Attached to: Poole)

DOLAN Paul David
Address: 30 Hine Way,
Hitchin, Hertfordshire
SG5 2SL
Tel: 01462 649779
(Attached to: Henlow)

DOLBY Pamela June (Mrs)
Address: Brickyard Farm,
Lower Road, Croydon, Royston,
Hertfordshire SG8 0HA
Tel: 01223 208004
(Attached to: Henlow)

DONLON Michael Patrick
Address: Three Acres,
Denny Beck, Lancaster,
Lancashire LA2 9HG
Tel: 07949 145528
(Unattached)

DONNELLY Stephen Michael
Address: South View Kennels,
78a Barkers Lane, Wythall,
Birmingham B47 6BU
Tel: 07982 073 457
(Attached to: Perry Barr)

DONOVAN Paul Martin
Address: Pretty Lane Kennels,
Pretty Lane, Coulsdon,
Surrey CR5 1NS
Tel: 01737 550473
(Attached to: Wimbledon)

DOUGAL Keith Albert
Address: Lydden Farm House,
Valley Road, Margate,
Kent CT9 4LF
Tel: 01843 822690
(Attached to: Sittingbourne)

DOUGLAS Sylvia Joan (Mrs)
Address: New Barremman Farm,
Clynder, Helensburgh,
Dunbartonshire G84 0QN
Tel: 01436 831902
(Unattached)

DOVE Steven
Address: Robin Hood, Clipstone
Road, Edwinstowe, Mansfield,
Nottinghamshire NG21 9JA
Tel: 01623 822 359
(Attached to: Doncaster)

DOWDEN Frances Helen (Mrs)
Address: Snedwod,
Burrowmoor Road, March,
Cambridgeshire PE15 0YX
Tel: 01354 656778
(Attached to: Henlow)

DOWMAN Martin Richard
Address: Burnside, Brigg Road,
Moortown, Market Rasen,
Lincolnshire LN7 6JA
Tel: 01652 678702
(Attached to: Doncaster)

DOYLE Bernard
Address: Ramat Kennels,
89 Denham Way,
Maple Cross, Rickmansworth,
Hertfordshire WD3 9SL
Tel: 01923 776 754
(Attached to: Wimbledon)

DOYLE Lewis
Address: Foresthead, Dalswinton
Road, Auldgirth, Dumfries,
Dumfriesshire DG2 0XP
Tel: 01387 740670
(Attached to: Shawfield)

DOYLE Tony Martin
Address: 44 Linford Lane,
Woolstone, Milton Keynes,
Buckinghamshire MK15 0BW
Tel: 01908 695443
(Unattached)

DRAKE John
Address: Monkroyd Farm,
Keighley Road, Laneshawbridge,
Colne, Lancashire BB8 7EJ
Tel: 01282 869520
(Attached to: Kinsley)

DRAKE Martin
Address: 38 Barker Crescent,
Melton Mowbray, Leicestershire
LE13 0QW
Tel: 01664 410860
(Attached to: Peterborough)

DRAPER Barrie
Address: Poultry Farm, Dalton
Magna, Rotherham, South
Yorkshire S65 3ST
Tel: 01709 851322
(Attached to: Sheffield)

DUGGAN Christopher
Address: Bodiam Farm,
St. Marys Lane, Upminster,
Essex RM14 3PB
Tel: 01708 642 123
(Unattached)

DUNBAR David
Address: 126 Main Street,
Auchinleck, Cumnock,
Ayrshire KA18 2AG
Tel: 01290 421686
(Attached to: Pelaw Grange)

DUNHAM Alice Ann (Mrs)
Address: The Bungalow, Chalk
Lane, Walpole St. Andrew,
Wisbech, Cambridgeshire
PE14 7JU
Tel: 01945 780 260
(Attached to: Peterborough)

DUNN Tommy
Address: 18 Donaldson Road,
Methill, Leven, Fife KY8 2LB
Tel: 01592 581 671
(Attached to: Shawfield)

EAGLESTONE Anthony Richard
Address: 15 Kirby Close,
Loughton, Essex IG10 3BA
Tel: 020 8508 8338
(Unattached)

EAGLETON Lesley (Mrs)
Address: Ridings Cottage,
Harperley Road, Stanley, County
Durham DH9 8TB
Tel: 01207 299311
(Attached to: Newcastle)

EDGAR Thomas George
Address: ubilee Cottage,
Northside Road, Northside,
Workington, Cumbria CA14 1BU
Tel: 01900 872776
(Attached to: Newcastle)

EDGE Peter Thomas
Address: Holly Gardens, St.
Olaves Road, Herringfleet,
Lowestoft, Suffolk NR32 5QU
Tel: 01502 732288
(Attached to: Yarmouth)

EDINGTON George
Address: 48 Dennison Crescent,
Birtley, Chester Le Street, County
Durham DH3 1NN
Tel: 0191 410 0494
(Attached to: Pelaw Grange)

EGAN David Joseph
Address: Oakview Farm,
Forest Road, Wokingham,
Berkshire RG40 5SA
Tel: 01189 776597
(Attached to: Reading)

ELCOCK David John
Address: 9 Teresa Gardens,
Waltham Cross,
Hertfordshire EN8 8EQ
Tel: 07715977554
(Unattached)

ELLIOTT Dennis Charles
Address: Franklyn, Dobbs Weir
Road, Roydon, Harlow,
Essex CM19 5JX
Tel: 01992 442 403
(Unattached)

ELLIOTT Donald Leslie Roy
Address: 35 Limes Avenue,
Swindon, Wiltshire SN2 1QQ
Tel: 07765 858326
(Attached to: Swindon)

ELLIS Gary
Address: 336 Norton Lane,
Earlswood, Solihull,
West Midlands B94 5LP
Tel: 01564 702708
(Attached to: Peterborough)

ELLIS George Richard
Address: Carr Farm Cottages,
Low Road, Norton Subcourse,
Norwich, Norfolk NR14 6SD
Tel: 01508 548265
(Unattached)

ELLIS Richard
Address: 69 Westlea, Bedlington,
Northumberland NE22 6DY
Tel: 01670 828 060
(Attached to: Pelaw Grange)

ELLISON Fred George William
Address: 35 Sherwood Avenue,
Askern, Doncaster, South
Yorkshire DN6 0QN
Tel: 01302 701149
(Unattached)

Elmer Norman Stuart
Address: 5 Brinkley Road,
Six Mile Bottom, Newmarket,
Suffolk CB8 0UN
Tel: 01638 570291
(Unattached)

ELSWORTH Barbara Susanne
(Mrs)
Address: Riverview,
Brackenbank, Wetheral,
Carlisle, Cumbria CA4 8HZ
Tel: 01228 560901
(Attached to: Pelaw Grange)

ELVIN Benjamin George
Address: 162 North Walsham
Road, Norwich, Norfolk NR6 7QJ
Tel: 01603 465756
(Attached to: Yarmouth)

EMBERTON Arthur
Address: Westfield Bridge House,
Westfield Road, Kirkhouse
Green, Doncaster, South
Yorkshire DN7 5TF
Tel: 01405 785640
(Attached to: Kinsley)

EVANS Carol Anne (Mrs)
Address: Nook View Farm,
Lumb Lane, Droylsden,
Manchester M43 7LN
Tel: 0161 370 5265
(Attached to: Doncaster)

EVANS Edward Leslie
Address: Granville Cottage,
Flexford Lane, Sway, Lymington,
Hampshire SO41 6DN
Tel: 01590 682457
(Attached to: Reading)

EVANS Garreth Bryn
Address: 29 Lonsdale Street,
Anlaby Road, Hull, North
Humberside HU3 6PA
Tel: 01482 563254
(Attached to: Hull)

EVANS Leslie John
Address: 40 Cleves Road,
Hemel Hempstead,
Hertfordshire HP2 7LH
Tel: 01442 215487
(Attached to: Henlow)

EVANS Raymond Rees
Address: 81 Callicroft Road,
Patchway, Bristol,
Avon BS34 5BU
Tel: 01179 759137
(Attached to: Swindon)

EVANS Raymond Thomas
Address: High View,
Darnford Lane, Lichfield,
Staffordshire WS14 9JQ
Tel: 01543 432101
(Unattached)

EVANS Roy David
Address: 3 Ashton Close,
Bishops Waltham, Southampton,
Hampshire SO32 1FP
Tel: 01489 890 638
(Attached to: Reading)

EVANS Roy John
Address: 8 Crossgate Road,
Dudley, West Midlands DY2 0SY
Tel: 01384 78214
(Unattached)

EVERETT Brian Charles
Address: Old Barn Stables, Stoke
Holy Cross Road, Nr.Lakenham,
Norwich, Norfolk
Tel: 07930 924268
(Attached to: Yarmouth)

EXCELL Ivor Fredric
Address: White House Farm,
Haveringland, Norwich,
Norfolk NR10 4PT
Tel: 01603 754662
(Attached to: Yarmouth)

FAINT Mr John
Address: Laurel Park,
Newgate Street Road, Goffs Oak,
Hertfordshire EN7 5RY
Tel: 01707 875 771
(Unattached)

FAIRLIE John
Address: Fairles Small Holding,
Kitchener Road, Whitburn,
Sunderland, Tyne and Wear
SR6 7NE
Tel: 07910 804 972
(Attached to: Pelaw Grange)

FANOUS Bishara Charles George
Address: Address: 257 Moor
Road, Papplewick, Nottingham,
Nottinghamshire NG15 8EP
Tel: 01159 680030
(Attached to: Doncaster)

FARMER Garry
Address: Fircroft, Dembleby,
Sleaford, Lincolnshire
NG34 0EH
Tel: 07718 602256
(Attached to: Peterborough)

FARRELL Thomas
Address: 18 Yew Tree Avenue,
Redcar, Cleveland TS10 4QG
Tel: 01642 471975
(Attached to: Pelaw Grange)

FARRELLY Sean Anthony
Address: 60 Havers Lane,
Bishop's Stortford, Hertfordshire
CM23 3PD
Tel: 01279 653168
(Attached to: Henlow)

FAWSITT Michael Henry
Address: Unit 10, Salamons Way,
Rainham, Essex RM13 9UL
Tel: 01708 553 880
(Unattached)

FEDORNAK Andrew Joseph
Address: Fox Corner, High Street,
Rampton, Cambridge,
Cambridgeshire CB4 8QF
Tel: 01954 252493
(Attached to: Henlow)

FENWICK James John
Address: Coopers Shop,
Bothal, Morpeth,
Northumberland NE61 6QW
Tel: 01670 853687
(Attached to: Newcastle)

FENWICK William (Snr)
Address: 35 Tennyson Avenue,
Boldon Colliery, Tyne and Wear
NE35 9EP
Tel: 01915 366 371
(Attached to: Pelaw Grange)

FERGUSON Amanda (Mrs)
Address: 15 Millands Road,
Thankerton, Biggar, Lanarkshire
ML12 6NX
Tel: 01899 308076
(Attached to: Pelaw Grange)

FERGUSON Kevin John
Address: The Old Dairy, Grange
Lane, Acomb, York, North
Yorkshire YO23 3QZ
Tel: 01904 786063
(Attached to: Doncaster)

FIELDING Richard Anthony
Address: Cutts Lane Kennels,
Cutts Lane, Hambleton,
Poulton-le-Fylde,
Lancashire FY6 9DF
Tel: 01253 701951
(Attached to: Belle Vue)

FINAL Alan David
Address: Greencourt Kennels,
Clue Hills Farm, Brill, Aylesbury,
Buckinghamshire HP18 9UZ
Tel: 01869 327810
(Unattached)

FINCH Colin George
Address: Kiln Lane Kennels, Kiln
Lane, Elmswell, Bury St.
Edmunds, Suffolk IP30 9QR
Tel: 01359 240750
(Unattached)

FINCH Joseph Alan
Address: 96 Old Park Road,
Dudley, West Midlands, DY1 3ND
Tel: 01902 679 442
(Unattached)

FINN Brian
Address: 15 Newlands Crescent,
Halifax, West Yorkshire HX3 7HU
Tel: 01422 200 061
(Attached to: Kinsley)

FINNIE Hugh
Address: 43 Station Road, Law,
Carluke, Lanarkshire ML8 5LN
Tel: 01698 351507
(Unattached)

FIRMAGER David Peter
Address: Glebe House, Scalford
Road, Melton Mowbray,
Leicestershire LE13 1LB
Tel: 01664 444632
(Attached to: Coventry)

FISHWICK Harry
Address: 70 Leyland Road,
Burnley, Lancashire BB11 3DP
Tel: 01282 420633
(Attached to: Kinsley)

FLAHERTY Patrick Joseph (Snr)
Address: Greenwell Kennels,
Baillieston, Glasgow G69 6UA
Tel: 0141 771 5774
(Unattached)

FLEMING Steven Shane
Address: 16 Burnside Cottages,
Kinglassie, Lochgelly,
Fife KY5 0XN
Tel: 01592 882708
(Attached to: Shawfield)

FLETCHER Mr Robert
Address: 58 Tudor Street,
Thurnscoe, Rotherham,
South Yorkshire S63 0DS
Tel: 01709 890770
(Attached to: Kinsley)

FOLEY Mark William
Address: Fawn Cottage,
Oxmardike, Gilberdyke,
Brough, North Humberside
HU15 2UY
Tel: 01430 441196
(Attached to: Kinsley)

FORD Bryan Reginald
Address: Bryns Kennels,
52a Sedge Fen, Brandon,
Suffolk IP27 9LH
Tel: 01353 675276
(Attached to: Peterborough)

FORDE Carol Anne (Miss)
Address: 49 Dorchester Road,
Maiden Newton, Dorchester,
Dorset DT2 0BD
Tel: 01300 320596
(Attached to: Poole)

FORMAN June Anne (Mrs)
Address: Illinois Farm, Hides
Lane, Addlethorpe, Skegness,
Lincolnshire PE24 4TY
Tel: 01754 763666
(Attached to: Peterborough)

FORREST Steven Peter
Address: Jesmond House,
Whitworth, Spennymoor,
County Durham DL16 7QY
Tel: 01388 813515
(Attached to: Pelaw Grange)

FORSTER Eric
Address: 20 Portland Crescent,
Meden Vale, Mansfield,
Nottinghamshire NG20 9PJ
Tel: 01623 847233
(Attached to: Doncaster)

Mr Alan FOSTER
Address: Derwentbrae, 1
Stewartsfield, Rowlands Gill,
Tyne and Wear NE39 1PE
Tel: 01207 544 152
(Attached to: Pelaw Grange)

FOSTER Jason Thomas
Address: Wimbledon Stadium
Ltd, The Kennels, Turners Lane,
Hersham, Walton-on-Thames,
Surrey KT12 4AW
Tel: 01932 226647
(Attached to: Wimbledon)

FOSTER Paul Robert
Address: Abbey Stadium
Kennels, Lady Lane, Blunsdon,
Swindon, Wiltshire SN25 4DN
Tel: 01793 703926
(Attached to: Swindon)

FRADGLEY Darryl John
Address: 32 Coniston Drive,
Townville, Castleford, West
Yorkshire WF10 3NL
Tel: 01977 736660
(Attached to: Doncaster)

FRADGLEY David Eric
Address: 16 Morley Avenue,
Knottingley, West Yorkshire
WF11 8RY
Tel: 01977 676654
(Attached to: Doncaster)

FRANCIS Stephen Christopher
Address: 1 North View, Easington
Lane, Houghton Le Spring,
Tyne and Wear DH5 0LY
Tel: 01915 267 120
(Attached to: Pelaw Grange)

FRANKS Robert
Address: 8 Finkle Street,
Bentley, Doncaster, South
Yorkshire DN5 0RP
Tel: 01302 817084
(Attached to: Doncaster)

FREEMAN David Edward
Address: Lodge Farm Kennels,
Bosty Lane, Walsall, West
Midlands WS9 0QQ
Tel: 07833578127
(Attached to: Perry Barr)

FREEMAN Michael John
Address: 3 Hyam Cottages,
Sherston Road,
Malmesbury, Wiltshire SN16 0RA
Tel: 01666 825418
(Attached to: Reading)

FRENCH Michael Richard
Address: 9 Oaklands Close,
Halvergate, Norwich,
Norfolk NR13 3PP
Tel: 01493 701102
(Unattached)

FREW Graeme Livingstone
Address: Elderslie House,
Annandale, Kilmarnock,
Ayrshire KA1 2RS
Tel: 01563 521579
(Unattached)

FRICKLETON William Jarvie
Address: Tappernail Farm,
Shieldmill Road, Redding,
Falkirk FK2 0DU
Tel: 01324 712870
(Attached to: Shawfield)

FRIEND Cyril George
Address: Knowle Lodge,
Knowle, Fareham,
Hampshire PO15 6DT
Tel: 01329 833235
(Attached to: Portsmouth)

FROOM Alan
Address: Farm Bungalow,
High Street, Brotton,
Saltburn-By-The-Sea,
Cleveland TS12 2QD
Tel: 01287 676 879
(Attached to: Kinsley)

FURY James
Address: 32 Kerrera Road,
Barlanark, Glasgow G33 4QZ
Tel: 0141 781 1102
(Unattached)

GAIN Rodney George
Address: Flightline,
Adsborough, Taunton,
Somerset TA2 8RR
Tel: 01823 413089
(Unattached)

GALE Barry Frank
Address: 8 Felden Close,
Watford, Hertfordshire WD2 6QW
Tel: 01923 441225
(Attached to: Henlow)

GALLACHER Robert Bryce
Address: 33 Glamis Drive,
Greenock, Renfrewshire
PA16 7NA
Tel: 01475 631543
(Attached to: Shawfield)

GALLANT Frank William John
Address: The Oaks,
School Road, Fritton, Norwich,
Norfolk NR15 2QN
Tel: 01508 498 244
(Attached to: Mildenhall)

GALLOWAY Andrew Thomas
Address: 70 Barskimming Road,
Mauchline, Ayrshire KA5 5DX
Tel: 01290 551 335
(Unattached)

GAMMON John Edmund
Address: Cosmic Kennels,
Maynards Green, Heathfield,
East Sussex TN21 0DJ
Tel: 01435 868021
(Attached to: Brighton & Hove)

GAMMON Stephen John
Address: Catford Racing
Kennels, Layhams Road,
Keston, Kent BR2 6AR
Tel: 01959 574428
(Attached to: Crayford)

GANT Kevin Paul
Address: 4 Bridge Rise,
Gissing, Diss, Norfolk
IP22 3UP
Tel: 01379 677318
(Unattached)

GARDINER Alan Edward
Address: Albourne Kennels,
Wheatsheaf Road, Albourne,
Henfield, West Sussex BN5 9BD
Tel: 01273 492916
(Attached to: Brighton & Hove)

GARLAND Paul Roger
Address: Birchgrove Kennels,
Sun Hill, Fawkham, Longfield,
Kent DA3 8NU
Tel: 01474 879532
(Attached to: Walthamstow)

GARRITY Janice Barbara (Mrs)
Address: 98 Poynders Hill,
Hemel Hempstead,
Hertfordshire HP2 4NR
Tel: 07788570643
(Attached to: Henlow)

GARTH Richard Anthony Clifford
Address: Westbrook Farm,
Layton Road, Rawdon, Leeds,
West Yorkshire LS19 6QS
Tel: 0113 259 0430
(Attached to: Kinsley)

GASKINErnest Alfred
Address: Winston Farm,
Hoe Lane, Nazeing, Waltham
Abbey, Essex EN9 2RJ
Tel: 01992 890 273
(Attached to: Romford)

GATES Robert
Address: Queta, Herringswell
Road, Kentford, Newmarket,
Suffolk CB8 7QR
Tel: 01638 750281
(Attached to: Mildenhall)

GAUGHAN Seamus
Address: Halls Farm,
George V Avenue, Pinner,
Middlesex HA5 5SU
Tel: 020 8954 9272
(Attached to: Henlow)

GEBSKI Krystyna Maria (Miss)
Address: Mayfield Kennels,
Mayfield Grove, Long Eaton,
Nottingham, Nottinghamshire
NG10 2AY
Tel: 0115 972 6760
(Attached to: Nottingham)

GEDDIS John James
Address: Nene Cottage,
101 South Brink, Wisbech,
Cambridgeshire PE14 0RJ
Tel: 01945 464260
(Unattached)

GENTLES Thomas Thornton
Address: 40 Glasgow Road,
Dennyloanhead, Bonnybridge,
Stirlingshire FK4 1QG
Tel: 01324 813035
(Unattached)

GIBBINSON George Thomas
Address: South Charlton Farm
Kennels, South Charlton Alnwick,
Northumberland NE66 2LY
Tel: 07859 888 384
(Attached to: Pelaw Grange)

GIBBONS Annette Lilian (Mrs)
Address: Cefn Llan Cottage,
Gwrhyd Road, Pontardawe,
Swansea, West Glamorgan
SA8 4TN
Tel: 01792 863876
(Unattached)

GIBBS Raymond
Address: 37 Molesham Way,
East Molesey, Surrey KT8 1NU
Tel: 020 8941 8009
(Unattached)

GIBSON Alan
Address: 1 Uphill Cottages,
Cambridge Road, Wadesmill,
Ware, Hertfordshire
SG12 0TR
Tel: 01920 468193
(Attached to: Henlow)

GIBSON James
Address: 68 Lancaster Lane,
Leyland, Lancashire PR25 5SP
Tel: 01772 431715
(Attached to: Belle Vue)

GIBSON John Thomas
Address: 26 Malvern Road,
Peterborough, Cambridgeshire
PE4 7TU
Tel: 01733 322746
(Attached to: Peterborough)

GIBSON William
Address: 41 The Arches,
Hadleigh Street, London E2 0LD
Tel: 020 7790 4703
(Unattached)

GIFKINS Anthony Bernard
Address: Elmcroft, London Road,
Capel St. Mary, Ipswich,
Suffolk IP9 2JJ
Tel: 01473 730584
(Unattached)

GILBERT Frederick
Address: Granby, Stafford Road,
Darlaston, West Midlands
WS10 8TZ
Tel: 0121 531 9138
(Attached to: Perry Barr)

GILBERT Lyndon
Address: 61 King Edward Street,
Wednesbury, West Midlands
WS10 8TN
Tel: 0121 526 6624
(Unattached)

GILBERT Martin John
Address: Lizvale Farm,
Goatswood Lane, Navestock,
Romford, Essex RM4 1HE
Tel: 0793 1177733
(Unattached)

GILES Robert
Address: Hare & Hound Kennels,
Lingfield Common Road,
Lingfield, Surrey RH7 6BZ
Tel: 01342 837355
(Unattached)

Sponsored by the BGRB

GILL Norman
Address: Woodlands, 28 Wood
End, Bluntisham, Huntingdon,
Cambridgeshire PE17 3LE
Tel: 01487 840934
(Attached to: Peterborough)

GILLARD Brian
Address: 56 Cornmill Lane,
Liversedge, West Yorkshire
F15 7DZ
Tel: 01924 408298
(Unattached)

GILLESPIE Margaret Smith (Mrs)
Address: Mayfield, Ednam Road,
Stichill, Kelso, Roxburghshire
TD5 7TD
Tel: 01573 470 262
(Unattached)

GILLETT Grant
Address: Bradborough Farm,
Lechlade Road,
Southrop, Lechlade,
Gloucestershire GL7 3PH
Tel: 01367 850473
(Attached to: Swindon)

GILLILAND Shirley Elizabeth
(Mrs)
Address: 197 Buckingham Road,
Bletchley, Milton Keynes,
Buckinghamshire MK3 5JF
Tel: 01908 641620
(Attached to: Henlow)

GILLING Robert John
Address: Ryehurst Kennels,
Ryehurst Lane, Binfield,
Bracknell, Berkshire RG42 5QZ
Tel: 01344 423126
(Attached to: Reading)

GITTENS Raymond Charles,
Address: 12 Tuns Road, Necton,
Swaffham, Norfolk PE37 8EH
Tel: 01760 725389
(Attached to: Yarmouth)

GLAYZER David Frank
Address: Fermoy Store,
Jay Lane, Lound, Lowestoft,
Suffolk NR32 5LH
Tel: 07946 161124
(Attached to: Yarmouth)

GODDARD Jacqueline Jane (Mrs)
Address: 7 Hillcrest,
Hampstead Norreys, Thatcham,
Berkshire RG18 0SH
Tel: 01635 201672
(Attached to: Reading)

GODWIN Elizabeth (Miss)
Address: 55 Aston Road,
Standon, Ware,
Hertfordshire SG11 1PY
Tel: 01920 822868
(Attached to: Henlow)

GOMERSALL Caroline Susan
(Mrs)
Address: 3 Grove Cottages,
Tadpole Lane, Blunsdon,
Swindon, Wiltshire SN25 2DY
Tel: 01793 729043
(Attached to: Swindon)

GOODCHILD Andrew Peter
Address: 50 Westmill Road,
Hitchin, Hertfordshire SG5 2SD
Tel: 01462 624790
(Attached to: Henlow)

GOODFELLOW Peter
Address: 61 Sutton Court Drive,
Rochford, Essex SS4 1HR
Tel: 01702 540 621
(Unattached)

GOODRUM Kevin Patrick
Address: Cornerways,
Hook Road, Wimblington,
March, Cambridgeshire
PE15 0QL
Tel: 01354 741450
(Attached to: Peterborough)

GOODWIN Geoffrey Paul
Address: Ferrybank Farm,
Northampton Road,
Orlingbury, Kettering,
Northamptonshire NN14 1JF
Tel: 01933 401 593
(Unattached)

GORDON Elaine Valerie (Mrs)
Address: 145 Lime Lane,
Walsall, West Midlands
WS3 5AW
Tel: 07963 028984
(Attached to: Perry Barr)

GOSS Peter Charles James
Address: Noahs Ark, 177 Merlin
Road, Welling, Kent DA16 2JS
Tel: 020 8304 1933
(Unattached)

GOWER Geoffrey James (Snr)
Address: 2 Lavender Close,
East Malling, West Malling,
Kent ME19 6EA
Tel: 01732 873 028
(Unattached)

GOWLER Enid (Mrs)
Address: Rutland Farm, Wisbech
Road, Whittlesey, Peterborough,
Cambridgeshire PE7 2DU
Tel: 01945 450636
(Attached to: Peterborough)

GRADY Mark
Address: Southcot, 54 Redehall
Road, Smallfield, Horley,
Surrey RH6 9QL
01342 844299
(Attached to: Sittingbourne)

GRAHAM James
Address: The Paddock,
Manse Brae, Cambuslang,
Glasgow G72 7XF
Tel: 01416 411 022
(Attached to: Shawfield)

GRAHAM Melvin John
Address: 19 White Apron Street,
South Kirkby, Pontefract, West
Yorkshire WF9 3LH
Tel: 01977 640605
(Unattached)

GRAINGE David James
Address: Hillside View, Church
Street, Well, Bedale, North
Yorkshire DL8 2PY
Tel: 01677 470542
(Attached to: Pelaw Grange)

GRANT John Roland
Address: Hillside, Tedburn St.
Mary, Exeter, Devon EX6 6EL
Tel: 01647 61255
(Attached to: Poole)

GRASSO Carol Ann (Mrs)
Address: 2 Highfield, Cranfield
Road, Moulsoe, Newport Pagnell,
Buckinghamshire MK16 0HL
Tel: 01908 610492
(Attached to: Henlow)

GRAY Geoffrey
Address: Graystoke, Treswell
Road, Rampton, Retford,
Nottinghamshire DN22 0HU
Tel: 01777 248 167
(Attached to: Hull)

GRAY John Robert
Address: 13 Sutton Crescent,
Barnet, Hertfordshire EN5 2SW
Tel: 020 8449 9855
(Attached to: Henlow)

GRAY Richard
Address: 14 Cross Lane,
Royston, Barnsley,
South Yorkshire S71 4AT
Tel: 01226 723766
(Attached to: Kinsley)

GRAY William Tees
Address: North Kirktonmoor
Farm, Eaglesham,
Glasgow G76 0QB
Tel: 01355 303461
(Unattached)

GREEN Albert George
Address: Valley View,
Claverhambury Road. Waltham
Abbey, Essex EN9 2BL
Tel: 07817 939143
(Attached to: Harlow)

GREEN Arun Clifford Bentle
Address: Lowlands Racing
Kennels, Lowlands Farm,
Freeks Lane, Burgess Hill, West
Sussex RH15 8DQ
Tel: 01444 233653
(Attached to: Crayford)

GREEN Bernard
Address: 8 Church Gate,
Gedney, Spalding,
Lincolnshire PE12 0BZ
Tel: 01406 364834
(Attached to: Peterborough)

GREEN Christopher James
Address: 42 Danelaw, Gt Lumley,
Chester-Le-Street, County
Durham DH3 4LU
Tel: 07986 503 629
(Attached to: Pelaw Grange)

GREEN Christopher John
Address: 15 High Street,
Haversham, Milton Keynes,
Buckinghamshire MK19 7DU
Tel: 01908 315656
(Attached to: Henlow)

GREEN Joseph George
Address: 8 Eton Way, Orrell,
Wigan, Lancashire WN5 8PN
Tel: 01942 214458
(Unattached)

GREEN Julie (Mrs)
Address: Silver Spring Arabians,
Paper Street, Yaxham, Dereham,
Norfolk NR19 1RY
Tel: 01362 695663
(Attached to: Yarmouth)

GREEN Kenneth
Address: 45 Chapel Lane,
Thurnscoe, Rotherham,
South Yorkshire S63 0HT
Tel: 01709 896 881
(Unattached)

GREEN Michael
Address: 9 Bernisdale Drive,
Glasgow G15 8BB
Tel: 0141 944 1330
(Attached to: Shawfield)

GREEN Philip Matthew
Address: Unit D, Burnt Oak
Farm, Burnt Oak Lane,
Newdigate, Dorking,
Surrey RH5 5BJ
Tel: 07843 447950
Portsmouth)

GREEN Valerie Andre (Mrs)
Address: Oaks Farm, Ashby
Road, Stapleton, Leicester,
Leicestershire LE9 8JE
Tel: 01455 290137
(Attached to: Nottingham)

GREENER Robert
Address: 15 Derwent View,
Blaydon-on-Tyne,
Tyne and Wear NE21 6LR
Tel: 01914 142 168
(Unattached)

GREENWELL Allan
Address: 6 William Street, Pelton
Fell, Chester Le Street, County
Durham DH2 2SF
Tel: 01913 702 757
(Attached to: Pelaw Grange)

GREENWOODJohn Alfred
Address: 18 Elmstead Gardens,
Worcester Park, Surrey KT4 7BD
Tel: 0208 330 3519
(Unattached)

GREGSON Paul William
Address: Pitts House Farm, Pitts
House Lane, Churchtown,
Southport, Merseyside PR9 7QT
Tel: 01704 228762
(Attached to: Belle Vue)

GRESHAM Shaun Robert
Address: Rollsbridge Farm, Ide,
Exeter, Devon EX2 9SU
Tel: 07901 823 269
(Attached to: Reading)

GREWCOCK Alex James
Address: Bromley Lane Farm,
Kings Bromley Lane, Rugeley,
Staffordshire WS15 4ED
Tel: 01543 490 904
(Attached to: Perry Barr)

GREY Ronald
Address: West Farm, Newton
Bewley, Billingham, Cleveland
TS22 5PQ
Tel: 07932 300377
(Attached to: Pelaw Grange)

GRIFFIN Roy Samuel
Address: Ivanhoe, Arterial Road,
Wickford, Essex SS12 9JF
Tel: 01268 727208
(Attached to: Sittingbourne)

GRIFFITHS Thomas
Address: Hoggersgate Farm,
Tursdale, Durham, County
Durham DH6 5NY
Tel: 07930 935 923
(Attached to: Pelaw Grange)

GRIGGS David Neil
Address: Uplands Farm,
Meggett Lane, South Alkham,
Dover, Kent CT15 7DG
Tel: 01303 892300
(Attached to: Sittingbourne)

GRIMSHAW Henry
Address: Greenacres, Rhoden
Road, Oswaldtwistle, Accrington,
Lancashire BB5 3QQ
Tel: 07904 956710
(Unattached)

GRINT Terence Rodney
Address: 48 Lower Packington
Road, Ashby-de-La-Zouch,
Leicestershire LE65 1GE
Tel: 01530 412000
(Unattached)

GURR Stephen
Address: Higher Trevell
Farmhouse, Lewannick,
Launceston, Cornwall PL15 7QW
Tel: 01566782842
(Attached to: Poole)

HACKETT Tony Vincent
Address: Hollygate Kennels,
Hollygate Lane, Cotgrave,
Nottingham, Nottinghamshire
NG12 3HE
Tel: 07966 100737
(Attached to: Coventry)

HALL Elizabeth (Miss)
Address: Sharp Hill Kennels,
Park Lane, Middleham, Leyburn,
North Yorkshire DL8 4QY
Tel: 07778 318 553
(Attached to: Pelaw Grange)

HALL Gary
Address: 28 Brooklands
Crescent, Havercroft, Wakefield,
West Yorkshire WF4 2HS
Tel: 01977 612852
(Attached to: Kinsley)

HALL James Robert
Address: Sunnycroft, 222 The
Long Shoot, Nuneaton,
Warwickshire CV11 6JW
Tel: 024 76383466
(Attached to: Hall Green)

HALL Leonard Thomas
Address: 15 Chestnut Street,
Grimethorpe, Barnsley,
South Yorkshire S72 7LQ
Tel: 07715 154959
(Attached to: Kinsley)

HALL Michael Charles
Address: Thorndon Racing
Kennels, Unit 2 Bird Lane,
Great Warley, Brentwood,
Essex CM13 3JU
Tel: 07899 958335
(Unattached)

HALLAM Jack
Address: 149 St. Marys Road,
Hyde, Cheshire SK14 4HE
Tel: 0161 366 8921
(Attached to: Kinsley)

HALLOWS Brian
Address: 108 Mayplace Road
East, Barnehurst,
Bexleyheath, Kent DA7 6EH
Tel: 01322 523443
(Unattached)

HAMILTON Gary Steven
Address: 18 Coleridge Road,
Ipswich, Suffolk IP1 6EH
Tel: 07939 570 819
(Attached to: Yarmouth)

HAMILTON Robert
Address: 55 Carlisle Road,
Cleland, Motherwell,
Lanarkshire ML1 5LR
Tel: 01698 356397
(Attached to: Shawfield)

HAMILTON Robert Paul
Address: 30 Eastleigh Road,
Peterborough,
Cambridgeshire PE1 5JQ
Tel: 01733 554821
(Attached to: Peterborough)

HAMMOND Darren John
Address: 312 Spittal Hardwick
Lane, Castleford, West Yorkshire
WF10 3QA
Tel: 01977 557075
(Unattached)

HAMPSON Darren John Francis
Address: Brookes Cottage, Holly
Bush Lane, Rixton, Warrington,
Cheshire WA3 6DZ
Tel: 01925 850864
(Attached to: Belle Vue)

HANCOX Graham Alfred
Address: 1 Newbold Road,
Wellesbourne, Warwick,
Warwickshire CV35 9NY
Tel: 01789 840500
(Unattached)

HANCOX Kenneth Henry James
Address: 2 The Glebe,
Church Lane, Corley, Coventry,
West Midlands CV7 8AY
Tel: 01676 541880
(Attached to: Coventry)

HANDY Kevin John
Address: 66 Yardley Close,
Oldbury, West Midlands B68 9DF
Tel: 0121 544 3439
(Attached to: Perry Barr)

HANNAH Leonard
Address: 10 Albert Road,
Waterloo, Liverpool L22 8QT
Tel: 0151 9285119
(Unattached)

HANNAN Robert Patrick
Address: Winnaway Kennels,
The Winnaway, Harwell, Didcot,
Oxfordshire OX11 0JQ
Tel: 01235 861 661
(Attached to: Oxford)

HARDIMAN Keith George
Address: 9 Morrison Road,
Hayes, Middlesex UB4 9JP
Tel: 020 8841 4579
(Attached to: Reading)

HARDY Robert Cyril
Address: 26 Newsam Road,
Kilnhurst, Rotherham, South
Yorkshire S64 5UN
Tel: 01709 583 924
(Attached to: Doncaster)

HARNDEN Peter Howard
Address: The Stud Kennels,
Flawforth House, Flawforth Lane,
Ruddington, Nottingham,
Nottinghamshire NG11 6NG
Tel: 07989 327 984
(Attached to: Nottingham)

HARRINGTON Michael Leonard
Address: 21 Oaklands Avenue,
Brookmans Park, Hatfield,
Hertfordshire AL9 7UH
Tel: 01707 663123
(Unattached)

HARRIS Michael
Address: Caynton Manor,
Caynton, Newport,
Shropshire TF10 8NF
Tel: 01952 550425
(Attached to: Monmore Green)

HARRIS Peter John
Address: 10 Painswick Close,
Paulsgrove, Portsmouth,
Hampshire PO6 3QD
Tel: 07946 623 569
(Attached to: Portsmouth)

HARRISON Steven Robert
Address: Lower Stoneroyd
Cottage, Healey Green Lane,
Huddersfield, West Yorkshire
HD5 0PB
Tel: 01924 499797
(Unattached)

HART Robert
Address: 4 Salcombe Close,
Tollesby Hall, Middlesbrough,
Cleveland TS8 9LZ
Tel: 01642 315194
(Attached to: Pelaw Grange)

HARVEY June Elizabeth (Mrs)
Address: Shelley Mead, Old
Salisbury Road, Ower, Romsey,
Hampshire SO51 6AN
Tel: 02380 812580
(Attached to: Poole)

HARVEY Robert
Address: 66 Morse Road,
Norwich, Norfolk NR1 4PL
Tel: 01603 438857
(Attached to: Yarmouth)

HARWOOD Albert George
Address: 27 Losinga Crescent,
Norwich, Norfolk NR3 2RR
Tel: 01603 468 255
(Attached to: Yarmouth)

HATTERSLEY Michael John
Address: 14 Byron Road,
Mexborough,
South Yorkshire S64 0DG
Tel: 01709 584 234
(Attached to: Kinsley)

HAWES Vivian Patricia (Mrs)
Address: Ash Tree Farm,
Padney Road, Wicken, Ely,
Cambridgeshire CB7 5YE
Tel: 01353 720512
(Attached to: Mildenhall)

HAWKES Derek Frank
Address: Harmony Kennels,
Spar Lane, Purleigh,
Chelmsford, Essex CM3 6QW
Tel: 01621 828563
(Attached to: Walthamstow)

HAY Liam
Address: Beechfield Lodge,
Clements End Road,
Studham, Dunstable,
Bedfordshire LU6 2NG
Tel: 01582 871 155
(Unattached)

HAY Terence William
Address: 29 Mayfield Crescent,
Lower Stondon, Henlow,
Bedfordshire SG16 6LE
Tel: 01462 851 626
(Attached to: Henlow)

HAYNES John
Address: Unit 2, Burnt Oak Farm,
Burnt Oak Lane, Newdigate,
Dorking, Surrey RH5 5BJ
Tel: 07973 917 921
(Unattached)

HAYWOOD Christopher Ian
Address: Brickhill Cottage,
63 Shaw Lane, Markfield,
Leicestershire LE67 9PU
Tel: 01530 242881
(Unattached)

HAZELTINE Keith
Address: 29 Greaves Road,
High Wycombe,
Buckinghamshire HP13 7JU
Tel: 01494 443 303
(Unattached)

HEALER Glynis Yvonne (Mrs)
Address: 20 Strangways Street,
Seaham, County Durham SR7
7LN Tel: 01915 817 846
(Attached to: Pelaw Grange)

HEARD Douglas Michael Kenneth
Address: 2 Pixie Laughter
Cottage, Old Morebath Station,
Bampton, Devon EX16 9BX
Tel: 01398 331776
(Attached to: Poole)

HEASMAN Ruth Pamela (Miss)
Address: Homeacre, Padgetts
Road, Christchurch, Wisbech,
Cambridgeshire PE14 9PL
Tel: 01354 638115
(Attached to: Henlow)

HEATH Charlie
Address: 83 Fletchers Lane,
Sidlesham Common, Chichester,
West Sussex PO20 7QG
Tel: 01243 641377
(Attached to: Portsmouth)

HEATH Dave
Address: Trotters Farm,
High Easter, Chelmsford,
Essex CM1 4RD
Tel: 01245 231 805
(Attached to: Harlow)

HEATON Beverley (Mrs)
Address: Lynwood,
Langley Road, Swinton,
Manchester M27 8SS
Tel: 0161 736 6923
(Attached to: Belle Vue)

HEBBS Paul Raymond
Address: 26 Paston Road,
Hemel Hempstead,
Hertfordshire HP2 5BA
Tel: 01442 241817
(Attached to: Henlow)

HEGGIE Mark Andrew
Address: 17 Stanley Grove,
Redcar, Cleveland TS10 3LN
Tel: 07976 750238
(Attached to: Pelaw Grange)

HELD Peter
Address: Turpins Cottage,
London Road, Binfield, Bracknell,
Berkshire RG42 4AB
Tel: 01344 642349
(Attached to: Portsmouth)

HEMSLEY John
Address: 43 Yarmouth Road,
Ormesby, Great Yarmouth,
Norfolk NR29 3QE
Tel: 01493 733891
(Attached to: Yarmouth)

HENMAN Peter Thomas
Address: 21 Rosebay Close,
Flitwick, Bedford,
Bedfordshire MK45 1PR
Tel: 01525 714004
(Attached to: Henlow)

HEPDEN Ghislaine Elaine (Mrs)
Address: Chase House,
Oxford Road, Old Chalford,
Chipping Norton,
Oxfordshire OX7 5QR
Tel: 07889 938948
(Attached to: Oxford)

HEPINSTALL Gillian Maria (Mrs)
Address: 58 Holgate Crescent,
Hemsworth, Pontefract,
West Yorkshire WF9 4NG
Tel: 01977 619297
(Attached to: Kinsley)

HEWITT Peter John
Address: 6a Long Lane,
Coalville, Leicestershire
LE67 4DZ
Tel: 01530 835 119
(Unattached)

HEWKIN Kenneth Charles
Address: 239 Alfreton Road,
Sutton-in-Ashfield,
Nottinghamshire NG17 1JP
Tel: 01623 516983
(Attached to: Hull)

HEYES Andrew Peter
Address: 1 Mount Pleasant
Cottages, Barmhouse Lane,
Hyde, Cheshire SK14 3BX
Tel: 0161 368 1662
(Attached to: Belle Vue)

HIGGINS John Patrick
Address: Beauleigh,
Cannon Lane, Maidenhead,
Berkshire SL6 3NR
Tel: 01628 828 467
(Attached to: Reading)

HILL Albert Colin
Address: Meadowsweet, Oak
Avenue, Crays Hill, Billericay,
Essex CM11 2YE
Tel: 0403 862369
(Unattached)

HINCHLIFFE Roger
Address: The Bungalow, Field
Lane, Killamarsh, Sheffield,
South Yorkshire S21 1AZ
Tel: 07833 345 461
(Attached to: Doncaster)

HITCH Arthur James
Address: Nuffield Farm,
Flaunden Lane, Bovingdon,
Hemel Hempstead,
Hertfordshire HP3 0PA
Tel: 01442 832271
(Unattached)

HENRY Joseph
Address: Hockaday, Church Villa,
North Road East, Wingate,
County Durham TS28 5AT
Tel: 01429 836863
(Attached to: Pelaw Grange)

HOLFORD Graham David
Address: Gaglebrook, Middleton
Road, Bucknell, Bicester,
Oxfordshire OX27 7LY
Tel: 01869 242643
(Attached to: Coventry)

HOLLAND Peter Michael
Address: 12b Sun Street,
Woodville, Burton On Trent,
Derbyshire DE11 7DP
Tel: 01283 210 843
(Attached to: Doncaster)

HOLMES Paul Anthony
Address: 73 West View,
Barlby Road, Selby, North
Yorkshire YO8 5BD
Tel: 01757 702 838
(Attached to: Doncaster)

HOLT Robert
Address: The Old Barn At
Moorcock, Black Dyke Lane,
Thornton, Bradford, West
Yorkshire BD13 3RR
Tel: 01274 833409
(Attached to: Doncaster)

HOMER Brian Neville
Address: Unit 2, Rear Of
Triptons, Oak Hill Road,
Stapleford Abbotts, Romford,
Essex RM4 1JJ
Tel: 07830 314800
(Unattached)

HOPKINS Craig
Address: Crosslea, Tinkers Hill,
Carlton-in-Lindrick, Worksop,
Nottinghamshire S81 9EP
Tel: 01909 733 733
(Attached to: Doncaster)

HOPTON Archibald
Address: 10 Holly Drive,
Old Basing, Basingstoke,
Hampshire RG24 7LE
Tel: 01256 818604
(Unattached)

HORNER David
Address: 9 Hopwood Grove,
Castleford, West Yorkshire
WF10 3AZ
Tel: 01977516810
(Unattached)

HOUFTON Jane Alison (Mrs)
Address: Field House Farm,
Dunham Road, Darlton, Newark,
Nottinghamshire NG22 0TA
Tel: 07785 258271
(Attached to: Sheffield)

HOUGH Ronald
Address: Sandrock Lodge
Kennels, Bawtry Road,
Tickhill, Doncaster, South
Yorkshire DN11 9HB
Tel: 01302 750834
(Attached to: Sheffield)

HOULDING Christopher John
Address: Henniker House, The
Street, Ashfield, Stowmarket,
Suffolk IP14 6LX
Tel: 01728 685 755
(Unattached)

HOUSTON Andrew
Address: Emscote Kennel,
Warwick Schooling Track,
Emscote Road, Warwick
Tel: 07980297418
(Attached to: Coventry)

HOWARD Edward Herbert
Address: 13 Newgate,
Shephall, Stevenage,
Hertfordshire SG2 9DS
Tel: 01438 232170
Henlow)

HOWARD Keith Harold
Address: Thrift Wood Farm,
Ockwells Road, Maidenhead,
Berkshire SL6 3AB
Tel: 01628 782155
(Attached to: Reading)

HOWARD Steven Anthony
Address: 10 Trefelin Crescent,
Port Talbot, West Glamorgan
SA13 1DZ
Tel: 01639 769 474
(Attached to: Reading)

HOWES Gary George
Address: Hall Gardens, Tower
Hill, Costessey, Norwich, Norfolk
Tel: 07713 817716
(Attached to: Yarmouth)

HOWLETT Johnny Francis
Address: 85 Verulam Way,
Cambridge, Cambridgeshire
CB4 2HJ
Tel: 01223 572911
(Unattached)

HOWSON Graham Alan
Address: 416 Warrington Road,
Leigh End, Glazebury,
Warrington, Cheshire WA3 5NX
Tel: 01942 678319
(Unattached)

HUGHES Albert
Address: 10 Min Yr Aber,
Bradley, Wrexham,
Clwyd LL11 4BH
Tel: 01978 755547
(Unattached)

HUGHES David Kenneth
Address: 198 Smithy Lane,
Scarisbrick, Ormskirk,
Lancashire L40 8HJ
Tel: 01704 840 028
(Unattached)

HUGHES Sonia Margaret (Mrs)
Address: Harwood Farm,
Withywood Lane,
Cranmore, Shepton Mallet,
Somerset BA4 4QR
Tel: 07971 931299
(Attached to: Swindon)

HUMPHREYS Kenrick Ellis
Address: Herston, Pencaer,
Goodwick, Dyfed SA64 0JA
Tel: 01348 875137
(Attached to: Reading)

HUNT Angela Susan (Mrs)
Address: Goodacre, Aimes
Green, Waltham Abbey,
Essex EN9 2BJ
Tel: 01992 890 169
(Attached to: Harlow)

HUNT Christopher Colin
Address: Triptons, Romford,
Essex RM4 1JJ
Tel: 01708 745 810
(Attached to: Mildenhall)

HUNT David Anthony
Address: New House Farm Stud,
Sawpit Lane, Apperley,
Gloucestershire GL19 4DW
Tel: 01452 780741
(Attached to: Perry Barr)

HUNTE Terence William
Address: 90 Wood Farm
Bungalow, Salhouse, Norwich,
Norfolk NR13 6JW
Tel: 01603 721335
(Attached to: Yarmouth)

HUNTINGDON Kevin
Address: 9 West End,
Hunwick, Crook,
County Durham DL15 0LH
Tel: 01388 602206
(Attached to: Pelaw Grange)

HUNWICKS Theresa Valerie (Mrs)
Address: Harrimans Farm
Cottage, Old Knarr Fen Drove,
Thorney, Peterborough,
Cambridgeshire PE6 0RJ
Tel: 01733 270066
(Attached to: Peterborough)

HURST Jamie Gavin
Address: 162 Whitehill Road,
Ellistown, Coalville,
Leicestershire LE67 1EP
Tel: 01530 263 737
(Attached to: Kinsley)

HURST Leslie
Address: 4 Bakewell Road,
Athersley, South Barnsley,
South Yorkshire S71 3SL
Tel: 01226 213967
(Attached to: Kinsley)

HURST Michael
Address: 42 Lincoln Road,
Cramlington, Northumberland
NE23 3XT
Tel: 01670 730 786
(Attached to: Pelaw Grange)

HURSTHOUSE Linda (Mrs)
Address: 8 Woodhay Walk,
Havant, Hampshire PO9 5RB
Tel: 02392 366 091
(Attached to: Portsmouth)

HUTCHINSON Andrew Buchan
(Snr)
Address: 38 Hazeldean Terrace,
Edinburgh EH16 5RT
Tel: 07989 020834
(Attached to: Shawfield)

HUTHART Geoffrey
Address: 12 Hurbuck Cottages,
Lanchester, Durham, County
Durham DH7 0RJ
Tel: 01207 508 138
(Attached to: Pelaw Grange)

HUTT Graham John
Address: Baltree Farm
Kennels, Hatchbank Road,
Kinross KY13 0LF
Tel: 01577 850367
(Unattached)

HUTTON Kevin Richard
Address: Signett Hill Farms,
Signet Hill, Burford,
Oxfordshire OX18 4JE
Tel: 07969 021 565
(Attached to: Swindon)

HYSLOP William James
Address: Fenceside Farm,
Crofthead Road, Kilmaurs,
Kilmarnock,
Ayrshire KA3 2RX
Tel: 01563 538748
(Unattached)

INGLE Ronald Dennis
Address: 40a Middleton Way,
Fen Drayton, Cambridge,
Cambridgeshire CB4 5SU
Tel: 01954 202027
(Attached to: Henlow)

INGRAM Alison Jean (Miss)
Address: Bersheda, Arterial
Road, Wickford,
Essex SS12 9JF
Tel: 01268 725649
(Attached to: Romford)

IRONS Barrie John
Address: 66 Ampthill Road,
Flitwick, Bedford, Bedfordshire
MK45 1AY Tel: 01525 712382
(Attached to: Yarmouth)

IRVING William Batey
Address: 40 St. Edmunds Park,
Carlisle, Cumbria CA2 6TS
Tel: 01228 526 593
(Unattached)

JACKSON James Barr
Address: 39 Gillburn Street,
Wishaw, Lanarkshire ML2 0QL
Tel: 01698 351889
(Unattached)

JACKSON Michael Roy
Address: Pixies Lodge, Dowsdale
Bank, Whaplode Drove, Spalding,
Lincolnshire PE12 0TZ
Tel: 01406 330 371
(Unattached)

JACKSON Vincent Ivan
Address: 103 Fairview Road,
Stevenage, Hertfordshire
SG1 2NP
Tel: 01438 722016
(Attached to: Henlow)

JAGO Richard Noel
Address: Grey Tiles,
11 Weybourne Road,
Farnham, Surrey GU9 9ER
Tel: 01252 330201
(Attached to: Reading)

JEFFERSON John David
Address: 19 Ladypark, Lowfell,
Gateshead, Tyne and Wear NE11
0HD Tel: 0191 487 0602
(Attached to: Pelaw Grange)

JENKINS Allan Kenneth
Address: White Oak Farm,
Tong Road, Bishopswood,
Stafford, Staffordshire
ST19 9AP
Tel: 07751 326196
(Attached to: Hall Green)

JINKS Diane Rosemary (Mrs)
Address: Rupen, Long Drove,
Parson Drove, Wisbech,
Cambridgeshire PE13 4JT
Tel: 0787 4023405
(Attached to: Peterborough)

JOBES William
Address: 48 Jack Lawson
Terrace, Wheatley Hill, Durham,
County Durham DH6 3RU
Tel: 07909 674 839
(Attached to: Pelaw Grange)

JOHNSON Andrew
Address: Meadow View,
Straight Mile, Four Ashes,
Wolverhampton,
West Midlands WV10 7DL
Tel: 01902 798 715
(Unattached)

JOHNSON Ann Lynn (Mrs)
Address: Beacon Park Farm,
Bridle Lane, Aldridge, Walsall,
West Midlands WS9 0RG
Tel: 0121 325 0750
(Attached to: Perry Barr)

JOHNSON Terence Douglas
Address: 6 Chapel Gardens,
Whaplode, Spalding,
Lincolnshire PE12 6UG
(Attached to: Peterborough)

JONAS Keith
Address: 35 Holland Park,
Cheveley, Newmarket,
Suffolk CB8 9DL
Tel: 01638 730535
(Attached to: Mildenhall)

JONES George Edward
Address: Orchards House,
Yarford, Kingston St. Mary,
Taunton, Somerset TA2 8AN
Tel: 07974 799916
(Attached to: Poole)

JONES Jennifer (Mrs)
Address: 59 Kings Drive,
Carnforth, Lancashire LA5 9AN
Tel: 01524 735 252
(Attached to: Doncaster)

JONES Lawrence John
Address: Winterfield Farm,
Winterfield Lane, Hulme,
Stoke-on-Trent, Staffordshire
ST3 5BG
Tel: 01782 305360
(Attached to: Belle Vue)

JONES Raymond Anthony
Address: Yorkley Court Farm,
Yorkley, Lydney,
Gloucestershire GL15 4TZ
Tel: 01594 563903
(Attached to: Swindon)

JONES Robert
Address: 18 Chapman Grove,
Corby, Northamptonshire
NN17 1HL
Tel: 01536 268299
(Attached to: Peterborough)

JOPLING George William
Address: 17 The Crescent,
Sherburn, Durham, County
Durham DH6 1EJ
Tel: 0191 372 3131
(Unattached)

JOPLING Heather (Miss)
Address: 22 Grange Avenue,
Houghton Le Spring,
Tyne and Wear DH4 6JQ
Tel: 01913 852 382
(Attached to: Pelaw Grange)

JOYCE Richard Henry
Address: 103 Wensleydale
Avenue, Ilford, Essex IG5 0ND
Tel: 0208 551 1880
(Attached to: Henlow)

JURY Robin
Address: 7 Priors Court
Cottages, Priors Court,
Hermitage, Thatcham,
Berkshire RG18 9JT
Tel: 01635 867969
(Attached to: Reading)

KALUS Julie May (Mrs)
Address: 85 Mayfair, Tilehurst,
Reading, Berkshire RG30 4RB
Tel: 07719472100
(Attached to: Reading)

Keane James
Address: 60 Binnacle Road,
Rochester, Kent ME1 2XP
Tel: 0634 842126
(Unattached)

KEANY Adrian
Address: 45 Darnley Avenue,
Wakefield, West Yorkshire
WF2 9QH
Tel: 01924 381109
(Unattached)

KEIGHTLEY Hayley (Mrs)
Address: Roxholme Grange, The
Green, Carlton-in-Lindrick,
Worksop, Nottinghamshire S81
9AQ Tel: 01909 732 065
(Unattached)

KELLY-PILGRIM Allison (Mrs)
Address: The Little Leys,
Coggeshall Road, Stisted,
Braintree, Essex CM77 8AB
Tel: 01376 323964
(Unattached)

KELSEY Brian Henry
Address: Kelfarm Kennels,
Jerry Bog, Laughton Warren,
Laughton, Gainsborough,
Lincolnshire DN21 3PU
Tel: 01427 628759
(Attached to: Doncaster)

KEMP Hazel Pamela Joyce (Mrs)
Address: Bodell, 144 Hungate
Road, Emneth, Wisbech,
Cambridgeshire PE14 8EQ
Tel: 01945 430391
(Attached to: Yarmouth)

KENNEDY Kenneth Alan
Address: Bank Foot Farm, West
Auckland, Bishop Auckland,
County Durham DL14 9PJ
Tel: 01388 83 5552
(Attached to: Pelaw Grange)

KENNEDY Patrick Francis
Address: 160 Parson Street,
Bedminster, Bristol,
Avon BS3 5QT
Tel: 01179 633341
(Unattached)

KENNEY James
Address: 37 Hillfoot Avenue,
Garshake, Dumbarton,
Dunbartonshire G82 3JX
Tel: 01389 732737
(Unattached)

KENNINGHAM Christopher
Charles Robert
Address: Dyers Hall Farm,
Sundon Road, Harlington,
Dunstable, Bedfordshire LU5 6LL
Tel: 07956 836748
(Attached to: Henlow)

KENNINGTON Edward James
Address: Harps Kennels,
Harps Hall Road, Walton
Highway, Wisbech,
Cambridgeshire PE14 7DL
Tel: 07723 357 006
(Unattached)

KEPPIE Alma Rosalind (Mrs)
Address: Two Oaks, Fletchwood
Lane, Totton, Southampton,
Hampshire SO40 7DZ
Tel: 07803 382571
(Attached to: Poole)

KERR James
459 Drumoyne Road,
Glasgow G51 4DD
Tel: 0141 4455673
Shawfield)

KERR Robert Hynds
Address: 4 Craig Cottage,
Crosshouse, Kilmarnock,
Ayrshire KA2 0BS
Tel: 07725 009227
(Unattached)

KERSHAW Charles Douglas
Address: 35 Hurst Lane,
Rawtenstall, Rossendale,
Lancashire BB4 7RE
Tel: 01706 228305
(Attached to: Kinsley)

KIBBLE Angela Maureen (Mrs)
Address: Hoskins Barn,
Buckland Road, Bampton,
Oxfordshire OX18 2EP
Tel: 01367 870581
(Attached to: Oxford)

KIBBLE Terry
Address: Horsenden Hill Kennels,
High Street, Tetsworth, Thame,
Oxfordshire OX9 7AD
Tel: 07786 034721
(Attached to: Oxford)

KIDD Christine Valerie (Mrs)
Address: 30 Cumberland Street,
Carlisle, Cumbria CA2 5JH
Tel: 01228 536 546
Pelaw Grange)

KILGANNON Brendan Oliver
Address: 42 Keynsham Road,
Eltham, London SE9 6QD
Tel: 020 8850 1641
(Attached to: Henlow)

KIMBERLEY Rosemary Ann (Mrs)
Address: The Cottage, Main
Road, Ratcliffe Culey, Atherstone,
Warwickshire CV9 3PD
Tel: 01827 716590
(Attached to: Perry Barr)

KING Caroline (Miss)
Address: Crossleigh Kennels,
Narcot Lane, Chalfont St. Giles,
Buckinghamshire HP8 4DX
Tel: 07748 032698
(Attached to: Reading)

KING Stephen John
Address: Unit 2, Burnt Oak Farm,
Burnt Oak Lane, Newdigate,
Dorking, Surrey RH5 5BJ
Tel: 01293 863 190
(Attached to: Portsmouth)

KIRBY Anne Marie (Mrs)
Address: Vicarage Farm Stud,
Kirtling, Newmarket, Suffolk
CB8 9HL
Tel: 01638 730129
(Unattached)

KIRK Rosalind (Mrs)
Address: Woodhorn View,
Woodhorn Road, Ashington,
Northumberland NE63 9ES
Tel: 01670 816940
(Attached to: Pelaw Grange)

KIRKLAND David
Address: 65 Robert Smillie
Crescent, Larkhall,
Lanarkshire ML9 1LF
Tel: 01698 309967
(Attached to: Shawfield)

KNIGHT Derek David
Address: Albourne Kennels,
Wheatsheaf Road,
Woodmancote, Henfield,
West Sussex BN5 9BD
Tel: 01273 494737
(Attached to: Brighton & Hove)

KOVAC Geraldine (Miss)
Address: Woodview Farm,
Landmere Lane, Ruddington,
Nottingham NG11 6ND
Tel: 0115 984 4538
(Attached to: Doncaster)

KUERES Otto Daniel
Address: Hatley Farm,
Bradley, Frodsham, Warrington,
Cheshire WA6 7EJ
Tel: 01928 733371
(Attached to: Belle Vue)

KULASZEWSKI Eric John
Address: 51 Linden Terrace,
Carlisle, Cumbria CA1 3PH
Tel: 01228 524112
(Attached to: Pelaw Grange)

LACEY Robert David
Address: Chestnut Lodge,
Gransden Road, Caxton,
Cambridge, Cambridgeshire
CB3 8PL
Tel: 01954 719821
(Unattached)

LAGAN Elizabeth Ann (Mrs)
Address: The Gables,
Daisy Bank, Lancaster,
Lancashire LA1 3JN
Tel: 01524 37458
(Unattached)

LAIRD David
Address: 19 The Crescent,
Blackpool, Lancashire FY4 1EQ
Tel: 01253 347549
(Unattached)

LAMBE John Patrick
Address: Weeford Kennels,
The Raconer, Weeford Road,
Birmingham, West Midlands
B75 5RF
Tel: 07734 791242
(Attached to: Perry Barr)

LANDLES Peter
Address: Sienna Stud,
Perkinsville, Pelton, Chester
Le Street, County Durham
DH2 1QW
Tel: 07771 781 923
(Attached to: Pelaw Grange)

LARTER Noel Luke
Address: Quoins, Kimberley
Road, Bacton, Norwich,
Norfolk NR12 0EN
Tel: 01692 651093
(Attached to: Yarmouth)

LAVENDER Frederick Mark
Address: Burnt Oak Farm,
Burnt Oak Lane, Newdigate,
Dorking, Surrey RH5 5BJ
Tel: 01293 862460
(Attached to: Portsmouth)

LAW Derek Maurice
Address: Tollgate House,
Leighton Road, Wing,
Leighton Buzzard,
Bedfordshire LU7 0PW
Tel: 01296 688454
(Attached to: Henlow)

LAWRENCE Leslie Joseph
Address: Ockendon Kennels,
Ockendon Road, North
Ockendon, Upminster,
Essex RM14 3PP
Tel: 01708 224593
(Attached to: Harlow)

LAWRENCE Paul William
Address: Lowfield House,
Doncaster Road, Denaby
Main, Doncaster, South
Yorkshire DN12 4ET
Tel: 01709 325064
(Attached to: Doncaster)

LAWRENCE Terry
Address: Greystones Kennels,
Cranesgate South ,
Holbeach, Spalding,
Lincolnshire PE12 8RJ
Tel: 01406 540382
(Unattached)

LAYCOCK Nigel Christopher
Address: Fulham House,
Fulham Lane, Womersley,
Doncaster, South Yorkshire
DN6 9BN
Tel: 01977 661 281
(Attached to: Doncaster)

LE ROUX Philippa Ann Pitt (Miss)
Address: Town Drove Bungalow,
Stow Road, Outwell, Wisbech,
Cambridgeshire PE14 8QL
Tel: 01945 773939
(Attached to: Peterborough)

LEE David William
Address: Canine Kennels,
Ockendon Kennels, Ockendon
Road, North Ockendon,
Upminster, Essex RM14 3PT
Tel: 01708 222733
(Attached to: Harlow)

LEE Victor Albert
Address: Ivycombe, Catley Cross
Road, Pebmarsh, Halstead,
Essex CO9 2PD
Tel: 01787 269 331
(Attached to: Mildenhall)

LEEKS Roy John
Address: Homefield, High Street,
Lavenham, Sudbury, Suffolk
CO10 9PT
Tel: 01787 247393
(Attached to: Mildenhall)

LEESON Christopher
Address: Hurle House Kennels,
Wynyard, Billingham,
Cleveland TS22 5NE
Tel: 01740 644 232
(Attached to: Sunderland)

LENTON Francis William
Address: 10 Winston Way,
Farcet, Peterborough,
Cambridgeshire PE7 3BU
Tel: 01733 244346
(Attached to: Peterborough)

LEVETT David John
21 Mill Road, Emneth, Wisbech,
Cambridgeshire PE14 8AE
Tel: 01945 474451
(Unattached)

LEVY Dawn Lynn (Mrs)
Address: 69 Elmcroft Avenue,
Edmonton, London N9 7DR
Tel: 020 8804 6628
(Unattached)

LEWIS Bryan
Address: 1 Laxford Birtley,
Chester Le Street, County
Durham DH3 2DR
Tel: 0191 410 9169
(Attached to: Pelaw Grange)

LEWIS David Nigel
Address: The Orchard, Three
Cross Road, West Moors,
Wimborne, Dorset BH21 6QW
Tel: 01202 855499
(Attached to: Poole)

LEWIS Susan Margaret
Address: 52 Connegar Leys,
Blisworth, Northampton,
Northamptonshire NN7
Tel: 01604 859801
(Attached to: Peterborough)

LEYDEN John Martin
Address: 41 Monckton Avenue,
Lowestoft, Suffolk NR32 3EG
Tel: 01502 563024
(Attached to: Yarmouth)

LIDDINGTON Robert William
Address: 39 Norton Crescent,
Towcester, Northamptonshire
NN12 6DW
Tel: 01327 350019
(Attached to: Reading)

LIDDLE Paul
Address: Lowgate Crossing
Farm, Lowgate, Balne,
Goole, North Humberside
DN14 0ED
Tel: 01405 862566
(Attached to: Sheffield)

LIMM Richard Sidney
Address: 71 Watling Street,
Dordon, Tamworth,
Staffordshire B78 1SY
Tel: 01827 704438
(Unattached)

LINDSAY Alfred Edward
Address: 9 Saywell Road,
Luton, Bedfordshire LU2 0TJ
Tel: 01582 416122
(Unattached)

LINDSAY Ian
Address: 54 Tillanburn Road,
Motherwell, Lanarkshire
ML1 5HZ
Tel: 07890 219 783
(Attached to: Shawfield)

LINK William Edward
Address: 65 Nursery Road,
Anston, Sheffield, South
Yorkshire S25 4BS
Tel: 01909 560805
(Attached to: Doncaster)

LINLEY Shirley (Mrs)
South View , North Otterington,
Northallerton, North Yorkshire
DL7 9JQ
Tel: 01609 776788
(Attached to: Sunderland)

LINWOOD Kevin William,
Old Bell Racing
Address: Kennels,
105 Field Crescent, Royston,
Hertfordshire SG8 7LB
Tel: 01763 220285
(Attached to: Henlow)

LISTER Charles Richard
Address: Mudros, Main Road,
North Clifton, Newark,
Nottinghamshire NG23 7AZ
Tel: 01777 228247
(Unattached)

LISTER Peter
Address: Lark Cottage,
Cornsay, Durham, County
Durham DH7 9EP
Tel: 01388 730482
(Attached to: Pelaw Grange)

LITTLE James Keith
Address: 28a Stone Lane,
Lydiard Millicent,
Swindon, Wiltshire SN5 3LD
Tel: 07751 191478
(Attached to: Swindon)

LITTLE Janice Ann (Mrs)
Address: Laal Wath,
Barracks Bridge, Silloth,
Wigton, Cumbria CA7 4NR
Tel: 016973 31387
(Attached to: Pelaw Grange)

LLEWELLIN Jill (Miss)
Address: Black Lion,
29 Welsh Row, Nantwich,
Cheshire CW5 5ED
Tel: 01270 628711
(Attached to: Coventry)

LLEWELLYN Cherie Diane (Mrs)
Address: Hilltop Farm,
Novers Hill, Knowle, Bristol
Tel: 0117 987 1448
(Attached to: Swindon)

LLOYD Henry
Address: 16 Trinity Road, St.
Johns Fen End, Wisbech,
Cambridgeshire PE14 8JA
Tel: 01945 430138
(Unattached)

LLOYD Robert
Address: 38 Winnipeg Road,
Bentley, Doncaster, South
Yorkshire DN5 0EB
Tel: 01302 875178
(Attached to: Doncaster)

LOCHRANE John
Address: 2 Collree Gardens,
Glasgow G34 9HF
Tel: 0141 771 4409
(Attached to: Shawfield)

LOCKE Maxine Louise (Miss)
Address: 4 Bonville Farm
Cottage, Arterial Road,
North Benfleet, Wickford,
Essex SS12 9JQ
Tel: 01268 728488
(Attached to: Romford)

LOMAX Brian
Address: 40 Cox Green Road,
Egerton, Bolton,
Lancashire BL7 9HF
Tel: 01204 305022
(Attached to: Kinsley)

LORAINS Stewart Edward
Address: Holywell Farm Cottage
Loftus,Saltburn-by-the-Sea,
Cleveland TS13 4UG
Tel: 01287 642148
(Unattached)

LOVEVincent
Address: 17 Bramber Drive,
Wombourne, Wolverhampton,
West Midlands WV5 8EQ
Tel: 01902 326164
(Unattached)

LOVERIDGE Anthony
Address: 143 Viola Avenue,
Staines, Middlesex TW19 7RZ
Tel: 01784 242794
(Attached to: Reading)

LOWE Joanne Marion (Miss)
Address: Aramoana Greyhound
Kennels, Hull Road, Seaton,
Hull, North Humberside
HU11 5RN Tel: 01964 534 088
(Attached to: Kinsley)

LOWTHER Mark Dixon
Rye Hill Farm, Icknield Way,
Drayton Holloway, Tring,
Hertfordshire HP23 4LB
Tel: 01442 822077
(Attached to: Henlow)

LUCAS Anthony Mark
Address: Hillside Greyhound
Kennels, Shere Road,
West Clandon, Guildford,
Surrey GU4 8SH
Tel: 01483 224018
(Attached to: Brighton & Hove)

LUCAS Margaret Eileen (Miss)
Address: Skibbereen Kennels,
Little Warley Hall Lane,
Little Warley, Brentwood,
Essex CM13 3EN
Tel: 01277 810500
(Attached to: Romford

LUCKHURST Julie Jane (Miss)
Address: Home Farm,
Couchman Green Lane,
Staplehurst, Tonbridge,
Kent TN12 0RU
Tel: 01580 891 579
(Attached to: Crayford)

LUMB Allen David
Address: 37 Ollerton Road,
Barnsley, South Yorkshire
S71 3DR
Tel: 07776 117245
(Attached to: Hull)

LUND Christopher Tom
Address: 32 Garden Lane,
Knottingley, West Yorkshire
WF11 9BS
Tel: 01977 675797
(Unattached)

LYNAS Glenn
Address: Escomb Poultry Farm,
Hallimond Road, Escomb,
Bishop Auckland, County
Durham DL14 7SS
Tel: 01388 603 087
(Attached to: Newcastle)

LYNCH Charles Thomas
Address: 7 Roch Crescent,
Whitefield, Manchester M45 8LR
Tel: 0161 280 1020
(Unattached)

LYNDS Susan Elsie (Mrs)
Address: 14 Crescent Road,
Hugglescote, Coalville,
Leicestershire LE67 2BB
Tel: 01530 839495
(Attached to: Coventry)

LYONS William Mark
Address: 8 Gordon Lane,
Ramshaw, Bishop Auckland,
County Durham DL14 0NL
Tel: 01388 835 004
(Attached to: Pelaw Grange)

MACARI Kelly Anne (Mrs)
Address: Greenside Farm, West
Lane, Trimdon, Trimdon Station,
County Durham TS29 6ND
Tel: 07900 920 459
(Attached to: Sunderland)

MACDONALD William
Address: 77 Gillburn Street,
Wishaw, Lanarkshire ML2 0QL
Tel: 01698 355588
(Attached to: Shawfield)

MACHIN Kenneth Richard
Address: 53 Moathouse
Lane East, Wednesfield,
Wolverhampton, West Midlands
WV11 3DD
Tel: 01902 735380
(Unattached)

MACKAY William Stuart
Address: 45 Henderson Avenue,
Cambuslang, Glasgow G72 7SB
Tel: 0141 641 5130
(Attached to: Shawfield)

MACKERELL Terry John
Address: 30 St. Andrews Way,
Blofield, Norwich,
Norfolk NR13 4LA
Tel: 01603 715985
(Attached to: Yarmouth)

MAGNASCO Luciano Luigi
Giovanni
Address: Fairview, Old London
Road, Milton Common, Thame,
Oxfordshire OX9 2JR
Tel: 01844 279480
(Attached to: Oxford)

MAIDEN Leslie
Address: Cedar Bungalow,
Langley Vale Road,
Epsom, Surrey KT18 5NQ
Tel: 01372 727865
(Attached to: Reading)

MALEY Peter Joseph
Address: 12 Normanby Hall
Park, Middlesbrough
Cleveland TS6 0SX
Tel: 01642 469961
(Attached to: Pelaw Grange)

MANLY John Arthur
Address: 14 Hetchleys,
Hemel Hempstead,
Hertfordshire HP1 3NX
Tel: 01442 257879
(Attached to: Henlow)

MANNING Maurice
Address: Wayside,
Breach Lane, Wilburton, Ely,
Cambridgeshire CB6 3SB
Tel: 01353 649418
(Attached to: Mildenhall)

MANTHORPE Scott
Address: 112 Morton Road,
Pakefield, Lowestoft,
Suffolk NR330JH
Tel: 01502 531017
(Unattached)

MARCH Jennifer Joan (Mrs)
Address: Wheatsheaf Farm,
41 Straight Road, Boxted,
Colchester, Essex CO4 5HN
Tel: 01206 272245
(Attached to: Peterborough)

MARKEY Frank
Address: 19 Albert Drive,
Larkhall, Lanarkshire ML9 2PU
Tel: 01698 887 186
(Attached to: Pelaw Grange)

MARKS Roy
Address: 32 Hamilton Road,
Newmarket, Suffolk CB8 0NY
Tel: 01638 661 210
(Attached to: Mildenhall)

MARLOW Kim Allison (Miss)
Address: Waterdell Kennels,
Flinthouse, Wangford, Brandon,
Suffolk IP27 0SJ
Tel: 01842 813419
(Attached to: Harlow)

MARRIOTT John Anthony
Address: Hesley Wood Cottage,
Hesley Lane,Thorpe
Hesley, Rotherham, South
Yorkshire S61 2SD
Tel: 01142 455092
(Unattached)

MARSH John Brian
Address: 9 Small Holdings,
Sherdley Road, St. Helens,
Merseyside WA9 5DQ
Tel: 01744 811432
(Unattached)

MARSHALL Alan David
Address: Sandhouse Farm,
Sand Lane, Susworth,
Scunthorpe DN17 3PR
Tel: 01724 783075
(Unattached)

MARSHALL Barry Clifford
Address: 4 Old West Estate,
Benwick, March,
Cambridgeshire PE15 0XE
Tel: 01354 677436
(Attached to: Peterborough)

MARTIN Clive Denver
Address: 23 New Road,
Chiseldon, Swindon,
Wiltshire SN4 0LX
Tel: 01793 740808
(Attached to: Swindon)

MARTIN David
Address: 56 Heathview Road,
Grays, Essex RM16 2RS
Tel: 01375 408 408
(Unattached)

MARTIN David Peter Foster
Address: Torne Gatehouse,
Epworth, Doncaster, South
Yorkshire DN9 1LE
Tel: 01427 875004
(Attached to: Doncaster)

MARTIN Geraldine (Mrs)
Address: 52 Central Avenue,
Enfield, Middlesex EN1 3QE
Tel: 020 8805 0204
(Unattached)

MARTIN Mervyn Russell
Address: 169 Wareham Road,
Corfe Mullen, Wimborne,
Dorset BH21 3LB
Tel: 01202 657 920
(Attached to: Poole)

MARTIN Stephen
Address: 60 Harridge Road,
Leigh-on-Sea, Essex SS9 4HE
Tel: 07754 260660
(Unattached)

MASON Michael William Edward
Address: 88 Lashford Lane,
Dry Sandford, Abingdon,
Oxfordshire OX13 6EB
Tel: 01865 739958
(Attached to: Reading)

MASON Rosemary (Mrs)
Address: Grange Cottage,
Fundenhall, Norwich
Norfolk NR16 1AH
Tel: 01508 488211
(Unattached)

MASON Stuart
Address: Whiteley Cottage,
Green Lane, Netherton,
Wakefield, West Yorkshire
WF4 4EX
Tel: 01924 230 865
(Attached to: Kinsley)

MASSEY Maurice Henry
Address: Windmill Cottage,
Blackthorn Hill, Blackthorn,
Bicester, Oxfordshire OX25 1TJ
Tel: 01869 253187
(Attached to: Oxford)

MAVRIAS Mick
Address: Thornton Farm
Kennels, Tilmanstone, Deal,
Kent CT14 0JN
Tel: 01304 620085
(Attached to: Sittingbourne)

MAVRIAS Spencer
Address: Thorndon Racing
Kennels, Unit 3, Bird Lane,
Great Warley, Brentwood,
Essex CM13 3JU
Tel: 07974 289986
(Attached to: Sittingbourne)

MAYO John Reginald
Address: Burwood, Menmarsh
Road, Worminghall, Aylesbury,
Buckinghamshire HP18 9UP
Tel: 01865 351627
(Attached to: Oxford)

MCARDLE James Bernard
Address: 48 Lester Piggott Way,
Newmarket, Suffolk CB8 0BJ
Tel: 01638 666332
(Attached to: Henlow)

MCCALLUM Gordon
Address: 76 Gray Street,
Elsecar, Barnsley,
South Yorkshire S74 8JL
Tel: 01226 360 342
(Attached to: Kinsley)

MCCARROLL Ann (Mrs)
Ashford Grove Stables, Ashford
Grove, Thornley, Durham,
County Durham DH6 3AD
Tel: 01429 821021
(Attached to: Pelaw Grange)

MCCARTHY Robert
Address: Percy Hunt Kennels,
Canongate, Alnwick,
Northumberland NE66 1NF
Tel: 01665 602 047
(Attached to: Pelaw Grange)

MCCAW Alan
Address: Misty Law,
Howwood, Johnstone,
Renfrewshire PA9 1DH
Tel: 01505 702421
(Attached to: Shawfield)

MCCLAIR Alexander George
Address: 114 Stephenson Way,
Corby, Northamptonshire
NN17 1DD
Tel: 01536 200 297
(Attached to: Peterborough)

MCCLURG Angela (Mrs)
Address: The Old School House,
Potsgrove, Milton Keynes,
Buckinghamshire MK17 9HG
Tel: 0797 1724526
(Attached to: Henlow)

MCCOMBE June Lilian (Mrs)
Address: Spring Gardens Farm,
Spring Gardens, Water,
Rossendale, Lancashire
BB4 9RD
Tel: 01706 214500
(Attached to: Belle Vue)

MCCONNELL Anthony Aidan
Address: Beverley House, Hall
Lane, Longton, Preston,
Lancashire PR4 5ZD
Tel: 01772 613003
(Attached to: Doncaster)

MCCULLOCH Gareth
Address: Redwood House,
1 Bickerton Crofts,
Hens Nest Road, East Whitburn,
West Lothian EH47 8RX
Tel: 01501 745 525
(Unattached)

MCDADE Thomas
Address: 5 Traquair Wynd,
Blantyre, Glasgow G72 0SQ
Tel: 01698 825 815
(Attached to: Shawfield)

MCDERMOTT Anthony David
Address: 12 Newport Road,
Hemsby, Great Yarmouth,
Norfolk NR29 4NN
Tel: 01493 730603
(Attached to: Yarmouth)

MCDONAGH Shirley Rose (Mrs)
Address: Brockley Hill Kennels,
Brockley Hill, Stanmore,
Middlesex HA7 4LN
Tel: 0208 954 7815
(Attached to: Henlow)

MCDONALD James Oliver
Address: 41 Acton Lane,
Harlesden, London NW10 8UX
Tel: 020 8961 1009
(Unattached)

MCDONNELL Patrick
Address: 491 Bursledon Road,
Southampton, Hampshire
SO19 8NJ
Tel: 02380 406891
(Attached to: Portsmouth)

MCDOWELL Alan Benjamin
Address: Crews House,
Brinkworth Road, Dauntsey,
Chippenham, Wiltshire SN15 4JL
Tel: 01666 510544
(Attached to: Swindon)

MCELLISTRIM Norah Eileen
Mary (Miss)
5 Burhill Kennels, Turners Lane,
Walton-on-Thames,
Surrey KT12 4AW Tel: 01932
221545
(Attached to: Wimbledon)

MCGLONE Patrick
Address: 66 Stonecraig Road,
Wishaw, Lanarkshire ML2 8BZ
Tel: 01698 359799
(Unattached)

MCGOLDRICK John
Address: 86 King Street,
Burton-on-Trent, Staffordshire
DE14 3AF
Tel: 07854 749 973
(Unattached)

MCGROGAN Barry
Address: 2 Fulmar Place,
Johnstone, Renfrewshire
PA5 0TA
Tel: 01505 348 388
(Attached to: Shawfield)

MCHUGH Susan Mary (Miss)
Address: 101 Mile Road,
Bedford, Bedfordshire
MK42 9UP
Tel: 01234 407750
(Attached to: Henlow)

MCKENNA Anthony
Address: Underhill Farm,
Underhill Lane, Sheffield,
South Yorkshire S6 1NL
Tel: 0114 2853889
(Attached to: Sheffield)

MCKENNA John Mark
Address: 62 Kendal Drive,
Castleford, West Yorkshire
WF10 3SP
Tel: 01977 515329
(Attached to: Hull)

MCKENZIE Ronald
Address: 17 Bigges Gardens,
Wallsend, Tyne and Wear
NE28 8BB
Tel: 0191 295 3835
(Attached to: Pelaw Grange)

MCKIE Thomas Collins
Address: 8 Main Road,
Springside, Irvine,
Ayrshire KA11 3AN
Tel: 01294 212440
(Unattached)

MCLAUGHLIN Peter
Address: Field House Farm,
Dalton Piercy, Hartlepool,
Cleveland TS27 3HY
Tel: 07764 695629
(Attached to: Pelaw Grange)

MCMANUS Mark
Address: 5 Corston Walk,
Manchester, M40 2FP
Tel: 01616 887 940
(Attached to: Kinsley)

MCNAIR Elizabeth (Mrs)
Address: Ellis Barn Farm,
Kenardington, Ashford,
Kent TN26 2LY
Tel: 01233 861 429
(Unattached)

MCNALLY Denis Joshua
Bridge Farm Kennels, Bridge
Farm, Fosse Way, Bretford,
Rugby Warwickshire CV23 9HA
Tel: 02476 542142
(Unattached)

MCNAMEE David
Address: Burnhope Farm,
Durham Lane, Elton,
Stockton-on-Tees,
Cleveland, TS21 1AA
Tel: 07904 966 505
(Attached to: Pelaw Grange)

MCNICHOLAS Angela Jeanette
(Mrs)
Address: Oak Tree Kennels,
Oak Tree Farm, Yarm Road,
Middleton St. George, Darlington,
County Durham DL2 1HN
Tel: 07740 643519
(Attached to: Sunderland)

MCTEAR Manus
Address: 15 Blackwoods
Crescent, Bellshill,
Lanarkshire ML4 2LS
Tel: 01698 748072
(Attached to: Shawfield)

MEAD Nicholas Paul
Address: Overend Green Farm,
Heath and Reach,
Leighton Buzzard,
Bedfordshire LU7 9LD
Tel: 01525 237905
(Attached to: Coventry)

MEAKIN Kevin
Address: Flagstaff Farm,
Nottingham Road, Ashby-de-la-
Zouch, Leicestershire LE65 1DS
Tel: 07796 555327
(Attached to: Monmore Green)

MEEK Anthony Charles
Address: Yew Tree Cottage,
Carters Piece, English Bicknor,
Coleford, Gloucestershire
GL16 7ES
Tel: 01594 86108
(Attached to: Hall Green)

MEEK Paul
Address: 23 Old Mill Gardens,
Walsall, West Midlands WS4 1BJ
Tel: 01922 860315
(Attached to: Perry Barr)

MELBOURNE Norman
Address: 62 Wesley Road,
Kiveton Park, Sheffield, South
Yorkshire S26 6RJ
Tel: 01909 772323
(Attached to: Sheffield)

MERCER Jason Lee
Address: Tylersley Farm,
Tylers Causeway, Newgate
Street, Hertford,
Hertfordshire SG13 8QN
Tel: 01844 281097
(Unattached)

MERCHANT David Michael
Address: 23 Hanger Road,
Tadley, Hampshire RG26 4QQ
Tel: 01189 815263
(Attached to: Portsmouth)

MERRIMAN David Arthur
Address: 207 Verity Way,
Stevenage, Hertfordshire
SG1 5PS
Tel: 01438 724812
(Attached to: Henlow)

PERRINS Richard Patrick
Address: 1 Kings Road, Long
Lawson, Melton Mowbray,
Leicestershire LE14 4NP
Tel: 01664 822967
(Unattached)

PERRY Elaine Susan (Mrs)
Address: Brookbank Farm,
Hackden, Holmes Chapel,
Crewe, Cheshire CW4 8BX
Tel: 07876 203010
(Doncaster)

MILAN Raymond John
9 Church Road, West
Kingsdown, Sevenoaks,
Kent TN15 6LL
Tel: 01474 853 144
(Unattached)

MILLARD John Alfred
Address: Waterdell Farm,
Springwell Lane, Harefield,
Uxbridge, Middlesex UB9 6PG
Tel: 01895 825034
(Attached to: Reading)

MILLER James
Address: 82 Lavender Drive,
East Kilbride, Glasgow G75 9JJ
Tel: 01355 245 471
(Attached to: Shawfield)

MILLER Paul
Address: 7 Etherley Bank, High
Etherley, Bishop Auckland,
County Durham DL14 0LG
Tel: 07957 200979
(Attached to: Sunderland)

MILLER Wendy Anne (Miss)
Address: Cleveland View,
Leasingthorne, Bishop Auckland,
County Durham DL14 8EH
Tel: 01388 722 219
(Attached to: Sunderland)

MILLION Anthony
Address: Linton House, Seaside
Lane, Easington, Peterlee,
County Durham SR8 3AS
Tel: 01915 270 039
(Attached to: Pelaw Grange)

MILLS Alexander Hamilton
Address: 12 Hilltown Terrace,
Woolmet, Dalkeith, Midlothian
EH22 1LG
Tel: 0782109935
(Unattached)

MILLS Ian William
Address: The Bungalow, Low
Road, Norton Subcourse,
Norwich, Norfolk NR14 6SA
Tel: 01508 548 353
(Attached to: Yarmouth)

MILLS Mandy Jayne (Miss)
Address: 5 Maltmas Drove,
Friday Bridge, Wisbech,
Cambridgeshire PE14 0HR
Tel: 01945 860666
(Attached to: Peterborough)

MILLWARD John Henry
Address: 70 Alton Avenue,
Willenhall, West Midlands
WV12 4NN
Tel: 01902 419382
(Unattached)

MINETT Ashley David Adam
Address: The Kennels,
Hubberts Bridge, Boston,
Lincolnshire PE20 3SZ
Tel: 01205 290 911
(Attached to: Sheffield)

MINGAY Peter
Address: 2 Station Cottages,
Shippea Hill, Ely,
Cambridgeshire CB7 4SP Tel:
07737 811 217
(Attached to: Mildenhall)

MITCHELL David George
Address: Blue Lias,
Furpits Lane, Langport,
Somerset TA10 9HJ
Tel: 01458 253766
(Attached to: Poole)

MITCHELL Kenneth Albert
Address: Clappers Kennels,
Grazeley, Reading, Berkshire
Tel: 07979 723509
(Attached to: Reading)

MITCHELSON Howard
Address: Cronkley Bank Farm
Cottage, Kiln Pit Hill, Consett,
County Durham DH8 9SD
Tel: 01207 255 255
(Attached to: Sunderland)

MOFFAT William Lawrence
Address: Rowan Cottage,
Baldinnie, Cupar,
Fife KY15 5LD Tel: 01334
840670
(Unattached)

MOORE Michael
Address: 55 West Avenue,
Southall, Middlesex
UB1 2AP
Tel: 0208 571 2032
(Attached to: Henlow)

MOORE Richard
Address: 7 Whipperley Way,
Luton, Bedfordshire LU1 5LA
Tel: 01582 419 473
(Attached to: Henlow)

MOORING Robert Charles
Address: 11 Paddock Close,
Norton, Malton,
North Yorkshire YO17 9AG
Tel: 01653 692554
(Unattached)

MORRIS Mark
Address: Loxdale Kennels,
52 Loxdale Drive,
Great Sutton, Ellesmere Port,
Merseyside CH65 7AN
Tel: 0151 357 2751
(Attached to: Kinsley)

MORRIS Yvonne (Mrs)
Address: 31 Corner Lane,
Leigh, Lancashire
WN7 5PY
Tel: 01942 256816
(Attached to: Doncaster)

MORRISEY James Michael
Address: 77 Low Grange Road,
Thurnscoe, Rotherham,
South Yorkshire S63 0LH
Tel: 01709 892228
(Attached to: Doncaster)

MORTIMER Margaret Ann (Mrs)
Address: 189 Havant Road,
Hayling Island, Hampshire
PO11 0LG
Tel: 02392 467550
(Attached to: Portsmouth)

MOSDALL Christopher Paul
Address: Unit 2,
Trotters Farm, High Easter,
Chelmsford,
Essex CM1 4RD
Tel: 07881 505 667
(Attached to: Harlow)

MOSS Joyce (Mrs)
Address: Folly Farm,
Crane Row Lane, Hamsterley,
Bishop Auckland, County
Durham DL13 3QU
Tel: 01388 488367
(Attached to: Pelaw Grange)

MOTTI Antonio
Address: 2 Underbridge
Cottages, Shipton Moyne,
Tetbury, Gloucestershire
GL8 8PJ
Tel: 07896 852 299
(Attached to: Reading)

MOULE Matthew
Address: Norfolk House,
Stanton Mereway, Willingham,
Cambridge, Cambridgeshire
CB4 5HJ
Tel: 01954 261855
(Attached to: Mildenhall)

MOULES David
Address: Address: 89 Kinross
Crescent, Luton, Bedfordshire
LU3 3JU
Tel: 01582 707866
(Attached to: Henlow)

MOYLE Victor (Snr)
Address: 56 Mellanear Road,
Hayle, Cornwall TR27 4QT
Tel: 01736 753221
(Attached to: Poole)

MUIR Henry Currie
Address: Craigmuir Farm,
Paisley, Renfrewshire PA2 8UT
Tel: 07703 435951
(Attached to: Shawfield)

MULLINS David
Address: Brookside, Arterial
Road, Wickford, Essex SS12 9JF
Tel: 01268 726583
(Attached to: Romford)

MULLINS John George
Address: Dillymore Cottage,
London Road, Capel St. Mary,
Ipswich, Suffolk IP9 2JZ
Tel: 01473 311069
(Unattached)

MULLINS Kelly
Address: Oldhall Kennels,
Green Lane, Mistley,
Manningtree, Essex CO11 2NL
Tel: 01206 392165
(Attached to: Walthamstow)

MUNKLEY David
Address: 211 Brierton Lane,
Hartlepool, Cleveland TS25 4AD
Tel: 01429 295 792
(Attached to: Pelaw Grange)

MUNNINGS Keith Anthony
Address: 9 Wright Close,
Stowmarket, Suffolk IP14 2BY
Tel: 01449 615804
(Unattached)

MUNSLOW Michael Terence
Address: Hillybank Kennels,
2 Chevin Side, Chevin Road,
Belper, Derbyshire DE56 2UN
Tel: 01773 822169
(Attached to: Nottingham)

MURPHY Patrick David
Address: 30 Langdale Drive,
Wakefield, West Yorkshire
WF2 9EW
Tel: 01924 211898
(Attached to: Kinsley)

MURPHY Terence
Address: 45 Kinsley House
Crescent, Fitzwilliam, Pontefract,
West Yorkshire WF9 5NB
Tel: 01977 612 646
(Attached to: Kinsley)

MURPHY Terence William
Address: 22 Brampton Close,
Cheshunt, Waltham Cross,
Hertfordshire EN7 6HZ
Tel: 01992 425035
(Unattached)

MURRAY John
Address: 14 Linnet Road, Bury
St. Edmunds, Suffolk IP33 3LL
Tel: 07760 304108
(Unattached)

MURRAY Thomas Spence
Address: 26 Netherwood Road,
Motherwell, Lanarkshire
ML1 2LE
Tel: 01698 252638
(Attached to: Shawfield)

MYLES Deborah (Miss)
Address: 9 Rogeri Place,
Hartlepool, Cleveland TS24 9NA
Tel: 01429 295 061
(Attached to: Pelaw Grange)

NELSON Ronald
Address: 1 Brookway, Greasby,
Wirral, Merseyside CH49 2NF
Tel: 01516 787 089
(Attached to: Kinsley)

NELSON Terence William
Address: 18 Chantry Croft,
Kinsley, Pontefract, West
Yorkshire WFf9 5JH
Tel: 01977 625 753
(Attached to: Kinsley)

NEWBERRY Mark
Address: 242 Coldhams Lane,
Cambridge, Cambridgeshire
CB1 3HN
Tel: 01223 571544
(Attached to: Mildenhall)

NEWBERRY Susan Lesley (Mrs)
Address: 238 Barlow Road,
Sileby, Leicestershire
LE12 7LR
Tel: 01509 813881
(Attached to: Coventry)

NEWMAN Maurice Thomas
Address: 8 Portmeers Close,
Lennox Road, Walthamstow,
London E17 8PT
Tel: 07939 692998
(Attached to: Harlow)

NICHOLLS Anthony Allam
Address: Jeanne, Rawcliffe
Road, Airmyn, Goole, North
Humberside DN14 8JN
Tel: 01405 763 412
(Unattached)

Norman NICHOLSON
Address: 11 Teesdale Place,
Knottingley, West Yorkshire
WF11 0LP
Tel: 01977 678404
(Attached to: Kinsley)

NOBLE Raymond
Address: 70 Ridley Road,
Carlisle, Cumbria CA2 4LD
Tel: 01228 531243
(Unattached)

NORTHALL Wayne
Address: 8 St. Helena Road,
Polesworth, Tamworth,
Staffordshire B78 1NW
Tel: 01827 896671
(Attached to: Coventry)

NORTHFIELD Justine (Mrs)
Nod Farm, 23 Cragg Road,
Chadderton, Oldham,
Lancashire OL1 2RY
Tel: 0161 633 4348
(Unattached)

NUNN Ian Douglas
Address: 22 Allington Walk,
Haverhill, Suffolk CB9 9AT
Tel: 01440 702 697
(Attached to: Henlow)

OAKES Sylvia (Mrs)
Address: 4 Lund Hill Lane,
Royston, Barnsley, South
Yorkshire S71 4BG
Tel: 01226 727767
(Attached to: Nottingham)

O'BRIEN Edward
Address: 51 Friern Barnet Lane,
London N11 3LL
Tel: 07867 926030
(Unattached)

O'BRIEN Michael (Snr)
Address: 4 Tangle Tree Close,
London N3 2TR
Tel: 07958 208795
(Unattached)

O'DONNELL Michael Anthony
Peter
Address: Ferry Top House,
Ferry Top Lane, Ryhill, Wakefield,
West Yorkshire WF4 2DS
Tel: 07802 974311
(Attached to: Sheffield)

O'DONNELL Robert
Address: 70 Househillmuir
Crescent, Pollok,
Glasgow G53 6HG
Tel: 0141 876 0214
(Unattached)

Michael OGDEN
Address: 8 Rowlett Road, Corby,
Northamptonshire NN17 2BW
Tel: 01536 407786
(Attached to: Peterborough)

O'GRADY Rosie (Mrs)
Address: O'Gradys,
72 Howard Street, Great
Yarmouth, Norfolk NR30 1LN
Tel: 07956 382 767
(Attached to: Yarmouth)

O'HARA Kevin Joseph
Address: 9 Windsor Road,
Batley, West Yorkshire WF17 0JX
Tel: 01924 443867
(Attached to: Doncaster)

O'REILLY Kevin
Address: Hillhead Farm,
Newcastleton, Roxburghshire
TD9 0TT
Tel: 01697 748 571
(Attached to: Pelaw Grange)

O'REILLY Malcolm Robert
Address: 10 Brewhouse Lane,
Soham, Ely,
Cambridgeshire CB7 5JE
Tel: 01353 722376
(Unattached)

ORGLES Robert Charles
Address: 4 Bloke Ockenden
Kennels, Ockendon Road,
North Ockendon, Upminster,
Essex RM14 3PT
Tel: 07957 341 314
(Attached to: Harlow)

ORME John
Address: Church Farm, Main
Street, Barrow, Oakham,
Leicestershire LE15 7PE
Tel: 01572 812205
(Attached to: Henlow)

O'ROURKE Patrick
Address: 116 Mosshall Street,
Motherwell, Lanarkshire
ML1 5HX
Tel: 01698 860 880
(Unattached)

O'ROURKE Timothy John
Address: 30 Turnpike Road,
Husborne, Crawley, Bedford,
Bedfordshire MK43 0XB
Tel: 01525 280636
(Attached to: Coventry)

OSBOURNE Gordon Samual
Address: 59 Bushfield Road,
Crewkerne, Somerset TA18 8HW
Tel: 01460 72338
(Attached to: Poole)

O'SULLIVAN Barry Desmond
Address: Oak Kennels,
Hazelwood, Sun Hill, Fawkham,
Longfield, Kent DA3 8NU
Tel: 01474 879949
(Attached to: Crayford)

OXLEY Yvonne
Address: Lyndias, 28 Ferry Road,
Barrow-upon-Humber,
South Humberside DN19 7DL
Tel: 01469 530338
(Unattached)

PACKHAM Colin William
Address: Mollifrend House,
Bath Road, Farmborough,
Bath, Avon BA3 1BY
Tel: 01761 470555
(Attached to: Reading)

PAGE Graham
Address: Oaklee, Knaves Green,
Brockford Green, Stowmarket,
Suffolk IP14 5NN
Tel: 01449 766651
(Unattached)

PAGE Joan Ann (Mrs)
Address: The Kennels, 2
Wrestlingworth Road, Potton,
Sandy, Bedfordshire SG19 2DP
Tel: 01767 261177
(Attached to: Henlow)

PALMER Andrew Charles
Address: Esperanza Croft,
Oak Road, Crays Hill, Billericay,
Essex CM11 2YL
Tel: 01268 523330
(Unattached)

PALMER Garry William
Address: The Bungalow, Mallets
Farm, London Road, Billericay,
Essex CM12 9HS
Tel: 01277 631210
(Attached to: Henlow)

PALMER Tony Alan
Address: 65 Thundridge Hill,
Thundridge, Ware,
Hertfordshire SG12 0UF
Tel: 01920 464921
(Unattached)

PARISI Andrew
Address: Azzurri Kennels,
145 Hamilton Road, Mount
Vernon, Glasgow G32 9QT
Tel: 07881 505068
(Unattached)

PARK Brian George
Address: Hares Hatch,
West Pelton, Stanley, County
Durham DH9 6RT
Tel: 0191 370 3493
(Attached to: Pelaw Grange)

PARKER Christine (Miss)
Address: 46 Honeywell Street,
Barnsley, South Yorkshire
S71 1PZ
Tel: 07788 716 665
(Attached to: Hull)

Elaine Teresa Parker (Mrs)
Address: Russanda, Station
Road, Hensall, Goole, North
Humberside DN14 0QU
Tel: 01977 662052
(Attached to: Sheffield)

PARKER George Frank
Address: 13 Lound Road,
Norwich, Norfolk NR4 7JQ
Tel: 01603 501317
(Attached to: Yarmouth)

PARKS Margaret (Mrs)
Address: 37 Dent Drive,
Eastmoor, Wakefield,
West Yorkshire WF1 4JG
Tel: 01924 361768
(Attached to: Kinsley)

PARR Keith Alfred
Address: 5 Bolton Row Cottages,
Peasemore, Newbury,
Berkshire RG20 7JW
Tel: 01635 248190
Attached to:Reading)

PARR Stephen
Address: 322 South Road,
South Ockendon,
Essex RM15 6EB
Tel: 01708850561
(Unattached)

PATERNOSTER Peter Albert
Address: Owls Tree Farm,
2 Hare & Hounds Corner,
Hemingstone, Ipswich,
Suffolk IP6 9RW
Tel: 01473 785840
(Attached to: Yarmouth)

PATERSON Ronald
Highfield View, Aislaby Road,
Eaglescliffe, Stockton-on-Tees,
Cleveland TS16 0QL
Tel: 07950 528 910
(Attached to: Sunderland)

PATRICK Thomas
Address: 14 Oakhill Drive,
Bonhill, Alexandria,
Dunbartonshire G83 9EF
Tel: 01389 720595
(Attached to: Shawfield)

PATTINSON Robert
Address: Hazels, London Road,
Vange, Basildon,
Essex SS16 4PX
Tel: 01268 553196
(Attached to: Sittingbourne)

PAUL Lynda Ann (Mrs)
Address: 20 The Street,
Hevingham, Norwich,
Norfolk NR10 5NA
Tel: 01603 754395
(Unattached)

PAYNE Graham Anthony
Address: 155 Hitchin Road,
Henlow, Bedfordshire SG16 6BA
Tel: 01462 811656
(Attached to: Henlow)

PAYNE Peter Francis
Address: Brooklyn Kennels,
Blackbush Lane, Horndon-on-
The-Hill, Stanford-le-Hope,
Essex SS17 8PT
Tel: 01375 891 614
(Attached to: Romford)

PEACH Christopher
Address: The Old Nursery,
Cromwell Road, Ringsfield,
Beccles, Suffolk NR34 8LR
Tel: 01502 715159
(Attached to: Yarmouth)

PEACOCK Andrew John
Address: Catford Racing
Kennels, Layhams Road,
Keston, Kent BR2 6AR
Tel: 01959 571926
(Attached to: Wimbledon)

PEARCE Deborah Oriel (Miss)
Address: Langley Lodge,
Longdown, Marchwood,
Southampton,
Hampshire SO40 4UH
Tel: 02380 293723
(Attached to: Poole)

PEARCE John
Address: Watch Kennels, Stave
Hall Farm, Fosse Way, Monks
Kirby, Rugby, Warwickshire CV23
ORL Tel: 01788 833213
(Attached to: Hall Green).

PEARSON Christopher
Address: Alameda Kennels,
Croft View, White Horse Lane,
Kent DA13 0UE
Tel: 01474 812 967
(Unattached)

PEARSON Julie (Mrs)
Address: Oak Grove Kennels,
Sedge Fen, Brandon,
Suffolk IP27 9LE
Tel: 01353 675234
(Unattached)

PECKOVER Ronald Harry
Address: 32 Salt Hill Drive,
Slough, Berkshire SL1 3TH
Tel: 01753 524472
(Attached to: Reading)

PEDDER Stewart James
Address: South View,
Harpers Drove, Ramsey Heights,
Huntingdon, Cambridgeshire
PE26 2RR
Tel: 01487 813619
(Unattached)

PEEK Kim Phyllis (Mrs)
Address: 5 Hillie Bunnies,
Earls Colne, Colchester,
Essex CO6 2RU
Tel: 01787 224187
(Unattached)

PENDALL Robert Albert
Address: Moors Kennels,
Moor Drove, Hockwold,
Thetford, Norfolk IP26 4JL
Tel: 07946 507769
(Attached to: Mildenhall)

PENNY Colin John
Address: Wingfield Drive,
Butt Lane, Burgh Castle,
Great Yarmouth,
Norfolk NR31 9QE
Tel: 01493 781 755
(Attached to: Yarmouth)

PERKINS Beryl Margaret (Mrs)
Address: 100 Pople Street,
Wymondham, Norfolk NR18 0LP
Tel: 01953 605892
(Attached to: Yarmouth)

PERKINS Rebecca Ellen (Miss),
Address: Little Weighton
Kennels, Highfield House,
Neat Marsh Road, Preston, Hull,
North Humberside HU12 8TR
Tel: 07896 013 491
(Attached to: Kinsley)

PERRIN Kenneth Edward
78 Vale Drive, Shirebrook,
Mansfield, Nottinghamshire
NG20 8RQ
Tel: 01623 746227
(Attached to: Nottingham)

PETERSON Michael Andrew
Address: Kings Farm, Piddington
Road, Ludgershall, Aylesbury,
Buckinghamshire HP18 9PJ
Tel: 07793 383 299
(Attached to: Oxford)

PETT Thomas Patrick
Address: Moors Hill Kennels,
Rusham Road, Shatterling,
Canterbury, Kent CT3 1JL
Tel: 07932 480061
(Unattached)

PHILPOT Richard Charles
106 Parsonage Road, Rainham,
Essex RM13 9LF
Tel: 01708 551689
(Attached to: Harlow)

PHILPOTT Paul Brian
Address: Sunnyfield Farm, Edge
Bank, Emneth, Wisbech,
Cambridgeshire PE14 8EJ
Tel: 01945 430425
(Unattached)

PICKERING Richard
Woodlington, Butt Lane,
Burgh Castle, Great Yarmouth,
Norfolk NR31 9PU
Tel: 01493 782108
(Unattached)

PICKWORTH Michael William
Address: Dotland Park, Hexham,
Northumberland NE46 1YD
Tel: 01434 603 419
(Attached to: Pelaw Grange)

PIKE Roy Leslie
Address: 3 Barn Close,
Todber, Sturminster Newton,
Dorset DT10 1HU
Tel: 01258 820731
(Attached to: Poole)

PILGRIM Stephen Ronald
Address: 94 Junction Road,
Hamworthy, Poole,
Dorset BH16 5AB
Tel: 01202 667 297
(Attached to: Poole)

PLEASANTS Raymond Arthur
Address: Malthouse Farm,
Old Norwich Road, Scottow,
Norwich, Norfolk NR10 5DB
Tel: 01603 424649
(Attached to: Yarmouth)

POAD Terence Roy
Address: Lower Eden,
Avonwick, South Brent,
Devon TQ10 9ES
Tel: 07742 005619
(Attached to: Poole)

POINTING Dorothy Mary (Mrs)
Address: 33 Sherburn Street,
Cawood, Selby,
North Yorkshire YO8 3SS
Tel: 01757 268601
(Attached to: Hull)

POMROY Stephen Roy
Address: 10 Oakridge Drive,
Willenhall, West Midlands
WV12 4DL
Tel: 07949 100 147
(Unattached)

POOLE Sheila (Mrs)
Address: The Hollies, 138 Moira
Road, Woodville, Swadlincote,
Derbyshire DE11 8EY
Tel: 01283 211931
(Attached to: Nottingham)

POOLEY Ian
New Farm, Blyton Carr,
Gainsborough, Lincolnshire
DN21 3EW
Tel: 07906444805
(Attached to: Nottingham)

POOTS Samuel
Address: High Gables,
Homestead Road, Ramsden
Bellhouse, Billericay,
Essex CM11 1RP
Tel: 01268 712 864
(Unattached)

PORTER Darryl Douglas
Address: Noon Trees,
Beacon Hill, Hilmarton, Calne,
Wiltshire SN11 9HT
Tel: 01249 760619
(Attached to: Swindon)

POTTER Nick John
Address: 2 Threehammer
Common, Neatishead, Norwich,
Norfolk NR12 8BP
Tel: 01692 630826
(Unattached)

POWER Denis
Address: 12 Coles Crescent,
Harrow, Middlesex HA2 0TP
Tel: 0208 864 3919
(Attached to: Henlow)

POWER George Scott
Address: 28 Maclean Place,
Gorebridge, Midlothian
EH23 4DX
Tel: 01875 822140
(Attached to: Shawfield)

POWER Michael William Walt
Address: Vale Lodge,
Gowthorpe Lane, Swainsthorpe,
Norwich, Norfolk NR14 8PT
Tel: 01508 578433
(Attached to: Yarmouth)

PRENDEVILLE Thomas Simon
Address: The Bungalow,
Ockendon Kennels, Ockendon
Road, North Ockendon,
Upminster, Essex RM14 3PT
Tel: 01708 221818
(Unattached)

PRENTICE David Jonathan
Address: Elm Tree Cottage,
Main Road, Lower Somersham,
Ipswich, Suffolk IP8 4QH
Tel: 01473 657707
(Attached to: Mildenhall)

PRICE Rita Ann (Mrs)
Meadowside, French Mill Lane,
Shaftesbury, Dorset SP7 8EU
Tel: 01747 854042
(Attached to: Poole)

PRINCE Karen Jane (Mrs)
Address: Stave Hall Farm,
Fosse Way, Monks Kirby, Rugby,
Warwickshire CV23 0RL
Tel: 01788 832991
(Attached to: Monmore Green)

PRINCE Wendy Anne (Mrs)
Address: 30 Doddington Road,
Benwick, March,
Cambridgeshire PE15 0UT
Tel:01354 677384
(Attached to: Peterborough)

PRIOR Paul
Address: 127 Broom Road,
Pemberton, Wigan,
Lancashire WN5 9QH
Tel: 01942 708255
(Attached to: Doncaster)

PRUHS David Richard
Address: The Willows, Burr Lane,
Spalding, Lincolnshire PE12 6AZ
Tel: 01775 724446
(Attached to: Peterborough)

PRUHS Deborah Karen (Miss)
Address: 12 Corner Farm,
Wisbech Road,
Thorney, Peterborough,
Cambridgeshire PE6 0TS
Tel: 0774 509 0634
(Unattached)

PRUHS Linda Janis (Miss)
Address: Bar Pasture Farm,
Willow Hall Lane,
Thorney, Peterborough,
Cambridgeshire PE6 0QN
Tel: 01733 222095
(Attached to: Henlow)

PUDDY David
Address: 33 Rydons Lane,
Coulsdon, Surrey CR5 1SU
Tel: 020 8668 2953
(Attached to: Reading)

PUGH Margaret Ann (Mrs)
Address: 3 Carr Green,
Bolton-upon-Dearne, Rotherham,
South Yorkshire S63 8AS
Tel: 01709 897171
(Attached to: Hull)

PURDY Michael
Address: 238 Cowick Road,
Tooting, London SW17 8LH
Tel: 020 8767 5473
(Unattached)

PUZEY Michael
1 Claverhambury Kennels,
Galley Hill, Waltham Abbey,
Essex EN9 2BL
Tel: 01992 893188
(Attached to: Walthamstow)

PYRAH Stephen Charles
Address: 45 Coniston Road,
Lancaster, Lancashire LA1 3NJ
Tel: 01524 68534
(Attached to: Doncaster)

RACE Steven
Address: Hill Farm Kennels,
Chesterfield Road, Unstone,
Dronfield, Derbyshire S18 4AF
Tel: 01246 415874
(Unattached)

RADEVA Zoya (Miss)
31 Tennyson Road, Great
Yarmouth, Norfolk NR30 4EY
Tel: 01493 301854
(Unattached)

RAE Matthew Leslie
Address: Peakstones Farm,
Soaper Lane, Shelf, Halifax,
West Yorkshire HX3 7PX
Tel: 07971 102 820
(Attached to: Pelaw Grange)

RAE William
Address: 46 Wingate Street,
Wishaw, Lanarkshire ML2 7RX
Tel: 07759 717316
(Attached to: Shawfield)

RAILTON Kevin
Address: 133 Garesfield
Gardens, Burnopfield,
Newcastle Upon Tyne,
Tyne and Wear NE16 6LQ
Tel: 01207 271 305
(Attached to: Pelaw Grange)

RALPH Sandra (Miss)
Address: Hay Head Farm,
Longwood Lane, Walsall,
West Midlands WS4 2JT
Tel: 01992 724009
(Attached to: Perry Barr)

RALPH Nicholas Paul (Jnr)
Address: Hillside Kennels,
The Pack, Market Street,
Winchcombe,
Gloucestershire GL54 5EL
Tel: 07784 088731
(Attached to: Reading)

RANKIN Graham
Address: 49 Bankhead Avenue,
Airdrie, Lanarkshire, ML6 8JG
Tel: 01236 750627
(Attached to: Shawfield)

RAWLINSON Frederick
Address: 262 Huddersfield Road,
Mirfield, West Yorkshire WF14
9PY Tel: 01924 408 567
(Attached to: Kinsley)

RAY Jason Mark
Address: 12 Elizabeth Avenue,
Staines, Middlesex TW18 1JP
Tel: 01784 885501
(Attached to: Henlow)

RAY Stuart
Address: Black House Farm,
Page Bank, Spennymoor,
County Durham DL16 7RB
Tel: 01388 811457
(Attached to: Newcastle)

RAYMENT Terence Michael
Terrys Kennels, Ockendon Road,
North Ockendon, Upminster,
Essex RM14 3PS
Tel: 01708 220 332
(Unattached)

RAYNERStephen James
Address: Eagles Farm, Cow
Lane, Gawcott, Buckingham,
Buckinghamshire MK18 4JJ
Tel: 01280 816585
(Attached to: Swindon)

READ Brian Peter
Address: 26 Ewden Rise,
Melton Mowbray,
Leicestershire LE13 0BU
Tel: 01664 565713
(Attached to: Peterborough)

REDDEN Colin
Address: 25 Lumley Drive,
Peterlee, County Durham
SR8 1NL
Tel: 0191 586 2483
(Unattached)

REDHEAD Andrew John
Address: 5 The Street,
Fersfield, Diss, Norfolk IP22 2BL
Tel: 07765 700 605
(Unattached)

REDPATH Elizabeth Garland (Mrs)
Address: Court Barn,
London Road, Rake, Liss,
Hampshire GU33 7JQ
Tel: 01730 893255
(Attached to: Portsmouth)

REED Robert James (Snr)
Address: Springwood Kennels,
Nestledown Complex,
Eastbourne Road, Blindley Heath,
Lingfield, Surrey RH7 6LG
Tel: 0797 0028427
(Attached to: Reading)

REES Philip Charles
Address: 3 Burhill Kennels,
Turners Lane, Walton-on-
Thames, Surrey KT12 4AW
Tel: 01932 222637
(Attached to: Wimbledon)

REEVES Mark Alan
Address: 12 Weardale Crescent,
Billingham, Cleveland TS23 1AZ
Tel: 07913 980 110
(Attached to: Pelaw Grange)

REGAN Kenneth
Address: Nant Melyn Farm,
Seven Sisters, Neath, West
Glamorgan SA10 9BW
Tel: 01639 700859
(Attached to: Reading)

REID Andrew Christine
Address: Lower Carbarn Farm,
Carbarns Road, Wishaw,
Lanarkshire ML2 0AU
Tel: 07843 584267
(Attached to: Shawfield)

REID John George
Address: 11 Tointons Road,
Upwell, Wisbech,
Cambridgeshire PE14 9HL
Tel: 01945 772701
(Attached to: Peterborough)

RENWICK Keith Mark (Jnr)
Address: 152 St. Anthonys Road,
Newcastle Upon Tyne,
Tyne and Wear NE6 2ND
Tel: 0191 275 9899
(Attached to: Pelaw Grange)

REYNOLDS James Weir
Address: Orchard Kennels,
Sandy Lane Farm,
Sandy Lane, South Ockendon,
Essex RM15 4XP
Tel: 01708 862016
(Attached to: Romford)

REYNOLDS Michael Shaw
Address: Auchenbowie Kennels,
Auchenbowie, Stirling,
Stirlingshire FK7 8HE
Tel: 01786 814773
(Attached to: Shawfield)

Sponsored by the BGRB

RICE Maurice John
Address: Sheltie Acre,
King John Bank, Walpole St.
Andrew, Wisbech,
Cambridgeshire PE14 7JP
Tel: 01945 780005
(Attached to: Peterborough)

RICH Peter James
Address: Upper Horton Farm
Kennels, New House Lane,
Canterbury,Kent CT4 7BN
Tel: 01227 731500
(Attached to: Walthamstow)

RICHARDS Nigel Gwyn
Address: 1 Clwtt Cottage,
Gyfelia, Wrexham,
Clwyd LL13 0YL
Tel: 01978 845695
(Unattached)

RICHES Simon Paul
Address: 9 Acre Kennels,
Brands Lane, Felthorpe,
Norwich, Norfolk NR10 4EA
Tel: 07881 821326
(Attached to: Yarmouth)

RICHMOND Harry
Address: Decoy Cottage,
Decoy Road, Ormesby, Great
Yarmouth, Norfolk NR29 3LZ
Tel: 01493 732536
(Attached to: Yarmouth)

RIDDIFORD Barry
Stanton Kennels, 2 Timlett
Cottages, Stanton Road, Shifnal,
Shropshire TF11 8PG
Tel: 01952 460995
(Attached to: Monmore Green)

RIDGWAY Terence Henry John
Address: 17 York Place,
Aylesbury, Buckinghamshire
HP21 8HP
Tel: 07785 797143
(Attached to: Henlow)

RIDING Philip
Address: Grange Cottage,
Grindley Lane, Stoke-on-Trent,
Staffordshire ST3 7TA
Tel: 01782 393117
(Unattached)

RIDLEY David Charles
Address: Sunningdale,
Horsham Road, Steyning,
West Sussex BN44 3AA
Tel: 01903 813 495
(Attached to: Portsmouth)

RIDLEY Julie (Mrs)
Address: Two Trees Farm,
Coventry Road, Aldermans
Green, Coventry,
West Midlands CV2 1NT
Tel: 02476 313442
(Attached to: Perry Barr)

RIGBY John
Address: 83 Main Road,
Higher Kinnerton, Chester,
Cheshire CH4 9AJ
Tel: 01244 661192
(Attached to: Coventry)

RIORDAN Daniel Christopher
Address: 3 Crow Lane, Romford,
Essex RM7 0EL
Tel: 01708 762033
(Attached to: Henlow)

RITCHIE Andrew
Address: 20 Holdings,
Barns of Claverhouse,
Dundee, Angus DD3 0QF
Tel: 01382 507522
(Attached to: Shawfield)

RITCHIE Craig
Address: Burnhead Kennels,
Burnhead House, Longridge,
Bathgate, West Lothian
EH47 9AB
Tel: 01501 772227
(Unattached)

ROBERTS Alan Stephen
Address: The Bungalow,
Pineview, Smestow, Swindon,
Dudley, West Midlands DY3 4PH
Tel: 01902 896370
(Unattached)

ROBERTS Dippy (Miss)
Address: Lodge Farm, Skeltons
Drove, Beck Row, Bury St.
Edmunds, Suffolk IP28 8DN
Tel: 01277 651139
(Attached to: Mildenhall)

ROBERTS Geoffrey Vaughan
Address: 10 Grindon Crescent,
Nottingham, Nottinghamshire
NG6 8BQ
Tel: 01159 754981
(Attached to: Kinsley)

ROBERTS John
Address: 2 Trinity Road, Stotfold,
Hitchin, Hertfordshire SG5 4EG
Tel: 01462 731029
(Attached to: Henlow)

ROBERTS Margaret Ann (Mrs)
Address: 231 Main Road,
Westwood, Nottingham,
Nottinghamshire NG16 5JB
Tel: 01773 602217
(Attached to: Nottingham)

ROBERTS Mark Paul
Address: 77 Festing Street,
Stoke-on-Trent Staffordshire
ST1 2HY
Tel: 01782 850628
(Unattached)

ROBERTS Paul Stuart
Address: Henlow Greyhound
Stadium, Bedford Road,
Lower Stondon, Henlow,
Bedfordshire SG16 6EA
Tel: 07970 931274
(Attached to: Henlow)

ROBERTS William Ernest (Jnr)
Address: 7 Lairs Close,
London N7 9TF
Tel: 0207 607 0912
(Unattached)

ROBINS Kim (Mrs)
Address: Toms Cabin Kennels,
1 Vale View, Tring Hill, Tring,
Hertfordshire HP23 4LD
Tel: 01442 890144
(Attached to: Henlow)

ROBINSON David
Address: 121 St Cutberts Drive,
Felling, Gateshead, Tyne And
Wear NE10 9AD
Tel: 0191 420 6314
(Attached to: Pelaw Grange)

ROBSON Trevor Douglas
Address: Nosbor Kennels,
Pasture Lane, Malton,
North Yorkshire YO17 7BS
Tel: 07861 675137
(Attached to: Hull)

ROCKE Geoffrey Gordon
Address: The Paddock,
Mayern Close, Leominster,
Herefordshire HR6 8PU
Tel: 07970 969932
(Attached to: Perry Barr)

ROGERS John Leslie
Address: Firs School Bungalow,
Station Road, Ampthill, Bedford,
Bedfordshire MK45 2QR
Tel: 01525 406020
(Unattached)

ROGERS Michael Kenneth
Address: 48 Eden Avenue,
Wakefield, West Yorkshire
WF2 9DJ
Tel: 01924 362289
(Unattached)

ROGERSON Alan
Address: 9 Cheshire Avenue,
Birtley, Chester Le Street,
County Durham DH3 2BA
Tel: 09194 923 806
(Attached to: Pelaw Grange)

ROLLASON Michael Roland
Address: 9 Dunelm Crescent,
Moorends, Doncaster,
South Yorkshire DN8 4PT
Tel: 01405 815442
(Attached to: Doncaster)

ROLLINSON Clive
Address: 50 Elm Road,
Skellow, Doncaster,
South Yorkshire DN6 8PH
Tel: 07979 460 107
(Attached to: Hull)

ROME Thomas Henry
Address: Dunmore, 1 Manse
Road, Terregles, Dumfries,
Dumfriesshire DG2 9RS
Tel: 01387 721314
Pelaw Grange)

ROSNEY Patrick James
5 Town Brow, Leyland,
Lancashire PR25 5SY
Tel: 01772 434589
(Attached to: Monmore Green)

ROTHERHAM Robert
22 Coalfell Avenue,
Carlisle, Cumbria CA2 7RY
Tel: 01228 590 036
(Attached to: Pelaw Grange)

ROWE George Colin
Horseshoe Cottage, West Drove
North, Walton Highway,
Wisbech, Cambridgeshire
PE14 7DP
Tel: 01945 880971
(Attached to: Mildenhall)

ROWE James Andrew
Sandlewood, Northwood Green,
Westbury-on-Severn,
Gloucestershire GL14 1NA
Tel: 01452 760 305
(Unattached)

RUDDICK Peter John
Rockhouse Farm, Old Ford,
Frome, Somerset BA11 2ND
Tel: 01373 462181
(Attached to: Poole)

Joseph RUDGEWICK
16a Heath Farm Road,
Red Lodge, Bury St. Edmunds,
Suffolk IP28 8LG
Tel: 01638 750729
(Attached to: Mildenhall)

RUMBELOW Ann Janna (Mrs)
Matchbox Farm, Wash Lane,
Aslacton, Norwich,
Norfolk NR15 2JR
Tel: 01379 677739
(Unattached)

RUSSELL William
Windley Farm, Crudgington
Green, Crudgington, Telford,
Shropshire TF6 6JY
Tel: 01952 540 919
(Attached to: Perry Barr)

RUTHERFORD Paul
North View, North Road,
Ponteland, Newcastle Upon Tyne,
Tyne and Wear NE20 0AA
Tel: 01661 872621
(Attached to: Newcastle)

RYDE Anna (Mrs)
Halls Green Farm,
Epping Road, Roydon, Harlow,
Essex CM19 5DG
Tel: 07752 859865
(Attached to: Harlow)

Sponsored by the BGRB

SABERTON Sharon Ann (Miss)
Brambleberry, Dozens Bank,
West Pinchbeck, Spalding,
Lincolnshire PE11 3ND
Tel: 07812 950 766
(Attached to: Peterborough)

SALLIS Gary Frederick
Unit 1, Fallowfield Kennels,
Grays Avenue, Basildon,
Essex SS16 5LP
Tel: 07719 423 052
(Attached to: Sittingbourne)

SALLIS Paul Anthony
Shortwood Farm, Green Lane,
Overseal, Swadlincote,
Derbyshire DE12 6JP
Tel: 01283 763920
(Attached to: Hall Green)

SALMON James Richard
34 Keir Hardie Terrace,
Dunfermline, Fife KY11 3BX
Tel: 01383 729047
(Unattached)

SAMS Lorraine Dawn (Miss)
2 Claverhambury Kennels,
Claverhambury Road,
Waltham Abbey,
Essex EN9 2BL
Tel: 01992 892 695
(Unattached)

SAMSON Russell Marc
205 Cowley Hill, Borehamwood,
Hertfordshire WD6 5ND
Tel: 0208 207 4468
(Unattached)

SAMUELS Erica Gail (Mrs)
79 Yarmouth Road,
Ormesby, Great Yarmouth,
Norfolk NR29 3QF
Tel: 07960929907
(Attached to: Yarmouth)

SANDBERG Justin John
187 School Road, Walton
Highway, Wisbech,
Cambridgeshire PE14 7DS
Tel: 01945 466082
(Attached to: Peterborough)

SAUNDERS James
Bramley House, 70 Wallingford
Road, Cholsey, Wallingford,
Oxfordshire OX10 9LA
Tel: 01491 651774
(Attached to: Reading)

SAUNDERS Nigel John
Saunders Dog Kennels,
Springcroft, 45 Hall Moss Lane,
Bramhall, Stockport,
Cheshire SK7 1RB
Tel: 0161 439 2639
(Attached to: Belle Vue)

SAUNDERS Terence William
Telford, 1 The Street, Hapton,
Norwich, Norfolk NR15 1AD
Tel: 07831 792383
(Unattached)

SAVAGE Gary
45 Chilmark Road, Norbury,
London SW16 5HB
Tel: 020 8764 7746
(Unattached)

SAVAGE Margaret Ann (Mrs)
Address: 82 Main Street,
Newthorpe, Nottingham,
Nottinghamshire NG16 2ET
Tel: 01773 760698
(Unattached)

SAVILLE Elaine (Mrs)
Address: Two Acres, Dunholme
Road, Scothern, Lincoln,
Lincolnshire LN2 2UE
Tel: 01673 860300
(Attached to: Nottingham)

SAVORY Charles John
Address: 25 Firth Park Avenue,
Sheffield, South Yorkshire
S5 6HF
Tel: 0114 256 2146
(Attached to: Nottingham)

SAVVA Nick
Address: Westmead Kennels,
Cow Lane, Edlesborough,
Dunstable, Bedfordshire
LU6 2HT
Tel: 01525 220450
(Attached to: Henlow)

SCANLON Joseph
Address: 183 Aldridge Road,
Perry Barr, Birmingham B42 2EY
Tel: 0121 356 3513
(Attached to: Perry Barr)

SCHOFIELD Peter
Address: 1 Peacocks, Great
Shelford, Cambridge,
Cambridgeshire CB2 5AT
Tel: 01223 845144
(Attached to: Henlow)

SCOLES Wendy Marilyn (Mrs)
Address: Berwensett, Allens
Drove, Gorefield, Wisbech,
Cambridgeshire PE13 4PB
Tel: 01945 410560
(Attached to: Peterborough)

SCOTT Jeffery
Address: 15 Wilmington,
Bedford Street, Hull, North
Humberside, HU8 8AP
Tel: 01482 226 732
(Attached to: Hull)

SCOTT Robert Donald
Address: Hawthorne Kennels,
Main Road, Upton, Nuneaton,
Warwickshire CV13 6JX
Tel: 07724 001 424
(Unattached)

SEAGRAVE John
Address: Rainbow Kennels,
Westgate Lane,
Old Malton, Malton,
North Yorkshire YO17 0SG
Tel: 01653 692623
(Attached to: Doncaster)

SENENKO Gillian (Mrs)
Address: 17 Herons Way,
Birdwell, Barnsley,
South Yorkshire S70 5SF
Tel: 01226 207 806
(Attached to: Doncaster)

SENIOR Russell
Address: Magnolia Bungalow,
Swineshead Road,
Kirton Holme, Boston,
Lincolnshire PE20 1SQ
Tel: 01205 290027
(Attached to: Peterborough)

SHAHIN Nicholas Boutros
Address: 28 Mayesbrook Road,
Dagenham, Essex RM8 2EB
Tel: 020 8599 7566
(Unattached)

SHARP Graham Lewis
Address: Peaceful Kennels,
Weald Bridge Road, North
Weald, Epping, Essex CM16 6AU
Tel: 01992 522317
(Attached to: Walthamstow)

SHAW George Charles
Address: 25 Branchalmuir
Crescent, Newmains, Wishaw,
Lanarkshire ML2 9DY
Tel: 01698 381779
(Unattached)

SHEARER Ian
Address: 20 Grasmere Avenue,
Padiham, Burnley, Lancashire
BB12 8PG
Tel: 01282 713 793
(Attached to: Doncaster)

SHEFFIELD Raymond Michael
Address: Green Barn, Tarbay
Lane, Oakley Green, Windsor,
Berkshire SL4 4QG
Tel: 07865 017 590
(Attached to: Reading)

SHELDON William
Address: 122 Houghton Road,
Hetton-le-Hole, Houghton Le
Spring, Tyne and Wear
DH5 9PL
Tel: 0191 526 5768
(Attached to: Pelaw Grange)

SHEPHERD Mark Stephen
Address: 11 Rheola Gardens,
Thornbury, Plymouth,
Devon PL6 8UB
Tel: 01752 770673
(Unattached)

SHERRY John
Address: Alders Farm,
Fyfield Road, Willingale,
Ongar, Essex CM5 0SQ
Tel: 01277 899 374
(Attached to: Walthamstow)

SHIELDS Mel
Address: Kimacoo, Green Lane
West, Rackheath, Norwich,
Norfolk NR13 6LT
Tel: 07717 211 529
(Attached to: Yarmouth)

SHORT Edward
Address: Tower Hill,
Alston, Cumbria CA9 3RR
Tel: 01434 381677
(Unattached)

SHORT Wendy Elizabeth (Mrs)
Address: Little Rowfold,
Coneyhurst Road, Billingshurst,
West Sussex RH14 9DF
Tel: 01403 784748
(Attached to: Brighton & Hove)

SHRIMPTON Keith Robert
Address: Whinfell House,
 Dog Drove, Holbeach Drove,
Spalding, Lincolnshire PE12 0RZ
Tel: 01406 330058
(Attached to: Peterborough)

SIDDALL Mark John
Address: Freedom Kennels,
Barnsley Road, Goldthorpe,
Rotherham, South Yorkshire
S63 9AW
Tel: 01709 884 583
(Attached to: Kinsley)

SILKMAN Barry
Address: Keedals, 101 Northaw
Road West, Northaw, Potters Bar,
Hertfordshire EN6 4NS
Tel: 01707 660 179
(Attached to: (Unattached)

SILLARS Elizabeth Ferguson (Mrs)
Address: Rowallandale Kennels,
Glasgow Road, Eaglesham,
Glasgow G76 0DN
Tel: 01355 302352
(Attached to: Shawfield)

SIM Karen (Mrs)
Address: Drum Farm, 684 Old
Dalkeith Road, Danderhall,
Dalkeith, Midlothian EH22 1RR
Tel: 0131 448 2251
(Unattached)

SIMMONDS Philip John
Address: The Kennels,
Cambridge Road,
Barton, Cambridge,
Cambridgeshire CB3 7AS
Tel: 01223 262 362
(Attached to: Harlow)

SIMMONS Leslie Charles
Address: Rozel, 11a Radlett
Road, Watford, Hertfordshire
WD2 4LH Tel: 01923 239446
(Unattached)

SIMMONS Trevor
Address: Old School House,
Corby Road, Irnham, Grantham,
Lincolnshire NG33 4JB
Tel: 01476 550308
(Attached to: Peterborough)

SIMPSON Dennis Edward
Address: 2 Windy Corner,
Leadenhall Road, Holbeach,
Spalding, Lincolnshire PE12 8EZ
Tel: 01406 701472
(Attached to: Peterborough)

SIMPSON Gordon Harry
Address: Greenways, The Green,
Penistone, Sheffield, South
Yorkshire S36 6BL
Tel: 01224 763285
(Attached to: Kinsley)

SIMPSON Janice (Mrs)
Address: Barn 1, Old Saw Mill,
Marton Road, Gargrave, Skipton,
North Yorkshire BD23 3NN
Tel: 01756 748 852
(Attached to: Doncaster)

SIMPSON John Stanley James
Address: Pipps Hill Farm, Pipps
Hill Road North, Crays Hill,
Billericay, Essex CM11 2UJ
Tel: 01268 289117
(Attached to: Wimbledon)

SIMPSON Patricia (Mrs)
Address: 27 Mardale Street,
Hetton-le-Hole, Houghton Le
Spring, Tyne and Wear DH5 0DH
Tel: 0191 526 2703
(Attached to: Pelaw Grange)

SIMPSON Russell Paul
Address: 52 Green End Road,
Kempston, Bedford,
Bedfordshire MK43 8RJ
Tel: 01234 857932
(Attached to: Henlow)

SKEECH Ernest Thomas
Address: 124 Crow Lane West,
Newton-le-Willows,
Merseyside, WA12 9YL
Tel: 01925 223122
(Unattached)

SKEGGS Tania Amelia Jayne
(Mrs)
Address: Renmar Nurseries,
Crown Lane, Tendring, Clacton-
on-Sea, Essex CO16 0BH
Tel: 01255 830988
(Attached to: Yarmouth)

SLATER Paul
Address: Oaken Hayes Farm,
Walsall Road,
Great Wyrley, Walsall,
West Midlands WS6 6AG
Tel: 07813 727821
(Attached to: Perry Barr)

SLOWLEY Neil Marc
Address: Lock Cottage Kennels,
Kingsbury Road, Marston,
Warwickshire
Tel: 01675 470 999
(Attached to: Perry Barr)

SMALLEY Brian Michael
Address: 24 Armada Close,
Wisbech, Cambridgeshire
PE13 3QF
Tel: 01945 489905
(Unattached)

SMEE Daniel Ronald
Address: 67 Markham Road,
Bournemouth, Dorset BH9 1JA
Tel: 01202 779947
(Attached to: Poole)

SMITH Anthony David
Address: 20 Newdigate Road,
Harefield, Uxbridge,
Middlesex UB9 6EL
Tel: 07947 136419
(Unattached)

SMITH Barbara Pauline (Mrs)
Address: Stave Hall Farm, Fosse
Way, Monks Kirby, Rugby,
Warwickshire CV23 0RL
Tel: 01788 833611
(Attached to: Hall Green)

SMITH David Ralph
Address: 92 Speedwell Road,
Colchester, Essex CO2 8DT
Tel: 01206 871618
(Attached to: Henlow)

SMITH James Edwin
Address: Outhouse Farm,
Redmarshall Road,
Bishopton, Stockton-on-Tees,
Cleveland TS21 1EX
Tel: 07867 850887
(Attached to: Pelaw Grange)

SMITH James Ronald
Address: Kimberwick Kennels,
Haggs Wood, Stainforth,
Doncaster, South Yorkshire
DN7 5HT
Tel: 01302 845 822
(Attached to: Sheffield)

SMITH John Henry
Address: Berkshire Kennels, 110
Dudley Street, West Bromwich,
West Midlands B70 9AJ
Tel: 07947 666 679
(Attached to: Coventry)

SMITH Kathleen (Mrs)
Address: Duchies Cottage,
Mill Lane, Pirbright,
Woking, Surrey GU24 0BT
Tel: 07919 270577
(Attached to: Reading)

SMITH Norman
Address: Unit 1, Mainsforth
Industrial Estate, Mainsforth
Road, Ferryhill, County Durham
DL17 9DE Tel: 07748 678 651
(Attached to: Pelaw Grange)

SMITH Robert Charles
Address: 51 Thrasher Road,
Aylesbury, Buckinghamshire
HP21 8DU
Tel: 01296 582750
(Attached to: Henlow)

SMITH Robert Paul
Address: Salem Villa, New
Brookend, Berkeley,
Gloucestershire GL13 9SF
Tel: 01453 811584
(Attached to: Swindon)

SMITH Robert William
Address: 23 Hillside Road,
Corfe Mullen, Wimborne,
Dorset H21 3SA
Tel: 01202 600766
(Attached to: Poole)

SMITH Ronald Welch
Address: Wych Farm Kennels,
Wych Lane, Adlington,
Macclesfield,
Cheshire SK10 4NB
Tel: 01625 827025
(Attached to: Belle Vue)

SMITH Simon
Address: 17 James Street
Caravan Site, James Street,
York, North Yorkshire YO10 3DT
Tel: 01904 415410
(Attached to: Hull)

SMITH Wayne Edward
Address: 6 Samuel Square,
Barnsley, South Yorkshire
S75 2NX
Tel: 01226 238559
(Attached to: Kinsley)

SMITH William
Address: Kilmany, The Clachan,
Campsie Glen, Glasgow
G66 7AB
Tel: 01360 310545
(Attached to: Shawfield)

SMITH John Leslie (Snr)
Address: 69 Raveloe Drive,
Caldwell, Nuneaton,
Warwickshire CV11 4QP
Tel: 02476 739278
(Unattached)

SMYLIE Anthony Paul
Address: 23 Craigleigh Grove,
Wirral, Merseyside CH62 9DJ
Tel: 0151 327 2450
(Unattached)

SNOW Allan
Address: 3 Stranfaer Close,
Swanwick, Alfreton,
Derbyshire DE55 1EE
Tel: 01773 602 860
(Unattached)

SOPPITT Edward
Address: 64 Woodland Crescent,
Kelloe, Durham,
County Durham DH6 4LX
Tel: 0191 377 2930
(Unattached)

SPELLMAN Geoffrey Francis
Address: 102 Chorley Old Road,
Whittle-le-Woods, Chorley,
Lancashire PR6 7LR
Tel: 01257 276279
(Attached to: Kinsley)

SPENCE John
Address: Westside Farm Cottage,
Symington, Biggar,
Lanarkshire ML12 6JU
Tel: 01899 308255
(Attached to: Shawfield)

SPENCER David Charles
Address: 79 Dereham Road,
Mattishall, Dereham,
Norfolk NR20 3NT
Tel: 01362 850 942
(Attached to: Yarmouth)

SPENDLOVE Jordan Andrew
Address: 4 Ethel Cottages,
London Road, Kessingland,
Lowestoft, Suffolk NR33 7PG
Tel: 01502 741483
(Attached to: Henlow)

SPIERS Sonja (Mrs)
Address: Upper Thruxted Farm,
Pennypot Lane, Waltham,
Canterbury, Kent CT4 7HA
Tel: 01227 730 276
(Attached to: Sittingbourne)

SPILLANE Gillian (Mrs)
Address: The Newlands, Wash
Road, Fosdyke, Boston,
Lincolnshire PE20 2DJ
Tel: 01205 260 272
(Attached to: Peterborough)

SPRACKLEN John Frederick
Address: Moreton Farm, Moreton
Lane, Northmoor, Witney,
Oxfordshire OX29 5SY
Tel: 01865 303042
(Unattached)

SPRAGG Pauline Rose (Mrs)
Address: The Kennels, Croft
Farm Ltd, Parrotts Grove,
Aldermans Green, Coventry,
West Midlands CV2 1NR
Tel: 07905 199159
(Attached to: Peterborough)

SPRAGGON David
Address: The Old Vicarage,
South Hetton, Durham,
County Durham DH6 2SW
Tel: 0191 5266726
(Unattached)

SPRINGALL Bernard Michael
Address: Crostwick Kennels,
North Walsham Road, Crostwick,
Norwich, Norfolk NR12 7BD
Tel: 01603 429480
(Attached to: Yarmouth)

Sponsored by the BGRB

SQUIRE Anthony
Address: Marston Cottage,
Marston Lane, Marston,
Stafford ST18 9SY
Tel: 07752 368 355
(Unattached)

STAMP Philip
Address: Parndon Kennels,
Reddish Vale Road, Stockport,
Cheshire SK5 7EU
Tel: 0161 368 2517
(Attached to: Sheffield)

STANTON Peter Andrew
Address: 123 Croft Road,
Upwell, Wisbech,
Cambridgeshire PE14 9HQ
Tel: 01945 772284
(Attached to: Mildenhall)

STANTON Robert
Address: Farm Bulidings, Mill
Lane, Oversley Green, Alcester,
Warwickshire B49 6LL
Tel: 07917 111 447
(Attached to: Perry Barr)

STAPLES David Colin
Address: 5 Washington Road,
Woodlands, Doncaster,
South Yorkshire DN6 7LQ
Tel: 07887864138
(Attached to: Kinsley)

STARK George Andrew
Address: 6 Abbey Place,
Forth, Lanark,
Lanarkshire ML11 8EB
Tel: 07960 633170
(Attached to: Pelaw Grange)

STEED Leon Frederick Ray
Address: Makeni, Wrabness
Road, Ramsey, Harwich,
Essex CO12 5NE
Tel: 01255 880659
(Unattached)

STEELE James
Address: Minerva Works,
Miller Street, Johnstone,
Renfrewshire PA5 8HP
Tel: 01505 344834
(Attached to: Shawfield)

STEELS Dilys Irene (Mrs)
Address: Glatton Kennels,
48 Quakers Drove,
Turves, Peterborough,
Cambridgeshire PE7 2DR
Tel: 01733 840534
(Attached to: Peterborough)

STEPHENS June (Mrs)
Address: 14 Yew Tree Road,
Witley, Godalming,
Surrey GU8 5RH
Tel: 01428681324
(Unattached)

STEPHENSON Lisa Jane (Miss)
Address: Sandwood, Eastoft
Road, Swinefleet, Goole, North
Humberside DN14 8EB
Tel: 01724 798267
(Attached to: Sheffield)

STERLAND Raymond
Address: 37 Grange Avenue,
Binley, Coventry,
West Midlands CV3 2ED
Tel: 02476 635 936
(Attached to: Coventry)

STEVENI Bernon
Address: Netherall Farm,
Netherhall Road, Roydon,
Harlow, Essex CM19 5JP
Tel: 01279 793529
(Unattached)

STEVENS Alan David
Address: Westfield Lodge,
Sleaford Road, Heckington,
Sleaford, Lincolnshire NG34 9QN
Tel: 01529 462988
(Unattached)

STEVENS George Dennis
Address: Barley Mow, Hooks
Green, Clothall, Baldock,
Hertfordshire SG7 6RF
Tel: 01462 790542
(Attached to: Henlow)

STEVENS Ian Peter
Address: Skibereen Kennels,
Rear of The Briars,
Hovefields Avenue, Wickford,
Essex SS12 9JA
Tel: 01268 727862
(Attached to: Crayford)

STEVENSON Denis Rober
Address: 63 Stonesby Avenue,
Leicester, Leicestershire LE2 6TX
Tel: 01162 242 880
(Unattached)

STEWARD Allan Leslie
Address: 47 Sandpiper Drive,
Park Farm, Peterborough,
Cambridgeshire PE2 8NX
Tel: 01733 894337
(Attached to: Peterborough)

STEWARD Scott Lee
Address: 25 Willow Avenue,
Peterborough, Cambridgeshire
PE1 4LX Tel: 07966 349427
(Attached to: Peterborough)

STICKLAND Gordon William
Address: Triangle Farm,
Stalbridge, Sturminster Newton,
Dorset DT10 2RT
Tel: 01963 362492
(Attached to: Poole)

STIRLING Anne (Mrs)
Address: Greenwell Farm,
125 Netherhouse Road,
Bargeddie, Glasgow G69 6UA
Tel: 0141 781 1423
(Attached to: Shawfield)

STOCKS Catherine Helen (Mrs)
Address: Roselea, Rectory Close,
Thurnscoe, Rotherham,
South Yorkshire S63 0RT
Tel: 01709 892819
(Unattached)

STONE Alec
Address: 71 Watling Street,
Nuneaton, Warwickshire
CV11 6JJ
Tel: 02476 745485
(Attached to: Perry Barr)

STONER Phillip
Address: Breezley, Palesides
Avenue, Ossett,
West Yorkshire WF5 9NL
Tel: 01924 264869
(Unattached)

STRANG Alexander
Address: 7 Tarbolton Path,
Larkhall, Lanarkshire ML9 1BX
Tel: 01698 306627
(Attached to: Shawfield)

STRATFORD Dianne (Mrs)
Address: 22 Witts Lane,
Purton, Swindon,
Wiltshire SN5 9ER
Tel: 01793 770424
(Unattached)

STRATFORD James Joseph
Address: 13 Townshott, Clophill,
Bedford, Bedfordshire MK45
4BN Tel: 01525 860560
(Attached to: Henlow)

STRINGER Gloria Felicity (Mrs)
Address: Shellgrove Farm,
Horton-cum-Studley, Oxford,
Oxfordshire OX33 1DE
Tel: 01865 351 757
(Attached to: Oxford)

STROUD Michael
Address: 28 Brookfield Road,
Wooburn Green, High Wycombe,
Buckinghamshire HP10 0PZ
Tel: 01628 526859
(Attached to: Reading)

SUMMERFIELD James Henry
Address: 14 Carshalton Road,
Kingstanding Birmingham
B44 0TG
Tel: 0121 354 6404
(Unattached)

SUTTON Judy (Mrs)
Address: 1-2 Spring Terrace,
Halifax, West Yorkshire HX2 7UB
Tel: 01422 247933
(Attached to: Kinsley)

SWADDEN Peter Vivian
Address: Model Farm,
Bupton, Hilmarton, Calne,
Wiltshire SN11 8SZ
Tel: 01249 760360
(Attached to: Swindon)

SYMONDS Christopher John
Address: Drogheda, Lynn Road,
Tilney All Saints, King's Lynn,
Norfolk PE34 4SA
Tel: 01553 829529
(Unattached)

TALBOT Daniel
Address: 43 Waverley Road,
Bolton, Lancashire BL1 6NW
Tel: 01204 411108
(Unattached)

TANNER Ronald Alfred
Address: Willow View, 51
Norwood Road, March,
Cambridgeshire PE15 8PX
Tel: 01354 659836
(Attached to: Peterborough)

TANNER Ronald Arthur
Address: 88 Lansdowne Road,
Lowestoft, Suffolk NR33 7ES
Tel: 01502 585694
(Attached to: Yarmouth)

TATE Eric George
Address: Old Park Farm,
Hambledon Road,
Denmead, Waterlooville,
Hampshire PO7 6XE
Tel: 0958 713354
(Attached to: Portsmouth)

TAYLOR Anthony John
Address: Catford Racing
Kennels, Layhams Road,
Keston, Kent BR2 6AR
Tel: 01959 574420
(Attached to: Wimbledon)

TAYLOR David George
Address: 101 Broomhill Avenue,
Knottingley, West Yorkshire
WF11 0EA
Tel: 01977 677409
(Unattached)

TAYLOR Kim Joanne (Mrs)
Address: Whybrows Farm,
Malting End, Kirtling,
Newmarket, Suffolk CB8 9HH
Tel: 01638 730403
(Attached to: Henlow)

TAYLOR Malcolm Robert
Address: 76 Smeaton Road,
Upton, Pontefract,
West Yorkshire WF9 1LF
Tel: 01977 644202
(Attached to: Kinsley)

TAYLOR Philip
Address: 121 West Bawtry
Road, Rotherham, South
Yorkshire S60 2XQ
Tel: 07711 479510
(Attached to: Doncaster)

TAYLORSON Louise Ann (Mrs)
Address: "LAT Kennels, Racing
Yard", Haggswood Stables,
Haggs Wood, Stainforth,
Doncaster, South Yorkshire
DN7 5PS
Tel: 07817354151
(Attached to: Sheffield)

TEAL Jacqueline Ann (Mrs)
Address: Linton Kennels,
Briardale Farm,
Scarborough Road, Malton,
North Yorkshire YO17 8AA
Tel: 01653 600198
(Attached to: Sunderland)

TESTER Kenneth John
Address: Grasmere, Church
Lane, Burstow, Horley,
Surrey RH6 9TG
Tel: 01293 784302
(Attached to: Brighton & Hove)

TEVERSHAM Gary David
Address: 4 Rookery Farm,
Sixteen Foot Bank,
Stonea, March,
Cambridgeshire PE15 0DU
Tel: 01354 688376
(Unattached)

THOMAS John Edward
Address: 31 Manor Close,
Witchford, Ely,
Cambridgeshire CB6 2JB
Tel: 01353 665 424
(Attached to: Mildenhall)

THOMAS William George
Address: Suffolk House,
Ashwells Road,
Pilgrims Hatch, Brentwood,
Essex CM15 9SG
Tel: 07980 093 384
(Unattached)

THOMPSON Clifford
Address: 13 Hamsterley
Crescent, Gateshead,
Tyne and Wear NE9 7LA
Tel: 01914 822 347
(Attached to: Pelaw Grange)

THOMPSON Gordon
Address: The Sidings,
Baggrow, Aspatria, Wigton,
Cumbria CA7 3QG
Tel: 016973 20003
(Unattached)

THOMPSON James Brian
Address: Outclough Farm,
Biddulph Road, Stoke-on-Trent,
Staffordshire ST6 8UW
Tel: 07788 943 969
(Attached to: Nottingham)

THOMPSON John Guy
Address: The Bungalow,
Killingwoldgrave Lane,
Bishop Burton, Beverley,
North Humberside HU17 8QX
Tel: 01964 550340
(Attached to: Hull)

THOMPSON Patricia Ann (Miss)
Address: Nestledown Kennels,
Hazelwood, Sun Hill,
Fawkham, Longfield,
Kent DA3 8N
Tel: 01474 872864
(Attached to: Crayford)

THOMPSON Richard John
Address: Crown Cottage,
Ellenthorpe, Boroughbridge, York,
North Yorkshire YO51 9HJ
Tel: 01423 322211
(Attached to: Hull)

THOMPSON Robert
Address: Pelaw Grange Kennels,
Pelaw Grange Greyhound),
Drum Road, Chester le Street,
County Durham DH3 2AF
Tel: 07980 136 692
(Attached to: Pelaw Grange)

THOMPSON Sharon Louise (Mrs)
Address: 1 Rutters Cottages,
Old Milton Road, Thurleigh,
Bedford, Bedfordshire MK44 2DJ
Tel: 01234 772281
(Attached to: Henlow)

THOMSON George
Address: 11 Jura Gardens,
Carluke, Lanarkshire ML8 4HU
Tel: 01555 770690
(Attached to: Shawfield)

THOMSON Kenneth William
Address: Highcroft, Sandy Lane,
East Tuddenham, Dereham,
Norfolk NR20 3JH
Tel: 01603 880283
(Unattached)

THORN Robin
Address: 33 Howard Road,
Sompting, Lancing,
West Sussex BN15 0LW
Tel: 01903 601359
(Attached to: Portsmouth)

THORPE Stephen
Address: 249 Edenfield Road,
Rochdale, Lancashire OL11 5AG
01706 646116
(Unattached)

THWAITES Kenneth John
Address: Barry Banks Farm,
Ugthorpe, Whitby, North
Yorkshire YO21 2BQ
Tel: 01947 840853
(Attached to: Pelaw Grange)

TIMMINS Paula (Mrs)
Address: Brook Farm, Talbot
Lane, Swannington, Coalville,
Leicestershire LE67 8QT
Tel: 07976 798 221
(Attached to: Nottingham)

TOMPKINS Robert
Address: 39a Gold Street,
Hanslope, Milton Keynes,
Buckinghamshire MK19 7LU
Tel: 01908 510249
(Unattached)

TOMPSETT Paul Andrew
Address: Park Farm Oast,
Smallbridge Road, Horsmonden,
Tonbridge, Kent TN12 8EP
Tel: 01892 722550
(Attached to: Crayford)

TONKS Alan
Address: Westerley House,
Thwing Road, Rudston, Driffield,
North Humberside YO25 4UQ
Tel: 01262 420798
(Attached to: Hull)

TORRANCE Graeme William
Address: 133 Carden Avenue,
Cardenden, Fife KY5 0EL
Tel: 01592 721 228
(Attached to: Shawfield)

TOVEY Brian Seward
Address: 6 Inglestone Road,
Wickwar, Wotton-under-Edge,
Gloucestershire GL12 8NH
Tel: 01454 294769
(Unattached)

TOWNER Roy John
Address: Ivy Farm Kennels,
Lidsing, Gillingham,
Kent ME7 3NL
Tel: 01634 232733
(Attached to: Brighton & Hove)

TOWNSEND Barbara Jean (Miss)
Address: Oak Tree Kennels,
Marshland Villa, School Road,
St. Johns Fen End, Wisbech,
Cambridgeshire PE14 8JR
Tel: 01945 430311
(Attached to: Peterborough)

TRANT Patrick Murray
Address: Stoneham Park House,
Stoneham Lane, Eastleigh,
Hampshire SO50 9HT
Tel: 02380 665544
(Attached to: Portsmouth)

TRETT Andrew Phillip
Address: 134 Beverley Road,
North Earlham, Norwich,
Norfolk NR5 8DW
Tel: 01603 454903
(Attached to: Yarmouth)

TREVISS Valerie Elizabeth (Mrs)
Address: 26 Kit Lane,
Owermoigne, Dorchester,
Dorset DT2 8HP
Tel: 01305 853 942
(Attached to: Poole)

TROUGHTON Leonard
Woodhaw, Back Lane,
Norton, Doncaster, South
Yorkshire DN6 9EA
Tel: 01302 700745
(Attached to: Hull)

TSIRIGOTIS Philip
Address: 26 Addison Avenue,
Oakwood, London N14 4AE
Tel: 020 8372 3237
(Unattached)

TTOFALLI Nicolas
Address: Barnlea, 2 Oundle
Road, Alwalton, Peterborough,
Cambridgeshire PE7 3UP
Tel: 01733 232429
(Attached to: Peterborough)

TUFFIN Anthony Peter
Address: 163 Hitchin Road,
Stotfold, Hitchin,
Hertfordshire SG5 4JH
Tel: 01462 835405
(Attached to: Henlow)

TUFFIN Laurence Graham
Address: Unit 1 Woodside Farm
Stables, Helmsley Road,
Rainworth, Mansfield,
Nottinghamshire NG21 0DG
Tel: 07980 303404
(Attached to: Nottingham)

TULLOCH Donald
Address: Auchans Farm,
Auchans Road,
Houston, Johnstone,
Renfrewshire PA6 7EE
Tel: 07939 840598
(Attached to: Shawfield)

TUNGATT Toni (Mrs)
Address: 7k Hillsley Road,
Portsmouth, Hampshire PO6 4LE
Tel: 02392 321034
(Unattached)

TURNBULL Kevin William
Address: 52 Stead Lane,
Bedlington, Northumberland
NE22 5QY
Tel: 01670 827 871
(Attached to: Pelaw Grange)

TURNER Albert Frank
Address: Keepers Cottage,
Coopers Lane, Saltby, Melton
Mowbray, Leicestershire
LE14 4QA
Tel: 01664 565239
(Attached to: Peterborough)

TURNER Bryan
Address: Burr Lodge, Burr Lane,
Spalding, Lincolnshire PE12 6AZ
Tel: 0775 711511
(Attached to: Peterborough)

TURNER Kirsten Despina (Miss)
Address: Mons Hill Cottage,
1 Mons Hill, Dudley,
West Midlands DY1 4LT
Tel: 01902 679 470
(Attached to: Perry Barr)

TURNEY Raymond John
Address: 41 Lanes End, Heath
and Reach, Leighton Buzzard,
Bedfordshire LU7 0AE
Tel: 01525 237770
(Attached to: Henlow)

UPTON Ernest
Address: Arbor Avenue,
Burnage, Manchester M19 1FU
Tel: 0161 432 3152
(Attached to: Doncaster)

VAIRA Luigi
Address: 69 Queens Road,
Peterborough, Cambridgeshire
PE2 8BS
Tel: 01733 553035
(Attached to: Peterborough)

VARLEY Amanda (Mrs)
Address: School House Farm,
Kiln Pit Hill, Consett, County
Durham DH8 9SB
Tel: 01434 673533
(Attached to: Newcastle)

VASS David Charles
Address: 56 The Causeway,
Staines, Middlesex TW18 3AX
Tel: 01784 456237
(Attached to: Reading)

VASS Gary Leonard
Address: Rossland,
Cheal Road, Gosberton,
Spalding, Lincolnshire
PE11 4JQ
Tel: 01775 750028
(Unattached)

VINCENT Paul Robert
Address: Glen Cottage, Clapham
Hill, Whitstable, Kent CT5 3DN
Tel: 01227274622
(Unattached)

WADE Thomas Charles Albert
Address: Dawn Ranch,
Blind Lane, Billericay,
Essex CM12 9SN
Tel: 01277 651809
(Attached to: Harlow)

WAGGOTT Alison Regina (Mrs)
Address: Hollin Hall Farm,
Fir Tree, Crook,
County Durham DL15 8DJ
Tel: 01388 768385
(Unattached)

WAINWRIGHT John
Address: 6 Woodfield Cottages,
Leicester Road,
Measham, Swadlincote,
Derbyshire DE12 7JQ
Tel: 01530 271611
(Unattached)

WAINWRIGHT Mona (Mrs)
Address: White Farm Kennels,
Broad Cut Road,
Calder Grove, Wakefield,
West Yorkshire WF4 3DT
Tel: 01924 274329
(Attached to: Sheffield)

WAKEFIELD James Henry
Address: No.2 Ockendon
Kennels, Ockendon Road,
North Ockendon, Upminster,
Essex RM14 3PT
Tel: 07952 620 364
(Unattached)

WALDEN Paul Stuart
Address: Foxhold Farm,
Thornford Road, Crookham
Common, Thatcham,
Berkshire RG19 8EL
Tel: 01635 268416
(Attached to: Swindon)

WALFORD Roger David
Address: Harwood Lodge
Cottage, Woolton Hill, Newbury,
Berkshire RG20 9TE
Tel: 01635 250711
(Attached to: Reading)

WALKER Ian Edward
Address: Flavel Farm Kennels,
Warton Lane, Austrey,
Atherstone, Warwickshire
CV9 3EJ
Tel: 07947 315 465
(Attached to: Perry Barr)

WALKER Judith (Mrs)
Address: 46 Gleneagles Road,
Dinnington, Sheffield,
South Yorkshire S25 2TD
Tel: 01909 566 035
(Unattached)

WALKER Matthew Joseph
Address: 26 Saffron Close,
East Hunsbury, Northampton,
Northamptonshire NN4 0SG
Tel: 01604 760535
(Unattached)

WALKER Neil John
Address: 11 Peartree Close,
Fenstanton, Huntingdon,
Cambridgeshire PE28 9LL
Tel: 01480 497149
(Attached to: Henlow)

WALL Geoffrey
Address: 8 Bluebell Road,
Darton, Barnsley,
South Yorkshire S75 5JG
Tel: 01226 386917
(Attached to: Doncaster)

WALLINGTON Leslie Dermot
Address: Bridgefield, Worcester
Road, Salford, Chipping Norton,
Oxfordshire OX7 5YQ
Tel: 01608 642739
(Attached to: Swindon)

WALLIS Mark Andrew
Address: Imperial Kennels,
Undley, Lakenheath,
Brandon, Suffolk IP27 9BY
Tel: 01842 860 579
(Attached to: Walthamstow)

WALLOND Ivan Charles
Address: Little Studley,
Chart Road, Sutton Valence,
Maidstone, Kent ME17 3AW
Tel: 01622 844956
(Attached to: Reading)

WALSH Doreen (Mrs)
Address: Brighton & Hove)
Kennels, Wheatsheaf Road,
Woodmancote, Henfield,
West Sussex BN5 9BD
Tel: 01273 494272
(Attached to: Brighton & Hove)

WALSH Maurice
Address: The Bampton Boarding
Kennels, Buckland Road,
Bampton, Oxfordshire
OX18 2AA
Tel: 01993 850671
(Attached to: Swindon)

WALSH Michael
Address: North View,
Grinsdale Bridge, Carlisle,
Cumbria CA5 6DP
Tel: 01228 576916
(Attached to: Pelaw Grange)

WALSH Sean Anthony
Address: Sacred Heart Cottage,
Oxford Road, Horndon-on-The-
Hill, Stanford-le-Hope,
Essex SS17 8PX
Tel: 01375 673 081
(Attached to: Harlow)

WALTERS Anita Jenny (Miss)
Address: Brookside Farm,
Broughton Hackett, Worcester,
Worcestershire WR7 4BE
Tel: 07704 122048
(Attached to: Hall Green)

WALTERS Gary
Address: 80 Hockliffe Street,
Leighton Buzzard,
Bedfordshire LU7 1HJ
Tel: 01525 636 287
(Unattached)

WALTON Anthony Thomas
Address: Beechwood Cottage,
Malton Road, York, North
Yorkshire YO32 9TH
Tel: 07788 626 511
(Attached to: Kinsley)

WALTON John
Address: Eastbank, Aspatria,
Wigton, Cumbria CA7 2JY
Tel: 01697 323153
(Attached to: Newcastle)

WALTON John Michael
Address: Blackrock Kennels,
"Blacklock, off Manchester
Road", Mossley, Ashton-under-
Lyne, Lancashire OL5 9QG
Tel: 01457 835 681
(Attached to: Belle Vue)

WALTON Stuart William
Address: 45 Vicarage Road,
Amblecote, Stourbridge,
West Midlands DY8 4JE
Tel: 01384 370158
(Attached to: Henlow)

WARD Aivar John
Address: 12 Johnson Rise,
Stoney Stanton, Leicester,
Leicestershire LE9 4BZ
Tel: 01455 274272
(Unattached)

WARD Alan James
Address: Unit 6, Ockendon
Kennels, Ockendon Road,
Upminster, Essex RM14 3PT
Tel: 07980 213140
(Unattached)

WARD Antony
Address: The Old Rectory,
Rectory Lane, Appleby
Magna, Swadlincote,
Derbyshire DE12 7BQ
Tel: 01530 515 311
(Unattached)

WARD David Alan
Address: 9 Redmoor Lane,
South Brink, Wisbech,
Cambridgeshire PE14 0RN
Tel: 01945 582335
(Attached to: Peterborough)

WARD Philip
Address: The Cottage,
Green Lane, Leverington,
Wisbech, Cambridgeshire
PE13 5EJ
Tel: 01945 870 590
(Attached to: Peterborough)

WARD Richard Graham
Address: Lindon, Rugby Road,
Long Lawford, Rugby,
Warwickshire, CV23 9DN
Tel: 01788 570427
(Attached to: Coventry)

WAREHAM Leslie Harry
Address: Little Haven, Ibsley
Drove, Ibsley, Ringwood,
Hampshire BH24 3NP
Tel: 01425 655041
(Attached to: Poole)

WARING Shane
Address: 6 Willow Close,
Gomersal, Cleckheaton,
West Yorkshire BD19 4JA
Tel: 01274 876 362
(Unattached)

WARREN Bernadette Patricia
(Miss)
Address: Shamrock Kennels,
10 Redmoor Lane, Wisbech,
Cambridgeshire PE14 0RN
Tel: 01945 582860
(Attached to: Peterborough)

WARREN Peter Paul
Address: 80 Station Road,
Snettisham, King's Lynn,
Norfolk PE31 7QS
Tel: 01485 541557
(Attached to: Mildenhall)

WARREN Russell
Address: Owlerton Sports
Kennels, Penistone Road,
Sheffield, South Yorkshire
S6 2DE
Tel: 0114 2343074
(Attached to: Sheffield)

WASS Frank George
Address: Keepers Cottage,
Bovingdon Hall, Bocking,
Braintree, Essex CM7 4AA
Tel: 01371 851 116
(Unattached)

WATSON Eleanor (Mrs)
Address: 1 Beltonfoot Way,
Netherton, Wishaw,
Lanarkshire ML2 0GA
Tel: 01698 351205
(Attached to: Shawfield)

WATSON James
Address: 9 Kyle Road,
Gateshead, Tyne and Wear
NE8 2YE
Tel: 01914 608 379
(Attached to: Pelaw Grange)

WATSON John
Address: 29 Tees Crescent,
Stanley, County Durham,
DH9 6HZ
Tel: 07913 171 194
(Attached to: Pelaw Grange)

WATSON Robert Henry
Address: 80 Strawfrank Road,
Carstairs Junction, Lanark,
Lanarkshire ML11 8RE
Tel: 01555 870886
(Attached to: Shawfield)

WATSON Stuart Matthew
Address: 392 Queen Elizabeth
Road, Nuneaton, Warwickshire
CV10 9DA
Tel: 02476 394517
(Unattached)

WATTS Brian John
Address: 13 Barrett-Lennard
Road, Horsford, Norwich,
Norfolk NR10 3EQ
Tel: 01603 898981
(Unattached)

WATTS James
Address: 132 Leicester Road,
Ibstock, Leicestershire
LE67 6HJ
Tel: 01530 263571
(Attached to: Coventry)

WAUGH James
Address: 34 Wortley Place,
Hemsworth, Pontefract,
West Yorkshire WF9 4NN
Tel: 01977 611129
(Attached to: Kinsley)

WEARING Edna Doreen (Mrs)
Address: Cravenia, Great North
Road, North Mymms, Hatfield,
Hertfordshire AL9 5SD
Tel: 01707 263803
(Unattached)

Carol Weatherall (Mrs)
Address: Coppice Kennels,
Frankton Lane, Stretton On
Dunsmore, Rugby,
Warwickshire CV23 9JQ
Tel: 01926 632 423
(Attached to: Henlow)

WEAVER Peter
Address: 84 Tiverton Road,
Tottenham, London N15 6RR
Tel: 020 8802 3800
(Attached to: Henlow)

WEBSTER Dennis
Address: 2 Modena Court,
Darfield, Barnsley, South
Yorkshire S73 9RD
Tel: 01226 752896
(Attached to: Doncaster)

WEBSTER Paul
32 Farrar Road, Droylsden,
Manchester M43 6EX
Tel: 07932 307 907
(Attached to: Doncaster)

WEIR Pamela (Mrs)
B & E Engineering, 101 Mill
Road, Allanton, Shotts,
Lanarkshire ML7 5DD
Tel: 07871820435
(Attached to: Newcastle)

WELLING John Paul
Shortwood Yard, Shortwood Hill,
Mangotsfield, Bristol,
Avon BS16 9PF
Tel: 0117 9373954
(Unattached)

WELLON Peter
Shady Hollow, Compton Green,
Redmarley, Gloucester,
Gloucestershire GL19 3JB
Tel: 01531 820520
(Unattached)

WEST Bernard Graham
63 Breck Lane,
Dinnington, Sheffield,
South Yorkshire S25 2LJ
Tel: 01909567318
(Attached to: Doncaster)

WEST Gordon (Jnr)
2 Churchlands Cottages,
Kirdford, Billingshurst,
West Sussex RH14 0LU
Tel: 01403 820549
(Attached to: Portsmouth)

WESTACOTT George Edward
74 Powys Avenue,
Townhill, Swansea, West
Glamorgan SA1 6PQ
Tel: 01792 646685
(Unattached)

WESTHEAD Andrew Paul
Bridge House, Monson Road,
Northorpe, Gainsborough,
Lincolnshire DN21 4AQ
Tel: 07979 873082
(Unattached)

WESTON Ian Paul Ashley
6 Selwyn Cottages, High Road,
Guyhirn, Wisbech,
Cambridgeshire PE13 4EQ
Tel: 01945 450417
(Attached to: Peterborough)

WESTWOOD Marlene Ena (Mrs)
Drovers Cottage, 1 Hatch,
Sandy, Bedfordshire SG19 1PT
Tel: 01767 692345
(Attached to: Henlow)

WHEATLEY Mark Antony
254 Station Road, New Waltham,
Grimsby, South Humberside
DN36 4PE
Tel: 01472 827945
(Attached to: Doncaster)

WHEELER Nicholas
1 Grove Cottages, Upperton,
Brightwell Baldwin, Watlington,
Oxfordshire OX49 5PA
Tel: 01491 613415
(Attached to: Reading)

WHITE Ernest
31 Southern Way,
Wolverton, Milton Keynes,
Buckinghamshire MK12 5EH
Tel: 01908 313 052
(Unattached)

WHITE Jane Anne (Mrs)
Brookbreasting Farm, Maxilla
Kennels, Watnall, Nottingham,
Nottinghamshire NG16 1HW
Tel: 07973 981836
(Attached to: Coventry)

WHITE Jenny Anne (Mrs)
Harts Hill, Holt Road, Horsford,
Norwich, Norfolk NR10 3AQ
Tel: 01603 401979
(Attached to: Yarmouth)

WHITE John William
B & J Kennels, Ockendon
Kennels, Ockendon Road,
Nr.Upminster, Essex RM14 3PS
Tel: 07989 283757
(Unattached)

WHITE Marc Antony
17 Millstream Close,
Creekmoor, Poole,
Dorset BH17 7EG Tel: 01202
387159
(Attached to: Poole)

WHITE Martin Joseph
Burlton Lane Farm, Myddle,
Shrewsbury, Shropshire
SY4 3RE
Tel: 01939 270 909
(Unattached)

WHITE Paul Craig
Foxearth House, Leek Road,
Werrington, Stoke-on-Trent,
Staffordshire ST9 0DG
Tel: 07836 655 852
(Attached to: Hall Green)

WHITE Peter John
42 Joys Bank, Holbeach,
Spalding, Lincolnshire PE12 8SD
Tel: 01406 540682
(Attached to: Peterborough)

WHITE Robert John
Lyon House, Hulfords Lane,
Hartley Wintney, Hook,
Hampshire RG27 8AG
Tel: 01252 843851
(Attached to: Reading)

WHITE Sean
37 Lewis Road, Mitcham,
Surrey CR4 3DF
Tel: 0208 640 6006
(Unattached)

WHITE Thomas Garham
Address: Green Acre Farm,
Hop Hills Lane, Dunscroft,
Doncaster, South Yorkshire
DN7 4JX
Tel: 01302 841652
(Attached to: Doncaster)

WHITEHOUSE Kevin Paul
Address: Oakhill, Romsley Lane,
Shatterford, Bewdley,
Worcestershire DY12 1RT
Tel: 01299 861632
(Attached to: Coventry)

WHITEHOUSE Susan Jane (Miss)
Address: The Bungalow,
Stourbridge Road,
Wombourne, Wolverhampton,
West Midlands WV5 0JN
Tel: 01902 893540
(Attached to: Perry Barr)

WHITING Gerald Jack
Address: High Hedges, Road
Green, Hempnall, Norwich,
Norfolk NR15 2NH
Tel: 01508 499704
(Attached to: Yarmouth)

WHITMARSH Charles
Address: 43 Heathview Road,
Grays, Essex RM16 2RS
Tel: 01375 387562
(Unattached)

WHITTON Darren Barry
Address: 104 Folly Road,
Mildenhall, Bury St. Edmunds,
Suffolk IP28 7BT
Tel: 07939 137250
(Attached to: Henlow)

WHITWOOD Paul Victor
Address: 12 Elizabeth Drive,
Necton, Swaffham, Norfolk
E37 8NB
Tel: 01760 440591
(Attached to: Yarmouth)

WICKENS Thomas Edward
Address: 83 Well Road, Barnet,
Hertfordshire EN5 3EA
Tel: 020 8440 8482
(Attached to: Henlow)

WIDMER Michael Scott
Address: Stone Mole House,
Low Street, Leeming Bar,
Northallerton,
North Yorkshire DL7 9LU
Tel: 01609 748392
(Unattached)

WIGHTMAN Mark Gregory
Address: 72 Bedford Road,
Sandy, Bedfordshire SG19 1EP
Tel: 01767 682012
(Attached to: Henlow)

WILCOCK Michael George
Address: 388 Worksop Road,
Mastin Moor, Chesterfield,
Derbyshire S43 3DJ
Tel: 01246 472762
(Unattached)

WILEMAN Barry Peter
Address: 47 Watling Street,
Dordon, Tamworth,
Staffordshire B78 1SY
Tel: 01827 709009
(Unattached)

WILEMAN Paul
Address: 59 Winchester Road,
Countesthorpe, Leicester,
Leicestershire LE8 5PN
Tel: 07711 835 061
(Attached to: Coventry)

WILEY Martyn Ernest
Address: The Gables,
Borwick Lane, Wickford,
Essex SS12 0QA
Tel: 01268 732039
(Attached to: Romford)

WILKES Raymond John
Address: Honey Brook Kennels,
Bridgnorth Road, Kidderminster,
Worcestershire DY11 5RR
Tel: 01562 754 076
(Unattached)

WILKINS Trevor
Address: 7 Oday Hill,
Drayton, Abingdon,
Oxfordshire OX14 4AB
Tel: 07763 569854
(Attached to: Reading)

WILKINSON David
Address: Cornforth Moor Farm,
Tursdale, County Durham
DH6 5NR
Tel: 0191 3772297
(Attached to: Pelaw Grange)

WILLEY Steven Carl
Address: 1 Monks Cottages,
Princess Margaret Road,
Linford, Stanford-le-Hope,
Essex SS17 0QU
Tel: 07852 126 237
(Unattached)

WILLIAMS Eric Leslie Trevellyan
Address: 24 Wallridge Drive,
Holywell, Whitley Bay, Tyne
and Wear NE25 0NL
Tel: 01912 375 591
(Attached to: Pelaw Grange)

WILLIAMS Harry Forrester
Address: White Gate House,
Witton Le Wear, Bishop
Auckland, County Durham DL14
0BP Tel: 013884 88446
(Attached to: Newcastle)

WILLIAMS Margaret (Mrs)
Address: Rosedene, Sandy Lane,
Wildmoor, Bromsgrove,
Worcestershire B61 0QU
Tel: 0121 453 8928
(Attached to: Perry Barr)

WILLIAMS Paul Frederick
Address: 3 Pusey Way, Lane
End, High Wycombe,
Buckinghamshire HP14 3LG
Tel: 01494 881189
(Unattached)

WILLS Norman Ian
Address: Keepers Cottage,
Wheatley Road, Forest Hill,
Oxford, Oxfordshire OX33 1EP
Tel: 07801 636284
(Attached to: Oxford)

WILSHAW Andrew James
Address: The Woodlands,
Kingsley Moor, Stoke On Trent,
Staffordshire ST10 2EN
Tel: 07977 732584
(Unattached)

WILSON Andrew Charles
Address: Nutty Ash, 8 Cromer
Road, Hainford, Norwich,
Norfolk NR10 3AT
Tel: 01603 891535
(Attached to: Yarmouth)

WILSON Barry
Address: 50 Hyde Meadows,
Bovingdon, Hemel Hempstead,
Hertfordshire HP3 0ES
Tel: 01442 380777
(Attached to: Henlow)

WILSON Clifford Anthony
Address: 1 Salters Land,
Salters Lane, Trimdon Grange,
County Durham TS29 6PE
Tel: 07725 237 228
(Attached to: Pelaw Grange)

WILSON Linda June (Mrs)
Address: Elm Tree Cottage,
Wakefield Road, Hampole,
Doncaster, South Yorkshire
DN6 7EX
Tel: 01302 728366
(Attached to: Doncaster)

WILSON Norman
Address: 2 Deanfield,
Bovingdon, Hemel Hempstead,
Hertfordshire HP3 0EW
Tel: 01442 380109
(Attached to: Henlow)

WILTON Colin Norman
Address: Sanhaven,
Bruntcliffe Road,
Morley, Leeds,
West Yorkshire LS27 0JZ
Tel: 01132 537441
(Attached to: Kinsley)

WINDRASS John Malcolm
Address: Brook House,
East Lutton, Malton,
North Yorkshire YO17 8TG
Tel: 01944 738607
(Attached to: Hull)

WINK Mark Stephen
Address: 27 Leam Gardens,
Gateshead, Tyne and Wear
NE10 8SU
Tel: 0191 438 1996
(Attached to: Pelaw Grange)

WINSPER Alan Keith
Address: Speedwell Farm,
Goodison Kennels,
Speedwell Lane, Baddesley
Ensor, Atherstone,
Warwickshire CV9 2DT
Tel: 01827 712977
(Attached to: Nottingham)

WISE Peter Graham
Address: 42 South Street,
Swanwick, Alfreton,
Derbyshire DE55 1BZ
Tel: 01773 609826
(Unattached)

WISEMAN June Maureen
Hermion
Address: 1 Mill Cottage,
St. Pauls Road South,
Walton Highway, Wisbech,
Cambridgeshire PE14 7DN
Tel: 01945 580135
(Attached to: Henlow)

WITCHELL Peter Brangwyn
Address: 53A Sedge Fen,
Brandon, Suffolk IP27 9LH
Tel: 01353 675456
(Attached to: Mildenhall)

WOOD Andrew
Address: 48 Burns Crescent,
Airdrie, Lanarkshire ML6 9PX
Tel: 01236766822
(Attached to: Shawfield)

WOOD Angela Karina (Mrs)
Address: Grange View,
Mill Lane, Hemingbrough,
Selby, North Yorkshire
YO8 6QX
Tel: 01757 704337
(Attached to: Hull)

WOOD Peter
Address: 82 Caithness Road,
Hartlepool, Cleveland TS25 3AL
Tel: 01429 291 006
(Attached to: Pelaw Grange)

WOOD David (Jnr)
Address: 31 Foulden Bastle
Holding, Berwick-upon-Tweed,
Northumberland TD15 1UL
Tel: 01289 386766
(Unattached)

WOODHOUSE Paul Francis
Address: The Kennels,
Romsey Road, Lyndhurst,
Hampshire SO43 7FN
Tel: 02380 282585
(Attached to: Poole)

WOODMAN Antony James
Address: Halls Green Farm,
Epping Road, Roydon,
Harlow, Essex CM19 5DG
Tel: 01279 793 200
(Unattached)

WOOLCOTT Michael Dennis
Address: Common Farm,
Chapel Road, Ramsey,
Huntingdon, Cambridgeshire
PE26 2RS
Tel: 01487 812594
(Attached to: Mildenhall)

WOOLF Roger Martin
Address: 109 Station Road,
Impington, Cambridge,
Cambridgeshire CB4 9NP
Tel: 01223 560614
(Unattached)

WOOLLEY Darren Lee
Address: Longcroft, 5 Station
Road, Catcliffe, Rotherham,
South Yorkshire S60 5ST
Tel: 01709 370 491
(Unattached)

WRAY Claudia Lauren (Miss)
Address: 108 Inmans Road,
Hedon, Hull,
North Humberside HU12 8NL
Tel: 01482 899074
(Attached to: Hull)

WRIGHT Anne (Mrs)
Address: 30a Ramsey Road,
Benwick, March,
Cambridgeshire PE15 0XD
Tel: 01354 677 499
(Attached to: Henlow)

WRIGHT Douglas William
Address: Elmfield Post Office,
234 Elmton Road, Creswell,
Worksop, Nottinghamshire
S80 4DZ Tel: 01909 721234
(Unattached)

WRIGHT Frank Charles
Address: Warstone Farm,
Old Warstone Lane,
Essington, Wolverhampton,
West Midlands WV11 2AS
Tel: 01922 411085
(Attached to: Coventry)

WRIGHT Graham Charles
Address: 126 Marsh Lane,
Yeovil, Somerset BA21 3BZ
Tel: 01935 426567
(Attached to: Poole)

WRIGHTING Wayne Richard
Address: Brighton & Hove
Kennels, Wheatsheaf Road,
Woodmancote, Henfield,
West Sussex BN5 9BD
Tel: 01273 492722
(Attached to: Brighton & Hove)

WYNN Leslie Harold
Address: 3 Old Rectory Close,
Powick, Worcester,
Worcestershire WR2 4QU
Tel: 01905 830303
(Unattached)

YATES Ernest
Address: Cherry Tree Court, High
Hoyland, Barnsley, South
Yorkshire S75 4BE
Tel: 01226 385619
(Unattached)

YEATES Richard Frank
Address: 185 Wycombe Road,
Prestwood, Great Missenden,
Buckinghamshire HP16 0HJ
Tel: 01494 863685
(Attached to: Reading)

YORK Roger Bruce
Address: Pitlochry,
Parsonage Road, Takeley,
Bishop's Stortford,
Hertfordshire CM22 6RA
Tel: 01279 870288
(Unattached)

YOUNG Henry
Address: 15 Hallinan Gardens,
Wishaw, Lanarkshire ML2 0JQ
Tel: 01698 360 262
(Unattached)

YOUNG Paul William
Address: Burton Lodge,
Borwick Lane, Wickford,
Essex SS12 0QA
Tel: 01268 733945
(Attached to: Romford)

YOUNG Thomas
Address: 59 Rowland Street,
Rugby, Warwickshire CV21 2BW
Tel: 01788 331723
(Unattached)

ZSIBRITA Jacqueline Susan (Mrs)
Address: 10 Sturgeons Way,
Hitchin, Hertfordshire SG4 0BL
Tel: 01462 635 032
(Attached to: Henlow)